Outsourcing Legal Aid in the Nordic Welfare States

Olaf Halvorsen Rønning
Ole Hammerslev
Editors

Outsourcing Legal Aid in the Nordic Welfare States

Editors
Olaf Halvorsen Rønning
Department of Criminology and
Sociology of Law
University of Oslo
Oslo, Norway

Ole Hammerslev
Department of Law
University of Southern Denmark
Odense M, Denmark

ISBN 978-3-319-46683-5   ISBN 978-3-319-46684-2 (eBook)
https://doi.org/10.1007/978-3-319-46684-2

Library of Congress Control Number: 2017955024

© The Editor(s) (if applicable) and The Author(s) 2018 This book is an open access publication.
Open Access This book is distributed under the terms of the Creative Commons Attribution 4.0 International License (http://creativecommons.org/licenses/by/4.0/), which permits use, duplication, adaptation, distribution, and reproduction in any medium or format, as long as you give appropriate credit to the original author(s) and the source, a link is provided to the Creative Commons license, and any changes made are indicated.
The images or other third party material in this book are included in the work's Creative Commons license, unless indicated otherwise in the credit line; if such material is not included in the work's Creative Commons license and the respective action is not permitted by statutory regulation, users will need to obtain permission from the license holder to duplicate, adapt or reproduce the material.
The use of general descriptive names, registered names, trademarks, service marks, etc. in this publication does not imply, even in the absence of a specific statement, that such names are exempt from the relevant protective laws and regulations and therefore free for general use.
The publisher, the authors and the editors are safe to assume that the advice and information in this book are believed to be true and accurate at the date of publication. Neither the publisher nor the authors or the editors give a warranty, express or implied, with respect to the material contained herein or for any errors or omissions that may have been made. The publisher remains neutral with regard to jurisdictional claims in published maps and institutional affiliations.

Cover illustration: Krohg, Christian/ Nasjonalmuseet for kunst, arkitektur og design/The National Museum of Art, Architecture and Design

Printed on acid-free paper

This Palgrave Macmillan imprint is published by Springer Nature
The registered company is Springer International Publishing AG
The registered company address is: Gewerbestrasse 11, 6330 Cham, Switzerland

"This book is dedicated to Kristian 'Kikki' Andenæs"

Preface

This book is dedicated to Kristian 'Kikki' Andenæs, on his retirement as professor at the University of Oslo. Throughout his career, Kikki has been deeply involved in legal aid for marginalised people. As a student, he was already involved in the student-run legal aid clinic *Juss-Buss*. While the Juss-Buss-initiative was still in its early days, Kikki helped set up a group offering legal aid to Roma people. He graduated from the Faculty of Law at the University of Oslo in 1974. After that he worked in the Ministry of Social Affairs and then as a deputy judge, before returning to academia. From 1978, he was employed as amanuensis at the Department of Social Science at the University of Tromsø, and then, in 1984, he joined the Department of Sociology of Law, Faculty of Law, University of Oslo, where he was awarded a Dr. philos. in 1992, for his thesis on the social care system in Norway. He became a professor in 1997. During his time at the Department of Sociology of Law, which later became the Department of Criminology and Sociology of Law, he was—amongst other things—head of department and supervisor of the Juss-Buss-project.

Kikki has published extensively on legal and socio-legal issues. His main fields of interest have been social law, legal aid, immigration law, education law, juridification, and other issues related to equality before the law. His main works include the book based on his doctoral thesis, *Sosialomsorg i gode og onde dager* [Social care—for better, for worse], his book *Sosialrett* [Social welfare law], and his work on juridification, published in various articles. Much of it has had a policy-based approach, emphasising the need for a better understanding of how the law affects society in general, and disadvantaged groups in particular.

But Kikki's importance cannot be measured by his scholarly output alone. He has been the supervisor of several PhD and MA students, project manager of Juss-Buss, head of department, and a great colleague at the Department of Criminology and Sociology of Law, University of Oslo; he has been closely involved in *Retfærd. Nordic Journal of Law and Justice*. All this means that he is a crucial figure in the development of sociology of law as an academic discipline not only in Norway but throughout the Nordic countries. His commitment reaches beyond the academic world: he is an active and committed contributor to legal aid projects such as Gatejuristen [The Street Lawyers] and Juss-Buss.

Apparently one of Kikki's favourite paintings is the picture on the cover of this book: 'Kampen for tilværelsen' [The Struggle for Survival] painted 1888-89 by the Norwegian artist Christian Krohg. Krohg used his art, and position as an artist, to depict social injustice and protest against it. 'Kampen for tilværelsen' shows hungry women and children waiting in the snow outside a bakery in the hope of getting stale bread. Social commitment and the determination to use science to battle against social injustice is also the hallmark of Kikki's academic life, where scientific work has been used as a platform to engage actively in marginalised people's struggle to improve their lives. We would like to thank Nasjonalmuseet for kunst, arkitektur og design [The National Museum of Art, Architecture and Design] in Oslo for giving us permission to use this work.

The editors would also like to thank all the contributors, Per Jørgen Ystehede, Turid Eikvam, and Heidi Mork Lomell for their sound advice and invaluable help, and Daphne Day for proof reading all the chapters with great care. We thank the Publishing fund for UiO researchers for providing us with funding to enable us to publish the collection as open access.

Oslo and Copenhagen   Olaf Halvorsen Rønning
November 2016   Ole Hammerslev

Contents

1. **Legal Aid in the Nordic Countries**   1
   Ole Hammerslev and Olaf Halvorsen Rønning

2. **Legal Aid in Norway**   15
   Olaf Halvorsen Rønning

3. **Legal Aid in Sweden**   43
   Isabel Schoultz

4. **Legal Aid in Finland**   77
   Antti Rissanen

5. **Legal Aid in Denmark**   99
   Bettina Lemann Kristiansen

6. **Legal Aid in Iceland**   125
   Hildur Fjóla Antonsdóttir

7	Juss-Buss [Law Bus]: A Student-run Legal Aid Clinic *Ole Hammerslev, Annette Olesen, and Olaf Halvorsen Rønning*	147
8	Gadejuristen [The Street Lawyers]: Offering Legal Aid to Socially Marginalised People *Stine Piilgaard Porner Nielsen and Ole Hammerslev*	169
9	Ex-prisoners' Need for Legal Aid in Denmark *Annette Olesen*	193
10	Nordic Legal Aid and 'Access to Justice' in Human Rights. A European Perspective *Jon T. Johnsen*	227
11	Legal Aid and Clinical Legal Education in Europe and the USA: Are They Compatible? *Richard J. Wilson*	263
12	Juridification, Marginalised Persons and Competence to Mobilise the Law *Knut Papendorf*	287
13	Outsourcing Legal Aid in the Nordic Welfare States *Ole Hammerslev and Olaf Halvorsen Rønning*	311
Index		329

List of Figures

Fig. 2.1	Legal assistance granted	26
Fig. 2.2	Annual spending on legal aid outside court	27
Fig. 2.3	Annual budgeted spending on legal advice	28
Diagram 3.1	The number of legal aid matter that has been concluded between 1997 and 2014, approved by either the Legal Aid Authority or by the Courts	60
Fig. 4.1	Services provided in PLA offices in 2014	83
Fig. 4.2	The distribution of cases in PLA offices in 2014	85
Fig. 4.3	The distribution of private lawyers' legal aid cases in 2014	87
Fig. 7.1	Number of cases in selected years	150
Fig. 7.2	Number of cases in key legal disciplines, 1999–2015	152
Fig. 8.1	Number of new users per year	174

List of Tables

Table 2.1	Number of legal aid cases, 2014	25
Table 3.1	Legal aid granted in 2014 by the Legal Aid Authority and the courts, based on the various concerns	62
Table 3.2	Distribution of the legal aid granted in 2014 on the basis of financial base of the claimant and the share of the total cost to be paid by the legal aid fee	64
Table 4.1	Monthly means and the basic excess that the applicant is liable to pay	81
Table 5.1	Expenditure. Legal aid by lawyers	117
Table 5.2	Expenditure. Legal aid offices	117
Table 5.3	Expenditure. Legal aid offices	118
Table 5.4	Expenditure. Free legal aid in regard to lawsuits	118
Table 5.5	Number of cases where free legal aid is granted	118
Table 6.1	Legal aid applications and grants (%) by year	138
Table 7.1	Number of cases in key legal disciplines, 1999–2015	151
Table 10.1	Legal aid budget per inhabitant, from the top 11 countries, in 2012	252
Table 10.2	Legal aid cases and costs per case	253

1

Legal Aid in the Nordic Countries

Ole Hammerslev and Olaf Halvorsen Rønning

The Nordic countries are among the highest spenders in Europe on legal aid, which provides people with legal services when they cannot otherwise afford legal assistance. Figures from 2012 provided by the European Commission for the Efficiency of Justice CEPEJ (2014) show that, of 47 European countries, Norway spends the most on legal aid per inhabitant, Sweden comes sixth, Denmark eighth, Finland tenth, and Iceland eleventh (for a full discussion, see Chap. 10). However, like many other Western European countries, Nordic countries also face political demands for cost savings, particularly in the face of the years of austerity following the 2008 financial crisis that impacted European welfare states. The welfare state was challenged by the entry of private actors into domains that

---

O. Hammerslev (✉)
Department of Law, University of Southern Denmark, Odense M, Denmark

Department of Criminology and Sociology of Law, University of Oslo, Oslo, Norway

O.H. Rønning
Department of Criminology and Sociology of Law, Faculty of Law, University of Oslo, Oslo, Norway

traditionally belonged to the state, and by market-orientated reforms partly inspired by neo-liberal ideas (Bonoli and Natali 2012; Kvist and Greve 2011). This has affected legal aid in Nordic countries, just as it has in countries throughout the world, where legal aid systems are challenged by funding cuts, and there are demands for the setting of new priorities when limited funds are available.

The most prominent of such developments has been the recent changes in England and Wales, which has seen dramatic cuts in funding that affect both the supply of legal aid, and those legal professionals providing it. Studies of English legal aid lawyers show how new public management focuses on efficiency, cost control, and external monitoring through various forms of quality assurance measurements and guidelines (Sommerlad 2001; Sommerlad and Sanderson 2013; Sommerlad and Wall 1999). One major effect of all this, Sommerlad argues, is that legal aid lawyers, once seen as moral or political lawyers—who, as Sarat and Scheingold (1998, p. 3) point out—help raise the moral status of the legal profession by reconnecting law and morality, and by manifesting 'the idea that lawyering is a "public profession"' —become a group of lawyers with low morale that damages the political project they set out to defend, namely that of empowering their clients and countering social injustice. Legal aid lawyers are downgraded in the legal hierarchy, are stressed by increasing workloads, earn less, and, finally, turn into burned-out, disillusioned welfare workers (Sommerlad 2001). Meanwhile, Eastern European countries also face challenges in developing legal aid schemes, mainly due to massive underfunding. Instead, legal clinics are linked with law schools and legal education (cf. for instance, Barendrecht et al. 2014, p. 82; Piana et al. 2013). The USA fares no better, struggling with an underdeveloped legal aid scheme for criminal cases, and with a civil legal aid system consisting of a wide variety of programmes beset with funding issues, and problems to do with federal versus state provision of legal aid (Houseman 2015). In Australia, there is a diverse set of legal aid initiatives, and severe challenges as regards provision for the indigenous population, and for rural areas, together with the problem of severe financial constraints (Hunter et al. 2009). Countries such as China and Japan seem to have introduced extensive legislation on legal aid but are experiencing challenges about putting it into practice (Qin and Tang 2013). In Brazil, there has been growing interest in the right to legal aid provided by the state, but, so far, it is still charitable organisations that seem to provide most of the legal aid (Alves 2014).

In this book, we set out to examine and compare civil legal aid in Nordic countries, as seen in relation to welfare state reforms, to determine if a unique model of Nordic legal aid exists. The Nordic welfare state model, common to all Nordic countries, is characterised by universal state-regulated welfare schemes, which give all citizens the right to assistance when they have various kinds of health or social problems. With the development of the Nordic welfare states after World War Two, the process of juridification accelerated, as legislation ensuring people's rights to welfare expanded. The growing complexity of welfare rights and regulation, as well as increasing bureaucracy, meant that ordinary people, especially poor people, had difficulty claiming their rights, both from the public administration and in the courts. Substantial legal aid schemes were developed to help people claim these rights, and in the Nordic countries legal aid came to be considered as part of the universal welfare ideology.

Nordic research on legal aid has most often been carried out against the backdrop of the ideology of universal welfare: researchers have generally considered legal aid as no different from traditional welfare state social support schemes, such as health care and social security, even though the market for legal services has been based primarily on market premises (Johnsen 1987). Though limited, Nordic legal aid research flourished in the 1970s and developed hand-in-hand with the emergence of new legal aid clinics in Norway and Denmark that were critical of public legal aid that was failing to satisfy unmet legal need among disadvantaged groups in society.

Nordic Legal Aid Research

With the strong social commitment of the 1970s, and the turn towards critical scholarship, if not Marxism, research inspirations and interests varied markedly in different Nordic countries. It was only in Norway that legal aid research developed into a strong field of socio-legal research in this decade, with pioneers such as Vilhelm Aubert, Thomas Mathiesen, Kristian 'Kikki' Andenæs, Torstein Eckhoff, and Jon T. Johnsen, in the Faculty of Law of the University of Oslo. They were inspired by US sociology, the sociology of law, and by cause lawyering (Mathiesen 2001). They succeeded in establishing several so-called action research projects that sought to combine scientific knowledge with practical action (Hammerslev and Mathiesen 2013). These projects had several aims. First, they established legal aid clinics in which law students gave free outreach legal aid to marginalised citizens. Not only did people in need get free legal advice, but law student volunteers got practical experience as a part of their education. Another aim was to document which types of legal need existed, and how social structures impacted different classes unevenly, so that the aid could be improved, and knowledge could be used to benefit those in need. They established attractive kinds of legal clinics in which future high profile lawyers and judges worked in during their studies. Through their visibility and use of academic capital, they successfully set the agenda on legal aid: factors that still make the legal clinic *Juss-Buss* an important and visible player in Norway (see Chap. 7). In Denmark, as in Finland, critical legal scholars were more concerned with changing social conditions for marginalised people by means of theoretical analysis of the law, and of the very concept of law (Hammerslev and Madsen 2014; Hammerslev and Madsen 2013). There were a few studies of legal aid, and some Danish research on various issues in Greenland, but their engagement with legal aid issues was not sufficient to make legal aid paradigmatic as a research topic, or as an important element in the public discourse, as had happened in Norway.

Noting the development of extensive welfare legislation giving all citizens rights in increasing areas, a series of Norwegian studies in the 1970s and 1980s examined the latent need for legal aid among marginalised people (Eidesen et al. 1975; Eskeland and Finne 1973; Johnsen 1994, 1987; Andenæs et al. 2005). Legal aid was defined thus: 'Aid which one person receives from another … when the aid worker has legal knowledge that can potentially have an impact on obtaining a desired result.' (Eskeland 1975, p. 12, our translation).

In several studies during the 1970s, including work on immigrant workers, Norwegian Romani, and the homeless, Norwegian scholars found that the need for legal aid was determined by social structures in industrialised society: everyone has a need for legal aid but the system for accessing legal assistance is uneven. The higher your position in the social hierarchy, the greater is the availability of legal aid—which means that the well-off, and companies, can have their needs met by the wide variety of legal services offered on the free market, while the more disadvantaged you are, less is available, and the more difficult it is to access legal aid. Mathiesen concluded that the need for legal aid was greater the lower the class one belonged to, and that the 'lumpenproletariat' had an especially acute need for legal aid in the areas of tax law, social security law, and the law on rent—core areas of the welfare state (Mathiesen 1975, p. 188). This showed that legal aid was symptomatic of social structures: on the one hand, even though welfare rights relate to basic subsistence, citizens are more likely to claim their rights the higher in the social hierarchy they are; on the other hand, many problems that the law is designed to solve cannot be solved by the law, since they arise from concrete difficult life situations (Eskeland and Finne 1973; Mathicsen 1975; Albrechtsen 1975). These studies generally followed work done in the USA and the UK (Hammerslev 2016; Smith 1919, Clark and Corstvet 1938; Pleasence et al. 2001; Dalberg-Larsen 1977; Abel-Smith et al. 1973).

Through the legal clinics, researchers were able to examine various barriers to legal aid, and the way legal aid, including outreach legal aid, was delivered; they were also in a position to make recommendations on the organisation of legal aid institutions. One reason why the law fails to give the legal protection it is designed to provide, it was argued, is the fact that welfare law is often written in difficult language, so that the rules are hard to understand for any lay person—and even more so for marginalised people, who often have little education. Another reason was that marginalised people could not afford legal assistance if it was not free (Sejr 1977). As society becomes ever more complex, and the amount of legislation becomes ever greater, this creates legal insecurity. To this should be added the increasing use of framework acts that delegate authority to public authorities for making decisions. The decisions and discretion of public authorities may well become dependent on financial or political criteria, making the most marginalised even more vulnerable (Beck and Sejr 1977, p. 213; see also Papendorf 2012).

Despite the existence of outreach legal aid for less well-off groups, there were barriers that prevented it reaching the target groups, because of the way aid was organised, and because of the target groups' lack of knowledge of legal aid, and their distrust of legal aid lawyers. To meet the needs of the most disadvantaged groups in society, Sejr (1977) concludes, legal aid ought to be delivered through informal institutions that have a close connection to local communities, and by means of outreach work. Institutions should be independent of the state and staffed by lawyers but should also have links with social workers and psychologists, because legal problems are often linked to other issues. Furthermore, legal aid should be free, and information about it should be made more available to target groups (Beck and Sejr 1977, p. 217). Legal aid was seen as a way to strengthen the rule of law and to enable citizens to take part in democratic decision-making processes (Beck and Sejr 1977, p. 219; see also Papendorf 2012).

Despite considerable state expenditure on legal aid, these early studies set the agenda for later legal aid research through their critical approach to the organisation of legal aid and the apparent unmet legal need among the poorest groups in society. In general, Nordic studies were characterised by an optimistic view of the law, and of free legal aid as the solution to various problems of less well-off groups in society. The studies assumed that they could uncover a latent—but real—need for legal assistance among certain groups of citizens. Thus, against a background of assumptions about a universal welfare state, unmet legal need in the Nordic populations is well documented (Dalberg-Larsen and Kristiansen 2014; Kristiansen 2013, 2009; Graver et al. 2001; Juss-Buss 2001; Juss-Buss and Rønning 2011). However, these studies rarely consider the normative side of their methodological approach. Behind the assessment of legal need was the assumption that people should use lawyers to solve their problems, and that when they did not use lawyers or other advisors, this constituted 'unmet legal need'. This made it easy to argue that further public funds were necessary (see also Pleasence et al. 2001). Hidden behind discussions of methods and empirical findings is the failure of the studies to recognise that, as Lewis (1973) pointed out: 'defining something as a legal problem is not a statement of fact, but a normative statement about how a problem ought to be solved.' The focus of the research, and the research design, has an embedded normativity (Habermas 1972).

Purpose of the Book

As illustrated by the literature review above, Nordic research on legal aid has not taken recent welfare state changes into consideration, nor have there been any comparative studies of all the Nordic countries. To serve several purposes, this volume therefore takes a different approach from that of traditional Nordic studies.

First, through chapters on individual countries, it seeks to compare all Nordic legal aid schemes—i.e., those of Denmark, Norway, Sweden, Finland, and Iceland—and to relate legal aid developments to those in the welfare states. The chapters explore some general questions about how legal aid schemes in the Nordic countries are organised and how they function. To what extent do the schemes match welfare state ideology, and are they changing alongside the changes in the welfare state?

Second, through discussions of the European 'access to justice perspective' set against the USA use of legal clinics, Chaps. 10, 11, and 12 examine the uniqueness of Nordic legal aid in a wider perspective. The overarching question is whether we can identify a Nordic model of legal aid. Through comparison of approaches within the Nordic countries, and the positioning of Nordic legal aid in the wider world, the conclusion will compare the Nordic schemes, their differences and similarities—and discuss if the Nordic welfare state approach to legal aid is unique.

Budget cuts also give rise to questions about how to design efficient legal aid programmes, and make alternative legal aid schemes more interesting: throughout the world there is a wide variety of alternative programmes exploring new ways of providing legal aid. As discussed above, Nordic legal aid research has also focused on, and recommended, the provision of alternative forms of legal aid. Thus a *third* purpose of this volume is to explore and discuss how legal aid institutions in the contemporary Nordic welfare states are organised and how they work. Chaps. 7, 8, and 9 examine some of the most notable alternative legal aid programmes in the Nordic countries: Juss-Buss, the Danish organisation The Street Lawyers, and various mentoring programmes for ex-prisoners. The aim of these case studies is to discuss alternative legal aid initiatives, and examine how the various programmes reach their target groups and help turn social problems into legal cases through legal aid in—to adopt the notion of Felstiner et al. (1980) —a naming, blaming, claiming process (for earlier studies discussing this process see, e.g., Carlin and Howard 1964–1965, p. 424; Johnsen 1987; Olesen et al. 2016, 2017).

Outline

Following the introduction, Chaps. 2, 3, 4, 5, and 6 will describe the national legal aid systems of the five Nordic countries. In this section, the public, state-organised legal aid schemes will be analysed, together with other notable legal aid initiatives in particular countries. The *Norwegian legal aid scheme*, as examined by Olaf Halvorsen Rønning, is largely based upon a well-funded public legal aid 'judicare' scheme. However, it is traditionally organised, with private-practice lawyers as the main providers, so it fails to fully meet some legal needs, especially those of disadvantaged groups. The public legal aid scheme is therefore complemented by a few high-capacity, outreach-focused legal aid initiatives directed at certain disadvantaged groups. These programmes are to some extent state-funded but are otherwise independent, and are connected to a Norwegian tradition of legal aid research and policy. The *Swedish legal aid scheme*—as described by Isabel Schoultz—has undergone a transformation: it used to be a public scheme comparable with Norway but now relies mainly on commercial legal aid insurance. Few alternative legal aid programmes exist. Insurance schemes mostly cover legal representation in trials, not legal advice or representation. Antti Rissanen examines legal aid in Finland. The *Finnish legal aid scheme* is perhaps the one most in tune with a welfare state ideology, as state-funded legal aid offices are the backbone of the scheme. It covers all legal problems, and has generous financial eligibility criteria. If necessary, the public legal aid offices can call on judicare lawyers. The Finnish legal aid system seems to work well but concerns have been raised that this system, too, will face more restrictions in coming years. The *Danish legal aid scheme*, as analysed by Bettina Lemann Kristiansen, has a mix of legal aid offices and judicare lawyers. The legal aid offices, organised by a private lawyers' and volunteers' initiative, but partly funded by the state, provide most of the legal advice, while legal representation, particularly in the courts, is provided by lawyers. The trend is now to cut expenditure on legal aid and on legal advice in particular. This is raising concerns about the accessibility of the legal aid system. Hildur Fjola Antonsdottir examines Icelandic legal aid. At present the *Icelandic legal aid scheme* is being affected by the financial crisis. It is based on a judicare model, with a measure of discretion regarding eligibility criteria, but the scheme is mostly limited to legal representation. The lack of accessible legal advice and information remains a concern.

After this analysis of the general legal aid systems, seen from a national perspective, Chaps. 7, 8, and 9 are devoted to in-depth case studies of particularly interesting examples of legal aid in the different countries. From Norway, there is a chapter by Ole Hammerslev, Annette Olesen, and Olaf Halvorsen Rønning on *Juss-Buss*, a student-run legal aid clinic. The establishment of the clinic was closely connected with pioneering legal aid research in Norway in the 1970s, and it is still in operation. Juss-Buss provides outreach legal aid to disadvantaged groups, such as prisoners and migrant workers, who are insufficiently covered by public schemes. Stine Piilgaard Porner Nielsen and Ole Hammerslev examines *Gadejuristen* [The Street Lawyers], which is a project in Denmark providing legal aid to vulnerable groups on the streets, such as drug addicts and sex workers. It is based on a holistic and novel outreach idea, and provides social and legal aid in an informal manner. The *legal needs of ex-prisoners*, and how the legal aid system functions in relation to them, are examined by Annette Olesen in the last chapter of this section. With background in the above-mentioned notion of Felstiner et al. 1980) of a naming, blaming, claiming process, which stresses how legal cases can emerge and transform, it highlights the inadequacy of the legal aid scheme to cope with the complexities of the legal problems prisoners face, and points to the need for more cross-functional legal aid programmes.

The final section, Chaps. 10, 11, and 12, will help contextualise the studies of the Nordic legal aid schemes. Johnsen's chapter on the *Nordic model of legal aid in Europe* compares the Finnish and Norwegian models of legal aid, and analyses them in relation to the ideologies of the welfare state, and against the background of European human rights. On the basis of theoretical perspectives on juridification, in particular in relation to Habermasian theories on the development of law in welfare states, Papendorf discusses the scope for disadvantaged groups to mobilise the law. Wilson discusses the differences between the USA and the European traditions of *legal aid clinics*, pointing out the current development of clinical legal education that is taking place in Europe.

The concluding chapter, Chap. 13, compares and analyses the legal aid systems in the Nordic countries, particularly in relation to the changes taking place in the welfare states, and discusses whether there is a unique Nordic model of legal aid.

References

Abel-Smith, B., Zander, M., & Brooke, R. (1973). *Legal problems and the citizen: A study in three London boroughs*. London: Heinemann.

Albrechtsen, E. H. (1975). Om advokater og advokatsøking. In A. Eidesen, S. Eskeland, & T. Mathiesen (Eds.), *Rettshjelp og samfunnsstruktur* (pp. 23–71). Oslo: Pax.

Alves, C. F. (2014). Contemporary challenges to legal aid in Brazil and England: Comparative perspectives on access to justice. *Amicus Curiae, 98*, 22–25.

Andenæs, K., Olsen-Nalum, H., Røed, M., & Westlund, J. (2005). *Kontoret for fri retshjælp: Retshjælp til ubemidlede: evaluering av en Oslo-institusjon gjennom 112 år*. Oslo.

Barendrecht, M., Kistemaker, L., Scholten, H. J., Schrader, R., & Wrzesinska, M. (2014). *Legal aid in Europe: Nine different ways to guarantee access to justice?* Amsterdam: Ministerie van Veilgheid en Justitie.

Beck, S., & Sejr, L. (1977). Retshjælpsbehov og retshjælpstilbud—en afsluttende teoretisk og retspolitisk diskussion.'. In L. Sejr (Ed.), *Retshjælp i et lokalområde* (pp. 201–221). Aarhus: Aarhus Universitet.

Bonoli, G., & Natali, D. (Eds.). (2012). *The politics of the new welfare state*. Oxford: Oxford University Press.

Carlin, J. E., & Howard, J. (1964–1965). Legal representation and class justice. *UCLA L. Rev., 12*, 381–437.

Clark, C. E., & Corstvet, E. (1938). The lawyer and the public: An A.A.L.S survey. *The Yale Law Journal, 47*, 1972–1993.

Dalberg-Larsen, J. (1977). Retshjælpsproblemer i et historisk perspektiv. Om behovet for retshjælp og om ideologi, praksis og forsning på retshjælpsområdet. In L. Sejr (Ed.), *Retshjælp i et lokalområde* (pp. 6–42). Aarhus Universitet.

Dalberg-Larsen, J., & Kristiansen, B. L. (2014). *Lovene og livet: En retssociologisk grundbog*. København: Jurist- og Økonomforbundets Forlag.

Eidesen, A., Eskeland, S., & Mathiesen, T. (1975). *Rettshjelp og samfunnsstruktur*. Oslo: Pax Forlag.

Eskeland, S. (1975). Innledning. In A. Eidesen, S. Eskeland, & T. Mathiesen (Eds.), *Rettshjelp og samfunnsstruktur* (pp. 10–22). Pax Forlag: Oslo.

Eskeland, S., & Finne, J. (1973). *Rettshjelp*. Oslo: Pax.

European Commission for the Efficiency of Justice. (2014). *European judicial systems. Efficiency and quality of justice*. Edition 2014 (2012 data). CEPEJ. Council of Europe. Strasbourg (CEPEJ 2014).

Felstiner, W. L. F., Abel, R. L., & Sarat, A. (1980). The emergence and transformation of disputes: Naming, blaming, claiming. *Law & Society Review, 15*(3/4), 631–654.

Graver, A. B., Skaug V., Strålberg, R., & Tangen, B. (2001). *Rettshjelp 2001: Behovet for rettshjelp i Oslos befolkning – deriblant et utvalg innvadrekvinner*. Universitetet i Oslo, Institutt for kriminologi og rettssosiologi.

Habermas, J. (1972). *Knowledge and human interests*. Boston: Beacon Press.

Hammerslev, O. (2016). Retshjælpsforskning. In H. V. G. Pedersen (Ed.), *Juridiske emner ved Syddansk Universitet 2015* (pp. 339–348). Jurist- og Økonomforbundets Forlag: København.

Hammerslev, O., & Madsen, M. R. (Eds.). (2013). *Retssociologi*. København: Hans Reitzels Forlag.

Hammerslev, O., & Madsen, M. R. (2014). The return of sociology in Danish socio-legal studies: A survey of recent trends. *International Journal of Law in Context, 10*(3), 397–415.

Hammerslev, O. & Mathiesen, T. (2013). Marxistisk retssociologi. In O. Hammerslev & R.M. Madsen (Eds.), *Klassisk og moderne retssociologi. Centrale temaer og tekster*. København: Hans Reitzels Forlag.

Houseman, A. W. (2015). *Civil legal aid in the United States: An update for 2015*. Washington, DC: National Equal Justice Library.

Hunter, R., Banks, C., & Giddings, J. (2009). Australian innovations in legal aid services: Lessons from an evaluation study. In P. Pleasence & N. J. Balmer (Eds.), *Reaching further: Innovation, access and quality in legal services*. London: TSO.

Johnsen, J. T. (1987). *Retten til juridisk bistand*. Oslo: Tano.

Johnsen, J. T. (1994). Nordic legal aid. *Maryland Journal of Contemporay Legal Issues, 5*(2), 301–331.

Juss-Buss. (2001). *Tvers igjennom lov til seier*. Oslo: Unipax.

Juss-Buss and O. H. Rønning (2011). *Med loven mot makta: Juss-Buss førti år*. Oslo: Novus Forlag.

Kristiansen, B. L. (2009). *Retshjælp i Danmark. Delrapport I: Beskrivelse af retshjælpstilbuddene*. Copenhagen: Justitsministeriets forskningsrapport.

Kristiansen, B. L. (2013). Retshjælp – fortsat et udækket behov? In T. Gammeltoft, I. E. Koch, B. L. Kristiansen, & S. Schaumburg-Müller (Eds.), *Protecting the rights of others* (pp. 83–101). København: DJØF-Forlag.

Kvist, J., & Greve, B. (2011). Has the Nordic welfare model been transformed? *Social Policy and Administration, 45*(2), 146–160.

Lewis, P. (1973). Social needs and legal action. In P. Morris, R. White, & P. Lewis (Eds.), *Social needs and legal action*. Oxford: Martin Roberston.

Mathiesen, T. (1975). Noen konlusjoner om rettshjelp, rettspolitikk og samfunnsstruktur. In A. Eidesen, S. Eskeland, & T. Mathiesen (Eds.), *Rettshjelp og samfunnsstruktur* (pp. 187–206). Oslo: Pax.

Mathiesen, T. (2001). Juss-Buss 30 år. In Juss-Buss (Ed.), *Tvers igjennom lov til seir* (pp. 16–19). Oslo: Pax Forlag.

Olesen, A., Minke, L. K., & Hammerslev, O. (2016). Det retlige møde. In *Festskrift til Sten Schaumburg-Müller*. København: Jurist- og Økonomforbundets Forlag.

Olesen, A., Nielsen, S.P.P. & Hammerslev, O. (2017). 'Gadejura – kunsten at fremelske gadefolkets oplevelse af at bære rettigheder.' In B.O.G. Mortensen et al. (Eds.), *Festskrift til Hans Viggo Godsk Pedersen*. København: Jurist- og Økonomforbundets Forlag.

Papendorf, K. (2012). *Rett for alle? Rettsliggjøring og rettsfjerne personers mulighet til å mobilisere retten*. Oslo: Novus forlag.

Piana, D., Langbroek, P., Berkmanas, T., Hammerslev, O., & Pacurari, O. (Eds.). (2013). *Legal and judicial training in Europe*. The Hague: Eleven International Publishing.

Pleasence, P., Buck, A., Goriely, T., Taylor, J., Perkins, H., & Quirk, H. (2001). *Local legal need*. London: Legal Services Research Centre.

Qin, Z., & Tang, J. (2013). Practical exploration and thoughts on model of clinical legal education–legal aid. In W. Du (Ed.), *Informatics and management science IV* (pp. 469–476). London: Springer London.

Sarat, A., & Scheingold, S. A. (1998). *Cause lawyering: Political commitments and professional responsibilities, Oxford socio-legal studies*. New York/Oxford: Oxford University Press.

Sejr, L. (Ed.). (1977). *Retshjælp i et lokalområde*. Aarhus: Aarhus Universitet.

Smith, R.H. (1919). *Justice and the poor: A study of the present denial of justice to the poor and of the agencies making more equal their position before the law, with particular reference to legal aid work in the United States*. Carnegie Foundation for the Advancement of Teaching.

Sommerlad, H. (2001). "I've lost the plot": An everyday story of the 'political' legal aid lawyer. *Journal of Law and Society, 28*(3), 335–360.

Sommerlad, H., & Sanderson, P. (2013). Social justice on the margins: The future of the not for profit sector as providers of legal advice in England and Wales. *Journal of Social Welfare and Family Law, 35*(3), 305–327.

Sommerlad, H., & Wall, D. (1999). *Legally aided clients and their solicitors: Qualitative perspectives on quality and legal aid*. London: The Law Society.

Open Access This chapter is distributed under the terms of the Creative Commons Attribution 4.0 International License (http://creativecommons.org/licenses/by/4.0/), which permits use, duplication, adaptation, distribution, and reproduction in any medium or format, as long as you give appropriate credit to the original author(s) and the source, a link is provided to the Creative Commons license, and any changes made are indicated.

The images or other third party material in this book are included in the work's Creative Commons license, unless indicated otherwise in the credit line; if such material is not included in the work's Creative Commons license and the respective action is not permitted by statutory regulation, users will need to obtain permission from the license holder to duplicate, adapt or reproduce the material.

2

Legal Aid in Norway

Olaf Halvorsen Rønning

Brief Overview and Introduction

The most prominent feature of legal aid in Norway is the public legal aid scheme. This is complemented by a few high-capacity alternative legal aid providers, such as public legal aid offices and legal aid clinics.

The public legal aid scheme, which receives the bulk of the public funding available for legal aid, is mainly provided through a 'judicare' scheme under which lawyers in private practice provide legal assistance to those granted such aid. The lawyers are remunerated through government funding. The conditions for granting legal aid under the scheme are strictly regulated by law, and aid is granted by civil service institutions or the courts. The civil legal aid scheme covers areas of law like divorce, unlawful dismissal, social security, and immigration, and in most cases a financial criterion determines eligibility for aid. The public legal aid judicare scheme is complemented by a few legal aid offices and first line services.

O.H. Rønning (✉)
Department of Criminology and Sociology of Law, Faculty of Law, University of Oslo, Oslo, Norway

In addition to the public judicare scheme, there are other legal aid providers. Some provide commercial legal assistance, such as legal aid insurance, while some are third sector initiatives. These are oriented around student legal aid clinics, interest organisations providing legal aid to certain groups (such as asylum seekers and drug users), consumer organisations, and labour unions. Some are fully, or partly, government funded, but they remain independently administered.

Legal aid in criminal matters, both to the accused and the victim, is mainly regulated by the criminal procedure code. In most criminal cases the accused is entitled to assistance from a publicly funded defender. The victim is entitled to legal aid in a range of cases, including those involving sexual assault, domestic violence, or serious bodily harm. Claims for compensation for the victim are incorporated in the criminal proceedings, and are argued either by the prosecution or by the victim's publicly funded lawyer (*bistandsadvokat*).

In what follows, this chapter will give a brief introduction to legal aid research in Norway.[1] Next, is a description of the civil public aid scheme's eligibility criteria, its providers, its administration, and how it is used. Alternative publicly funded and administered legal aid schemes, such as public legal aid offices, will then be dealt with. Finally, the chapter will discuss alternative legal aid initiatives, such as legal aid clinics and legal aid provided by public interest organisations.

Research on Legal Aid in Norway

There has been a considerable amount of research into legal aid, and legal needs, in Norway. This research has examined unmet legal need, doctrinal, and socio-legal analysis of the legal situation of disadvantaged groups, as well as the functioning of different legal aid initiatives. Here, only a brief overview of the most relevant research is given.

The first scientific examination of legal aid issues was *Rettshjelp* ('Legal aid') (Eskeland and Finne 1973), which showed an unmet legal need in Norway and how the legal aid schemes then in place failed to reach disadvantaged groups. The research on unmet legal need was continued and expanded in Jon T. Johnsen's (1987) *Retten til juridisk bistand*, which consisted of broad empirical, theoretical, and policy-oriented analysis of the extent and causes of unmet legal needs, and of how legal aid schemes could be designed to deal with such issues. The tradition of research into unmet legal needs has continued in several empirical studies (Graver et al. 2002; Haugen and Vigerust 1992; Jordal and Hasle 2014), which all found extensive unmet legal need.

Research has also been conducted on various legal aid initiatives, such as student-run legal aid clinics like *Juss-Buss*, or *Gatejuristen* (The Street Lawyers). This research has focused on doctrinal and socio-legal analysis of the legal problems faced by the client groups, and the working methods and effects of legal aid initiatives (see e.g., Johnsen and Anti 1997; Lied 2013; Bratholm and Sundby 1976; Eskeland et al. 1975; Juss-Buss 1996, 2001; Rui and Jusshjelpa i Nord-Norge 2009; Rønning and Juss-Buss 2011, Graver 1979; Johnsen 1980; Lid 1981; Rønning and Bentsen 2008).

There has been a considerable number of analyses of features of the legal aid scheme, with comparative analysis of international legal aid schemes (Johnsen 2009a), and evaluations of current or pilot legal aid schemes (Andenæs et al. 2005; Botheim et al. 2008; Oxford Research 2013, 2015).

The Public Legal Aid Judicare Scheme

The civil public legal aid scheme in Norway is based on a 'judicare' model. Lawyers in private practice provide legal aid to eligible clients and are remunerated out of public funds. The scheme is regulated by the Legal Aid Act, which lays down the eligibility criteria; both financial and material that have to be fulfilled in order to get legal aid.

The Norwegian public legal aid scheme's stated purpose is to be a 'social support scheme to ensure that the necessary legal assistance is provided to people without means, so they have access to legal advice and representation in cases of great personal and welfare importance.' This avowed purpose serves as a guideline for the interpretation and application of the Act and also explicitly identifies the welfare ideology inspiring it. The issue of the Act's welfare ideology, and whether it actually conforms to this ideology, is discussed in Chap. 10.

History

There have been elements of regulation of legal assistance in Norway since Viking times (approx. eighth to eleventh century AD), and the first formal laws of Norway, from the late 1200s, had provisions for royal ombudsmen, who were entitled to file suits on behalf of those without sufficient knowledge or power to represent themselves (NOU 1976, p. 38). During the 1500s and 1600s, officially appointed lawyers—procurators—were obliged to represent 'the poor, widows, the insane, and the defenceless' before the courts, without other remuneration than a percentage of the claim received if the client won the case. This scheme, with only minor adjustments, continued into the 1800s. After 1893, the Ministry of Justice took over the administration of the legal aid scheme, and had discretionary power to grant legal representation in court cases. This was transferred to the courts in 1937. Legal aid outside court cases was not considered a state matter, but in the major cities municipal legal aid offices were established to provide legal aid. The first was the office for legal aid in Oslo, established in 1893; it was inspired by the Danish 'Studentersamfundets Retshjælp for Ubemidlede.' This office is still in operation, see below. Similar offices existed in Bergen, Trondheim, and Stavanger but these have since closed.

The legal aid scheme was informal and discretionary, and only regulated by a circular from the Ministry of Justice, until reform work began in the early 1970s. In 1980, the Legal Aid Act was passed; it implemented the current public legal aid scheme (Legal Aid Act 1981). The law provided for wide eligibility, especially since it contained no restriction on which types of cases could be granted legal aid. However, after only a few years, the Act was amended, and restrictions on eligibility were introduced. Although the Act has been amended several times, the basic structure of the scheme remains the same.

Eligibility

Under the current public legal aid scheme, legal aid will only be granted if the eligibility criteria of the Legal Aid Act are met. There are both financial and material criteria for eligibility, and restrictions on subject, necessity, and subsidiarity.

Financial Eligibility

In most instances, there is a financial eligibility criterion that must be met if legal aid funded by the public legal aid scheme is to be granted. However, there are no such criteria in cases involving matters considered to be particularly important, such as domestic violence, the use of force in psychiatric health care, or child welfare cases (Legal Aid Act, section 11 and section 16).

When financial eligibility is assessed, both income and assets are taken into account, as well as whether the applicant has a spouse/co-habitant or not. There is then no further assessment of the applicant's actual ability to fund legal aid by themselves: no adjustments are made, for instance, on the basis of the total cost of legal assistance needed, or any particularly high outgoings the applicant has, such as child maintenance or medical expenses.

A person must have less than 246,000 Norwegian Kroner—NOK (27,300 €) in gross annual income, or, if they are cohabiting, the gross annual income of the household must be below 369,000 NOK (40,750 €), in order to be eligible for legal aid. For comparison, the average gross annual income in Norway is currently 518,000 NOK (57,000 €) (SSB 2016). In addition, a person must have net assets below 100,000 NOK (11,000 €). Assets, such as cars or holiday cottages, are included in the assessment (Justis- og politidepartementet 2012, section 3.4).

If either of these financial eligibility criteria is not fulfilled, legal aid can be granted under a discretionary exemption clause (Legal Aid Act 1981, section 11 subsection 3, and section 16 subsection 3) but it is rarely employed, except for exemptions of housing of normal value (Rønning and Bentsen 2008).

These financial criteria have not been changed since 1 January 2009. This has in effect reduced the income threshold for financial eligibility for legal aid, as average salaries have increased since that time.

Material Criteria

The Legal Aid Act contains clear cut provisions identifying those cases in which an applicant would be eligible for legal aid. In general, only if the applicant's case falls within the areas of law specifically mentioned in the Act will legal aid be granted.

Coverage under the law has been steadily developed since it came into force. The overarching principle is said to be that cases of importance for the welfare of the applicant should be prioritised. The original preparatory work of the Legal Aid Act that established the current system, states that the rationale for choosing certain areas of law was that these were ones commonly seen as being most significant to people, and affecting their personal relations the most. Typically they involved employment, children, family, divorce, tenancy, and social security. In subsequent years, there has been little reform of the scope of the law. A few areas of law have been added, in particular ones relating to mental health care and immigration issues.

The Act distinguishes between legal aid cases involving means testing (where the financial eligibility criteria apply) and cases without means testing.

In certain matters deemed to be of 'great personal or welfare importance for a person' (Justis- og politidepartementet 2004, p. 29), legal aid is granted without means testing (Legal Aid Act 1981, section 11 subsection 1, and section 16 subsection 1). This includes the following:

- Immigration cases
- Child welfare cases
- Claims for compensation or redress for unlawful criminal prosecution
- Claims for compensation from the perpetrator of a criminal offence
- Domestic violence cases
- Cases regarding forced marriage
- Cases where coercion is involved, for instance, in psychiatric health care
- Cases concerning conscientious objection to military service

In other areas, legal aid is only granted if the financial criteria are fulfilled (Legal Aid Act 1981, section 11 subsection 2, and section 16 subsection 2). These are matters considered to be of crucial importance to the welfare of the person concerned.

They include:

- Marital cases
- Custody cases
- Personal injury cases
- Tenancy cases regarding termination of contract and eviction
- Employment cases regarding unfair dismissal
- Compensation for victims of violent crime
- Complaints/appeals concerning social security

In matters other than those specified in the Legal Aid Act, legal aid will not normally be granted. There is, however, an exemption clause from this, which allows the County Governor or the court to grant legal aid in any legal matter, though the use of this clause is very limited (Justis- og politidepartementet 2012; Rønning and Bentsen 2008).

The scope of the scheme has been extensively criticised (see the review in Botheim et al. 2008, p. 100; Justis- og politidepartementet 2008, p. 67). The criticism has mostly been that the general scope of the scheme is too limited and that it is poorly adjusted to the legal need that research and practitioners suggest exists in the population. In addition, the delimitation of the areas covered under the scheme has been criticised for being random (Rønning and Bentsen 2008). An example of such randomness is that legal aid is granted in tenancy cases if the applicant's contract has been terminated due to a normal breach of contract but not if it has been terminated due to a gross breach of contract. Similarly, legal aid is provided in cases involving deportation following a breach of the immigration act but not when deportation follows a breach of the criminal code.

Other Criteria

Coverage under the public legal aid scheme is subsidiary. Thus legal aid will generally only be granted if the need for legal aid is not covered by anything else, such as legal expense insurance, public information offices such as consumer advice centres, or the administrative obligation to give guidance to the public (Legal Aid Act 1981, section 11 subsection 2, and section 16 subsection 2). This significantly limits the availability of legal aid in administrative matters, as under the Norwegian administrative procedure act, public officials have a wide-ranging obligation to give guidance to individuals. This is one of the more contested issues regarding the Norwegian Legal Aid Act. Many of the most disadvantaged groups, such as prisoners, often have legal disputes with administrative bodies but under this rule are excluded from the legal aid scheme.

There are general necessity criteria in the Legal Aid Act, which limit the scope of the Act in cases where legal aid is unnecessary in a particular situation, because the problem is not a legal one, or because legal aid cannot contribute to solving the problem. For legal aid in the form of representation in court cases, the Legal Aid Act stipulates that the granting of legal aid has to be reasonable. This entails a consideration of various issues, including the cost of the case in relation to the value at issue, and the proceedability of the court case.

As a central principle the Legal Aid Act limits cover to physical persons (Legal Aid Act 1981, section 4): commercial entities are excluded from the scheme.

Grants and Providers of Legal Aid

If legal aid is granted, the applicant is entitled to either legal assistance outside court, or legal representation in court proceedings. The legal aid will be provided by a lawyer, who will be remunerated from state funds.

If legal assistance is granted, the lawyer will be paid for the work according to set rates for the hours needed for the case—so-called fixed fees. For instance, in most immigration cases, one will receive legal aid for between three and seven hours, while in family cases involving divorce one will receive legal aid for 12 hours. The number of hours allotted for different issues are set by the Ministry of Justice. The client is entitled to the necessary legal assistance from the legal aid lawyer, regardless of whether the case is more complicated than provided for in the fixed fees. This means that lawyers working on such cases would receive less than the nominal hourly fee for legal aid cases.

If legal representation is granted, the applicant will receive as much legal aid as is necessary to conduct the case in a reasonable manner. The courts, or the County Governor's office, will check the hours claimed, and will cap the number of hours payable if they exceed what is reasonable.

If legal aid is granted, court fees will also be covered under the legal aid scheme, together with costs of interpretation and costs relating to evidentiary issues. A grant for legal aid will not cover the legal expenses of the opposing party, which the legal aid client will generally be obliged to pay if he or she loses a court case.

The hourly fee for lawyers working under the scheme is currently 995 NOK (110 €) (Justis- og politidepartementet 2015, section 1). In 2013, the average hourly fee for lawyers in Norway was 1403 NOK (155 €) (Den Norske Advokatforening 2014, p. 21),[2] while the average hourly fee for lawyers with mostly private (as opposed to corporate) clients was 1254 NOK (140 €).

The client has to pay a contribution. The rate is currently 995 NOK (110 €) for legal aid outside court. For legal aid in court proceedings, the contribution is 25% of the cost but is capped at 4975 NOK (550 €) (Regulation to the Legal Aid Act 2005, section 2–1).

As the providers under the scheme are lawyers in private practice, the scheme provides traditional legal assistance comparable to that which any self-funding client would have. All providers under the scheme are licensed advocates or deputy advocates, bound by the common regulatory framework and ethical codes covering lawyers in Norway. However, the use of private practice lawyers rather than traditional legal aid lawyers means that it is harder to remove traditional barriers to accessing legal assistance, such as lack of problem awareness (Eskeland and Finne 1973, p. 212), cultural issues (Johnsen 1987, p. 503), lack of language skills (Andenæs et al. 2001, p. 21), lack of knowledge of the legal aid schemes (Gautun 1997, p. 75), and the geographical distribution of legal services. Less resourceful clients also lack the legal knowledge to assess the performance of their lawyer, so the quality assurance system, with disciplinary boards organised by the Bar Association (or other supervisory boards) does not necessarily ensure the quality of the legal aid work done by the lawyers (NOU 2002:18). In this regard the fixed fees, which encourage the lawyer to spend as little time as possible on cases, give rise to concern about the quality of the scheme. The Bar Association also claims that low payment under the scheme discourages lawyers from doing legal aid work: they prefer more profitable self-funding clients (Den Norske Advokatforening 2015). The contention is that this impacts the general quality of the legal aid work done by lawyers, as the best lawyers prefer other types of work, and that it hinders recruitment to that section of the profession. The political debate on the level of legal aid fee has been heated, and resulted in the Bar Association staging a week-long strike in Spring 2015 (Sæther 2015).

Administration of the Legal Aid Scheme for Civil Matters

The Norwegian Ministry of Justice and Public Security is responsible for administering legal aid in Norway. As most of the publicly funded legal aid scheme is regulated by the Legal Aid Act, most changes to the scheme require an Act of Parliament.

The County Governors (Fylkesmannen) are the decision-making body of first instance for applications for legal aid. They mostly deal with applications for legal aid outside the courts, and cases regarding the use of the exemption clause in the Legal Aid Act, which gives them discretionary power to grant legal aid even if the standard criteria are not met. Decisions can be appealed to The Civil Affairs Authority, and, in turn, be subject to judicial review by the courts.

Lawyers themselves are entitled to grant legal aid outside court, if all the criteria for legal aid are satisfied. Most applications for legal aid outside the courts are handled in this manner. In 2014, 15,235 of 18,617 grants for legal aid were decided by the lawyers themselves (Fylkesmannen i Oslo og Akershus 2015). When payment is made, the decisions of the lawyers are reviewed by the County Governor, who has the power to overturn the lawyers' decision.

The courts decide on most applications for legal aid before the courts. The decisions are made by the judge preparing the case. Decisions regarding legal aid can be appealed.

Use of Public Legal Aid Schemes

Precise statistics for the use of the public legal aid schemes are not available. However, I will point out certain figures that might shed light on the issues.

Use of the Judicare Scheme for Legal Assistance Outside Court

Under the publicly funded legal aid 'judicare' scheme, about 18,617 applications for legal assistance outside court were granted in 2014. This amounts to 37.34 cases per 10,000 inhabitants. The ten areas of law for which most legal aid was granted are listed in Table 2.1 as:

As we can see, a considerable proportion of the legal aid applications granted relates to various legal issues regarding immigration: these are 36% of all cases. Various family law matters, particularly those relating to termination of marriage, constitute 23% of cases.

If we look at changes in the number of cases for which legal assistance was granted (Fig. 2.1), we see an increase in 2009 and 2010. This is mostly due to a sharp increase in the number of applications for legal aid in asylum cases and other immigration cases, which corresponds to the rise in asylum applications in Norway during those years. Apart from this, the number of legal aid applications granted each year is relatively stable but slowly decreasing. The downward trend might be explained by the fixed financial criteria for income, which have not been changed since 2009.

Table 2.1 Number of legal aid cases, 2014

Asylum	4094	22%
Child custody	2257	12%
Complaints about social security decisions	1730	9%
Immigration cases (deportation, etc.)	1559	8%
Divorce	1217	7%
Consideration of reporting certain crimes	890	5%
Asylum cases involving minors	871	5%
Employment	835	5%
Compensation for wrongful prosecution	798	4%
Other family cases	670	4%

Source: Unpublished statistics from the Civil Affairs Authority

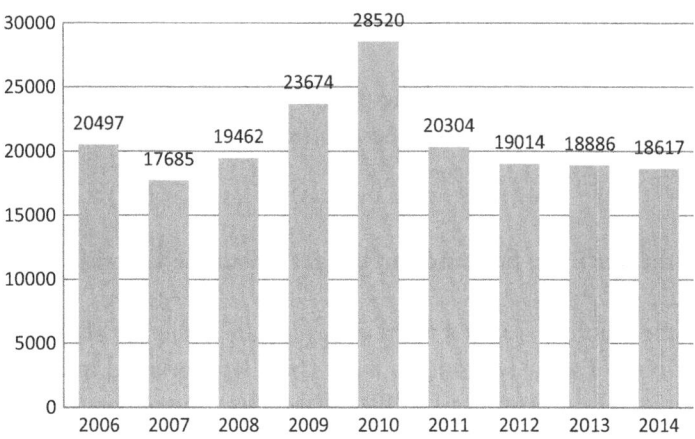

Fig. 2.1 Legal assistance granted (Figures from unpublished statistics from the Civil Affairs authority)

Use of the Judicare Scheme for Legal Aid in Court Proceedings

There are no published statistics on the current use of legal aid in civil cases before the courts. However, some figures might shed some light on the scope of legal aid grants.

According to the Council of Europe's Commission for the Protection and Efficiency of Justice (CEPEJ 2014), Norway states there were 6429 cases before the courts for which legal aid was granted in Norway in 2012. This amounts to 1289 legal aid cases per 10,000 inhabitants. To put this in context, in 2012 there were 15,576 civil cases before courts of first instance, 1951 before the appellate courts and 82 before the Supreme Court. Thus the proportion of civil cases brought to the courts with legal aid can be said to be quite high.

In preparation for the most recent Government Policy paper on legal aid, published in 2009, an overview of the use of the legal aid scheme was presented. This reports that in 2007 there were 5420 cases in which legal representation before the courts was granted. This represents approximately 1153 cases per 10,000 inhabitants. Over 50% of these were child custody cases, 15% were cases relating to the use of force in psychiatric treatment, and 10% related to issues regarding divorce, such as child custody. Other matters thus constitute only a very small part of the total use of the scheme. Tenancy cases, for instance, were only 0.4% of the legal representation granted (Justis- og politidepartementet 2008, p. 24).

Legal Aid Expenditure

Legal aid expenditure in Norway is demand-led—in principle legal aid would be granted to all entitled to it under the Legal Aid Act, regardless of budget caps. From an international perspective, Norwegian legal aid expenditure is high: it is the country spending most on legal aid (in civil and criminal cases combined) among Council of Europe members, (53.55 € per inhabitant in 2012) (European Commission for the Efficiency of Justice 2014, 47 f.). Legal aid expenditure as a percentage of GDP is 0.07%, placing it as one of the top five countries in Europe.

Expenditure on Legal Assistance Outside Courts

Figure 2.2 shows expenditure on legal assistance outside court, in nominal figures (NOK). In 2014, spending was 135 million NOK (11,500,000 €).

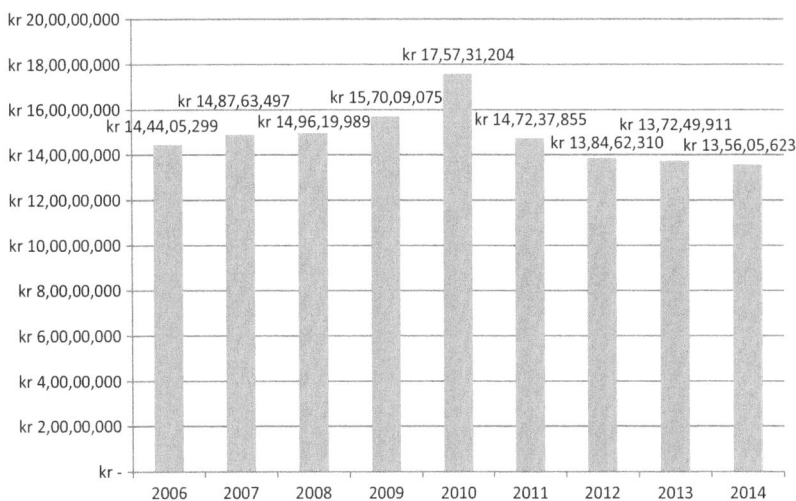

Fig. 2.2 Annual spending on legal aid outside court (Figures from statistics from the Civil Affairs Authority)

We see an increase in legal aid expenditure in 2010, mostly attributable to a sharp rise in legal aid applications for asylum cases, which corresponds to fluctuations in the number of asylum seekers coming to Norway. The cost of legal assistance to asylum seekers was four times higher in 2010 than in 2006.

Legal Representation Under the Judicare Scheme

No statistical information is published on legal aid expenditure on legal representation in court cases. The State Budget, however, predicts how much will be spent on legal representation, and can serve as an indicator of legal aid spending. As mentioned above, legal aid expenditure in Norway is demand-driven, and there is no cap on grants of legal aid.

The total amount of legal aid expenditure in civil cases budgeted for in 2015 was 797,451,000 NOK (88,605,000 €) (Justis- og beredskapsdepartementet 2015), a nominal increase of 12% from 2014.

Fig. 2.3 is a representation of budgeted legal aid spending in NOK. As can be seen, budgeted spending is quite stable, but, in nominal figures, gradually increasing.[3] The cost of legal aid before the courts is roughly six times as much as that of legal aid outside court, so court cases are considerably more expensive.

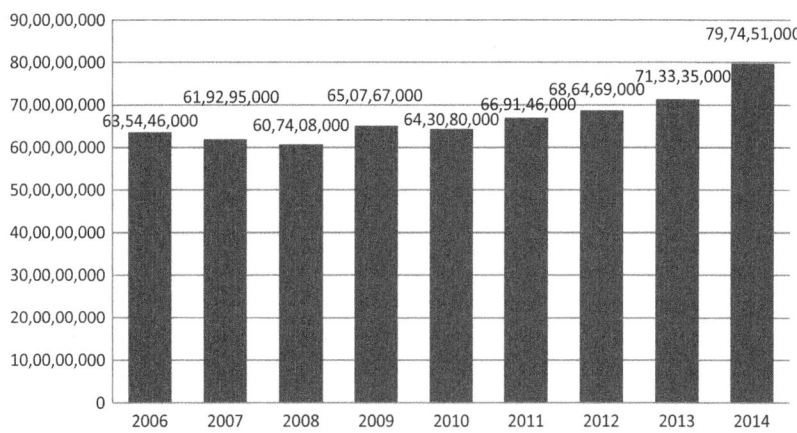

Fig. 2.3 Annual budgeted spending on legal advice (Figures from State Budget chap 470:72)

Although there are no figures available for the use of the scheme, the steadily growing budgets for legal aid before the courts probably mirror an increase in demand for legal aid, though some of the increase might also be attributable to the increasing cost of legal aid cases.

Expenditure on Alternative Legal Aid Schemes

The publicly funded judicare scheme is allotted the bulk of the funding available from the legal aid budget of the Ministry of Justice (Justis- og beredskapsdepartementet 2015). A comparatively small portion is assigned to other legal aid schemes, as will be described below. In the State Budget for 2015, the figure was 32,333,000 NOK (3,592,000 €). This is 4% of the total budget for legal aid.

Public Legal Aid Offices

There is currently one public legal aid office in Norway, called Fri Rettshjelp (Free Legal Aid). It is situated in the inner city of Oslo and is oriented particularly towards meeting the legal needs of the inner city population, especially of immigrant groups. The office has been in operation since 1893. It is funded by the government and the municipality.

The public legal aid office is staffed by private practice lawyers who work there part time. The clients are mostly from disadvantaged groups. Almost 80% have a non-Norwegian background, and almost 96% have incomes low enough to qualify for legal aid (Roli 2015). The inner city location, the informal manner of client communication, and the way the office wins the confidence of the client group stand out as reasons why it manages to reach such disadvantaged groups (Andenæs et al. 2005). In addition, clients are exempt from paying the contribution normally applicable to all legal aid given under the public scheme. This exemption also affects how the office manages to reach out to clients (Roli 2015).

The legal aid office generally handles cases in the way laid down in the Legal Aid Act—only supplying legal aid if the client meets the eligibility criteria. However, it has a far less restrictive approach when applying the exemption clause of the Act, and will grant legal aid in cases not normally covered by the Act if the client is considered to be in great need. In 2014, the office handled 3235 cases. Of these, 54.6% were outside the material scope of eligibility of the Legal Aid Act. The majority of cases involve the law relating to the family, immigration, housing, social security, or employment. The office identifies cases involving unpaid wages, social security, and housing as areas where there is great need for legal aid, and which are not covered by the Legal Aid Act (Roli 2015).

The office is unable to meet the demand for legal aid—in 2015, 700 clients who contacted the office had to be rejected due to lack of capacity.

Legal Expenses Insurance

Legal expenses insurance, where the cost of legal assistance is covered through commercial insurance schemes, is one of many ways of providing access to legal aid. As has been mentioned, the public legal aid scheme is subsidiary to legal aid provided by legal expenses insurance, so this constitutes an important restriction on the legal aid scheme. Some companies set up specifically to provide legal expenses insurance, employ in-house lawyers to give legal aid to policyholders.

Legal expenses insurance is normally part of the cover provided by more comprehensive policies, such as house or car insurance. House insurance covers quite a wide range of risks but does not generally cover legal expenses involving family law, labour law, or administrative law. Legal expenses insurance can also be bought as a separate policy.

Legal expenses insurance is obtainable not just for court cases, but for all levels of legal aid, as long as a dispute is involved. Cover will normally be limited to 80,000 or 100,000 NOK, (8800–11,100 €), and the client will normally pay a contribution. In 2014, legal expenses policyholders filed 11,293 claims, and the payout was 272 million NOK (30,220,000 €) (Finans Norge 2015).

In addition to the legal expenses insurance just described, another common type of legal expenses policy provides conveyancing insurance. These policies normally cover all expenses arising from disputes regarding the property, including legal fees. In the light of current legislation on conveyancing, such policies have been criticised for increasing the number of disputes.

Alternative Legal Aid Schemes

In the following, I will highlight some of the more notable alternative legal aid schemes (for a complete review, see Johnsen 2009b). I will focus on those fully or partly funded by the Ministry of Justice. Most of these are generally quite independent but the grants for legal aid given by the Ministry mean it has some control of these initiatives. Legal aid is also given by a wide range of other providers: trades unions, special interest organisations, or ombudsmen.

A vast amount of legal aid is provided by such initiatives. Johnsen (2009b, pp. 72–78) estimates that at least 250,000 cases involving legal aid were handled outside the public legal aid scheme. He considers this to be a conservative estimate, and suggests the actual figure might be twice as high, or more. The public legal aid scheme handles around 33,000 cases, so the role of the government legal aid scheme seems to be comparatively modest.

There is no central coordination of, or policy for, the wide range of commercial, public and not-for-profit legal aid providers. This might lead to a problem of overlapping legal aid initiatives in some areas, and gaps in legal aid coverage in others (Johnsen 2009b, p. 78).

Pro Bono Work

The largest pro bono scheme is *Advokatvakten*, which is organised by the Norwegian Bar Association in most municipalities throughout the country. Under the scheme lawyers provide free legal aid in 30 minute consultations, in all kinds of cases, and to all types of people. The legal aid is normally dispensed in public buildings, such as town halls or libraries. It is estimated that 2000–4000 cases are handled annually (Johnsen 2009b).

There have also been several pro bono initiatives aiming to public interest cases before the courts. The first was called 'Advokatforeningens prosedyregruppe i utlendingsrett' (the Bar Association's Group for Procedures in Immigration Law), established in 2007. The initiative aims to provide expert legal aid to immigrants, in order to try important or principled cases decided by the immigration administrative bodies before the courts. A secretariat of law students, headed by experienced immigration lawyers, received and screened a number of immigration cases, and selected a few for trial. Between 2007 and 2011 the group received around 1020 cases, and of the 24 that had been finally decided in 2011, 18 were decided in favour of the immigrant. This included several cases thought to be setting important precedence (Humlen and Myhre 2011).

Some major law firms have *pro bono* agreements with other legal aid initiatives, promising to take to court (or at least consider) cases that the initiatives do not have the resources to handle themselves. This would apply to student legal aid clinics, which are not allowed to go to court. The most extensive agreement is perhaps the one between the Norwegian Association for Asylum Seekers (NOAS) and the law firm Wiersholm (Austenå 2015), one of the largest and most high-profile commercial law firms in Norway.

Student-Run Legal Aid Clinics

There are currently five student-run legal aid clinics, situated in the four biggest cities in Norway. Most are affiliated to a university. The legal aid clinics are staffed mostly by senior law students, with some form of supervision by the law faculties.

Juss-Buss, which literally translates as 'Law Bus' is the oldest and most active today, see Chap. 7. The clinic started in 1971, inspired by outreach initiatives in the USA, and was part of the radical student movement in Norway in the 70s (Andenæs 1975; Capua 1975, 2001; Johnsen 2003). Similar clinics were started in other major Norwegian cities in the 70s and in 1980.

The student legal aid clinics all share a goal of providing outreach legal aid to vulnerable groups, while educating students in practical legal work.

Several of the clinics also do legal policy work, and gather data and conduct research on the legal situation of their client groups.

Student legal aid clinics are mainly staffed and administered by senior students, who handle most of the case work and administration, without faculty supervision of individual cases. The work is based on a collective approach: one case worker is responsible for preparing cases through client interviews and legal research but a group of students go through all the cases and make sure the work is done in a responsible manner. Each clinic consists of between 17–30 students.

Their approach to providing legal aid is especially focused on offering a low-threshold alternative, thus removing the barriers to seeking legal assistance met by vulnerable groups. This is mainly done through an extensive outreach programme. The students regularly visit prisons in their local region. In the case of clinics situated in the more rural parts of Norway, such as 'Jusshjelpa i Nord-Norge' in the north, outreach work is done to provide legal aid in areas where there are few lawyers. In addition they visit adult education centres, shelters for the homeless, information centres for foreign workers, and similar institutions (Skårberg 2016, p. 43).

The clinics do not just provide legal aid in individual cases. Most have extensive programmes of legal information and education. Since the 1970s, a key concern has been to increase legal awareness among client groups, thereby improving the clients' situation by enabling them to avoid legal disputes, or handle them without aid. Such work is being done through lectures and do-it-yourself courses on legal issues, by publishing books or leaflets offering practical advice in clear and simple language, or by training in the client groups. The latter has proven particularly effective in reaching minority women, which is the aim of the clinic specialising in legal aid for women (JURK) (Hellum and Taj 2014).

In addition to legal aid, all the clinics do a considerable amount of legal policy work, which is regarded as a way to improve the legal situation for the client groups. All clinics work on reforming the public legal aid scheme, and on reform issues within chosen fields of law.

The student-run legal aid clinics handle a great number of cases, compared to the judicare scheme. Approximately 17,000 cases each year are handled by the five legal aid clinics.[4] Given that public spending on such clinics is about 12 million NOK (1,330,000 €) annually (Justis- og beredskapsdepartementet 2015), they provide very cost effective legal aid.

Gatejuristen

'*Gatejuristen-prosjektet*' (The Street Lawyers) is a legal aid initiative aiming to supply legal aid to people with drug addiction. It is run by a small professional secretariat, and volunteers, mostly lawyers, providing outreach legal aid. Administratively it is a part of The Church City Mission, a charitable social work organisation with links to the Norwegian Church. It was set up in Oslo, in 2005, and was partly inspired by a similar project in Denmark (see Chap. 8), and by the outreach legal aid work done by the Norwegian legal aid clinics (Lied 2013). At present, *Gatejuristen* operates in ten cities around the country, and provides legal aid in over 2500 cases annually (Mørch 2015).

Legal aid is provided to everyone in the defined client group—people with drug addiction. This is done by various kinds of outreach work: for example, by attending social care centres or health centres, or just by walking the streets talking to people in the drug community. Through its years of operation, *Gatejuristen* has become well-known and trusted among the client groups, and thus clients often seek legal aid at *Gatejuristen*'s office, although they would not contact a traditional legal aid lawyer (Lied 2013).

The cases handled are mostly outside the scope of the public legal aid scheme. In Oslo, cases involving social security law, health law, criminal law, compensation and insurance law, and debt law are most frequent. In addition to providing legal advice and assistance, *Gatejuristen* handles cases before the courts, particularly cases that might set precedence. In 2014, 969 cases were handled by the 70 volunteers working in Oslo. In addition to legal aid in individual cases, *Gatejuristen* also does general information work, legal policy work, and basic research into the legal needs of the client group (Mørch 2015).

The funding for *Gatejuristen* comes mostly from the Ministry of Justice, the municipalities, and from donations from commercial businesses and charitable organisations. In addition, most of the legal aid work is done by volunteer lawyers.

Norwegian Association for Asylum Seekers: NOAS

NOAS is an example of a special interest organisation involved with legal aid. It is an independent charitable organisation working to protect institution of asylum and the interests of individual asylum seekers. They do information work, policy work, and provide legal aid in individual cases.

Legal aid work has become an increasingly important part of NOAS's work. In 2014, they handled 1354 asylum cases, and provided legal aid in 230 of them. Legal aid is given at all stages of the asylum process, but the organisation is mostly contacted by people whose application has been rejected by the immigration authorities. NOAS struggles to meet the demand for legal aid, and is forced to prioritise certain cases for which to provide aid. In cases where NOAS has given legal aid, 46% have gained a positive decision. The largest area of work for NOAS is their information project, through which newly arrived refugees are given legal information on the asylum procedure. In 2014, they gave information to 9453 refugees (Austenå 2015). The funding for the organisation comes from members' fees, project support from various public aid schemes, and contributions from individuals and charitable funds.

Legal Aid Policy and Legal Aid Reform

As we have seen, several aspects of the Norwegian public legal aid scheme have been politically contested. Much of the criticism directed against the scheme regards eligibility, which, it is claimed, is too restrictive and does not match unmet legal needs, especially those of the most disadvantaged groups. The structure of the public legal aid scheme has been criticised for encouraging lawyers to do substandard work, or to work without remuneration. It is claimed that this affects both the quality of the legal aid provided under the scheme, and recruitment to the part of the legal profession working on legal aid cases. The lack of outreach elements and other alternative ways of providing legal aid, in a way that will reach disadvantaged groups, has also been criticised.

The Norwegian legal aid scheme has also been criticised by international human rights bodies. In the 6th Periodic Cycle of review of

Norway's compliance with its obligations under the UN Convention on Civil and Political Rights (CCPR), undertaken in October 2011, The UN Human Rights Committee expressed concern as to whether the current legal aid system was adequate to meet the requirements of CCPR article 14, and encouraged the Norwegian government to review it in order to ensure full compliance.[5] In the review of the combined 6 and 7 periodic reports from Norway to the UN Committee Against Torture, undertaken in November 2012, the Committee expressed concern about the limited legal aid available to persons facing deportation or return (CAT 2011). The legal aid scheme was also part of the assessment of compliance with access to justice standards in the context of Norway's use of solitary confinement. The Norwegian legal aid scheme has been subject to scrutiny by the European Court of Human Rights, in regard to ECHR article 35 issues on the exhaustion of domestic remedies and legal aid. However, the issue was not decided upon, as the application to the Court was dismissed as manifestly ill-founded for other reasons (Agalar vs Norway 2011). Several similar Norwegian cases involving legal aid in immigration cases have been subject to ECHR consideration, where the ECHR applied similar tests, but the arguments were struck down for other reasons.[6]

The deficiencies of the public legal aid scheme have to some extent been recognised. Most political parties in Norway have for a period of time pledged to reform and improve the legal aid scheme. However, there have been few practical changes.

Conclusions

The broad image of the Norwegian legal aid scheme emerges as being based on a comprehensive, traditionally oriented, and costly public legal aid scheme, with several deficiencies as to how the scheme manages to meet the legal aid needs of the population. In particular, the public scheme's lack of outreach and limited coverage of legal areas make it incapable of ensuring access to legal assistance for all. The most disadvantaged groups are particularly ill served. This is partly due to the reliance on traditional providers. The shortcomings of the public scheme mean it is incompatible with the traditional belief in a welfare state ensuring inclusion and social security for everyone. The considerable role of alternative legal aid providers is likewise at odds with the welfare ideology. This goes for both the extent of the sector, which is very much greater than that of the public schemes and their role; without such initiatives, many of the most disadvantaged would completely lack means of accessing and utilising the legal system. The role of alternative legal aid providers also includes innovation. They employ new, untraditional means to enhance access to legal assistance, on the basis of knowledge of the needs of client groups, the effectiveness of different legal aid strategies, and the workings of the legal system. This might provide a basis for the reform of the public system that would make it into a public legal aid scheme which, in keeping with welfare state ideology, provides access to the law for everyone.

Notes

1. I have presented parts of this chapter as a national report at the International Legal Aid Group conference in the Hague in 2013.
2. Figures are from 2013, when the legal aid fee was 970 NOK (108 €).
3. The increase from 713,335,000 NOK (75,087,894 €) in the 2013 budget to 797,451,000 NOK (83,942, 210 €) in the 2014 budget seems to represent an increase in demand for legal aid for 2014 that was unaccounted for in the budget, as the budget was adjusted during 2014, and thus the apparent increase appears to be more gradual than the budget figures indicate.
4. Based on information from the annual reports of the clinics.
5. CCPR/C/NOR/CO/6: '6. The Committee is concerned that means tested legal aid fails to take account of the actual circumstances of the applicants, and is assessed without regard to the actual cost of the legal service being sought. Moreover, legal aid is not available at all with regard to certain categories of case. (art. 14)
   The State party should review its free legal aid scheme to provide for free legal assistance in any case where the interests of justice so require.'
6. Cf. for instance, ABDOLLAHPOUR vs. Norway app. 57,440/10 (Dec.) and ALI vs Norway app. 22,669/10 (Dec.)

Bibliography

Agalar vs Norway. (2011). *Aglar vs Norway app. No 55120/09 (Dec.)*. Strasbourg: European Court of Human Rights.
Andenæs, K. (1975). Rettshjelp til norske sigøynere. In A. Eidesen, S. Eskeland, & T. Mathiesen (Eds.), *Rettshjelp og samfunnsstruktur* (pp. 118–152). Oslo: Pax.
Andenæs, K., Gotaas, N., Nilsen, A. B., & Papendorf, K. (2001). *Språk og rett: om utlendingers og språklige minoriteters møte med rettsvesenet*. Oslo: Unipax.
Andenæs, K., Nalum-Olsen, H., Røed, M., & Westlund, J. (2005). *Kontoret for fri retshjælp: Retshjælp til ubemidlede": evaluering av en Oslo-institusjon gjennom 112 år*. Oslo.
Austenå, A.-M. (2015). *NOAS Årsrapport 2014*. Oslo: Norsk organisasjon for asylsøkere.
Botheim, I., Hyllseth, E., & Vik, G. (2008). *Kartlegging av rådgivnings- og konfliktløsningstilbudet i Norge* (Vol. nr. 2008:1). Oslo: Statskonsult.
Bratholm, A., & Sundby, N. K. (1976). *Kritisk juss*. Oslo: Pax.
Capua, G. D. (1975). Juss-Buss – Et rettshjelpstilbud for "vanlige folk"? In A. Eidesen, S. Eskeland, & T. Mathiesen (Eds.), *Rettshjelp og samfunnsstruktur* (pp. 72–94). Oslo: Pax.
Capua, G. D. (2001). *Om å legge ut på dypet* (Vol. nr 69). Oslo: Institutt for kriminologi og rettssosiologi, Avdeling for rettssosiologi, Universitetet i Oslo.
CAT. (2011). *Combined sixth and seventh periodic reports of States parties due in 2011, submitted in response to the list of issues (CAT/C/NOR/Q/7) transmitted to the State party pursuant to the optional reporting procedure (A/62/44, paras. 3 and 24) – Norway*. Geneva: Committee Against Torture.
Den Norske Advokatforening. (2014). *Rapport fra BRANSJEUNDERSØKELSEN 2014*. Oslo: Den Norske Advokatforening.
Den Norske Advokatforening. (2015). *Krav og varsel om aksjon*.
Eskeland, S., & Finne, J. (1973). *'Rettshjelp': en analyse og empirisk undersøkelse av tradisjonell rettshjelps muligheter og begrensningersærlig for folk som lever under vanskelige økonomiske eller sosiale kår*. Oslo: Pax.
Eskeland, S., Mathiesen, T., & Eidesen, A. (1975). *Rettshjelp og samfunnsstruktur*. Oslo: Pax.
European Commission for the Efficiency of Justice. (2014). *Report on 'European judicial systems – Edition 2014 (2012 data): Efficiency and quality of justice'*. European Commission for the Efficiency of Justice.
Finans Norge. (2015). *Skadestatistikk for landbasert forsikring*. Retrieved April 19, 2016, from Finans Norge https://www.fno.no/statistikk/skadeforsikring/Kvartalsvise-statistikk-publikasjoner/skadestatistikk-for-landbasert-forsikring/

Fylkesmannen i Oslo og Akershus. (2015). *Statistikkskjema for fri rettshjelp 2014*. Oslo: Fylkesmannen i Oslo og Akershus.
Gautun, H. (1997). *Hjelp til rett?: en evaluering av ordningen med fri rettshjelp* (Vol. 219). Oslo: Fafo.
Graver, H. P. (1979). *Rettshjelp i Kanada* (Vol. 3). Oslo: Universitetet i Oslo, Inst.for rettssosiologi.
Graver, A. B., Skaug, V., Strålberg, R., & Tangen, B. (2002). *Rettshjelp 2001: behovet for rettshjelp i Oslos befolkning - deriblant et utvalg innvandrerkvinner* (Vol. nr 85). Oslo: Universitetet i Oslo, Institutt for kriminologi og rettssosiologi, Avdeling for rettssosiologi.
Haugen, M. S., & Vigerust, E. (1992). *Det udekkede behov for rettshjelp: et uløst problem: rapport fra en undersøkelse i Oslo og Akershus i 1991* (Vol. 59). Oslo: Universitetet i Oslo.
Hellum, A., & Taj, F. (2014). Norsk-pakistanske kvinner i rettslig klemme: om å gjøre rettighetsinformasjon tilgjengelig, forståelig og anvendelig. In A. Hellum & J. Köhler-Olsen (Eds.), *Like rettigheter – ulike liv: rettslig kompleksitet i kvinne-, barne-, og innvandrerperspektiv* (pp. 389–414). Oslo: Gyldendal juridisk.
Humlen, A., & Myhre, J. W. (2011). 'Advokatforeningens aksjons- og prosedyregruppe i utlendingsrett – status etter 4 års drift.' In Rønning, O. H. & Juss-Buss (Eds.), *Med loven mot makta. Juss-Buss 40 år*. Oslo: Novus, pp. 125–155.
Jensen, A. P. (2015). *STATENS SIVILRETTSFORVALTNING – ÅRSRAPPORT 2014*. Oslo: Statens sivilrettsforvaltning.
Johnsen, J. T. (1980). *Behovet for offentlige rettshjelpkontorer*. Oslo: Juss-Buss.
Johnsen, J. T. (1987). *Retten til juridisk bistand: en rettspolitisk studie*. Oslo: Tano.
Johnsen, J. T. (2003). *Juss-buss – et fagkritisk eksperiment: idégrunnlag, arbeidsprinsipper og erfaringer: veiledning for medarbeidere i Juss-Buss*. Oslo: Juss-Buss.
Johnsen, J. T. (2009a). Drar de norske rettshjelpsreformene tilstrekkelig nytte av lærdommene fr Finland og England?: Kommentarer til stortingsmelding nr. 26 "Om offentlig rettshjelp. Rett hjelp". *Kritisk juss., 35*(2), 157–195.
Johnsen, J. T. (2009b). *Hva kan vi lære av finsk rettshjelp? En sammenligning av rettshjelpsordningene i Norge og Finland*. Oslo: Justis- og politidepartementet.
Johnsen, J. T., & Anti, T. (1997). *Samisk rettshjelp: en analyse av Rettshjelpkontoret Indre Finnmark*. Oslo: Tano-Aschehoug.
Jordal, I., & Hasle, S. S. (2014). *Rettshjelp 2013*. Oslo: Juss-Buss.
Juss-Buss. (1996). *Juss-buss 25 år: 1971–1996: jubileumsfestskrift*. Oslo: Juss-buss.
Juss-Buss. (2001). *Tvers igjennom lov til seier*. Oslo: Unipax.

Justis- og beredskapsdepartementet. (2015). *Prop. 1 S (2015–2016) Proposisjon til Stortinget (forslag til stortingsvedtak) for budsjettåret 2016.* Oslo: Justis- og beredskapsdepartementet.
Justis- og politidepartementet. (2004). *Ot.prp nr 91 (2003–2004) Om lov om endringer i lov 13. juni 1980 nr. 35 om fri rettshjelp m.m.* Oslo: Justis- og politidepartementet.
Justis- og politidepartementet. (2008). *Om offentleg rettshjelp: rett hjelp. Stortingsmelding nr 26 (2008–2009)* (Vol. nr. 26(2008–2009)). Oslo: Justis- og politidepartementet.
Justis- og politidepartementet. (2012). *G-12/05 Rundskriv om fri rettshjelp (Circular on legal aid).*
Justis- og politidepartementet. (2015). *G-2015-5 Ny salærsats for advokater mv. i straffesaker og i rettshjelpssaker og nye stykkprissatser for medisinsk sakkyndige.*
Legal Aid Act. (1981). *Act on legal aid of 13. June 1980 nr 35.*
Lid, B. (1981). *Fangers rettshjelpsbehov.* Oslo: Universitetet i Oslo, Inst.for rettssosiologi.
Lied, C. (2013). *Gatejurister: oppsøkende rettshjelp til folk med rusrelaterte problemer.* Oslo: Akademika forl.
Mørch, A. C. (2015). *Gatejuristen Årsrapport for 2014.* Oslo: Gatejuristen.
NOU 1976:38. (1976). *Fri rettshjelp i Norge.* Oslo: Justisdepartementet.
NOU 2002:18. (2002). *Rett til rett: en vurdering av konkurranseforholdene i markedet for juridiske tjenester.* (8258306685). Oslo: Justis- og politidepartementet,.
Oxford Research. (2013). *Evaluering av pilotprosjekt om førstelinjerettshjelp.* Kristiansand: Oxford Research.
Oxford Research. (2015). *Som bestilt. Evaluering av spesielle rettshjelpstiltak.* Oxford Research: Kristiansand.
Regulation to the Legal Aid Act. (2005). *Regulation to the legal aid act FOR-2005-12-12-1443.*
Roli, B. O. (2015). *Fri Rettshjelp årsrapport 2014.* Oslo: Oslo kommune. Velferdsetaten.
Rønning, O. H., & Bentsen, H. K. (2008). *Bruken av unntaksbestemmelsene i lov om fri rettshjelp.* Oslo: Institutt for kriminologi og rettssosiologi, Det juridiske fakultet, Universitetet i Oslo.
Rønning, O. H., & Juss-Buss (Eds.). (2011). *Med loven mot makta: Juss-buss førti år.* Oslo: Novus.
Rui, J. P., & Jusshjelpa i Nord-Norge (Eds.). (2009). *Rettshjelp fra kyst til vidde: festskrift til Jusshjelpa i Nord-Norge 20 år.* Oslo: Gyldendal akademisk.

Sæther, A. S. (2015, 12 April). *Advokatene aksjonerer – vil ikke ta klienter i fengslingsmøter*. VG. Retrieved from http://www.vg.no/nyheter/innenriks/domstol/advokatene-aksjonerer-vil-ikke-ta-klienter-i-fengslingsmoeter/a/23510751/

Skårberg, H. H. (2016). *Årsrapport for Juss-Buss 2015*. Oslo: Juss-Buss.

SSB. (2014). *Organisasjonsaktivitet, politisk deltakelse og sosialt nettverk, levekårsundersøkelsen, 2014*. Retrieved April 18, 2016, from http://www.ssb.no/kultur-og-fritid/statistikker/orgakt/hvert-3-aar

SSB. (2016). *Lønn, alle ansatte, 2015*. Retrieved March 15, 2016, from https://www.ssb.no/lonnansatt

Open Access This chapter is distributed under the terms of the Creative Commons Attribution 4.0 International License (http://creativecommons.org/licenses/by/4.0/), which permits use, duplication, adaptation, distribution, and reproduction in any medium or format, as long as you give appropriate credit to the original author(s) and the source, a link is provided to the Creative Commons license, and any changes made are indicated.

The images or other third party material in this book are included in the work's Creative Commons license, unless indicated otherwise in the credit line; if such material is not included in the work's Creative Commons license and the respective action is not permitted by statutory regulation, users will need to obtain permission from the license holder to duplicate, adapt or reproduce the material.

3

Legal Aid in Sweden

Isabel Schoultz

Introduction

Today, Sweden has a combination of public and private cover for legal expenses in civil cases. Legal expenses insurance (*Rättsskydd*) is part of household insurance policies, and it can pay part of the costs of legal representation in certain types of case under litigation. Those without household insurance, or if the insurance does not cover the particular case, can, under certain circumstances, be entitled to publicly funded legal aid (*Rättshjälp*). In order to obtain legal aid you have to apply to the Legal Aid Authority, which provides legal aid under the Legal Aid Act, or directly to the court if the case is already before the court. To be eligible for publicly funded legal aid you have to meet certain criteria: for example your financial base must be less than 28,000 € (260,000 Swedish Krona—SEK)[1] a year and you must not have legal expenses insurance covering the issue. Legal aid is not granted if your financial situation would have enabled you to take out insurance. Legal aid also applies primarily to private individuals.

I. Schoultz (✉)
Sociology of Law Department, Lund University, Lund, Sweden

This means that legal aid legislation is based on the assumption that the market supplies appropriate insurance policies, and that individuals actually take out insurance (Swedish National Courts Administration 2009). Today, 96% of the Swedish population above the age of 16 has household insurance. In other words, most of the Swedish population is protected by legal expenses insurance. However, young people (16–34 years) and people born abroad are significantly less likely than the average population to have household insurance.[2] Legal expenses insurance and legal aid have been described as two sides of the same coin (Kilian and Regan 2004) but there are significant differences that will be discussed in this chapter.

Civil procedural rules in Sweden have been described as 'creating a defendant-friendly forum', and increasing the economic risk for the plaintiffs (Carlson 2012, p. 135). The civil litigation process also includes an allocation of legal costs and fees whereby the losing side in the majority of cases has to pay costs and fees for both sides (Carlson 2012). In relation to legal aid, economic obstacles limiting individuals' access to information and adequate representation is highly relevant (Cappelletti 1993). Access to justice could also be seen as a major element of the welfare state. Cappelletti and Garth (1978) point to barriers in the legal system that may be of relevance to an understanding of the need for legal aid: the costs of litigation, time, and party capability (including the competence to recognise and pursue claims, and experience of the judicial system). Thus, getting access to justice in practice, rather than merely at a theoretical level, may require legal aid to overcome these significant barriers.

This chapter aims to review the current state of legal aid in Sweden, with emphasis on the public legal aid scheme and legal expenses insurance. The text also discusses the function of the legal aid scheme in relation to the welfare state and, from an access to justice perspective, identifies strengths and weaknesses in legal aid policies and practices. In an attempt to give the reader the necessary background to the current legal aid scheme in the country, the history is presented first, followed by a review of the meagre research on legal aid in Sweden. A section on legal expenses insurance follows, since this is the primary source of legal protection. Thereafter, public legal aid is described, with the focus on entitlement criteria, general restrictions and procedural issues, the providers supplying the aid, statistics on the use of public legal aid, and the cost of the scheme. The two following sections examine legal aid provided by the unions, and alternative legal aid provided by *pro bono* lawyers and student legal clinics. The chapter ends with a concluding discussion.

Historical Background

In 1919, Sweden passed the first legislation providing free legal aid to poor people (Johnsen 1994). Subsequently, at the end of the 1960s, legal aid policy was influenced by Scandinavian welfare ideology, providing both litigation aid and legal aid assistance (Johnsen 1994). However, prior to 1973 there was no statutorily unified system of legal aid in Sweden (Muther 1975). The purpose of the Legal Aid Act (1972:429) that came into force in 1973 was to equalise access to legal services by enabling everyone to obtain legal assistance in any case where legal aid was needed (Muther 1975). The legal aid of that time was part of the generous welfare programmes developed in the early 1970s, and included assistance for most legal problems including advice and minor assistance. It was also open to most of the population (Kilian and Regan 2004).

The Swedish legal aid scheme up until the middle of the 1990s has been described as 'probably the most generous and comprehensive scheme internationally' (Kilian and Regan 2004, p. 247). However, legal aid in Sweden was described by Johnsen (1994) as limited in comparison with other Nordic countries' legal aid schemes at that time. The limitation mainly regarded the low number of cases eligible per 10,000 people, the preponderance of matrimonial cases, and the limited cover of other legal problems (Johnsen 1994, p. 329). These conflicting opinions have at least two explanations. First, Kilian and Regan (2004) were not specifically comparing Sweden with other Nordic countries: if they had done so the conclusion about Sweden may have been different. Second, Kilian and Regan (2004) include protection given by public legal aid as well as by legal expenses insurance, while Johnsen (1994) only discusses public legal aid. Legal expenses insurance was integrated into household insurance policies in response to pressure from the labour movement in the 1960s. It was designed to fill gaps in public legal aid by providing legal aid to middle-income earners who might be excluded from public legal aid because of their income, and to cover costs that were not covered by public aid, such as costs awarded by the court in unsuccessful civil cases. At this time, legal expenses insurance was not widely used, and most Swedes relied on public legal aid (Regan 2003). However, by including legal expenses insurance, Kilian and Regan (2004) reach their conclusion that the Swedish legal aid system was probably the most generous legal aid scheme in the world.

In the current Legal Aid Act (1996:1619), which came into force in December 1997, the Swedish government introduced a reform to legal aid policy in an effort to cut public spending, and, by extension, to change the way Swedes responded to common legal problems. One of the goals of the legal aid reform was to achieve major cost savings, since Sweden was undergoing the worst recession since the 1930s (Regan 2003). The more limited resources were mainly to be allocated to those in most need of legal aid (Swedish National Courts Administration 2009). Regan (2003) notes that the reform did not affect all forms of legal aid: aid in criminal cases and to victims was maintained. Other welfare policies were not changed as much as legal aid policies (Regan 2003). The overarching change in the reform was to make the legal aid scheme secondary to the legal expenses cover provided by individuals' household insurance. This means that the claimant in a dispute should first turn to their insurance company. Anyone who had legal expenses insurance covering the case in question would not receive legal aid (Swedish National Courts Administration 2009). However, the reform did not, as Regan (2003) points out, include a requirement on insurance companies to expand the cover they were offering. The reform presupposed that insurance companies would continue to offer legal expenses insurance to existing policy-holders in the future. Despite major changes in the legal aid scheme, the reform caused little public protest, apart from that voiced by the Swedish Bar Association (Regan 2003). The reform also separated legal aid from other forms of legal assistance, such as public defenders, public counsel, and counsel for injured parties (Renfors et al. 2012).

Another aim of the legal aid reform was to make the legal aid fee vary according to the income of the applicant; it was to be calculated in relation to the costs of legal counsel and paid regularly to the appointed counsel (Swedish National Courts Administration 2009). The new law also included other changes to the entitlement criteria for legal aid. Among other things, up to two hours' counselling had to precede an application for legal aid. The annual income limit for entitlement to legal aid was reduced from 26,800 to 22,600 € (249,000 to 210,000 SEK). Even so, more than 80% of the population was entitled to legal aid, on the basis of their income (SOU 2014). In 1999, the income limit for entitlement to legal aid was raised to 28,000 € (260,000 SEK) (Swedish National Courts Administration 2009).

The 1997 Legal Aid Act also introduced requirements for special grounds for legal aid to be granted in cases relating to divorce and related issues, to child maintenance, to business owners as regards business activities, and to cases handled abroad (Swedish National Courts Administration 2009, p. 18). Many family law disputes no longer qualified for legal aid in the new legal aid scheme and an alternative form of dispute resolution was introduced. The allowance for employing counsel was also limited to a maximum of 100 hours, with very limited opportunity for increase (Swedish National Courts Administration 2009).

In the middle of the 1990s, prior to the reform of legal aid, Sweden had more than one hundred publicly employed lawyers working in twenty-eight bureaus at the county level (Johnsen 1994, p. 309). The state-financed legal aid bureaus were closed down in 1999 on the grounds that the state should no longer engage in the practice of law (Departementsserien 1992).

As regards the welfare state, the 1997 reform of the Legal Aid Act singled out legal services from other welfare reforms in the 1990s in the retreat from quasi-universal and comprehensive coverage, as well as the shift from public to private protection (Regan 2003). The current legal aid law is fundamentally different from the previous law in that sense that, from being tax-funded legal aid in the previous law, it has become mainly privately funded through insurance premiums.

Previous Research on Legal Aid in Sweden

There are only a few academic publications to be found on legal aid in Sweden. It is noteworthy that these journal articles on legal aid in Sweden are all written by non-Swedes. Muther (1975) wrote a paper on the legal aid act reform of 1973. In 1994, Johnsen (1994) published a more extensive piece on Nordic legal aid, in which he compares the systems in Sweden, Finland, and Norway. Thereafter, Regan (2000, 2003) published two papers on the 1997 reform and on the mix of private and public legal protection. A few years later Kilian and Regan (2004) published a paper in which they compare legal expenses insurance and legal aid schemes in Sweden and Germany. However, this comparison seems to be based on Regan's previous work on Sweden.

In addition to these studies, Renfors et al. (2012) and Stangendahl (1998) have published comments on the Legal Aid Act (1996:1619). Bruder (1998) has written a book on issues relating to legal counsel in the context of the legal expense insurance and the Legal Aid Act. These pieces are naturally limited to summaries and explanations of the law, and do not contain any empirical research on legal aid.

The legal aid scheme in Sweden has also been subject to several government initiated investigations, both prior to the 1997 reform (see for example SOU 1977, 1984, 1995; The Swedish National Audit Office 1992, 1993) and after (Departementsserien 2003a, b; SOU 2014). The current legal aid act has also been evaluated twice by the Swedish National Courts Administration (2001, 2009).

To sum up, legal aid in Sweden has been the object of several governmental investigations, but academic publications are few. It is hard to know why legal aid research has been underdeveloped in Sweden, particularly in contrast to the extensive research on legal aid done in neighbouring countries, such as Norway. This chapter therefore aims to fill part of the gap in the literature on legal aid in Sweden by providing a description and discussion of the current legal aid scheme in relation to access to justice and the function of the welfare state.

Legal Expenses Insurance

Today, legal expenses insurance is the primary source of legal protection in Sweden. Household insurance has contained a legal expenses element since the 1960s, and, prior to the 1997 reform, claimants could obtain legal protection both through insurance and through public legal aid.

Nowadays it is a matter of either or—anyone who has legal expenses insurance covering the case in question will not receive legal aid.

Johnsen (1994) differentiates between *litigation aid* and *legal assistance aid*. Legal expenses insurance only covers the former, i.e., cases under litigation. One of the significant limitations of legal expenses insurance is the lack of cover for legal advice and minor legal assistance (Kilian and Regan 2004). In general, insurance covers hearings in a District Court, a Land and Environmental Court, a Court of Appeal, or the Supreme Court. Insurance does not apply to criminal cases or disputes that may be examined by administrative authorities, specialist courts, or the administrative courts (Swedish National Courts Administration 2009). The administrative courts have their own investigative responsibility (Carlson 2012) and therefore the need for legal representation is not deemed to be the same (Swedish National Courts Administration 2009).

Legal expenses insurance is incorporated into household policies, and is not offered as an 'add on' or separate 'stand-alone' insurance. As a rule, insurance companies require that the policy has been taken out for at least two years before use can be made of the legal expenses insurance (Swedish National Courts Administration 2009). Generally, too, legal protection through the insurance is not granted if the value of the case is less than half a base sum which represents 2400 € (22,250 SEK) in 2015. Insurance does not generally apply to disputes having to do with divorce or the dissolution of partnerships, or to disputes relating to the insured's employment or other professional duties (Swedish National Courts Administration 2009). The costs for the individual can vary since insurance companies have different conditions but liability for 20% of the base amount and 20% of the damages costs exceeding 20% of the base amount is common (Swedish National Courts Administration 2009). In practice, liability can end up as much as 5000 €.

In addition, different insurance companies have different exceptions and rules. Some companies exclude child custody, child maintenance, and similar issues. Others have a withdrawal period of a year or two after the marriage, partnership, or relationship ends before the legal protection can be utilised in these disputes. Several insurance companies do not cover litigation under the Group Proceedings Act (2002, p. 599) (Swedish National Courts Administration 2009). The Swedish

National Courts Administration (2009) found in their evaluation that, even though the insurance criteria differed somewhat between insurance companies, insurance policies have not changed since the reform came in to place to a degree that would imply that the system is no longer functioning as it is supposed to.

As a rule, the legal representative hired must be operating close to the insured party's home, or the place where the hearing takes place. The legal representative must be a lawyer or an associate employed in a law firm. The possibility of appointing other appropriate legal representation exists but needs to be approved by the Board for Legal Protection Insurance Issues (Swedish National Courts Administration 2009). Generally, the insurance company pays the legal representative's fees and costs in accordance with an hourly rate norm, the costs of the investigation and collection of evidence, and administrative costs in court. Legal expenses insurance generally also covers situations when the insured is compelled to pay legal expenses to the opposing party or to the State, as well as settlements (if it is likely that the Court would have decided on a higher amount) (Swedish National Courts Administration 2009). In 2015 the maximum amount of legal protection varied between insurance companies, from 13,000 to 27,000 € (120,000 to 250,000 SEK) (The Swedish Consumers' Insurance Bureau 2015).

In a survey conducted by Swedish National Courts Administration (2009) directed at lawyers, several negative consequences of legal expenses insurance were highlighted. More than 90% of lawyers think that there is a need for the possibility of public legal aid being given in cases where legal protection through insurance has been exhausted (Swedish National Courts Administration 2009). Another issue brought to light by the lawyers, is the need for legal advice. For legal expenses insurance to be used the issue has to be formally considered a legal dispute (when a claim has been wholly or partly rejected by the other party) but legal advice may be necessary prior to that (Swedish National Courts Administration 2009).

In 2014, legal expenses insurance was used in 12,879 cases at an estimated cost of 38 million € (356 million SEK).[3] In 1997, the amount paid by legal expenses insurance was estimated at 17 million € (157 million SEK) distributed among 11,401 insurance cases. Ten years later, in 2007, the equivalent sum was estimated at 29 million € (271 million SEK) distributed among 13,046 insurance cases (Swedish National

Courts Administration 2009). These figures include legal expenses insurance in both household insurance and second/holiday home insurance. The costs have increased significantly but interestingly the developments indicate that the number of insurance cases has not increased to the extent that you might expect, given that legal aid reform made legal expenses insurance the primary source of legal protection. The increased costs are probably related to rises in legal costs in general, and the fact that insurance companies have raised the ceiling for the amount of legal costs being reimbursed. The number of policyholders who received compensation peaked in 1999, with more than 15,000 disbursements for legal expenses (Swedish National Courts Administration 2009). In relation to developments between in 1997 and 2007 Regan (2003, p. 58f) concludes that, since the increase in the insurance industry's costs were much smaller than the decrease in public expenditure after the reform, legal disputes are either being funded by alternative means, or more cases are abandoned before they go to court. Many of the 'missing cases' are probably family law cases that are now dealt with through negotiation or do-it-yourself divorces. However, Regan (2003) suggests that some are cases where people have been discouraged from seeking legal advice since it is too costly. The issue raised by Regan (2003) may still be valid: the legal aid reform may have discouraged citizens from using lawyers and going to court. From an access to justice perspective, the figures may indicate that effective equality in the sense of equal opportunities (see Cappelletti 1992), is not being achieved.

The Public Legal Aid Scheme

Entitlement Criteria

The right to legal aid is governed by the Legal Aid Act (1996:1619). Public legal aid covers all legal matters (*rättslig angelägenhet*) not specifically excluded in the law (the restrictions are presented later in this section). While legal expenses insurance is limited to cases under litigation, public legal aid has a wider application. However, Renfors et al. (2012) argues that, in practice, it does not make much difference since many of the issues that would come into question as 'legal matters' not requiring litigation, for example, marriage contracts and wills, are nonetheless excluded in the Legal Aid Act.

According to section 6 in the Legal Aid Act, legal aid can be granted to a person whose financial base does not exceed 28,000 € (260,000 SEK) a year. This limit was last changed in 1999. The financial base includes annual income after allowances for maintenance obligations, including 2700 € (25,000 SEK) per child, to a maximum of 8100 € (75,000 SEK), assets and debts (Legal Aid Act section 38). Generally, assets exceeding 5400 € (50,000 SEK) are taken into account and half of this amount will be added to the annual income. The value of the residence where the claimant lives permanently is not counted as an asset (Renfors et al. 2012). It is difficult to tell exactly what percentage of the Swedish population qualifies for legal aid in relation to their financial base. In 2013, the median income (including income from pensions, sickness benefit, and other taxable payments from the Social insurance agency) of the Swedish population aged between 20 and 64 was 30,600 € (284,001 SEK) a year, while for people under 20 it was 27,000 € (252,540 SEK) (Statistics Sweden 2015). However, these numbers include neither maintenance obligations, nor assets or debts. Based on the income level for 2013, a government investigation concluded that about 43% of the Swedish population is eligible for legal aid (SOU 2014). The government-initiated report suggests that the income limit should be raised to 43,100 € (400,000 SEK), in order to meet the intentions of the law that about 80% of the population should be eligible for legal aid based on their income (SOU 2014). However, no such steps have been taken.

A person granted legal aid would have to pay between 2% and 40% of the costs to the legal representative in a legal aid fee. The size of the legal aid fee is based on the financial base and the total costs of the legal representative. The idea is that individuals should contribute to the costs to the extent they can afford (Legal Aid Authority 2015a). If the claimant is a minor the legal aid fee may be waived if the applicant's financial circumstances justify it (SOU 2014).

As stated by section 7 in the Legal Aid Act, legal aid cannot be granted if legal assistance can be obtained in another way. In the centre of the paragraph is the claimant's need for a legal counsel; if the individual can protect his or her own interests, no need for legal counsel is considered to exist. This includes an assessment of personal qualifications and the seriousness of the issue, for example, a trained lawyer may be considered not to have a need for a legal counsel (Renfors et al. 2012). Legal aid can also not be granted if the matter in hand gives entitlement to other forms of legal assistance, such as public defenders or public counsel (appointed for example in cases concerning compulsory care and deportations). Similarly, legal aid is not granted if the claimant can obtain it from trade unions or other organisations, such as tenants' organisations (Renfors et al. 2012).

Section 8 in the Legal Aid Act makes it clear that legal aid may be granted only when, considering the nature and importance of the matter, the value of the dispute and other circumstances, it is reasonable that the state should contribute to the costs. In practice, the nature of the case can mean that an application for legal aid is rejected if it is obvious that the case has no prospect, or that the dispute concerns a matter that is considered to involve larger financial transactions unrelated to the claimant's everyday welfare. For example, if the dispute relates to an expensive hobby, the purchase of luxury objects or equities, art speculation, tax avoidance, or transactions involving the grey areas between the permissible and impermissible, legal aid may not be granted (Renfors et al. 2012). Renfors et al. (2012) state that according to the explanatory statement of the law the feasibility assessments should be made with caution and balance, taking into account all the circumstances relating to the matter. In addition, like legal expenses insurance, legal aid is not normally granted if the value of the dispute is considered small: a special reason is needed if the amount does not exceed half a basic amount (2400 € in 2015). Another circumstance that may negatively influence the right to legal aid arises if it is considered that the claimant has obstructed the investigation of the matter (Renfors et al. 2012).

To be granted legal aid the applicant must not have legal expenses insurance covering the legal matter (Legal Aid Act section 9). The same applies if the applicant should have had legal expenses insurance. As already discussed, this is the fundamental difference between the current legal aid scheme and the previous one. The *should have had* a legal expenses insurance rule is important here. If the applicant does not have legal expenses insurance but if, given their insurance coverage in general, or their financial and personal circumstances, they should have had such protection, legal aid is granted only if there are special reasons as regards the nature of the issue or the importance of the claimant. This rule was inserted to discourage people from not taking out insurance and relying that legal aid would be granted (Renfors et al. 2012). Renfors et al. (2012) refers to the preparatory work for the legal aid act regarding what 'financial circumstances' means in practice, and concludes that those located near or within the upper half limit of eligibility for legal aid, are to be considered people who *should have had* insurance. This means that if you have a financial base close to or within the range of 13,000–28,000 € (120,000–260,000 SEK) your application may be rejected. Legal practice in this area indicates that if the applicant can prove that he/she is living in certain circumstances (if, for example, they have only just received housing as a result of divorce or release from prison) and therefore have not had time to take out insurance he/she can be granted legal aid (Renfors et al. 2012). In a specific case where a man had neglected to renew his insurance, the court concluded that, given his financial and personal circumstances, he should have had insurance, but he was still granted legal aid since the matter in question (child custody), and other circumstance, could be classified as a special reason (Swedish National Courts Administration 2009). This rule has been criticised by several of the lawyers participating in the Swedish National Courts Administration survey evaluating the Legal Aid Act. One of them said:

> 'It is not uncommon for individuals to lack legal expenses insurance, and for it to be held that they should have had insurance. They are then completely without protection and have no opportunity to litigate with the help of a legal counsel.' (Swedish National Courts Administration 2009, p. 353, response no. 24, my translation).

Given that most Swedes do have legal expenses insurance, this problem only applies to a small part of the population. Nonetheless, this rule can cause significant limitations as far as access to justice principles go. Even though those who fall between the cracks have an income, economic obstacles may limit their access to the courts.

General Restrictions

As mentioned, all legal matters qualify for legal aid, unless specifically excluded. However, there are various limitations to the right to legal aid in certain areas: the preparation of tax returns, the writing of wills, prenuptial agreements, estate inventories, and cases relating to debt restructuring do not get legal aid (Legal Aid Act section 10). The argument here is that people can handle certain simpler issues on their own (Renfors et al. 2012). As described above, the legal aid reform also abolished legal aid in most family law disputes, replacing it with negotiation in disputes involving children and do-it-yourself application forms for divorce (Regan 2003). Thus the current Legal Aid Act (section 11) requires special reasons to grant legal aid in family-related matters, such as divorce and child maintenance support. For example, in divorce cases a prerequisite is that the case is considered to be more complicated and to require more legal counselling than is normally required in cases of divorce (Renfors et al. 2012).

Section 11 in the Legal Aid Act requires special reasons in cases concerning taxation, customs fees or other similar charges, as well as small claims (mentioned above), and matters handled abroad. Victims of sexual assault abroad are an exception, no special reasons being required (Legal Aid Act section 21). Legal aid is generally not approved for cases in the European Court of Human rights or the UN commissions (Renfors et al. 2012). For anyone who is not a Swedish citizen and has not previously been resident in Sweden, legal aid is limited to matters dealt with in Sweden (Swedish National Courts Administration 2009, p. 21f).

Another highly relevant limitation to legal aid is the fact that legal aid is not generally granted for hearings before the Administrative courts (see Legal Aid Act section 7 on the need for legal assistance). Such cases are also excluded from legal expenses insurance (Renfors et al. 2012). As mentioned previously, there is not deemed to be the same need for legal representation, since the administrative courts have their own investigative responsibility. Cases involving individual freedom and personal integrity, such as those involving the deportation of asylum seekers or the deprivation of liberty due to mental illness or addiction have public counsel appointed by the state. However, since the 1997 reform, these provisions are no longer included in the Legal Aid Act (Renfors et al. 2012). In the government-initiated evaluation of the Legal Aid Act, lawyers addressed the limited possibility of receiving legal aid in administrative courts. One lawyer participating in the survey highlights this issue:

'Administrative law cases, involving, for example, the withdrawal of sickness benefit, the right to life annuities for accidents at work or recovery of paid claims of the kind specified, are routinely denied legal aid (legal protection through insurance is exempted by insurance criteria) and thus parties cannot hire a legal representative.' (Swedish National Courts Administration 2009, p. 409, response no. 8, my translation).

These experiences indicate that access to justice is limited in administrative cases. All the more so because administrative law cases are excluded from legal expenses insurance policies. In cases concerning, for example, the withdrawal of social benefits, people could be assumed to have a very limited ability to pay for legal services themselves. This means that an individual may, without knowledge and experience, have to fight a case where a government agency is the opposing party. Administrative cases regarding, for example, the right to social benefits may have a great impact on people's lives. The evaluation of the Legal Aid Act suggests that there are grounds for reviewing the possibility of legal aid in administrative law cases (Swedish National Courts Administration 2009); however, no such review seems to be taking place.

Legal aid is, in general, not granted to business owners in matters arising from business activities, unless there are special reasons relating to the nature and limited extent of his or her economic and personal conditions and circumstances (Swedish National Courts Administration 2009). In addition, the requirement in section 6 of the Legal Aid Act that legal aid applies to private individuals denies legal aid to organisations and groups of individuals.

Procedural Issues

Applications for legal aid are decided by the Legal Aid Authority, unless the matter is already before a court. In that case, it is the court that decides on legal aid. Section 2 of the Legal Aid Act states that an application for legal aid must be preceded by consultation with a lawyer or other legal practitioner (for a minimum of one hour and a maximum of two hours). Exceptions may be made if it is clear that such consultation is unnecessary. The consultation fee paid by the applicant is a set at 175 € (1628 SEK) per hour in 2015. The fee can be reduced to half if the individual's income is less than 8100 € (75,000 SEK) per year. In the case of people under the age of 18, and those with no income or wealth, the consultation can be waived by the Legal Aid Authority (2015b). The application for legal aid is filed together with the legal counsel undertaking the consultation.

The benefit of legal aid counsel covers work to a maximum of 100 hours, with some limited opportunity for increase. The state pays the costs of evidence in the public court, the Labour Court, and the Market Court. The state also pays the costs of an investigation up to 1100 € (10,000 SEK), except for investigation of a matter that should be heard by an administrative court or an administrative authority (Swedish National Courts Administration 2009).

The majority of lawyers participating in the above-mentioned survey say that often, or very often, 100 hours is not sufficient (Swedish National Courts Administration 2009). One of three things usually happens when legal aid ceases: the client pays the excess, or the legal representative does not charge more, or the client drops the case (Swedish National Courts Administration 2009). While legal aid is limited to 100 hours, continued legal aid may be granted for the hours required to complete a process. In legal expenses insurance, a similar possibility does not exist. In order to avoid these differences in the systems, the Swedish National Courts Administration is proposing to give the Supreme Court and the Supreme Administrative Court the ability to grant extended legal assistance at public expense (Swedish National Courts Administration 2009). However, the suggestion has not been implemented.

Decisions taken by the Legal Aid Authority can be appealed to the Legal Aid Board. The Board consists of five members: a chairman who is a judge, two lawyers, and two other members, all appointed by the government. The decisions taken by the Legal Aid Board cannot be appealed. In 2014, 6.3% of all applications were appealed to the Legal Aid Board (Swedish National Courts Administration 2015b).

Conclusions on Entitlement to Public Legal Aid

Our description of the entitlement criteria, general restrictions, and procedural issues relating to public legal aid has revealed the strengths and limitations of the Swedish legal aid scheme. Public legal aid covers those on average to low incomes who do not have insurance, and have not failed to take out insurance when they ought to have done so. The above description does not however reveal that nowadays the percentage of the population that is eligible for legal aid has decreased significantly, and that this goes against the intentions of the law (SOU 2014).

The legal aid scheme does potentially cover some issues not generally covered by legal expenses insurance, such as more complicated child custody and child maintenance cases, and work related issues. A significant difference between public legal aid and legal expenses insurance is the coverage of costs when a case is lost in court. Public legal aid does not cover the opposing party's legal expenses in the way legal expenses insurance does. On the other hand, in the survey of lawyers conducted by Swedish National Courts Administration (2009), several respondents raised the issue that individuals using their legal expenses insurance may have to pay a considerably higher fee than people with the same income who have been granted public legal aid. One lawyer said: 'people who have no or a very low income pay 20–25% of the legal counsel's fee [when using their legal expenses insurance]. If they had been granted legal aid, it would have been about 2–10%' (Swedish National Courts Administration 2009, my translation). In such cases, it is a disadvantage to have legal expenses insurance.

According to Regan (2003) the reform of legal aid has significantly downgraded access to legal advice and minor assistance in legal cases, and thus actively discouraged many Swedes from seeking advice or assistance from lawyers for legal problems. The legal aid scheme places considerable responsibility on the individual to identify the legal problem and pay for legal assistance to access legal advice. Even though the legal advice fee can be reduced or waived for those with no, or a very low, income, others have to pay quite a high fee to receive legal advice. In other words, the support that people might need to work out whether they have a legal problem or not, and how it could be solved, is costly. This is inconsistent with the fact that most people need assistance with every-day non-litigation legal problems (Eidesen et al. 1975; Kilian and Regan 2004). This is a significant example of limited access to justice. Legal advice and assistance can play an important role in tackling social exclusion (Buck et al. 2005; Currie 2009).

Furthermore, a prerequisite for obtaining legal aid is that citizens are aware of their right to legal assistance. A survey conducted by the Swedish National Courts Administration reveals that awareness of legal protection is low; most people cannot distinguish between legal aid and the legal protection provided by household insurance. Most are not even aware of the extent to which they have such insurance. The Courts Administration therefore proposes that information about the opportunities for legal assistance must be made more widely available (Swedish National Courts Administration 2009).

As this section has shown, there is a range of limitations to the granting of legal aid. These limitations will also be apparent when we look at how many are granted legal aid. Before that we will look briefly at the providers of legal aid.

Providers Under the Scheme

Johnsen (1994) differentiates between *judicare,* which is legal aid delivered by private lawyers, and *salaried* legal aid provided by public employees. Salaried legal aid no longer exists in Sweden: citizens are only offered judicare. According to section 26 of the Legal Aid Act, the legal aid counsel appointed can be a lawyer, an associate in a law firm, or any other appropriate person. In other words, no formal qualifications are required. However, the Legal Aid Authority or the court assesses legal counsels who are not lawyers or associates of a law firm for their suitability as representatives (Legal Aid Authority 2015c).

The legal representative's remuneration is based on an hourly rate adopted by the government. In 2015, this was 140 € (1302 SEK) (excluding VAT) for those approved for Swedish F-tax (entrepreneurs who pay their own preliminary tax and social security contributions) and 107 € (991 SEK) (excluding VAT) for those not approved for F-tax (Swedish

National Courts Administration 2015a). According to section 27 of the Legal Aid Act, the hourly rate may deviate from the standard rate if this is justified by the skill and care with which the assignment has been carried out, or by other relevant factors. The hourly rate represents the minimum amount that a lawyer will charge per hour in ordinary cases not covered by legal aid; double the rate would hardly raise an eyebrow in business law.

Use of Legal Aid[4]

Diagram 3.1 shows the use of legal aid approved by the Legal Aid Authority and the courts (when the case was already before a court) between 1997 and 2014. It also shows the use of legal consultation partly or fully funded by the Legal Aid Authority from 2000 to 2014, since no statistics before 2000 on legal consultation exist.

If a legal aid case has been concluded it means that the Legal Aid Authority has decided on the division of the legal aid costs (Swedish National Courts Administration 2015b); in other words the legal aid case is closed. The diagram reveals several interesting developments in legal aid. The most noteworthy is the steep decline in legal aid after the legal aid

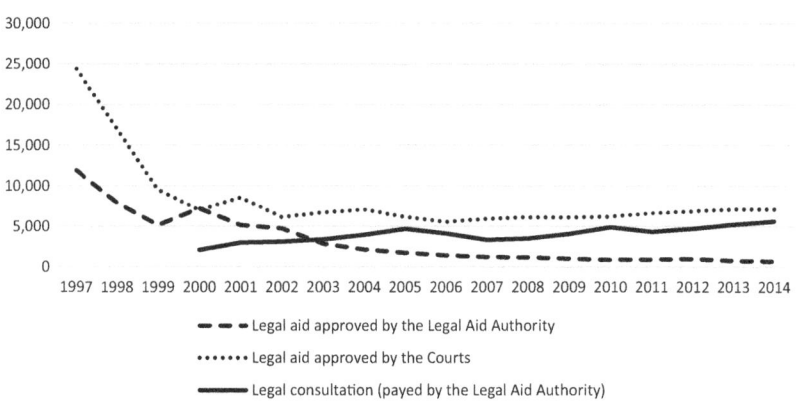

Diagram 3.1 The number of legal aid matter that has been concluded between 1997 and 2014, approved by either the Legal Aid Authority or by the Courts (Source: Statistics from the Legal Aid Authority)

reform. Between 1997 and 2000, the total amount of legal aid cases concluded fell from 36,301 to 14,242 (figures arrived at by adding those approved by the Legal Aid Authority to those approved by the courts). From the beginning of the millennium, the total number of legal aid cases concluded steadily declined to 7952 in 2014. However, if we compare the legal aid approved by the Legal Aid Authority with the legal aid approved by the courts, the former shows the drop, while the latter has remained relatively unchanged since 2000. In fact, legal aid approved by the Legal Aid Authority declined from 7235 cases in 2000 to 740 cases in 2014. Examining the figures closely, we can see that, of the 7235 cases in 2000, only 1411 were granted under the current Legal Aid Act. In other words, in the year 2000 the Legal Aid Authority was still concluding legal aid proceedings from the former Legal Aid Act. However, taking into account only those granted legal aid under the current Legal Aid Act, the number of cases concluded has still almost halved, from 1411 in 2000 to 740 in 2014 (Swedish National Courts Administration 2003, 2015b). The decline is not surprising, given that the number of applications also steadily declined, from 2587 in 2000 to 1154 in 2014 (Swedish National Courts Administration 2015b). These figures leave us with two obvious questions: (1) Why have applications to the Legal Aid Authority fallen so significantly? (2) Why has the approval of legal aid in the courts not declined in line with the rate of approval by the Legal Aid Authority? The answer to the first question is most likely connected to the fact that the income limit for entitlement to legal aid has not been revisited since 1999. In other words, fewer people satisfy the entitlement criteria. It might seem reasonable to expect that the income limit would affect the approval of legal aid in court in a similar manner, but it has not. Unfortunately, there are no statistics on the number of applications for legal aid coming in to the courts so we cannot tell how applications to the courts have developed during the same period. The second question is, therefore, difficult to answer. We do know, however, that family law cases in the courts (which is a large part of the legal aid granted in courts) increased by 85% between 2001 and 2014, which may be part of the explanation.

Looking again at Diagram 3.1, one sees that the number of legal consultations includes consultations where, due to individual financial constraints, the fee has been partly or fully waived. Here, there is an upward trend. In 2000, the Legal Aid Authority paid for 2113 consultations while in 2014 it paid for 5664. These numbers do not reveal if the use of legal consultations has increased in general, only that the number of people who had the fee partly or fully waived due to individual financial constraints has increased significantly. The increase is relevant in relation to the previous discussion on access to legal advice being reduced by legal aid reform. What these numbers indicate is that an increasing number of people cannot afford the legal consultations that are necessary if one is to be granted legal aid.

Table 3.1 presents the types of cases granted legal aid in 2014 by the Legal Aid Authority and the courts. There is a massive preponderance of family law oriented cases. However, this category includes a range of issues, such as divorce (lawsuits), child custody, alimony, and various other family-related issues. The preponderance can perhaps be understood in the light of the fact that some insurance companies have excluded the issues of child custody, child maintenance, and the like, while others have a withdrawal period of a year or two after the end of the marriage, partnership or relationship before legal protection can be utilised in these disputes.

The most common issues not related to family law, are those to do with labour law and claims/demands (concerning for example a dispute where someone claims payment, and the other person rejects the claim).

Table 3.1 Legal aid granted in 2014 by the Legal Aid Authority and the courts, based on the various concerns

Concerns	Legal Aid Authority	Court	Total
Family law	405	6295	**6700**
Labour law	189	150	**339**
Claims, demands	56	274	**330**
Damages	23	102	**125**
Rental dispute	2	66	**68**
Another concern	8	48	**56**
Other civil	7	31	**38**
Other administrative matters	3	31	**34**
Inheritance	6	18	**24**
Victims of crime abroad	10		**10**
Property dispute	1	8	**9**
Social Security	1	1	**2**
Total	**711**	**7024**	**7735**

Source: Statistics from the Legal Aid Authority

As discussed previously, issues involving administrative law are not very often granted legal aid. Table 3.1 also reveals differences between legal aid granted by the Legal Aid Authority and that granted by the courts. First, the courts grant ten times as much legal aid, which means most cases are already before a court when legal aid is granted. Given the number of applications to the Legal Aid Authority presented above, it seems that most people granted legal aid in court did not apply to the Legal Aid Authority before the case went to court. One possible explanation might be that some people at least, did not know about the possibility of legal aid before the court proceedings. Second, if one looks at the issues concerned in percentage terms, labour law constitutes a considerable part (27%) of the legal aid granted by the Legal Aid Authority but not of that granted by the courts (only 2%). In general, family law issues are much more dominant in the cases granted legal aid by the courts. If one looks at aid granted over time, family law issues have predominated since 1997. Still, given that family law oriented cases represent 87% of all legal aid granted, Regan (2003, p. 50) may have a point when he argues that the legal aid policy introduced in 1997 has restricted 'assistance to a relatively narrow range of court cases.' It is difficult to tell to what extent the granting of legal aid matches the legal problems people experience in their daily lives. For example, in Table 3.1, rental disputes account for quite a small share of legal aid granted in 2014, while classical legal aid studies have shown that people frequently have housing problems, but that these do not necessarily qualify as legal cases (Eidesen et al. 1975; Eskeland and Finne 1973). Other attempts to measure civil justice problems indicate that consumer issues and those relating to employment, neighbours, and debt were most common (Buck et al. 2005; Currie 2009). However, others have pointed out that divorce problems are one of those issues for which legal advice is most commonly sought (Genn and Paterson 2001). Previous research indicates that the fact that public legal aid in Sweden is dominated by family law court cases does not necessarily correspond to the legal problems people have. Norwegian studies (Eidesen et al. 1975; Eskeland and Finne 1973) also emphasise the need for legal aid programs that reach out to people rather than waiting for them to seek help, and then ask what their 'real problems' are.

Table 3.2 Distribution of the legal aid granted in 2014 on the basis of financial base of the claimant and the share of the total cost to be paid by the legal aid fee

Financial base of the claimant of legal aid	Share of the costs payed by the claimant of legal aid	Proportion of those granted legal aid in 2014
Minors without income	0%	10%
0–5400 €	2%	29%
5400–10,800 €	5%	20%
10,800–13,000 €	10%	8%
13,000–16,200 €	20%	9%
16,200–21,600 €	30%	12%
21,600–28,000 €	40%	11%

Source: Statistics from the Legal Aid Authority

The statistics on those granted legal aid also show the share of the total cost the applicant had to pay, calculated on their financial base (see Table 3.2). We find two thirds of those granted legal aid belong in the lower income range: those who pay 0 to 10% of legal expenses in a legal aid fee. This distribution may have to do with the fact that those with an income above 13,000 € are generally considered able to afford household insurance that includes cover for legal expenses, and are therefore largely denied public legal aid.

Spending on the Scheme

As already mentioned, one of the main aims of the legal aid reform that came into force in 1997 was to cut public spending (Regan 2003). This was indeed achieved (Swedish National Courts Administration 2001). Spending decreased between 1998 and 2005 because the legal aid scheme was made secondary to legal expenses insurance. Thereafter, costs began to increase again, because the number of cases did not decrease at the same rate as in previous years, while the hourly cost of legal counsel increased (Swedish National Courts Administration 2009). In 2014, legal aid under the Legal Aid Act cost the state approximately 27 million € (248 million SEK). These costs do not include the 1 million € (8.5 million SEK) costs of legal consultations where the fee was partly or wholly waived due to individual financial constraints. In the same year, the state received revenue from legal aid fees of about 4 million € (41 million SEK) (Swedish National Courts Administration 2015b). Taking this revenue into account, the total cost of legal aid, including legal consultations, was 23 million €—which represents slightly more than 2 € per capita during 2014. The public legal aid figures do not include other forms of legal assistance, such as public counsels in administrative cases involving individual freedom and personal integrity, counsel for injured parties, or public defenders in criminal cases, since these provisions are not included in the Legal Aid Act.

Legal Aid Through Trade Unions

Work-related issues are not covered by legal expenses insurance but can qualify for public legal aid if a person is not unionised, or if the union cannot help. Members of a trade union have the right, under certain conditions, to obtain legal aid in matters connected with, or relevant to, his or her work. Before you can obtain legal aid the union may require you to have been a member for a certain period of time. The dispute must be related to work: matters such as wage disputes, redundancy, the right to occupational injury or disease benefits, or work-related criminal charges. Legal aid through the union can be granted if there is deemed to be a reasonable chance of winning the case. For those who are granted legal aid the union pays all legal costs if the case goes to court and the costs for both sides if the case is lost. In addition to legal costs, lost earnings and any accommodation and travel costs incurred in connection with the proceedings may be paid.

The trade union confederations LO[5] and TCO,[6] as well as some of the unions in the third confederation Saco,[7] employ the same law firm (LO-TCO Rättsskydd) to take legal proceedings relating to social insurance and labour law. The firm is primarily owned by LO. According to its own statistics, in 2014, more than 40 trade unions employed the firm on about 1000 cases, including ones relating to labour and social insurance law.[8] These numbers are a minimum of those receiving legal aid though the unions, since each case can include more than one person and several trade unions handle their own cases.

Union membership has declined since the mid-1990s, from 85% of all wage earners (excluding full-time students working while studying) in 1995 to 70% in 2014 (Kjellberg 2015). From an international perspective, union membership in Sweden is still among the highest in the Organisation for Economic Co-operation and Development (OECD) countries (OECD 2015). Union membership differs greatly with age, from 35% in the 16–24 age bracket to 80% for those aged 45–64. Union membership among foreign-born workers is somewhat lower than among workers born in Sweden. The union confederation that caters mainly for blue-collar workers (LO) has seen a greater decline since the mid-1990s than the other two main union confederations (Kjellberg 2015). The decline in union membership is relevant from a legal aid perspective because legal expenses insurance does not normally cover labour law disputes. As already mentioned, if people are not unionised, or if the union cannot help, it may sometimes be possible to obtain legal aid though the Legal Aid Act. However, those who are not members of a union and have a financial base exceeding 28,000 € per year, have nowhere to turn in disputes relating to their work.

Alternative Legal Aid Initiatives

There is a range of legal aid alternatives in Sweden, although they are not as well known or comprehensive as in Norway, for example. In the following section, I will discuss *pro bono* legal services and voluntary student legal clinics. There are, however, other forms of alternative aid, for example, public institutions offering consumers legal aid (see Johnsen 1994) that I will not discuss.

Pro Bono Legal Assistance

According to Regan (2001), pro bono work by lawyers diminished after the comprehensive 1973 legal aid reform, since the Legal Aid Act covered most legal advice and minor assistance as well as legal representation in most courts. At this time, legal services could be obtained from both private and public lawyers. With the second reform in 1997, a renewed need for pro bono legal assistance arose.

Since 1998, the Swedish Bar Association has organised free legal advice offered by lawyers working in their spare time in several cities in Sweden. One of these services offers consultations with a lawyer for about

15 minutes on certain dates at local libraries and civic centres. They can be found in more than 30 places in the Stockholm area and in eight other cities in Sweden. During the consultation the lawyer does not draw up legal documents, or take any other direct action, but offers advice on how the client can move forward with their issue (Advokatsamfundet 2015).

There are also legal firms offering free legal advice on immigration law. For example, the Swedish Refugee Advice Centre in Stockholm provides free legal advice on issues relating to asylum, family reunification, and Swedish citizenship, and on other matters relating to Swedish immigration law. In 2015, they registered 350 new cases (Rådgivningsbyrån för asylsökande och flyktingar 2016). Similar asylum advice centres exist in other cities (see, for example, Stadsmissionen 2015).

Another form of pro bono work is offered by a well-known law firm operating as a foundation supported by donations and grants from individuals. The firm takes on cases pro bono if they concern equal treatment (non-discrimination), freedom of association, property rights, freedom of trade, rule of law, and personal privacy, where the state, municipality, trade union or the employer is the opposing party (Centrum för rättvisa 2015). They only deal with a few cases each year—ones, for example, in the European Court of Human Rights, or class actions on gender discrimination in the national courts.

Cappelletti (1992, p. 29) discusses pro bono work from an access to justice perspective and argues that it is a sign of a 'political laissez-faire philosophy', where the state has not undertaken necessary measures to solve a known problem. However, the way the programme is structured by the Swedish Bar Association enables it to meet, to some extent at least, the criterion Cappelletti (1992) discusses, namely geographical availability, even though the programme is not available nationwide and is concentrated in medium-sized and large cities. Since lawyers offer legal advice in local libraries and civic centres, they at least come somewhat closer to being able to 'reach out to the poor' (Cappelletti 1992, p. 30).

Voluntary Student Legal Clinics

There are several voluntary student legal clinics in Sweden. Both Stockholm and Gothenburg have ones connected to the editorial office of a magazine sold by the homeless and specifically targeting homeless and other socially disadvantaged people. The clinics are sponsored by larger legal firms (Faktumjuristerna 2015; Gatujuristerna 2015). There is a similar legal clinic targeting homeless and other socially disadvantaged people in Lund. This one, however, seems to be working without the support of larger law firms (Juridikcentrum 2015). These three legal clinics are quite new initiatives, which started in the years from 2005 to 2013.

Other law student-initiated aid schemes are more general, such as *Juristjouren* in Lund and Uppsala. The work of the clinic in Lund will be discussed further below. It was formed in 1978 to offer free legal advice and information to the public. *Juristjouren* in Lund is an independent non-profit organisation run by law students from Lund University. Their office in the town centre is financed by the municipality. During a visit to *Juristjouren*, I was able to interview two of the students working there.[9] The Lund legal clinic offers legal advice in face-to face meetings or on the phone. (The similar clinic in Uppsala also offers advice via e-mail.) Meetings take place either in their office in Lund, where they have a drop-in hour, four days a week, or in local libraries or civic centres in the region of Malmö and Lund. The students' travel expenses are paid by the civic centres.

Individuals and small businesses are offered a 30 minute consultation. While other student-initiated legal clinics may provide help with drawing up documents and contacting authorities, *Juristjouren* does neither of these things; focusing instead on offering legal information covering a wide variety of areas. Today they have about 80 members taking part in the activities of the legal clinic as volunteers, while pursuing their studies. They are at various stages in their law studies but the clinic requires that students should have passed the third semester before joining. They offered help in about 600 cases in 2014, either in face-to-face meeting or on the phone. To advertise their services they use social media and their web site; they offer lectures to various stakeholders and hand out leaflets on the street. Recently they have been putting up posters in six languages to reach groups that do not speak Swedish.

Among the most common issues handled by *Juristjouren* are those to do with family law (e.g., divorce, cohabitation agreements, child custody), inheritance law, housing, consumer law (e.g., the purchase of various types of services and contractual interpretation), criminal law, and administrative law (matters concerning the Social Insurance Agency and Social Services). *Juristjouren* can be understood as a first resort: 'Many people come to us to see if they have a case at all, before turning to a lawyer, since it is very expensive to turn to a lawyer', one of the students, Robin, explains. He describes the nature of many of the cases they help with: 'A lot of cases are not that difficult really, but people do not know how to handle them.' The other student, Agnes, expands on this: 'People do not really know what they are entitled to.' In this type of case, the legal clinic can inform people about their rights and what they can expect from, for example, the authorities. The classic Norwegian legal aid study (Eskeland and Finne 1973) and more recent international studies (Curran and Noone 2008; Denvir et al. 2013) indicate that people rarely know their rights or what they are entitled to. Furthermore, research has shown that people often do not see their problems as legal ones (Sandefur 2009). In line with the students' experiences, Eidesen et al. (1975) found that the legal aid citizens need seldom involved complicated legal issues but had to do with concrete problems in a legal framework.

Sometimes a case brought to the student legal clinic in Lund, is very specialised, or involves something requiring legal proceedings, and they have to refer the client to a law firm. Since they are not sponsored by any law firm, they never suggest a specific firm to their clients. Instead, they can point clients to the judicial area in which they should try to find a suitable firm. However, they think that most people who seek help get it in one way or another. They, at least, get advice on how to proceed with their case. Sometimes they request their clients to take the first step (for example, to make a phone call to an organisation) and then get back to them.

The students identify another area where information is often sufficient. Agnes described people's lack of knowledge about their entitlement to legal services: 'Something that people rarely know about is that they may be entitled to help through their household insurance. We provide that information quite often.' Robin said: 'That's right, they should check the terms of their household insurance if they want to sue someone or are being sued.' Their experience that few people know about legal expenses insurance is significant to an access to justice perspective, where knowledge of your rights is a cornerstone (Curran and Noone 2008). If Swedes generally do not know if or how they are covered, this becomes a problem if they end up in a litigation process. A prerequisite for the use of legal aid is that citizens are aware of their rights.

Like the pro bono programme organised by the Swedish Bar Association, the student clinic initiative in the Lund and Malmö area, strives to achieve geographical availability by offering services in the Lund office as well as in local libraries and civic centres. From an access to justice perspective, the student legal clinics are evidently filling a gap that the general legal aid scheme is not able to fill, namely the provision of legal information and, to some extent, legal advice.

Concluding Discussion

As the current legal aid scheme in Sweden is currently structured, most of the population relies on legal expenses insurance, rather than public legal aid. Thus, the legal protection offered today is primarily through people's private household insurance and secondarily through publicly funded legal aid. Legal expenses insurance limits the type of legal services provided, since it only covers legal problems that involve litigation in court. The figures presented in this chapter on the use of legal aid in Sweden show that the great majority (90%) of those granted public legal aid are already before the courts when they are granted legal aid, and the rest will most likely also eventually end up in court. In other words, out-of-court cases lose out when it comes to entitlement to legal protection, both through legal expenses insurance and public legal aid. The legal problems, even quite mundane ones, people experience with government agencies, employers, neighbours, and landlords can have serious consequences if not resolved (Sandefur 2009). Thus, offering legal advice services can prevent legal problems from escalating. As previously pointed out in this chapter, the hourly rate for a legal consultation (the prerequisite to applying for legal aid) is high enough to discourage people from seeking advice, and it can only be reduced or waived in retrospect for those with no income, or a very low one. The increasing numbers of people having the fee partly or fully waived due to their financial constraints indicates that more and more people cannot afford the legal consultations that are a prerequisite to being granted legal aid.

Limited access to legal advice and minor assistance for problems outside of litigation is a consequence of the legal aid reform in 1997 (Regan 2003). Prior to the reform Sweden was known as a country coming close 'to attaining the ideal of equal access to legal services for all' (Kilian and Regan 2004, p. 246). Regan (2001) argues that the reform brought back the need for pro bono work by lawyers, which today provides the free legal advice (although limited to 15 minute consultations in specific locations in Sweden) that the public legal aid does not. Student legal clinics to some extent also cover the need for legal information and legal advice. Nonetheless, the structure of the current legal aid scheme in Sweden places a considerable responsibility on the individual to identify the legal problem. In other words, the form of support that people might need to decide whether they have a legal problem or not, and how it can be solved, is costly.

The chapter has also highlighted how the reform of the legal aid policy has left some groups without help for their legal problems: for example, those with moderate means who do not have legal expenses insurance, are not poor enough to qualify for legal aid but may still not be able to afford a private lawyer. The same goes for those with moderate means who are not eligible for legal aid for work-related legal problems and who do not belong to a union. Taking into account the fact that fewer people meet the income criteria in the Legal Aid Act (SOU 2014), the number of people who fall between the cracks will increase if the income ceiling is not raised. In addition, the chapter has shown that access to legal aid in administrative cases is limited. This could indicate limited access to justice in legal matters, where an individual may have to pursue a case in court against a government agency. Such individuals may have a very limited ability to pay for legal service. The fact that administrative law cases are excluded from legal expenses insurance policies, results in higher dependence on public legal aid. These examples cast a dark shadow on the promises of the welfare state, and can be argued to contribute to weakening access to justice for certain groups of people.

Notes

1. All amounts in Swedish Krona are converted to Euro based on the exchange rate 24 January 2016: 1 € equals 9.28 Swedish Krona. All amounts in Euro are rounded up to the nearest hundred.
2. The most recent figures for the percentage of the population with home insurance were received through e-mail from Philip Ando at Statistics Sweden (SCB) (2015-09-28).
3. The figures from 2014 were received from Lena Westerberg at Insurance Sweden (Svensk Försäkring). These numbers exclude legal expenses insurance for businesses and real estate. In 2014, 6445 insurances cases concerning businesses and real estate received legal expenses compensation to an estimated value of 219 million SEK.
4. The author would like to thank Ylva Boström-Berglund at Rättshjälpsmyndigheten (the Legal Aid Authority) for providing all the statistics on public legal aid.
5. LO stands for the Swedish Trade Union Confederation, which is the central organisation for 14 affiliates that organise workers in both the private and the public sectors.
6. TCO stands for the Swedish Confederation of Professional Employees and comprises 14 affiliated trade unions.
7. Saco stands for the Swedish Confederation of Professional Associations and is a trade union confederation of 22 affiliated associations.
8. Based on e-mail correspondence with Sussanne Lundberg and Claes Jansson at LO-TCO Legal AB by 2015-10-12 respectively 2015-10-15.
9. The interview was conducted in 15 October 2015 with Robin E. Göbel and Agnes Emaus Günzel at *Juristjouren* in Lund.

References

Advokatsamfundet. (2015). *Advokatjouren*. Retrieved October 28, 2015, from https://www.advokatsamfundet.se/Behover-du-advokat/Advokatjouren/

Bruder, I. (1998). *Rättsskydd och rättshjälp: nödvändiga och skäliga kostnader m m*. Stockholm: IFU utbildnings AB.

Buck, A., Balmer, N., & Pleasence, P. (2005). Social exclusion and civil law: Experience of civil justice problems among vulnerable groups. *Social Policy and Administration, 39*(3), 302–322.
Cappelletti, M. (1992). Access to justice as a theoretical approach to law and a practical programme for reform. *South African Law Journal, 109*(1), 22–39.
Cappelletti, M. (1993) Alternative Dispute Resolution Processes within the Framework of the World-Wide Access-to-Justice Movement. *The Modern Law Review, 56*(3):282–296.
Cappelletti, M., & Garth, B. (1978). Access to justice: The newest wave in the worldwide movement to make rights effective. *Buffalo Law Review, 27*(2), 181–292.
Carlson, L. (2012). *The fundamentals of swedish law: A guide for foreign lawyers and students*. Lund: Studentlitteratur.
Centrum för rättvisa. (2015). *Vårt uppdrag*. Retrieved October 27, 2015, from http://centrumforrattvisa.se/om-oss-2/
Curran, L., & Noone, M. A. (2008). Access to justice: A new approach using human rights standards. *International Journal of the Legal Profession, 15*(3), 195–229.
Currie, A. (2009). The legal problems of everyday life. In R. Sandefur (Ed.), *Access to justice* (Vol. 12, pp. 1–41). Bingley: Emerald Group Publishing.
Denvir, C., Balmer, N. J., & Pleasence, P. (2013). When legal rights are not a reality: Do individuals know their rights and how can we tell? *Journal of Social Welfare & Family Law, 35*(1), 139–160.
Departementsserien. (1992). *De allmänna advokatbyråerna: principförslag om avveckling av det statliga engagemanget (Ds 1992:51)*. Stockholm: Allmänna förl.
Departementsserien. (2003a). *Rättshjälp i gränsöverskridande rättsliga angelägenheter: genomförande av EG:s rättshjälpsdirektiv (Ds 2003:53)*. Stockholm: Fritzes offentliga publikationer.
Departementsserien. (2003b). *Rättshjälp och ersättning till rättsliga biträden (Ds 2003:55)*. Stockholm: Fritzes offentliga publikationer.
Eidesen, A., Eskeland, S., & Mathiesen, T. (1975). *Rettshjelp og samfunnsstruktur*. Oslo: Pax.
Eskeland, S., & Finne, J. (1973). *'Rettshjelp': en analyse og empirisk undersøkelse av tradisjonell rettshjelps muligheter og begrensninger – særlig for folk som lever under vanskelige økonomiske eller sosiale kår*. Oslo: Pax.
Faktumjuristerna. (2015). *Om Faktumjuristerna*. Retrieved October 26, 2015, from http://faktum.se/faktumjuristerna/

Gatujuristerna. (2015). *Vårt arbete*. Retrieved October 26, 2015, from http://www.gatujuristerna.se/?page_id=2

Genn, H. G., & Paterson, A. (2001). *Paths to justice in Scotland: What people in Scotland think and do about going to law*. Oxford: Hart Publishing Limited.

Johnsen, J. T. (1994). Nordic legal aid. *Maryland Journal of Contemporay Legal Issues, 5*(2), 301–331.

Juridikcentrum. (2015). *Välkommen*. Retrieved October 26, 2015, from http://juridikcentrum.com/

Kilian, M., & Regan, F. (2004). Legal expenses insurance and legal aid – two sides of the same coin? The experience from Germany and Sweden. *International Journal of the Legal Profession, 11*(3), 233–255.

Kjellberg, A. (2015). 'Kollektivavtalens täckningsgrad samt organisationsgraden hos arbetsgivarförbund och fackförbund.' *Studies in Social Policy, Industrial Relations, Working Life and Mobility*. Research Reports 2013:1. Updated 17 November 2015. Department of Sociology, Lund University.

Legal Aid Authority. (2015a). *Ansökan och avgifter*. Retrieved September 17, 2015, from http://www.rattshjalpsmyndigheten.se/Vad-ar-rattshjalp/Ansokan-och-avgifter/.

Legal Aid Authority. (2015b). *Har du rätt till rättshjälp?* Retrieved September 17, 2015, from http://www.rattshjalpsmyndigheten.se/Vad-ar-rattshjalp/Har-du-ratt-till-rattshjalp/

Legal Aid Authority. (2015c). *Juridiska ombud – vem är vad?* Retrieved September 19, 2015, from http://www.rattshjalpsmyndigheten.se/Vad-ar-rattshjalp/Juridiska-ombud---vem-ar-vad/

Muther, P. S. (1975). The reform of legal aid in Sweden. *International Lawyer, 9*(3), 475–498.

OECD. (2015). *Trade union density*. Retrieved December 21, 2015, from https://stats.oecd.org/Index.aspx?DataSetCode=UN_DEN

Rådgivningsbyrån för asylsökande och flyktingar. (2016). *Nyhetsbrev 1 2016*. from http://sweref.org/wp-content/uploads/2016/02/Nyhetsbrev-1-2016.pdf

Regan, F. (2000). Retreat from equal justice? Assessing the recent Swedish legal aid and family law reforms. *Civil Justice Quarterly, 19*, 168–184.

Regan, F. (2001). How and why is pro bono flourishing: A comparison of recent developments in Sweden and China. *Law in Context, 19*, 148–162.

Regan, F. (2003). The Swedish legal services policy remix: The shift from public legal aid to private legal expense insurance. *Journal of Law and Society, 30*(1), 49–65.

Renfors, C., Sverne Arvill, E., & Sverne, E. (2012). *Rättshjälpslagen och annan lagstiftning om rättsligt bistånd: en kommentar*. Stockholm: Norstedts juridik.
Sandefur, R. L. (2009). Access to justice: Classical approaches and new directions. In R. L. Sandefur (Ed.), *Access to justice*. Bingley: Emerald Group Publishing, ix–xvii.
SOU. (1977). *Översyn av rättshjälpssystemet: betänkande (SOU 1977:49)*. Stockholm: Liber/Allmänna förl.
SOU. (1984). *Den allmänna rättshjälpen: huvudbetänkande (SOU 1984:66)*. Stockholm: Liber/Allmänna förl.
SOU. (1995). *Ny rättshjälpslag och andra bestämmelser om rättsligt bistånd: betänkande. (SOU 1995:81)*. Stockholm: Fritze.
SOU. (2014). *Rättvisans pris: betänkande (SOU 2014:86)*. Stockholm: Fritze.
Stadsmissionen. (2015). Asylrådgivning i Västsverige. Retrieved October 27, 2015, from http://www.stadsmissionen.org/asylradgivning-vastsverige
Stangendahl, P. (1998). *Rättshjälp: ny lag 1 december 1997: rådgivning, behov av biträde, rimlighetsprövning, förhållande till rättsskydd, ersättning till biträde, rättshjälpsavgift*. Göteborg: Tholin & Larsson.
Statistics Sweden. (2015). *Sammanräknad förvärvsinkomst 2013*. Retrieved October 26, 2015, from http://www.scb.se/sv_/Hitta-statistik/Statistik-efter-amne/Hushallens-ekonomi/Inkomster-och-inkomstfordelning/Inkomster-och-skatter/Aktuell-pong/302201/Inkomster--Individer/Riket/303237/
Swedish National Courts Administration. (2001). *Domstolsverkets utvärdering av rättshjälpslagen* (1996:1619). DV-rapport 2001:6. Jönköping: Domstolsverket.
Swedish National Courts Administration. (2003). *Årsredovisning 2002*. http://www.domstol.se/Publikationer/Arsredovisning/redovisning_2002.pdf
Swedish National Courts Administration. (2009). *Översyn av rättshjälpslagen – ett regeringsuppdrag*. Jönköping: Domstolsverket.
Swedish National Courts Administration. (2015a). *Rättshjälp och taxor 2015*. http://www.domstol.se/Publikationer/Rattshjalp_och_taxor/rattshjalp_och_taxor_2015.pdf
Swedish National Courts Administration. (2015b). *Årsredovisning 2014*. http://www.domstol.se/Publikationer/Arsredovisning/sveriges_domstolar_ar_2014_webb.pdf
The Swedish Consumers' Insurance Bureau. (2015). *Jämför hemförsäkringar*. Retrieved September 25, 2015, from http://www.konsumenternas.se/forsakring/olika-forsakringar/om-hemforsakringar/jamfor-hemforsakringar

The Swedish National Audit Office. (1992). *Rättshjälpens effektivitet: regeringsuppdrag*. Riksrevisionsverket (RRV): Stockholm.
The Swedish National Audit Office. (1993). *Rättshjälp – till vilken kostnad?: översyn av beräkningsgrunderna för fastställande av timkostnadsnorm m m: regeringsuppdrag*. Stockholm: Riksrevisionsverket.

Open Access This chapter is distributed under the terms of the Creative Commons Attribution 4.0 International License (http://creativecommons.org/licenses/by/4.0/), which permits use, duplication, adaptation, distribution, and reproduction in any medium or format, as long as you give appropriate credit to the original author(s) and the source, a link is provided to the Creative Commons license, and any changes made are indicated.

The images or other third party material in this book are included in the work's Creative Commons license, unless indicated otherwise in the credit line; if such material is not included in the work's Creative Commons license and the respective action is not permitted by statutory regulation, users will need to obtain permission from the license holder to duplicate, adapt or reproduce the material.

4

Legal Aid in Finland

Antti Rissanen

Introduction

In Finland, public legal aid is governed by the Legal Aid Act, the Act on State Legal Aid Offices, and three government decrees: one on legal aid, one on legal aid fee criteria, and one on state legal aid offices. Legal aid is administered by the Ministry of Justice and is granted mainly through the state legal aid offices or the decisions of the courts. Legal aid services in Finland employ both public and private service providers. Public legal aid (PLA) offices work the same way regardless of their geographical location, and their main task is to provide a wide range of legal services, from legal counselling to court duties. Under the legal aid system, public legal aid lawyers working in PLA offices provide all kinds of legal help, from court representation to out-of-court proceedings, such as document drafting and legal advice, whereas private lawyers can represent legal aid clients only in court proceedings. Legal aid work by private lawyers needs

A. Rissanen (✉)
Institute of Criminology and Legal Policy, University of Helsinki, Helsinki, Finland

to be first approved by a legal aid decision from the PLA office, after which they are paid out of state funds. Legal aid is provided in basically all cases where there is a need for legal aid, excluding cases of little importance such as uncontested divorces, or criminal cases where only a fine is anticipated. Legal aid is either free of charge, or provided with an excess and is not available to companies or corporations.

The origins of the Finnish legal aid scheme go back to the 1950s. In 1956, a law ensuring free trial took effect in Finland. Its aim was to provide citizens with state-funded legal representation in the courts by private lawyers. Matters outside such litigation were left out of the new Act, mainly for fiscal reasons (Jokela 1995). The new law concerning free trial and the first municipal legal aid act came into force in 1973, thereby expanding the scope of the cost-free procedure and establishing communal legal aid offices (Jokela 1995; Rosti et al. 2008). This reform created the current mixed-model system in which public legal aid lawyers, working in public legal aid offices, as well as private lawyers, provided legal aid services. The main reason for creating salaried legal aid offices was to make it possible to provide legal aid throughout the whole country. In the late 1980s, a revision of the law expanded legal aid to cover many out-of-court civil cases (especially those related to divorce and child custody), as well as preliminary investigations in criminal cases.

The next notable structural change was made in the late 1990s, when public legal aid offices were transferred from the municipalities to the Finnish state. The reform also introduced the possibility of partial payment for legal aid where the client's liability was determined by means and merit testing (Rosti et al. 2008, p. 64). A larger modification took place in 2002, when the new Legal Aid Act came into force. Now, public and private legal aid providers were placed under the same law, and the state's legal aid offices were tasked with making all decisions related to granting legal aid. This clarified the system from the clients' point of view; now the only gateway to the system was through public legal aid offices. During 2002, on the basis of the new Legal Aid Act, the financial criteria for publicly-funded legal aid were also altered. This change extended the availability of legal aid, which had been mostly used by the poor, to middle-income clients. In the legislative drafting of the new Legal Aid Act, it was estimated that the proportion of the population eligible for at least partially subsidised legal aid would expand with this act from 45% to 75% (Finnish Government 2001). The decision-makers' view was that legal services should be equally accessible to all citizens, irrespective of their financial means. What was unique about this reform by international standards was the major contribution of state salaried public legal aid lawyers and other office staff (Regan and Johnsen 2007).

Since publicly-funded legal aid is primarily designed for the needy, and to some in the middle-class, for the majority of Finns the usual way to cover legal proceedings is legal expenses insurance (LEI) provided by private insurance companies. LEI was first introduced in 1968, and it is usually automatically included with household insurance, which explains its prevalence; according to reliable estimates, around 90% of Finns are covered by it (Lasola and Rissanen 2013). According to Finnish legislation, LEI takes precedence over public legal aid. This principle has been followed since the 2002 legal aid reform (Rosti et al. 2008).

Compared to those in many common law jurisdictions, legal aid services in Finland and citizens' access to justice overall have not been systematically researched. The reasons are many, but a major one is that Finnish scholars and academics have focused more on other aspects of socio-legal studies rather than access to justice (e.g., Ervasti 2008). However, a few academic articles have been published on the Finnish legal aid system, both in Finnish and in English. Probably the most notable research has been conducted by Francis Regan and Jon T. Johnsen, who evaluated the Finnish legal aid system from an international perspective in the first decade of the 2000s (Regan and Johnsen 2007). Since that time, publications addressed to an international audience have been produced by Rosti et al. (2008), who offer a more technical description of Finnish legal aid, and Johnsen (2011), who compared the Finnish and the Norwegian legal aid systems. In the past few years, the former National Institute of Legal Policy[1] has published a set of studies (in Finnish only) about the current state of the Finnish legal aid system (Rissanen and Rantala 2013; Lasola and Rissanen 2014; Rissanen and Lasola 2014).

The aim of this chapter is to offer an up-to-date description of the Finnish legal aid system and its functions in the welfare state. In addition to the more technical description of Finnish legal aid, the aim is to explore how various legal aid initiatives implement access to justice goals, and to determine what effects these policies will have from the perspective of potential legal aid clients. In the following sections, I will first provide a detailed overview of the legal aid services in Finland. This includes explaining entitlement criteria for legal aid (material and financial), procedural issues, providers, use, and expenditure. Second, I briefly describe alternative legal aid initiatives. Third, I will show how public legal aid is currently addressed from the decision-makers' point of view and describe the kinds of reforms currently being faced in a time of austerity. Thereafter, I discuss the current challenges of the mixed legal aid model. Finally, I will briefly summarise the discussion and address the future of legal aid services in Finland.

Details and Function of the Finnish Legal Aid System

Entitlement and Eligibility

By international standards, the Finnish PLA system is often seen as generous and comprehensive (Regan and Johnsen 2007; Rosti et al. 2008; Barendrecht et al. 2014). Legal aid is granted to all inhabitants having a need for expert assistance in legal matters. However, legal aid is not granted if the applicant has legal expenses insurance that covers the matter in hand.

Legal aid can be applied for either by submitting a legal aid application straight to the PLA offices or by filling in an electronic legal aid application form on the internet. When applicants contact the PLA office to meet with a PLA lawyer, they are advised to arrive with all the necessary documents on their income, wealth, and debt since these are required when legal aid is being considered. If an applicant has chosen to use the services of a private lawyer, the usual procedure is to fill in the legal aid application with the lawyer with the help of all the aforementioned documents. If the legal aid application is made using the electronic application form no documents on income, wealth, or debt can be attached to it. The electronic application forms are verified by using spot checks, and the applicant is obligated to provide the necessary documents if they are asked for by the PLA office. In addition, PLA offices are entitled to obtain information about the applicant's financial status from state and municipal officials, as well as from private institutions such as pension funds and insurance companies.

Legal aid eligibility is based on the applicant's available means. This is assessed by calculating their net monthly income. Net income is calculated from the monthly combination of the applicant's income after taxes, wealth, and expenditure. Expenditure is calculated by deducting from disposable income, housing costs (no instalment of a mortgage), childcare fees, alimony, recovery proceedings, and loan arrangements. Wealth is calculated after liabilities attached to its value are reduced. Wealth that is not taken into account in determining the supplementary excess consists of a family's primary residence and a car, provided that their value is reasonable in proportion to the family's size and need. If the applicant is married or cohabits, the incomes of both spouses are taken into account in the calculation.

If the monthly funds available to a single applicant are 600 € or less, legal aid will be granted for free (Table 4.1). If their funds lie between 601 € and 1300 €, the applicant has to pay an excess, determined by sliding eligibility scales. This type of scale gradually reduces the share contributed by the state, in proportion to the client's income and wealth. In addition, those who pay an excess also have to pay a legal aid charge of

Table 4.1 Monthly means and the basic excess that the applicant is liable to pay

Income/single person	Excess	Income/spouses, per person	Excess
600 € at the most	0%	550 € at the most	0%
800 € at the most	20%	700 € at the most	20%
900 € at the most	30%	800 € at the most	30%
1050 € at the most	40%	1000 € at the most	40%
1150 € at the most	55%	1100 € at the most	55%
1300 € at the most	75%	1200 € at the most	75%

Figures from the Finnish Ministry of Justice web pages, http://www.oikeus.fi/oikeusapu/en/index/hakeminen/mitaoikeusapumaksaa.html, obtained 16 January 2016

70 €. The supplementary excess consists of 50% of the assets of the applicant and of his or her spouse, insofar as these exceed 5000 €. One reason for the personal contribution is to encourage clients to weigh carefully the costs and benefits of legal proceedings, thereby discouraging frivolous cases. Fees paid by PLA office clients amounted to approximately 5.3 million € in 2015. Of this sum, 3.2 million € was collected from clients paying an excess. Just under 500,000 € was from the compensation paid by the losing party in the legal dispute. PLA offices also collected 1.5 million € from so-called self-paying clients, who fund their legal help completely by themselves. In rural areas, where there are no private lawyer service nearby, PLA offices can take on clients who are not entitled to state paid legal aid according to their means and merits. In these situation clients are obligated to pay to the PLA office the current median hourly fee for private lawyer services.

Financial eligibility is reviewed when the applicant files a legal aid application. If the application is rejected, then the applicant may appeal the decision by filing a re-submission. In this event, the PLA office can itself rectify the decision or forward the re-submission to the court. As mentioned in the previous section, PLA offices essentially have a monopoly on out-of-court legal aid issues. If the applicant has a legal issue involving litigation, she/he can choose whether to use the services of a PLA office or a private lawyer. However, a legal aid decision to use a private lawyer can be granted in out-of-court matters only in special cases, that is, if the particular issue requires some sort of juridical knowledge that the PLA office lacks, or if the PLA office lacks sufficient resources to handle the question. In addition, the two parties in a dispute cannot seek help from the same PLA office. This disqualifies the PLA office from handling the other party's case, and she/he will need to get help from another PLA office or a private lawyer.

In a legal dispute, legal aid covers the costs of the party receiving legal aid but not the costs of the other party. Thus, if the legal aid client ends up losing the case, she/he may have to pay the costs of the winning party. Likewise, if the legal aid client wins the case, the other party is liable to pay the state's costs (Rosti et al. 2008: p. 69.). In addition to the lawyer's fees, legal aid covers any translation or interpretation services required, expenses for evidence (e.g., medical certificates), and witnesses' fees.

Legal Aid in PLA Offices

At present there are 23 state legal aid offices in Finland, which operate in 165 locations around the country. These locations are branch offices where PLA lawyers are usually on call by agreement. The offices are most often in the vicinity of the district courts. The offices are geographically divided among six legal aid districts, with a Head of District manager in charge of each district.[2] The districts were selected on the basis of the regional need for legal aid services. Legal aid offices have from 4 to 30 employees, of which approximately half are lawyers and the rest are office staff (Muilu 2015).

In 2014, PLA offices dealt with around 46,500 legal aid cases. This is less than in the first decade of 2000s when PLA offices on average dealt with close to 55,000 cases per year. Despite the decrease in the number of cases handled, the case structure itself has not altered. Over half of all legal aid cases in PLA offices are out-of-court issues. In 2014, the most common service was legal advice, which accounted for just under 40% of all services (Fig. 4.1). The second most common service was document drafting (22%), and the third was court hearings (19%). The category

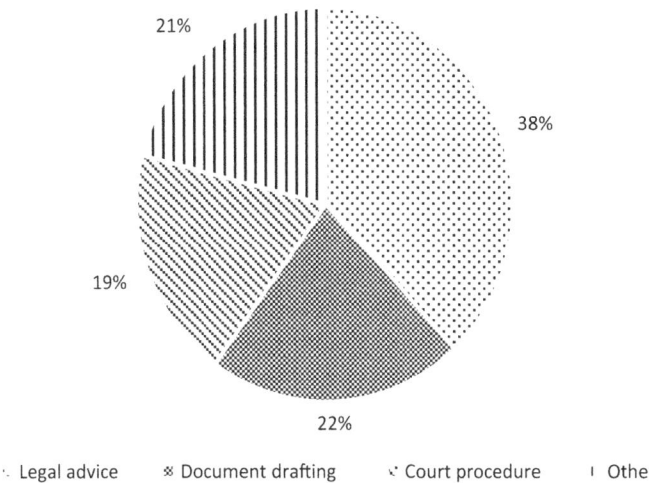

Fig. 4.1 Services provided in PLA offices in 2014 (Ministry of Justice (MoJ) 2015a)

'other' includes, for example, procedures involving administrative authorities, trade confirmations, and assistance to asylum seekers.

Legal advice in PLA offices is divided between giving face-to-face advice and telephone counselling. Of all the advice given, only a little over half was in face-to-face encounters. The key feature of telephone counselling is that it is always free for everybody: there is neither means nor merit testing, as there is for face-to-face advice. Telephone counselling is a relatively new service in PLA offices; it was piloted in 2005 and became available nationwide in 2009; since that time it has become one of the most widely used means of obtaining legal assistance from PLA offices. Because of this universally available telephone counselling, the role of PLA offices has moved towards being a legal 'triage' service, providing the first steps in a legal diagnosis. In other words, after the initial contact, the PLA office provides either a comprehensive legal diagnosis or, at least a preliminary one, together with referral to someone who can provide a fuller diagnosis (Pleasence et al. 2014). However, according to PLA lawyers, many people who are first helped over the phone will eventually end up booking face-to-face meetings with the lawyer, because of the complexity of their legal issue (Rissanen and Rantala 2014).

Family and inheritance issues are the most common problems handled in PLA offices (Fig. 4.2). In 2014, these made up approximately one half of all cases. Other traditional civil law cases, which comprise the third largest group (21%), concern real estate issues, debt, rent, compensatory damages, employment contracts, and torts. In recent years, the single most common issue for PLA offices has been drafting estate inventories. In 2012, such inventories made up 12% of the issues handled by PLA offices.

The distribution of cases also suggests that PLA offices have the profile of a primary legal aid provider, that is, they seek to prevent legal problems from escalating into a courtroom conflict. Since the majority of cases they handle are non-litigation matters, PLA offices fulfil an important screening function by tackling disputes and other legal problems at an early stage, thereby diminishing the possibility of escalation, and minimising social and personal costs. The majority of their clients receive their legal aid for free. In 2014, around 70% of all clients received legal assistance free of charge, and 23% paid an excess. Seven per cent of PLA clients were so-called self-paying customers, who paid the full cost of their legal aid.

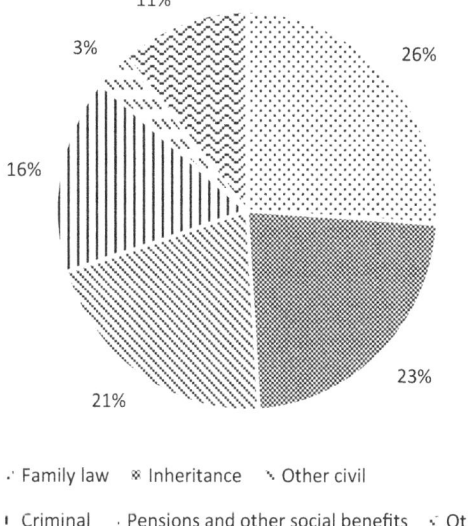

Fig. 4.2 The distribution of cases in PLA offices in 2014 (MoJ 2015a)

According to a 2013 study (Rissanen and Rantala 2013), users of PLA services mainly find the service in one of three ways: (1) they hear about it from other officials (from the courts, police, or social services); (2) it is recommended by their friends or relatives; (3) they find it on the internet. PLA offices themselves do not actively advertise their services. They have sometimes been criticised for their long waiting times: the time that elapses between the client first contacting the office to make an appointment and the actual meeting with a lawyer. In 2008, the average waiting time was 11 days; in 2014 it was 13 days.

Finland is a sparsely populated country,[3] which has challenges in providing its citizens with legal aid services and access to justice. Thus, geographical factors are pivotal in considering legal aid services. At present, the geographical distribution of the 23 PLA offices and their operational locations can be considered quite comprehensive, ranging from the southern coast to northern-most Lapland. However, it has been argued that in some parts of the country there is actually a failure to meet the demand for legal aid. These areas are mainly in south-east Finland (Rissanen and Lasola 2014).

There are also regional differences in the use of legal aid services as regards the choice of the PLA or private lawyers. In rural areas, PLA offices handle the majority of all legal aid cases, whereas in urban areas, cases are distributed quite evenly between the two service providers. The main reason behind this division is that private law firms are usually concentrated in population centres.

Legal Aid Cases Handled by Private Attorneys

Unlike the situation in many other countries, in Finland the Finnish Bar Association (FBA) does not have a monopoly on providing legal services. Legal aid from private lawyers is provided either by advocates who are members of the bar, or by someone with a master's degree in law from a Finnish university, or the equivalent from an EEA country,[4] who is registered by an independent legal counselling board. Prior to 2013, only members of the FBA (as advocates) were under recognised supervision,[5] but, since then, all lawyers who wish to represent their clients in court have been overseen by an independent disciplinary board. Current estimates suggest that there are around 2000 advocates who are FBA members, and around 1500 licenced lawyers who have a permit to act as a registered legal counsel.[6] In 2013, there were some 840 private law firms that had handled at least one state-funded legal aid issue that year; 420 of these had handled over ten legal aid issues (Lasola and Rissanen 2014). A great many of these law firms were concentrated in or near Finland's five largest cities.[7] Private offices handling legal aid cases are generally small, employing on average 1.5 lawyers per office. In recent years, the proportion of private lawyers handling legal aid cases has been around one third. Advocates have handled around 60% of the total, and other lawyers the remaining 40% (Rissanen and Lasola 2014).

In 2014, private lawyers handled around 32,000 legal aid cases, of which approximately 66% were criminal matters, 14% were cases under the Aliens Act (mostly asylum seekers), and 11% were family matters (Fig. 4.3). In recent years, the most notable change in the case structure has been the growing number of cases under the Aliens Act. This is due to new legislation introduced in 2013, which placed asylum seekers' legal

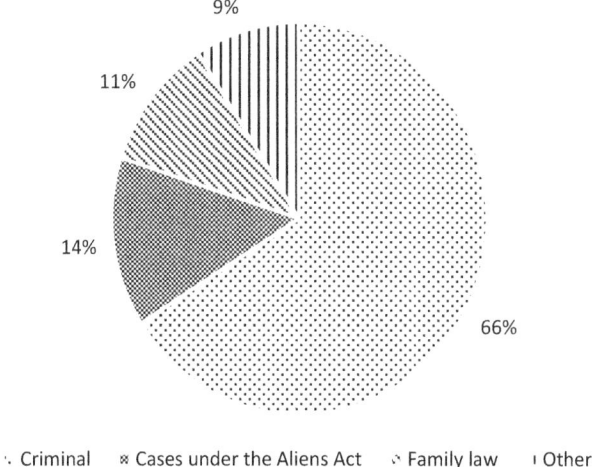

Fig. 4.3 The distribution of private lawyers' legal aid cases in 2014 (MoJ 2015a)

aid solely under the Legal Aid Act.[8] Cases under the Aliens Act already constitute the second largest case group for private lawyers. The Legal Aid Act gives entitlement to the services of a private lawyer for a maximum of 80 hours. The ceiling of 80 hours is calculated for each issue separately, and includes counselling outside the court as well as representation during trials (Rosti et al. 2008, p. 82).

The preponderance of criminal matters is explained by the fact that, as previously mentioned, private lawyers are only allowed to handle cases involving litigation. However, under special conditions private lawyers can also handle out-of-court legal aid issues. These most often arise when the PLA office is too busy to take on new clients, or is disqualified from handling the matter due to a problem of independence, or lacks the expertise required for the particular case.

Overall the role of private lawyers in the legal aid field, compared to that of PLA offices, is closer to fire-fighting than to preventing legal problems from escalating. This also reflects their customer base: around 90% of private lawyers' legal aid clients receive services free of charge. Guidance from other officials (in PLA offices, the police, and so on) and from the grapevine are the two main channels by which legal aid clients find their way to private lawyers' offices (Rissanen and Lasola 2014). According to both PLA staff and private lawyers, in recent years, PLA offices have increasingly referred clients with demanding and time-consuming legal problems to private lawyers in order to reduce their overall work burden (Rissanen and Rantala 2013: Rissanen and Lasola 2014).

Expenditure[9]

The public legal aid system is entirely funded by the Ministry of Justice (MoJ). In 2014, expenditure on legal aid amounted to 71.8 million €. Of this sum, 21.4 million € was spent on running legal aid offices, and 50.4 million € was paid in fees and remuneration in legal aid matters to private lawyers (Muilu 2015) Eighty-two percent of the fees and remuneration payable to private lawyers was incurred in the general courts, and 12% in the administrative courts. Six per cent of the fees were related to out-of-court procedures. The fees paid to private lawyers are partly determined on the basis of the time taken to handle legal aid cases (an hourly fee), and partly on the basis of fixed amounts.

Since 2008, the hourly rate paid to private attorneys has been raised twice, first from 91 € to 100 € per hour in 2008, and then from 100 € to 110 € per hour in 2014.[10] Fixed fees are applied in the district courts' hearings of criminal matters, where the fixed fee is 415 €, or 615 € if the hearing lasts over three hours. In civil and petitionary matters, the fees are 515 € and 715 € respectively. The rates are set by governmental directives. At the end of a legal aid case, private lawyers' invoices have to be approved by the presiding judge. Legal aid fees are considerably lower than those paid by clients not entitled to publicly-funded legal aid. The average hourly fee for self-funding clients in recent years has been either side of 200 €, the highest hourly fees for lawyer services being charged in the Helsinki region.

The costs of legal aid have risen in recent years, a rise directly associated with increased payments to private lawyers (Muilu 2015). Annual expenditure on legal aid has increased by around 17 million € since 2008. Another factor in the rise is the transition that took place in 2013, whereby all legal issues involving asylum seekers were moved to the legal aid system. However, spending on PLA offices decreased during the years between 2010 and 2013. The main reason for this was the implementation of structural changes, which reduced the number of person-years in PLA offices from 445 to 404, and shrank the PLA office network. Barendrecht et al. (2014) calculated that, overall, legal aid costs in Finland per capita are around 13 €, and comprise approximately 0.03% of GDP. In the European context, the Finnish legal aid system is considered very cost effective (ibid.).

Alternative Legal Aid Initiatives

Legal Expenses Insurance

For individuals in need of legal help, LEI is the primary means of covering legal costs. Someone who has LEI that covers a particular issue is not entitled to state-funded legal aid. However, LEI is a very different kind of provider of access to justice. It is managed by insurance companies as an automatic add-on to household insurance. The annual cost of LEI varies from 20 € to 50 €, depending on the insurance company. The usual maximum cover under normal policy conditions is around 8500 €. The basic precondition for LEI is often that it applies to a legal dispute that can be resolved in court. However, LEI also offers some coverage if the case is settled before a courtroom hearing. In such cases 50% of all expenses are usually paid.

Legal counselling and legal advice are excluded from LEI. In recent years, insurance companies have tightened LEI policy conditions governing the type of case covered. For example, family and inheritance issues are generally excluded, or they have to meet strictly defined criteria.

In recent years, the cover offered by LEI has decreased. In addition to tightened policy conditions, the maximum amount of basic insurance has long remained the same, around 8500 €, despite increases in legal costs. In property and housing disputes, for example, it is not uncommon for the entire cover to be used up even before the case goes before a judge in court (Lasola and Rissanen 2014).

Even though public legal aid is not usually granted if the applicant has LEI, there are a few exceptions. One example is when the applicant receives state-assisted legal aid in order to pay the excess of a LEI policy. Also, in some cases clients may be entitled to legal aid for costs that exceed the maximum coverage provided by LEI. Although a condition for legal aid to be granted is that the applicant does not have a valid LEI policy that would cover the issue in question, PLA and LEI are not overlapping systems. Insurance is more a kind of solution for pre-defined legal issues, while state-funded legal aid basically covers any legal problem, without limits on indemnity.

Other Legal Aid Initiatives

On the whole, the range of alternative legal aid initiatives in Finland is somewhat narrow. There are no law clinics or paralegals that offer assistance with people's legal problems. However, many trade unions offer legal aid services or LEI policies to their members for labour law matters, including this in the price of the membership fee. Unions provide legal assistance to their members if disputes occur between employees and employers. The role of trade unions in labour law cases can be quite significant, as around three out of four working-age Finns belong to a trade union.

Finland also has various ombudsmen. These include the Parliamentary Ombudsman, the Ombudsman for Minorities, the Ombudsman for Equality, a Consumer Ombudsman, a Data Protection Ombudsman, a Patient Ombudsman, and a Social Welfare Ombudsman. In 2014, the Parliamentary Ombudsman and his two deputies received around 4600 complaints. The majority concerned social welfare, the police, health care, and prison administration. Around 16% of the complaints led to action being taken by an ombudsman.[11] Unlike that of the Parliamentary Ombudsman, the duty of the Special Ombudsmen is to monitor how the interests and rights involved in their field are implemented in general policies, laws, and practices. Rosti et al. (2008) concludes that, as regards legal services, it is important to note that advice to members of the public is a vital part of each ombudsman's activity. According to the study by Rosti et al. (2008), ombudsmen differ in how they carry out this duty in practice. Much of their advice is given over the telephone, in relatively informal discussions.

Finnish advocates have not traditionally been known to engage in pro bono activity. According to Rosti et al. (2008), during the past few years big law offices have taken on a certain number of pro bono activities. Unfortunately, there is no data or information on what types of legal matters these are, or to whom these pro bono services are given. However, the FBA offers free legal consultations in twelve localities around the country. In these consultations lawyers offer general guidance, advising the client on whether a particular issue requires more specialised legal help. They also assist people with looking for help in the right place. In 2013, the FBA assisted some 1400 people in this way. It can be argued that the lack of pro bono services is mainly due to the comprehensive PLA system, and the service provided by PLA offices in particular. Regarding pro bono services in the Nordic countries, Johnsen (2011, p. 175) says 'the private profession can be seen advocating for a comprehensive judicare system since it functions as a secondary market as well as reduces the risk of economy failure and on top of that diminishes society's demand on the profession for pro bono work.'

Recent Policy Developments and Strategies for Publicly-funded Legal Aid

In recent years, the Finnish legal aid system has seen the biggest changes since the 2002 legal aid reform. The most concrete change, driven by the worsening financial situation as well as by demographic changes in the population, has been the reduction of the number of PLA offices, which has dropped from 60 in 2008 to the current 23. Changes in the public legal aid structure are part of a bigger reform involving the entire area of legal services and their quality in Finland. This includes goals for shortening the length of judicial proceedings and strengthening legal protection. The current government has also introduced a plan to cut the number of district courts from 27 to 20 in coming years. As part of this comprehensive reform, legal aid itself has been listed as one of the top priorities.

More concretely, to deal with the above-mentioned cuts, the Finnish Ministry of Justice is increasingly investing in e-services and remote services. The reform emphasises that, from a citizen's perspective, the current challenge is to find the right service, and to be able to evaluate its quality and reliability (MoJ 2015a, b). Particular attention is being paid to the timely delivery of legal aid services and preventing legal problems from escalating, which itself acts as a vital part of the state's effort to contain costs (Buck et al. 2008; Doust 2011). In the first wave of these non-traditional service models was the above-mentioned nationwide telephone counselling, introduced in 2009. Now, the emphasis is on video counselling, online reservations for PLA lawyer call backs, helping clients via online chats, and launching an electronic application system (MoJ 2015a, b). In part, greater emphasis on technological services is also intended to reduce situations where parties of the dispute end up seeking help from the same PLA office. At present, video counselling is offered by five PLA offices.

According to Ministry of Justice plans, in future a greater part of legal aid expenditure will be covered by client contributions. Although there is no specific timetable for this, it would essentially mean raising the current legal aid fee (currently 70 € per client) or altering the scales of excesses. The Ministry is also revising legal aid case criteria, to determine if some legal problems should no longer be eligible for legal aid.[12] (MoJ 2015a, b) Finally, the new legal aid plans also include introducing the stricter implementation of fixed fees in some legal aid cases, to curb costs (ibid.).

The Debate on the Mixed Legal Aid Model in the Twenty-first Century

In recent years, the FBA has probably been the most vocal critic of the current state-funded legal aid system. Their criticism focuses largely on remuneration and the monopoly on non-litigation issues by PLA offices. The level of remuneration to private advisers for legal aid lags behind the normal hourly fees, which causes discontent among lawyers and other legal professionals (Rissanen and Lasola 2014). Many private lawyers complain that the discrepancy between normal legal fees and legal aid fees is too great: private lawyers would like to see legal aid fees around 130–150 € per hour (Rissanen and Lasola 2014). In addition, PLA offices are exempted from VAT, which arouses resentment among private practitioners.[13]

In Finland the determination of lawyer fees has been left to free competition and market mechanisms. Rather than enforcing fee regulation, the Finnish public legal aid system tries to influence market failures (high prices) in the provision of legal services by giving public subsidies to those citizens who otherwise could not afford to have legal issues dealt with properly (Kilian and Regan 2004). The lower fees for legal aid cases have been justified by the argument that these rein in the costs to the public sector but they also protect those legal aid clients who pay part of the fees themselves (Viitanen 2011, p. 286). The discussion of remuneration is part of a bigger picture about which the FBA has expressed concern: many rural areas are already facing, or will soon face, an acute need for competent lawyers to handle legal aid cases. In recent years, private lawyers have mainly been concentrated in the capital and the surrounding region, and especially in big corporate law firms. At the same time, divisions within the legal profession have increased: according to a survey by the FBA (2012), 70% of bar members under 40 years of age mainly practise business law. Among those aged over 50, the share of business lawyers is 40%. This shift is also being seen in the global context (Abbott 1981; Heinz et al. 1998; Sandefur 2001; Heinz et al. 2005). In addition to the question of fees, the FBA argues that legal aid regulators create market conditions that are unfair to the private profession by maintaining a monopoly on non-litigation cases, and therefore limiting the client's choice of lawyers. The FBA has even recommended that PLA offices should be turned into public legal advice centres and that all other legal aid matters should be handled by private lawyers.

Conclusion

By comparison with international trends, the Finnish PLA system has not tightened constraints on its legal aid criteria in recent years (regarding, for example, income limits or case eligibility). On the contrary, the

Finnish PLA system has more or less continued to offer access to justice in a quasi-universal way (Regan and Johnsen 2007; Rosti et al. 2008; Rissanen and Rantala 2013; Barendrecht et al. 2014). The decrease in the number of PLA offices has had some effects: there has been a slight decrease in the number of clients as well as a slight increase in client waiting times. These minor changes, however, have led to a growing number of cases being delegated to private lawyers. Overall, the effects have been modest compared to those seen in many other legal aid systems in Europe. In general, an efficient and integrated legal aid model is the main reason that the Finnish legal aid system has been able to maintain its comprehensive coverage and internationally recognised reputation. (Regan and Johnsen 2007; Rosti et al. 2008; Barendrecht et al. 2014). Both PLA offices and private lawyers have important roles and duties in the system; PLA offices offer more holistic legal services, whereas private lawyers concentrate on legal disputes.

As seen above, with less money coming in, the Finnish legal aid system is trying to improve access to justice by using less conventional means than those employed in traditional legal services. This is indicated by a move to integrated frameworks of techniques and pathways, instead of concentrating solely on lawyer-led court pathways. The emphasis is on developing e-services and remote services, and on people being pro-active in identifying their legal problems at an earlier stage. This means that the focus is on counselling—preventing the escalation of problems—rather than preparing clients for the litigation process. Thus, the publicly funded legal aid system is taking steps to build confidence rather than to provide too much paternalistic direction.

Finally, it is clear that there is a need for more robust interdisciplinary discussion in Finland about the factors that actually influence people's right to have access to justice. The academic focus has hitherto been on the procedural principles of access to justice (Ervo 2005; Viitanen 2011) and participants' experiences in court processes (Ervasti and Aaltonen 2013; de Godzinsky and Aaltonen 2013). In a time of austerity, the role of diverse academic information is especially important, because it is not feasible to subsidise full-scale legal assistance for every problem that might be brought before the law.

Notes

1. Now called the Institute of Criminology and Legal Policy, the University of Helsinki.
2. The districts are Helsinki, Eastern-Finland, Kouvola, Rovaniemi, Turku, and Vaasa.
3. An area of 340, 000 square km has a population of 5.5 million.
4. European Economic Area.
5. Supervised by the Bar Committee.
6. Figures from September 2015.
7. Helsinki, Espoo, Tampere, Vantaa, and Oulu.
8. Asylum seekers have the right to free legal advice and are able to choose between the legal aid offices maintained by the state and the services offered by private law firms.
9. All the figures in this section were provided by the Ministry of Justice.
10. All fees are represented without VAT (value added tax), which is 24%.
11. http://www.oikeusasiamies.fi/Resource.phx/pubman/templates/2.htx?id=1115
12. The Ministry of Justice is tentatively considering whether debt counselling and repeated custody disputes could be excluded from the legal aid scheme.
13. For example, in the case of a customer who is obligated to pay an excess.

References

Abbott, A. (1981, January). Status and strain in the profession. *American Journal of Sociology, 86*(4), pp. 819–835.

Barendrecht, M., Kistemaker, L., Scholten, H. J., Schrader, R., & Wrzesinska, M. (2014). *Legal aid in Europe: Nine different ways to guarantee access to justice? The Hague institute for internationalisation of law*. Tilburg: University of Tilburg.

Buck, A., Pleasence, P., & Balmer, N.J. (2008, October). Do citizens know how to deal with issues? Some empirical insights. *Journal of Social Policy, 37*(4), pp. 661–681.

Doust, L.T. (2011). Foundation for change. *Report of the Public Commission on Legal Aid in British Columbia*. Vancouver: Public Commission on Legal Aid.

Ervasti, K. (2008). Sociology of law as a multidisciplinary field of research. In U. Bernitz, S. Mahmoudi, & P. Seipel (Eds.), *Law and society. Scandinavian studies in law* (Vol. 53). Stockholm: The Stockholm University Law Faculty.

Ervasti, K., & Aaltonen, M. (2013). *Osapuolten kokemuksia siviilioikeudenkäynneistä. Research Communications 118*. Helsinki: National Institute of Legal Policy.

Ervo, L. (2005). *Oikeudenmukainen oikeudenkäynti*. Helsinki: WSOY.

Finnish Government. (2001). *Government bill 82/2001*.

de Godzinsky, V., & Aaltonen, M. (2013). *Koettu oikeudenmukaisuus hallintoprosesseissa. Research Communications 121*. Helsinki: National Research Institute of Legal Policy.

Heinz, J. P., Nelson, R. L., Laumann, E. O., & Michelson, E. (1998). The changing character of lawyers' work: Chicago in 1975 and 1995. *Law and Society Review, 32*(4), 751–775.

Heinz, J. P., Nelson, R. L., Sandefur, R. L., & Laumann, E. O. (2005). *Urban lawyers. The new social structure of the bar*. Chicago: University of Chicago Press.

Johnsen, J. T. (2011). How do the private professions in Finland and Norway impact on legal aid delivery? In A. Uzelac & C. H. van Rhee (Eds.), *The landscape of legal professions in Europe and the USA: Continuity and change*. Cambridge: Intersentia.

Jokela, A. (1995). *Oikeudenkäyntikulut ja maksuton oikeusapu*. Lakimiesliiton kustannus: Helsinki.

Kilian, M., & Regan, F. (2004). Legal expenses insurance and legal aid – Two sides of the same coin? The experience from Germany and Sweden. *International Journal of the Legal Profession, 11*(3), 233–255.

Lasola, M., & Rissanen, A. (2013). *Oikeusturvavakuutus ja julkinen oikeusapu* (Research communications 119). Helsinki: The National Research Institute of Legal Policy.

Lasola, M., & Rissanen, A. (2014). *Oikeusturvavakuutus ja julkinen oikeusapu. Research Communications 119*. Helsinki: National Institute of Legal Policy.

Ministry of Justice, Finland (MoJ). (2015a). 'Oikeusavun kokonaissuunnitelma'.

Ministry of Justice, Finland (MoJ). (2015b). 'Oikeusministeriön kirjanpitöyksikön (KPY 150) tilinpäätös vuodelta'.

Muilu, M. (2015). *National report, Finland*. Edinburgh: International Legal Aid Group's conference.

Pleasence, P., Coumarelos, C., Forell, S., & McDonald, H. M. (2014). *Reshaping legal assistance services: Building on the evidence base*. Sydney: Law and Justice Foundation of New South Wales.

Regan, F., & Johnsen, J. T. (2007). Are Finland's recent legal services policy reforms Swimming against the Tide of international reforms? *Civil Justice Quarterly, 26*(July), 341–357.

Rissanen, A., & Rantala, K. (2013). *Julkisen oikeusavun kohdentuminen. Research communications 117*. Helsinki: National Institute of Legal Policy.

Rissanen, A., & Rantala, K. (2014). Oikeusapujärjestelmä ja oikeudensaantimahdollisuudet. *Oikeus, 43*(4), 397–413.

Rissanen, A., & Lasola, M. (2014). *Julkinen oikeusapu: Yksityisten avustajien toiminta. Research communications 124*. Helsinki: National Institute of Legal Policy.

Rosti, H., Niemi, J., & Lasola, M. (2008). *Legal Aid and Legal Services in Finland. Research report 237*. Helsinki: National Research Institute of Legal Policy.

Sandefur, R. L. (2001). Work and honor in the law: Prestige and the division of lawyers' labor. *American Sociological Review, 66*(3), 382–403.

Viitanen, K. (2011). *Asianajaja palkkiot – kilpailu vai sääntely?* Helsinki: Edita Publishing.

Open Access This chapter is distributed under the terms of the Creative Commons Attribution 4.0 International License (http://creativecommons.org/licenses/by/4.0/), which permits use, duplication, adaptation, distribution, and reproduction in any medium or format, as long as you give appropriate credit to the original author(s) and the source, a link is provided to the Creative Commons license, and any changes made are indicated.

The images or other third party material in this book are included in the work's Creative Commons license, unless indicated otherwise in the credit line; if such material is not included in the work's Creative Commons license and the respective action is not permitted by statutory regulation, users will need to obtain permission from the license holder to duplicate, adapt or reproduce the material.

5

Legal Aid in Denmark

Bettina Lemann Kristiansen

Introduction and Historical Background

While equality before the law is a basic legal principle, it is often very costly to bring a case before the court and to employ lawyers. This means that many people, for all practical purposes, are deprived of legal aid if it is not free of charge, or almost free of charge.

If the need for legal aid is to be satisfied, this implies that citizens should know their legal position and their rights, or have a way of finding out about this, and that they should have the means to achieve these rights—if necessary through a court case. This entails finding out whether there is in fact a legal claim that can be tried by the courts, an administrative tribunal, or some other body. And finally, the claim must actually be made.

Enabling people to know their legal position is demanding for legislators as well as for the administrative authorities. Regulations have to be formulated in such a way that it is possible for citizens to know their legal

---

B. Lemann Kristiansen (✉)
Law School, Jurisprudence, Aarhus University, Aarhus, Denmark

© The Author(s) 2018
O. Halvorsen Rønning, O. Hammerslev (eds.), *Outsourcing Legal Aid in the Nordic Welfare States*, https://doi.org/10.1007/978-3-319-46684-2_5

positions.[1] It should at least be possible for the citizen to know where to go (which authority to go to) for further guidance. Furthermore, knowledge of the law is one thing; it is quite another thing to know one's legal position. This very often requires knowledge about administrative practice, which is not always available or accessible. This is often the case, for example, in regard to welfare regulation.

The ability to get your rights requires clarification of whether you actually have a case—a claim that can be brought before the court—and requires you to be able to bring the case to court. Although access to the court system is a core value in our society, actual access depends on various factors. A number of barriers face citizens bringing a case before the court—financial and others. Quite often citizens need help to get their rights.

In what follows, the term *legal aid* is used to refer to both pre-trial legal aid and legal aid in regard to lawsuits. The official scheme for legal aid distinguishes between these forms of legal aid, and the providers of the two types of legal aid are also different.

For centuries, there has been a strong tradition of legal aid in the Scandinavian countries, including Denmark. The point of origin was private and voluntary legal aid. Originally, legal aid was offered to people of limited financial means, that is, those who could not pay for the professional legal assistance they needed.

In Denmark, Danske Lov (Danish Act) (D.L. 1-9-12) stated in 1683 that lawyers, when ordered by the state authorities, were obliged to give legal aid to poor people such as widows, lunatics, and the defenceless, free of charge. This regulation was, of course, not very popular with the lawyers and thus this had little practical effect. This form of legal aid, stipulating free legal aid to poor people in regard to court cases, continued into the nineteenth century, but legal aid was restricted to legal aid for court cases.

In the eighteenth and nineteenth centuries the requirement for free legal aid to be given for lawsuits was expanded. Free legal aid depended on the citizen meeting certain financial conditions, and on the fact that it was deemed reasonable (by the authorities) to take the case to court (Betænkning 404/ 1966). Since 1827, the basic principles for granting free legal aid for lawsuits have been that the citizen had a good reason for taking the case to court, and that the citizen did not have the financial means to do so if public funding was not available.

It was not until the general regulation on the Administration of Justice (Retsplejeloven), in 1916, that there was a law on free legal aid in regard to lawsuits. According to it, lawyers who had beneficium (who were on the list of court-assigned lawyers in criminal cases) were also obliged to give legal aid to people of limited financial means (Betænkning 404/1966, pp. 8–13).

The establishment and development of the constitutional state in the nineteenth century, with its core values and ideals of equality before the law, did not lead to changes in, or improvements of, the access to justice of ordinary people. A large part of the population still had no real access to justice. In the twentieth century, the legislative goal was real access to justice by means of public funding, subsidies or grants to ensure access to legal advice, and to cover legal fees and costs when bringing a case before the court.

In the 1960s, the regulations on free legal aid for lawsuits were adjusted. At the same time pre-trial legal aid was introduced. Citizens were given the right to free legal aid by lawyers if they met certain, mainly financial, criteria. However, awareness of this was not very widespread within the general population.

However, the need for legal aid is not limited to court cases. In Denmark, there is a strong tradition of legal aid in a broader sense.

In 1885, the first private legal aid office was established in Copenhagen by a group of students who were outraged by the lack of help for the poor (see also Chap. 12). This legal aid office is still active and is the largest in Denmark—it is now called the Copenhagen Legal Aid Office (Københavns retshjælp).

Since then, a number of similar private legal aid offices have been established. They are usually situated near universities or other institutions that provide the necessary volunteers—primarily law students or social work students.

In the 1970s, various measures were taken to improve legal aid. Three of the most important of these were: first, as part of a very ambitious new law on social welfare (Bistandsloven 333/1974 section 28), local authorities now had a general obligation to provide citizens with free advice in order to help them overcome (social) obstacles. Although the focus was on weak or vulnerable families, this meant (at least in theory) free advice for all citizens, not just people in need of social welfare benefits; second, a special complaints tribunal was established to give citizens an easier and cheaper way of solving conflicts, by providing an alternative to court cases such as the Consumer Complaints Board (Forbrugerklagenævnet); and third, a lawyer-based free legal aid scheme was established in 1978. Lawyer-based legal aid offices (Advokatvagter) were established in a number of larger cities, where lawyers give free legal aid in the form of a short consultation and verbal advice.

Some of these measures are part of the welfare state. Legal aid is to some extent perceived as a public responsibility. The authorities are expected to help citizens gain knowledge of their legal position, are also expected to help citizens in regard to cases within the administrative system, so no further legal aid is needed. As we will see below, there is, in fact, a need for legal aid to supplement help from the authorities—in both areas.

Thus, lawyer-based legal aid offices and private legal aid offices are still at the core of the legal aid given outside of court cases.

As mentioned above legal aid has traditionally originated from the goodwill of lawyers and law students. And this is still the case, since legal aid to a great extent depends on voluntary action. In both lawyer-based legal aid offices (Advokatvagter) and private legal aid offices, lawyers and law students work without payment. To some extent the costs of office space and office supplies can be covered by a public grant. Most of lawyer-based legal aid offices are situated in law offices or, more commonly, work from public libraries or the like.

A brief introduction to legal aid research in Denmark is given below. After this, the public legal aid scheme in Denmark is described. The various providers of legal aid are presented and the use of the different forms of legal aid is described. Then, there is a description of the administration and costs of the legal aid system.

Legal Aid Research

In Denmark, there have only been a few studies on legal aid. Most of them focus on the need—and especially the unmet need—for legal aid. Others are focused on specific providers of legal aid and their users.

In the 1970s, there was research on legal aid throughout the Nordic countries (Eskeland and Finne 1973; Eidesen et al. 1975; Sejr et al. 1977). In Denmark, this took the form of research into the need for legal aid. When researching the unmet need for legal aid, the starting point was to examine the existing legal aid possibilities. One of the most comprehensive studies was carried out between 1975 and 1977, in Aarhus (the second largest city in Denmark); on the hidden and unmet need for legal aid (Sejr et al. 1977). The study found a great need for legal aid and that it was for the most part unmet. Further details about this study are below.

The findings of this Danish study are very similar to those of studies on legal aid in other Nordic countries. Jon Johnsen (1987) carried out a historical, empirical, and legal political study of the field of legal aid, in which he also summarised existing legal aid studies. By putting together one Danish study and three Norwegian ones, he created a very comprehensive basis for his research. These studies concluded that there was an unmet need for legal aid: the research showed that 60% of the households included in the various studies had an unsatisfied need for legal aid. It was also found that people of the lower social classes were in greater need of legal aid than those better off.

These findings have been confirmed by later research (Norges offentlige utredninger (NOU) 2002, p. 18; Rui 2009; Broch Graver et al. 2001; Gadejuristen 2011). There is a need for legal aid in vital areas of life, and the studies show that people without means (financial and others) are in the greatest need. The need for legal aid is greatest in cases concerning various types of rights.

The most recent Danish study was carried out in 2009—i.e., 30 years after the first empirical research into legal aid in Gellerupparken. This study is based on a survey of a number of different legal aid offices—both lawyer-based and private (Lemann Kristiansen 2009a). The study examines who the clients are, what their need for legal aid is, i.e., what type of legal questions they have, and what help they are given. Comparison of this data with general statistics makes it possible to assess the unmet need for legal aid. This study is detailed below.

After a reform in 2007 relating to civil court cases, there was a drastic decrease in spending on legal aid. The government advisory board on legal matters carried out an inquiry into the consequences of the reform. A number of these were found to relate to the legal aid system. The Association of Lawyers hired a consultant bureau to examine this further. Surveys and interviews showed a clear shift away from legal aid by lawyers to aid provided in legal aid offices. Thus, this reform was very significant for legal aid in Denmark. More about the reform and its consequences follows.

Over the years, the Association of Lawyers has also carried out studies of various aspects of lawyers' legal aid work (Danske Advokater and Advokatsamfundet 2011; Advokatsamfundet 2011). Surveys show that only a few lawyers have legal aid as part of their daily work, and that many are very reluctant to take on legal aid cases, see below.

Different Legal Aid Schemes[2]

Someone who has legal questions or is in need of legal aid may be helped in various ways. Often, they may contact the administrative authorities and obtain information and, to some extent, advice. As regards court cases, the courts are obliged to provide guidance for citizens. Various types of private sector possibilities for legal aid are also available—first and foremost, lawyers and legal aid offices, but also private actors, such as trade unions and tenant associations.

The Administration of Justice Act (Retsplejeloven), section 323, stipulates that everybody has a right to basic verbal legal advice free of charge. Also, if certain financial criteria are met, there is a right to further legal aid. This form of legal aid is subsidised by the state.

The legislation provides for free legal aid for lawsuits if certain criteria are met: those set by the Danish Administration of Justice Act (Retsplejeloven, section 330 ff.). Free legal aid may be given by supplying a lawyer or by covering the costs of a trial by public funding or insurance.

Besides this distinction between pre-trial legal aid and legal aid in connection with legal proceedings or lawsuits there are also important distinctions between different providers of legal aid.

In the following, my starting point is the legislation on *pre-trial legal aid*. After this, the different *providers* of legal aid are examined and there is a description of the legislation on *free legal aid*, i.e., legal aid in connection with legal proceedings and court cases.

Pre-trial Legal Aid

Pre-trial legal aid is about giving citizens information about their legal position, and about how to get their rights (and help them do so if necessary). As mentioned above, the Administration of Justice Act (Retsplejeloven), section 323, stipulates that everybody has a *right* to basic verbal legal advice free of charge.

The public legal aid scheme is described in detail in administrative regulations which distinguish between different levels of legal aid—referred to as *steps*.[3]

Step 1 legal aid aims to clarify whether there is a legal problem or case. It is conceived of as a 'legal A&E department', where you can find out whether you have a legal claim or not, and if so, what your possibilities are for pursuing your claim, and (if necessary) what the chances of financial aid are if you want to take it to court. The legal aid is limited to verbal advice. There used to be a list of subjects or types of cases that were excluded from legal aid (criminal cases, tax cases, and cases related to trade). Legal aid was also contingent on financial criteria. However, this basic form of legal aid now includes all citizens (regardless of income) and all legal questions (regardless of subject).

If further legal aid is needed, public funding depends on the citizen/client meeting certain financial criteria. The financial limits are changed yearly by administrative order. The financial criteria are the same as those governing free legal aid in connection with lawsuits (see below). There are also certain non-financial criteria. The financial criteria are supplemented by a list of subjects or types of cases that are excluded from step 2 and 3 legal aid: criminal cases and cases related to trade or business are excluded.

Step 2 legal aid covers extended verbal legal advice, drawing up letters, summonses or subpoenas, the settlement of estates in divorces or simple wills or (pre)nuptial agreements. *Step 3* legal aid covers disputes where a settlement or compromise is thought to be a possible outcome of the legal aid, so this type of legal aid is aimed mainly at preventing lawsuits.

An important change was made in the administrative order regulating legal aid offices in 2014 (Bekendtgørelse 637/2014 om Retshjælp); this excluded cases involving administrative authorities from step 2 and step 3 legal aid. There is a general rule in Danish administrative law stipulating that administrative authorities are obliged to provide guidance within their area of responsibility (The Public Administration Act (Forvaltningsloven), section 7). If the citizen is dissatisfied with a decision of the administrative authorities, there are various ways to complain and have the case re-examined. In recent years, however, complaint tribunals have been abolished, and the possibilities for filing a complaint have been reduced. Legal aid can be provided to help file a complaint but, once a complaint has been filed, citizens are expected to manage without further legal aid. It is presumed that the guidance from the complaint tribunal is sufficient.

Legal Aid Providers

As regards pre-trial legal aid, the main providers are lawyers and legal aid offices. Most of the actors in the field of legal aid are private entities. Lawyers have traditionally been the linchpin of this system of legal aid. The general principle is that you must pay (yourself) for the lawyer's services, and the principal rule is that the citizens must pay for professional legal aid, for example, that provided by lawyers. Nevertheless, there are a number of public legal aid schemes that ensure that people without means are not prevented from getting the legal aid they need (see below).

As mentioned above, there is a strong tradition of legal aid in Denmark and of legal aid based on voluntary work. This has resulted in the establishing of various types of legal aid offices. The ones relevant to the legislation on legal aid are two types of legal aid offices: lawyer-based legal aid offices (Advokatvagter) and private legal aid offices (retshjælpskontorer). These both supplement the legal aid given by lawyers.

The private legal aid offices are the oldest ones. As mentioned previously, private legal aid offices were established by lawyers and law students who volunteered to give legal aid to people without means. The Copenhagen Legal Aid Office (Københavns Retshjælp) is the oldest one in Denmark. It was established in 1885 by law students who saw the need for legal aid, and that people without financial means often lacked the help they required. In 1936, a similar legal aid office was established in Aarhus (Århus Retshjælp). Since then, other legal aid offices have been established—typically near institutions of legal or social work education. The aim of these legal aid offices was to help people of limited means. However, later, these financial criteria were supplemented by criteria regarding subject—mostly in the form of a list of subjects or types of cases for which legal aid would not be given; this list has varied over time. It is not possible to say how many of these private legal aid offices there are, since they vary greatly in regard to background, structure, and the form of legal aid given. Those operating according to the legislation on legal aid can apply for public funding. There are about 30 of these.

Since the 1970s, there have been a number of legal aid offices staffed by lawyers, which provide free legal advice (Advokatvagt, which I here call lawyer-based legal aid offices). The lawyer-based legal aid offices were established on the lawyers' own initiative. By now, this type of legal aid office can be found in most of the larger cities in Denmark.

The establishment of these lawyer-based legal aid offices was made possible by a general improvement in the legal aid system which resulted from a reform in 1978. According to an EU (European Union) initiative, lawyers' services became subject to value added tax (Act 204/1978). The Danish Parliament then decided that this revenue should be devoted to increasing the subsidies on legal aid. The result was a relaxation of the financial criteria for granting free legal aid in regard to lawsuits, so more people were eligible for free legal aid. The subsidies for legal aid offices were also increased. As a result more legal aid offices—especially more lawyer-based offices—were established. They were seen as legal 'A&E departments' giving free legal advice but they did (and do) not provide representation, or draft letters, *et cetera*. Only lawyers, and graduates who assist them, work in these legal aid offices. The work is voluntary and unpaid. Public subsidies cover some office supplies. Usually the lawyers' offices accommodate the legal aid offices, or the legal aid is offered at the local library.

As mentioned above, there is a distinction between various forms of legal aid.

Step 1 legal aid, i.e., free verbal advice, is provided by lawyer-based legal aid offices and private legal aid offices. There is no public funding for *lawyers* giving this type of legal aid. If a lawyer provides this type of legal aid, it is either free of charge or the client has to pay for it—it is not subsidised. Some lawyers give this type of legal aid pro bono and thus free of charge for the client.

Step 2 and 3 legal aid is offered by private legal aid offices and by lawyers (but not lawyer-based legal aid offices). A public subsidy covers part of the bill from the lawyer, and the citizen/client pays the other part. Lawyers are paid 1030 DKK (Danish Krone)/137 € for level 2 legal aid. The client pays 25% of this. The lawyer is paid 2350 DKK/313 € for level 3 legal aid, of which the client pays half. Legal aid given by private legal aid offices, on the other hand, is free of charge.

To sum up, the citizen's right to legal aid under the legislation is quite substantial—in theory. However, as we will see, in practice there are limitations and obstacles. This leads to an unmet need for legal aid, as we also know from research regarding legal aid.

Both lawyer-based legal aid (lawyers and lawyer-based legal aid offices) and private legal aid offices are subsidised by the Government and are subject to different kinds of regulation regarding the criteria for legal aid, auditing (of accounts and of statistics), and annual accounts. See below.

Alongside these public legal aid schemes, there is an increasing number of different *alternative* legal aid initiatives. This includes a variety of institutions and organisations—mainly private entities and non-profit organisations. Often, they give legal advice in a specific field of law, for example, trade unions or tenant associations; others have a specific target group, such as artists or refugees. Some of these require subscription, membership, or payment of fees—others are free of charge. These alternative private legal aid initiatives seldom have public funding or subsidies. They are, therefore, not subject to the regulation of legal aid, including the financial and other criteria. A rather new form of legal aid is street level legal aid (Gadejuristen). This targets people such as the homeless or substance abusers. The idea here is to meet the clients where they exist—in the street (see Chap. 8).

A lot of legal aid offices are thus private entities or non-profit organisations with private funding and no public subsidies, meaning that there is no clear picture as to how many there are. The quality and extent of the legal aid supplied by them is also unknown.

To sum up, there are a great variety of legal aid providers in Denmark. With regard to legal aid covered by the legislation, and the administrative regulation of it, which lays down the criteria for legal aid—in so far as it is subsidised by public means—the primary providers are lawyers (law firms and lawyer-based legal aid offices) and private legal aid offices, which are subject to the regulation.

The Use of Pre-trial Legal Aid

Since the providers of pre-trial legal aid are many and very varied, and since not all apply for subsidies, there is no clear picture as to their use. However, focusing on the more official legal aid offices, namely the lawyer-based offices and the private offices, which work under the legislation and which have public funding (to some extent), it is possible to say something about how these are used.

Private legal aid offices have been studied by researchers. As mentioned above, one study was carried out in the 1970s. The basis of this study was the setting up of a legal aid office in a new residential area in Aarhus (Gellerupparken). Advertisements were placed in various locations in the area. The result was that a large number of people consulted the legal aid office—people who otherwise were not likely to seek professional legal aid. In the first two years (the period of the study) more than 1600 people contacted the legal aid office. In 55% of the cases, advice was provided; in 45% of the cases more help was needed and obtained. In 63% of the cases that were concluded within the period of the study the client won the case in full, and a further 19% of the cases were won to some extent. Besides the legal aid office, a representative section of the population within the area was canvassed as to their legal problems. Two thirds of the population had legal problems and the average was 1.4 problems per household. These were legal problems for which they were not planning to seek help or advice. The legal aid office in Gellerupparken is still open.

What follows is based on my own research on legal aid in Denmark (Lemann Kristiansen 2009a). I carried out a survey in a number of selected legal aid offices; some lawyer–based and some private. The lawyers and legal advisers filled in a form for every new application seeking help over a period of 3–6 months. A total of 2398 responses were collected, and 262 cases (step 2 and 3 legal aid) were followed from beginning to end. In each of these cases a supplementary survey was made of the handling, the communication between the parties, and so forth. The results of the survey were compared with public general statistics. The primary purpose of the study was to examine existing legal aid offices: Who are the clients? What are the legal problems? What kind of help is needed and provided?

The study shows that 46% of the clients are men and 54% are women. The typical client is 40–49 years old; this group clearly over-represented, whereas the young and the old are under-represented. The typical client has a medium-length education and is a wage earner. Wage earners, even though they represent 48% of all clients, are still under-represented when compared with the general statistics for the areas in question. Pensioners and social welfare clients are slightly over-represented. The average income of legal aid clients is below that of the population in general.

The reason for contacting the legal aid office varies according to the type of legal aid office in question. In private legal aid offices questions regarding rental law are predominant (25%); family law (18%) and contract law (16%) questions are also very common. In lawyer-based legal aid offices the clients mostly ask questions about tort law, tax law, criminal law, and debt problems. A lot of clients also ask about inheritance law and problems concerning the administration of estates.

Different groups of clients have different legal problems. Young people mainly have problems regarding rental law and contracts. Family law problems predominate among the 30–60-year-old clients. Older clients very often ask about inheritance law. So, legal problems change through life. Legal problems also vary depending on educational and occupational factors.

Most of the legal aid needed is legal advice (step 1 legal aid). In 83% of cases, legal aid involves guidance or legal advice. 70% of the clients need information about their legal position, and 50% are expected to be able to cope on their own, once they have obtained advice (help to self-help). In this connection, the education level of the client is an important factor. The better-educated client is more often expected to be able to self-help. In 20% of the cases, further legal aid is needed (step 2 or 3 legal aid). Clients with a lower level of education, in particular, need this type of legal aid. In more than 50% of cases, Step 2 or 3 legal aid either leads to the client winning the case or to a settlement. This is a clear indication of the necessity for the legal aid, and that it is worthwhile for this type of help to be given. In the remainder of the cases, it has often proved impossible to proceed further, due to legal reasons or lack of evidence. One in eight cases is dropped by the client because of the time and inconvenience involved in proceeding with it. Only very rarely are economic reasons given for giving up a case.

To sum up, this study finds that there is a widespread need for legal aid, that legal aid clients come from a very broad section of the population, and that legal aid makes a difference. In short, it is well-established in research that a need for legal aid still exists.

It is also well-established that there is a great unmet need for legal aid. The unmet need can be seen in the growing number of people contacting legal aid offices. The annual reports of legal aid offices all show a substantial increase in the number of people demanding legal aid (Københavns Retshjælp 2010, 2011; Århus Retshjælp 2010, 2011, 2012; Gellerupparkens Retshjælp 2011; Silkeborg Retshjælp 2011). To give an example, the number of people who contacted Århus Retshjælp increased by 59% in the period 2008–2011 (Århus retshjælp 2012). The two largest private legal aid offices in Denmark provided legal aid to 18,000 people in 2011.[4]

An unmet need is also demonstrated by the above mentioned study. It is a fair assumption that people living in cities other than Aarhus and Copenhagen have a similar need for legal aid and that there is therefore an unmet need for legal aid, since legal aid offices (both private and lawyer-based) are few and far between. The question remains how this need for legal aid is satisfied—or to what extent.

As we will see below, there has been a remarkable decrease in public expenditure on pre-trial legal aid provided by lawyers (step 2 and 3 legal aid). It is a fair assumption that there has been a similar decrease in its use but there are no data on this. Inquiries by the Association of Lawyers showed that only 18% of lawyers were involved in legal aid as part of their daily business (of which 12% were obliged to do so as part of being public defenders); 50% never gave legal advice under these regulations (Danske Advokater and Advokatsamfundet 2011; Advokatsamfundet 2011).

Lawyers said that they did not find legal aid profitable. However, there are other factors at play. Law firms have changed in the way they are organised, and in the legal fields on which they focus. Law firms are larger than previously and have moved to the largest cities. This is partly due to a reform in the court system resulting in fewer courts, which are concentrated near the larger cities. Lawyers are primarily focused on and very specialised in fields of business law, and their clients are usually business corporations and firms. This results in a withdrawal from citizens' everyday law problems. And the possibilities for getting legal advice—let alone free legal aid—from lawyers are very limited.

There has also been a reduction in the number of lawyer-based legal aid offices. In 2004, there were approximately 100 such offices in Denmark. However, by 2011, the number had decreased to approximately 88 offices. This is due to a number of factors, including aforementioned general developments in the work of lawyers, and consequential difficulties in recruiting lawyers for legal aid offices. Lawyer-based legal aid offices experience great difficulties regarding the recruitment of volunteers (Advokatsamfundet 2011). There is no longer the same incentive. In the past, lawyers could keep up with different areas of law, and perhaps meet potential clients in the legal aid office, thus generating business for the firm. However, lawyers have now become more specialised, and do not have the same interest in keeping up with different areas of law; the typical clientele in law firms has also changed. Statistics from the lawyer-based legal aid offices showed that approximately 25,000 people per year used them in the period 1985–2001. However, since 2001, no statistics have been available (Betænkning 1436/ 2004).

In what follows, the legislation on free legal aid in connection to legal proceedings is described.

Free Legal Aid (Fri Proces): Legal Aid in Regard to Lawsuits and Legal Proceedings

The courts have a general obligation to provide advice on cases that might be brought before them. This mainly involves procedural advice in connection with filing a court case, taking out of a summons, and similar matters.

In 2007, a reform was made concerning civil court cases. The purpose of this was to provide better access to justice. Its cornerstone was the introduction of *small claims procedures*. These give citizens a simple way to have their small claims (up to 50,000 DKK/6666 € and all cases with no financial issues) heard by the courts in summary proceedings without lawyers, in which citizens represent themselves.

The courts have an extended obligation to give guidance in certain types of cases, for example, in the administration of estates and execution of claims. However, the court has to tread cautiously when providing guidance and advice, because they must maintain impartiality. They, therefore, primarily give advice regarding procedural matters. This excludes all the more material questions, for example, what evidence and what arguments to present to the court. Advice regarding material questions can only be given when both parties are present (Betænkning 1436/ 2004, p. 321ff). This means that there is a general need for legal aid in the form of professional help with lawsuits and legal proceedings (Lemann Kristiansen 2009b).

If the case has to be taken to court various forms of legal aid can be provided. In some cases a lawyer can be assigned. The lawyer's fee is then paid by the state. In criminal cases, cases of coercive measures and certain cases regarding child custody the Court will appoint a lawyer.

Most Danish citizens (about 90%) have insurance covering legal aid, i.e., primarily court fees and costs (Betænkning 1436/ 2004, p. 166f.; Betænkning 1113/ 1987, pp. 113–114; Betænkning 1341/ 1997, p. 644), although a study has shown that only 27% are aware of this (Retshjælpsordninger i Danmark 2002). The insurance does not cover the above mentioned pre-trial legal aid. Legal aid insurance is an obligatory and integrated element in various types of insurance, for example, car insurance or family/household insurance. However, there are a number of limits to this insurance. First, cover is usually limited (typically around 125,000 DKK/16,666 €) and excess (typically around 2500 DKK/333 €). Different types of insurance and different insurance companies have different rules on these financial limitations to legal aid. Second—and more importantly—there is a list of subjects/types of cases not covered by the insurance. This list is the same for all insurance companies and means that, for example, family law cases and cases to do with employment are not covered. So, in reality, some of the most common and important cases seen from the citizen/client/policy holder perspective are not covered by the insurance. Cases brought before (administrative) complaint tribunals are not covered either. In small-claims court cases only the court fees and a very limited fee to the lawyers are covered. The initial court proceedings and the preparation of the case are also excluded. Third, a legal assessment of the case has to be made, usually by a lawyer, before the insurance company will agree to cover it.

If a person does not have legal aid insurance, or the insurance does not cover the case, he or she can apply for free legal aid for the lawsuit (fri proces), provided they meet the criteria for this. The legislation regarding free legal aid is found in the Administration of Justice Act (Retsplejeloven).

First you have to meet certain financial criteria set forth in the Administration of Justice Act (Retsplejeloven) section 325. The financial criteria are changed yearly by administrative order. According to the current financial criteria you can apply for free legal aid if your income is below 304,000 DKK/40,533 € (386,000 DKK/51,466 € for couples); you can add 53,000 DKK/7066 € for every dependent child under the age of 18.

In connection with the preparatory work on reforms to civil court cases, it has been estimated how much of the population actually meet these financial criteria. In 1966, the figure was 85% (Betænkning 404/1966, p. 30). However, since then, the number has fallen dramatically. In the 1980s, the estimate was 35% of the population (Betænkning 1436/2004, p. 154). In 1988, the criteria were changed, so that 60% became eligible. Since then, the criteria have been adjusted every year. In 1995, however, it was estimated that barely 50% met the criteria (Betænkning1341/ 1997, p. 477). And most likely the figure has dropped further since then.

You must also have a good reason to file the lawsuit, which means that you have to have a fair chance of winning the case. However, in some types of cases (for example those involving housing or employment, or if you have won a case in a tribunal) this criterion is eased, so that you basically only have to meet the financial criteria. This is regulated in the Administration of Justice Act (Retsplejeloven), section 327.

These two basic criteria have been the same since the beginning of the nineteenth century but, of course, the contents of these criteria and their administration have changed many times. The aforementioned reform in civil court cases in 2007 brought about some important changes. The coordination and connection between legal aid insurance and free legal aid was strengthened, so that insurance is primary, and you can only get free legal aid if you do not have insurance, or if the insurance does not cover the case, or if the costs of the case exceed what is covered by the insurance. The administration of free legal aid was also changed. Since 2007, responsibility for administering the regulation on free legal aid is divided between the Ministry of Justice and the Courts. Appeals on free legal aid can be brought before a special administrative body (Procesbevillingsnævnet).

When there is a clear case for free legal aid, (the Administration of Justice Act, section 327) because a previous decision has been in favour of the citizen applying for free legal aid, e.g., either one by an administrative authority or by an approved private dispute tribunal, the Court can grant free legal aid if the financial criteria (The Administration of Justice Act, section 325) are met. In other cases, the Ministry of Justice decides if free legal aid is to be granted. The administration is placed in The Department of Civil Affairs (Civilstyrelsen), which is an agency under the Ministry of Justice. In these cases, the material criteria come into effect (Mavrogenis 2012). Among these are the importance of the case for the citizen; in tenancy cases, custody cases, employment cases, or cases concerning health issues, the criteria are eased. Other criteria are the chances of winning the case, the size of the claim (trifling cases are rejected, typically when the claim is below 3500 DKK/467 €); whether the costs of the case are deemed unreasonably high, and whether it can be heard by an approved tribunal—if so, the citizen is advised to take the case to this tribunal (after which you can go to court if necessary). The aforementioned Consumer Complaints Board is one of these (18) approved tribunals.

If free legal aid is granted, the state will cover all costs incurred by the trial, regardless of whether you win or lose the case.

To sum up, the criteria for free legal aid being granted for lawsuits are quite strict in Denmark, compared with the neighbouring countries, but if free legal aid is granted, all costs are covered, which is a comparatively generous system.

The Use of Free Legal Aid in Lawsuits

Since the 2007 reform, there has been a marked fall in the number of cases where free legal aid is granted. In the period from 2010 to 2015, the number of cases where the Courts granted free legal aid dropped by 60%.[8] For free legal aid decisions from The Ministry of Justice/The Department for Civil Affairs there has been a decrease of 26% in the number of applications for free legal aid. Free legal aid is granted in approximately 30% of cases.[9]

The factors behind this decrease in free legal aid are manifold. Some of the main reasons include: First, the small claims proceedings that were introduced in the 2007 reform has led to more cases where citizens represent themselves, and many cases are settled before they come to court. Second, changes to do with authorities, for example, in regard to cases concerning the administration of estates, have resulted in decisions on free legal aid being moved from the Ministry of Justice to the courts. Third, the reform meant that, when people applied for legal aid although they had insurance cover for legal expenses, their application was rejected—it took some time for people to adjust to the new regulation. However, apart from all this, there has also been a remarkable decrease in civil court cases. Since the reform in 2007, civil lawsuits in City Courts have fallen markedly. In the period from 2008 to 2013, there was a 25% drop.[10]

To sum up, the use of free legal aid in court cases has decreased. However, as we will see, expenditure has not decreased.

The Administration of, and Expenditure on, Legal Aid

The Ministry of Justice is responsible for the administration of legal aid.

As mentioned above, free legal aid in regard to lawsuits is granted either by the Court or by The Department for Civil Affairs (by delegation from the Ministry of Justice).

In regard to pre-trial legal aid, the State Budget has an appropriation for legal aid. Or rather, there are two appropriations: one is for subsidies for legal aid by lawyers (offentlig retshjælp ved advokat), where the actual costs are covered, so it is demand-led. Legal aid is given to all those who apply and meet the criteria. The other appropriation is for legal aid offices (lawyer-based legal aid offices (advokatvagter) and private legal aid offices (retshjælpskontorerne)) —here the budget is fixed. This appropriation is distributed among the legal aid offices which apply and meet the criteria. There is also an appropriation for free legal aid (fri proces).

The tables below show expenditure on the different forms of legal aid in the period 2004–2011. This period is chosen to show the significance of the 2007 reform.

The first two figures show spending on pre-trial legal aid. Table 5.1 shows legal aid by lawyers and Table 5.2 shows legal aid by legal aid offices (both lawyer-based, and private legal aid offices).

As one can see, there is a quite substantial reduction in expenditure. As mentioned above, the factors behind this are manifold.

Since the civil court cases reform in 2007, there has been a marked reduction in spending on public subsidies for legal aid by lawyers (Offentlig retshjælp ved advokat), i.e., the subsidies covering part of the lawyer's fee. According to the administrative authorities' statistics, spending on this type of legal aid fell from 24.6 million DKK/ 346,666 € a year to 5.8 million DKK/773,000 € a year in the first four years after the reform.

Lawyer-based legal aid offices (advokatvagter) and private legal aid offices (retshjælpskontorer) can apply for a grant once a year. In May each year, the available money is distributed among the legal aid offices that have applied and meet the criteria. This means that legal aid offices do

Table 5.1 Expenditure. Legal aid by lawyers

Mill. DDK.	2004	2005	2006	2007	2008	2009	2010	2011
Step 2	8·9	8·6	7·8	4·2	3·4	3·0	2·4	2·6
Step 3	15·6	14·7	13·7	6·4	4·7	4·3	3·7	3·2
Total	24·6	23·3	21·5	10·6	8·1	7·3	6·1	5·8

(Source: Domstolsstyrelsen)

Table 5.2 Expenditure. Legal aid offices

Mill. DKK	2004	2005	2006	2007	2008	2009	2010	2011
	8·8	8·9	9·1	10·4	10·9	11·3	12·5	12·8

(Source: The State Budget and Retsplejerådet) (Lawyer-based legal aid offices providing step 1 legal aid and private legal aid offices providing step 1, 2 and 3 legal aid)

not know how much they will get until then. This makes for great uncertainty, and difficulties in regard to planning. About 90 legal aid offices apply yearly.

The subsidies depend on certain conditions. Legal aid offices have to satisfy requirements regarding their management, and the quality of legal aid and information given. They have to be open for a minimum number of hours.

As one can see, there has been an increase in the appropriation for this type of legal aid. However, the total sum still represents a considerable reduction. This led to criticism in the media. In 2012, a political agreement was reached that the annual appropriation should be increased by 7.5 million DKK/1 million € for legal aid offices. This agreement was extended in 2014 (Aktstykke 58, of 2014). The appropriation for legal aid offices is now approximately 21 million DKK/2.8 million € per year.

Thus, expenditure over recent years is (Table 5.3):

Expenditure on free legal aid for lawsuits is as follows (Table 5.4):

As can be seen, there has been an increase in expenditure. However, in the same period, the number of cases where at least one of the parties has been granted free legal aid is considerably smaller (Table 5.5):

Table 5.3 Expenditure. Legal aid offices

Mill. DKK	2012	2013	2014	2015	2016
	18·6	20·7	21	21·1	21·9

(Source: The State Budget)

Table 5.4 Expenditure. Free legal aid in regard to lawsuits

Mill. DKK	2004	2005	2006	2007	2008	2009	2010	2011
	318·1	312·5	343·7	281·2	322·8	367·8	432·7	460·0

(Source: Domstolsstyrelsen)

Table 5.5 Number of cases where free legal aid is granted

Number of cases	2004	2005	2006	2007	2008	2009	2010	2011
Ordinary cases	2.941	2.888	2.674	1.703	1.059	927	915	803
Rental cases	1.235	1.128	1.081	560	254	214	176	161
Family law/marital cases	5.592	4.863	4.354	2.171	1.441	994	723	418
Other cases	224	253	249	177	689	2.840	2.477	1.535
Total	9.992	9.132	8.358	4.611	3.443	4.975	4.291	2.917

(Source: Domstolsstyrelsen)

So, although there has been a fall in the total number of civil court cases, and although there has been a reduction in the number of cases where free legal aid is granted, expenditure has still increased, showing that spending on individual cases must have increased.

As one can see, the reduction in case numbers since the reform is quite substantial. And this is true for all types of cases—except for 'other' cases: examples of these are small claims cases (where an increase was to be expected), cases where court decisions are executed, cases before the bailiff, and probate court cases. The reform also led to a shift towards bailiffs and probate courts. Since the reform, when there is no dispute, i.e., where the claim is not disputed and the problem involved is merely its execution, it can be brought before the bailiff without a prior court decision. This was originally limited to cases of up to 50,000 DKK/6666 € (i.e., the same as for small claims proceedings). In 2011 this was changed, so that cases of up to 100,000 DKK/13,333 € can be executed directly, if not disputed. This, of course, results in the shifting of a great number of cases from traditional civil court proceedings to execution. Free legal aid is much less frequently granted for these types of cases.

To sum up, total expenditure on pre-trial legal aid in particular has decreased substantially. There is no obvious cause for the decrease. The main factors, however, are, as mentioned above, the 2007 civil court cases reform and the introduction of small claims proceedings. Another factor is the fact that lawyers have reservations about legal aid. A third factor is the shift from legal aid by lawyers to legal aid offices (Retsplejerådet 2011).

Concluding Remarks

The Administration of Justice Act (Retsplejeloven), section 323, stipulates that everybody has a right to basic verbal legal advice free of charge and, if certain financial criteria are met, there is a right to further legal aid.

Research has shown a widespread need for legal aid, and that legal aid makes a difference. Research has established that this need continues to be unmet.

In general, it has become easier for Danish citizens to acquire information about their legal position, since this is very often accessible via the internet. However, not all citizens are able to find the correct information in this way. The administrative authorities are often very good at giving information via their homepages but, typically, they provide general information based on 'normal' or 'simple' cases. There is no indication as to what you can do if your case is atypical. So, citizens often find that their problems do not fit with the information available, which does not always match the complexity of the real problem. Very rarely does the information offered take into consideration the correlation between different areas of the law. Advice or guidance is often needed to make information usable, so that it can provide a basis for informed decision-making.

The supply of, and access to, pre-trial or pre-procedural free legal aid has changed over the years. Legal aid by lawyers subsidised by the Government is practically non-existent for the vast majority of citizens. A major factor is that the lawyers do not find legal aid profitable. However, other factors are also at play. The law firms have changed in the way they are organised and the legal fields that they focus on have also changed. Firms have relocated to the big cities, largely because of a reform in the court system that has led to fewer courts. Lawyers are primarily focused on and become specialised in fields of business law, and their clients are mainly business corporations and firms. This means they are no longer interested in citizens' everyday legal problems.

The lawyer-based legal aid offices have great difficulty in recruiting volunteers (Advokatsamfundet 2011). There is no longer the same incentive. There are fewer lawyer based legal aid offices, and the lawyers working there are often unfamiliar with the kind of legal questions they meet, since their primary work is related to business law.

Lawyers are still, however, an essential part of the Danish legal aid system, but there has been a clear shift away from legal aid provided by lawyers to legal aid offices (Retsplejerådet 2011 and Copenhagen Economics 2012).

The very few private legal aid offices providing general legal aid (as opposed to more specialised legal aid offices) are concentrated in the major cities, close to institutions of legal education where the necessary volunteers are found. Since these private legal aid offices only exist in a few places, access to this form of legal aid is very uneven and unequal.

Some private legal aid offices provide legal advice over the telephone or by email, and, in this respect; you might say that their legal aid is nationwide. This type of legal aid is, however, usually limited to step 1 legal aid—verbal advice. The clients are, in fact, predominantly local (Lemann Kristiansen 2009a).[5] Another problem or challenge is to ensure the quality of the legal aid. When law students or social work students are the main work force, close supervision by experienced lawyers is required. This is not always available free of charge, and the financial resources of these institutions are very limited.

Thus, part of the population is in reality cut-off from (free) legal aid. This is also true as regards the very basic form of legal aid. This has been a well-known fact for some time, and there has been some discussion of reforms to the civil procedure regulations (Betænkning 1436/ 2004, pp. 312–313, p. 334; Betænkning 1341/ 1997, pp. 437–439). The geographical differences are described as unfortunate but any more comprehensive reform of legal aid is deemed unrealistic—primarily for financial reasons.

The civil courts cases reform of 2007 has resulted in a change in the need for legal aid, and in a remarkable reduction in spending on it. The purpose of the reform was to give better access to justice; its cornerstone is the introduction of small claims proceedings, in which citizens represent themselves. However, this new form of court procedure has created new inequalities in access to justice. Not all citizens are able to determine on their own whether they in fact have 'a case', or to download the correct forms, fill them in, decide on what evidence to present before the court, and finally litigate the case. Thus a new need for legal aid has been created—but not met. Since the 2007 reform, there has been a marked fall in cases where free legal aid for lawsuits is granted.

In many ways citizens are expected to be self-reliant. This is also true in regard to cases involving administrative authorities. They are expected to find the relevant information, hand in the relevant applications, contribute the relevant facts and enter into negotiations or deliberations with the authorities. The gap between the resourceful and the disadvantaged citizen is growing.

This is also true in regard to legal aid. It is harder to find the legal aid you need if you are not a resourceful citizen, or if you do not live in one of the larger cities in Denmark. The need for legal aid is increasing and changing. Developments in the administrative system and the courts have not been reflected in the public legal aid schemes. There is a great need for further research and a coherent legal-political discussion in regard to legal aid (Johnsen 1978 and Vedsted-Hansen and Pedersen 1982).[6] The legal aid scheme needs to be brought into line with the general developments in society, so that it provides nationwide and high-quality legal aid.

Notes

1. For these demands on the legislator see Evald (2009), pp. 33–52.
2. This section is based on Lemann Kristiansen (2009b) and (2013).
3. It is optional for private legal aid offices whether they operate according to this distinction but it is a condition for getting public funding.
4. In comparison from statistics from the (100) lawyer-based legal aid offices showed that in 2001 they had approx. 25,000 clients. The lawyer-based legal aid offices no longer maintain statistics on their clients but, since then, the number of lawyer-based legal aid offices has decreased by 20%, and, thus, I presume that the same is the case as regards the number of clients.
5. This survey showed that clients in the legal aid offices live very close by. A survey made in Århus Retshjælp (2012) focusing on the legal aid over the telephone showed the same pattern. Very few calls came from municipalities.
6. Here such a coherent legal political overhaul was demanded. Here it is pointed out that legal aid has been in a legal political vacuum for more than 70 years.

References

Advokatsamfundet. (2011). *Rapport om advokatvagter i Danmark*.
Århus Retshjælp. (2010). *Århus Retshjælp Årsberetning*.
Århus Retshjælp. (2011). *Århus Retshjælp Årsberetning*.
Århus Retshjælp. (2012). *Århus Retshjælp Årsberetning*.
Betænkning 1113. (1987). *Betænkning om advokatretshjælp, fri proces og retshjælpsforsikring m.v.* Afgivet af Justitsministeriets udvalg vedrørende Retshjælp m.v.

Betænkning 1341. (1997). *Småsagsudvalgets betænkning: småsagsproces, inkassoproces*. Justitsministeriet.
Betænkning 1436. (2004). *Reform af den civile retspleje/afgivet af Retsplejerådet*. Vol. 3: Adgang til domstolene.
Betænkning 404. (1966). *Betænkning om ændring af reglerne om fri proces og organisationen af den vederlagsfri retshjælp*. Afgivet af det af Justitsministeriet den 2. November 1960 nedsatte udvalg.
Bistandsloven (Law on Social Welfare) L333. (1974).
Broch Graver, A., (et al.). (2001). *Rettshjelp*. Oslo: Institutt for kriminologi og rettssosiologi, Avdeling for rettssosiologi, Universitetet i Oslo.
Copenhagen Economics, Danske Advokater & Advokatsamfundet. (2012). *Retshjælp i nød? En analyse af udviklingen siden 2007 og dens konsekvenser*.
Danske Advokater og Advokatsamfundet. (2011). *Advokaters syn på offentlig retshjælp ved advokat, fri proces og retshjælpsforsikring* (SFI Survey).
Eidesen, A., Eskeland, S., & Mathiesen, T. (Eds.). (1975). *Rettshjelp og samfunnsstruktur*. Oslo: Pax.
Eskeland, S., & Finne, J. (1973). *Rettshjelp*. Oslo: Pax.
Evald, J. (2009). Lovsprogets tilgængelighed. In P. Andersen (Ed.), *Om rettens tilgængelighed* (pp. 33–52). Copenhagen: Jurist- og Økonomforbundets Forlag.
Gadejuristen. (2011). *Dokumentationsprojektet—en undersøgelse af udsattes retshjælpsbehov*. Accessible via the homepage: www.gadejuristen.dk
Gallup. (2002). *Retshjælpsordninger i Danmark*. Rapport.
Gellerupparkens Retshjælp. (2011). *Årsberetning*.
Johnsen, J. T. (1978). Den norske rettshjelpsutredningen. En kritisk kommentar. *Retfærd, 8*, 18–31.
Johnsen, J. T. (1987). *Retten til juridisk bistand. En rettspolitisk studie*. Oslo: Tano.
Københavns Retshjælp. (2010). *Årsberetning*.
Københavns Retshjælp. (2011). *Årsberetning*.
Lemann Kristiansen, B. (2009a). *Retshjælp i Danmark. Delrapport I: Beskrivelse af retshjælpstilbuddene*, http://www.justitsministeriet.dk/forskning/rapporter-vedr-forskningspuljen/
Lemann Kristiansen, B. (2009b). Domstolenes tilgængelighed. In P. Andersen (Ed.), *Om Rettens tilgængelighed* (pp. 87–119). Copenhagen: Jurist- og Økonomforbundets Forlag.
Lemann Kristiansen, B. (2013). Retshjælp—fortsat et udækket behov? In T. Gammeltoft-Hansen, I. E. Koch, B. Lemann Kristiansen, & S. Schaumburg-Müller (Eds.), *Protecting the Rights of Others. Festskrift til Jens Vedsted-Hansen* (pp. 83–101). Copenhagen: DJØF Publishing.

Mavrogenis, A. (2012). *Fri proces. Retshjælp*. Copenhagen: Jurist- og Økonomforbundets Forlag.

Norges offentlige utredninger. (2002). NOU 2002:18 *Rett til rett. Vurdering av konkurranseforholdene i markedet for juridiske tjenester*. Utredning fra Advokatkonkurranseutvalget, avgitt til Justis- og politidepartmentet.

Retsplejerådet. (2011). Retsplejerådets rapport, *Redegørelse om retshjælp ved advokat m.v.*

Rui, J. P. (Ed.). (2009). *Rettshjelp fra kyst til vidde. Festskrift til Jusshjelpa i Nord-Norge 20 år*. Oslo: Gyldendal akademisk.

Sejr, L. et al. (1977). *Retshjælp i et lokalområde*. Forskningsrapport, Aarhus: Aarhus Universitet.

Silkeborg Retshjælp. (2011). *Årsberetning for Silkeborg Retshjælp*.

Vedsted-Hansen, J., & Pedersen, A. S. (1982). Hvor blev retshjælpspolitikken af?—Fra retspolitik til retsplejeteknokrati. *Retfærd, 22*, 66–82.

Open Access This chapter is distributed under the terms of the Creative Commons Attribution 4.0 International License (http://creativecommons.org/licenses/by/4.0/), which permits use, duplication, adaptation, distribution, and reproduction in any medium or format, as long as you give appropriate credit to the original author(s) and the source, a link is provided to the Creative Commons license, and any changes made are indicated.

The images or other third party material in this book are included in the work's Creative Commons license, unless indicated otherwise in the credit line; if such material is not included in the work's Creative Commons license and the respective action is not permitted by statutory regulation, users will need to obtain permission from the license holder to duplicate, adapt or reproduce the material.

6

Legal Aid in Iceland

Hildur Fjóla Antonsdóttir

Introduction

The aim of this chapter is to give an overview of the public legal aid provision for civil cases in Iceland: how it has developed, and the main issues that appear to have been, and remain, contentious. It is safe to say that the framing of public legal aid in civil cases in Iceland has primarily been in terms of the law. Mostly lawyers have discussed the topic of legal aid and there is little evidence of a socio-legal debate, or even a policy debate on the issue in terms of the broader aims and purposes of legal aid in society, and the social significance of access to justice.

I will begin by giving a brief background to the historical development of legal aid in Iceland. I will then outline the current legislation and administration of legal aid and describe recent discussions in terms of legislative changes on legal aid, against the backdrop of the economic and

---

I would like to thank Margrét Steinarsdóttir, lawyer and Director of the Icelandic Human Rights Centre, for her helpful comments on this chapter.

H.F. Antonsdóttir (✉)
Sociology of Law Department, Lund University, Lund, Sweden

© The Author(s) 2018
O. Halvorsen Rønning, O. Hammerslev (eds.), *Outsourcing Legal Aid in the Nordic Welfare States*, https://doi.org/10.1007/978-3-319-46684-2_6

political turmoil that has characterised Icelandic society over the last 10 years. I will then proceed to give an account of the applicants for, and recipients of, legal aid. Following this, I will briefly describe the legal expenses insurance, now found in some of the standard home and family insurance packages offered by the main insurance companies. Finally, I will briefly discuss access to free legal counselling and out-of-court legal assistance services provided by members' organisations and the voluntary sector.

To say that literature on access to legal aid in Iceland is scarce is an understatement. It would seem that only a handful of lawyers have written on the subject over the years, and a few reports have been written on various aspects of legal aid. There have been a few student theses, mostly in law, on the topic, and a number of short articles in Icelandic legal journals. Very little, if any, information on legal aid in Iceland can be found in other languages.

Historical Background to the Development of the Law on Legal Aid

The first legal provision for free legal assistance in Iceland was included in the procedural rules of the Norwegian and Danish laws that were enacted in Iceland from 1718 to 1732. The authorities were authorised to appoint a spokesperson to represent, free of charge, poor widows, people with mental health problems, and people without legal guardians. Under a directive from Norway in 1797, new provisions on legal assistance came into force. Their main aim was to assist the poor in claiming their most obvious rights. The eligibility criteria for legal assistance seem to have been very strict, so it was obviously only intended for those who could not provide for themselves (Gíslason 1994).

In 1907, specific laws on legal aid (gjafsókn) came into force, according to which the government was responsible for providing legal aid to churches, hospitals, and institutions that provided support to the poor. Legal aid could also be granted to people who had been certified as poor by the local authorities, or by parish priests. However, before an applicant was granted legal aid, the merits of the case had to be considered, although no further guidelines were provided on that point. As before, the law was based on the notion that legal aid was a form of charity (Gíslason 1994).

In 1936, a new law on civil procedure (no. 85/1936) was enacted that included a chapter on legal aid similar to the previous law. This law stipulated that the concept of legal aid (gjafsókn) should apply to both plaintiffs and defendants, and that, before legal aid was granted, the merits of the case should be assessed. The criteria for those who could apply for legal aid were also extended to include schools and municipalities, as well as churches, hospitals, and charities. In special cases, applicants could be granted legal aid if they were in dire straits financially, even if they were not considered poor. In addition to the law on legal aid, there were provisions, in other laws, on people's rights to legal aid under certain circumstances (Gíslason 1994).[1]

No further legislative changes were made to the law on legal aid until the Law on Civil Procedure (no. 91/1991) came into force in 1992, which I will discuss in more detail in the next section. By that time, lawyers and non-lawyers alike had drawn attention to the need for law reform in the area of legal aid (Gíslason 1994). It was pointed out that, due to the increasing complexity of modern societies, there was a greater need for legal information and assistance. It was noted that access to legal aid in the other Nordic countries was considerably more extensive than in Iceland, and that there was a need not only for access to legal aid to pursue court cases, but also for access to legal information and assistance (Eydal 1973; Rafnar 1981).

In 1979, a bill was brought before Parliament that would have established the right to receive necessary legal counselling and assistance outside the court but it was not passed. At the general meeting of the Icelandic Bar Association in 1986, a proposal to expand the provision of legal aid and ensure access to legal aid outside court was accepted. The Minister for Judicial Affairs subsequently appointed a committee charged with drawing up a bill on public legal aid. This bill was brought before Parliament in 1989–1990 and included wider eligibility criteria for legal aid for pursuing cases in court (which the current legislation is based on), together with provisions on the right to general legal information and assistance outside the court in specific cases. However, like the previous bill, this one was not enacted (Gíslason 1994). So far, there is still no provision in Icelandic law for legal aid in the form of legal counselling and out-of-court assistance.

The Current Legislation on Legal Aid in Civil Cases and its Administration

In 1992, the current legislation on legal aid in civil cases came into force with the enactment of the Law on Civil Procedure (no. 91/1991). Chapter XX of this Law, entitled Legal Aid (Gjafsókn), sets out the provisions on legal aid in Articles 125–128, whose contents I will now outline.

The definition of legal aid (gjafsókn) includes legal aid for both plaintiffs and defendants, as was also the case under the previous law. The current law makes the Minister for Judicial Affairs responsible for appointing three lawyers to make up a Legal Aid Committee to review applications and make recommendations on which applicants should be granted legal aid.[2] While it is the Minister who grants legal aid, he cannot do so unless the Legal Aid Committee has recommended that the application should be funded; however, he has the authority to deny an applicant legal aid, contrary to the recommendations of the Legal Aid Committee. The Minister is also authorised to provide more detailed guidelines on the legal aid eligibility criteria and the workings of the Legal Aid Committee in regulations.[3]

Legal aid is only to be granted if the applicant has sufficient reason to initiate proceedings or defend themselves in civil proceedings, and if one of the following conditions is fulfilled:

A. The applicant's financial situation is such that they could not afford to defend their interests, and the case is of such a nature that it would be considered appropriate that legal aid for it should be financed by public funds,
B. The outcome of the case would have great general significance, or would be of great importance for the employment, social status or other personal status of the applicant.

The provisions in section B are taken from the previous bill on legal aid that was brought before parliament in 1989–1990. The rationale put forward in the previous bill for this criterion is that it would apply, in particular, when the case involved basic issues concerning legal interpretation, or when it was of significant public interest, or when it had great significance for the socio-economic position of the applicant. In such cases, it could be considered unfair that the applicant should need to bear significant costs.

The state is obliged to pay those costs that the legal aid recipient is responsible for, i.e., the costs of legal services, etc. However, legal aid can be limited to covering only a certain component of the case, or to a certain amount. The lawyer's fees are to be decided by the judge, which means that the state is not obliged to pay the legal costs as charged by the lawyer. The legal aid recipient is exempt from all treasury charges arising from the case, including charges for official certificates and other documents that are a part of the case. The legal aid also covers the enforcement of the recipient's rights, unless otherwise stated in the legal aid licence. Being granted legal aid does not exempt the recipient from paying the legal costs of the other party to the case.

Lawyers are free to set their own fees, and rates can vary between law firms. According to the Icelandic Bar Association's Code of Ethics, lawyers should draw their client's attention to the possibility of legal aid where applicable (The Icelandic Bar Association, n.d.-a). One of the issues that has been raised in relation to fees in legal aid cases is that the amount decided by the judge is often lower than the fees charged by the lawyer, and the decision is not usually accompanied by detailed justification. It has been the norm for lawyers to forgo their legal fees, either entirely, or in part (Magnusson 2005). This arrangement has frequently been criticised by lawyers, who claim that judges do not appreciate the expenses involved in running law firms (Björnsson 2005). This arrangement might mean that lawyers keep their work to a minimum and therefore do not represent their clients in the best way possible, which in effect restricts clients' access to the courts (Jónsson 2005). Another objection is that, due to this arrangement, lawyers will increasingly make special agreements with their clients whereby the clients pay the difference between the fees charged by the lawyer and the amount decided by the judge (Sævarsson 2005). In 2010, the Judicial Council (dómstólaráð) issued announcement no. 5/2009 stipulating that the hourly rate for legal fees in legal aid cases was 10,000 Icelandic Kronor (ISK) (56 €) excluding VAT but the announcement is no longer valid.[4]

It is important to note that, in certain cases, individuals have a legal right to legal aid from the state. Such provisions can be found in various laws.[5] In a report commissioned by the Icelandic Bar Association on legal aid, this state of affairs has been criticised on the grounds that it is not always clear why legal aid is available in some types of cases but not others. The authors query whether the equality principle is being followed in these circumstances (Jónsson and Harðardóttir 2008). It remains the case, however, that, by law, those who are entitled to legal aid have to submit an application to the Legal Aid Committee.

The regulations issued by the Minister for Judicial Affairs describe in more detail the eligibility criteria for legal aid, and the workings of the Legal Aid Committee. An application to the committee must include the following: the main documents concerning the case; a copy of the applicant's tax returns for the past two years (and the applicant's partner's tax returns, if applicable); information about the applicant's income since the last tax return (and information about the income of the applicant's partner, if applicable); and other relevant documents. The Legal Aid Committee has to be notified if the applicant has an insurance policy that provides legal costs insurance. It is further stipulated that legal aid is only awarded to pursue a case in an Icelandic court, so it is not possibly to apply for legal aid to take legal action in international courts.

The regulations set out in more detail how the law's eligibility criteria should be interpreted. As stated in Article 126 of the Law, the applicant has to have sufficient reason to initiate proceedings, or defend herself or himself in civil proceedings. Furthermore, the case must be of such a nature that it is acceptable for it to be paid for out of public funds; it should be clear that a lawsuit is necessary and that its timing is appropriate; and the case must be likely to be successful. If the case involves a dispute that is already before the courts, in another case that will likely set a precedent, legal aid can be refused until it is possible to see whether the case is likely to succeed.

The section A criteria allow applications based on the applicant's low economic status. The regulation further stipulates that the annual income criteria for legal aid is 2 million ISK (12,687 €) before tax per single person and 3 million ISK (19,030 €) per couple. Additional income of 250,000 ISK (1586 €) is allowed for each dependent child. It is worth mentioning here that the income tax threshold in 2014 was 1,692,295 ISK (10,735 €) suggesting that the income criterion is set just above the income tax threshold, which seems to have been a benchmark for granting legal aid since the current legislation came in to force in 1992 (Gíslason 1994).[6] In 2014, the average annual income for men in Iceland was 5,818,000 ISK (36,906 €), and for women 4,310,000 ISK (27,340 €) (Statistics Iceland 2015a).[7] This criterion, however, is not fixed and the regulation lists factors to be considered when deciding whether to grant legal aid even if the applicant's income is higher than the set amount.

The report commissioned by the Icelandic Bar Association mentioned above was critical of the inclusion of a fixed income criterion in the legal aid regulations. Based on a comparison with the other Nordic countries, the authors point out that the income criterion in Iceland is not index-linked and that there is no mention of it being regularly evaluated. They are also critical of the fact that the income criterion is to be decided by the Minister for Judicial Affairs at any given time, as opposed to being fixed by law (Jónsson and Harðardóttir 2008).

The section B conditions for granting legal aid require that the outcome of the case should have great general significance, or be of great importance for the employment, social status, or other personal status of the applicant. The regulations further specify that when applications are evaluated on that basis, the Legal Aid Committee should consider whether the case would be thought important, and would matter significantly to a number of people, and whether the courts have previously settled a comparable or similar case. The regulations also specify that, when deciding if the outcome of the case would have a great impact on the employment, social status, or other personal status of the applicant, the Legal Aid Committee should assess how significant this impact would be.

Backlash During the Boom Years

The law on legal aid remained more or less unchanged until 2005, when the eligibility criteria were tightened considerably by legislation and regulations. Since 1995, Iceland had been ruled by a right-wing coalition government that had been pursuing a neo-liberal economic agenda coupled with a statist approach, which involved selective deregulation and privatisation.[8] The privatisation of the banks, coupled with lax financial regulations, resulted in the banks' unprecedented growth some of which was redistributed back into the country, resulting in an economic boom (Wade and Sigurgeirsdottir 2012).[9] While state spending had increased during the boom years—though not as a percentage of GDP—and the rate of income tax percentage had been lowered, the tax burden on low and middle-income groups increased, due to the impairment of the tax threshold (Ólafsson 2007, 2010).

Against this political and economic backdrop, the Law on Civil Procedure no. 7/2005 was amended. The main changes to the general provisions on the eligibility criteria for legal aid were, first, further restrictions to legal aid in section A where, in addition to low income, the case now must be of such a nature that it would be considered appropriate that legal aid for it be financed by public funds. The second change was the cancelling of the conditions for legal aid laid down in section B, i.e. that the outcome of the case should have great general significance or be of great importance for the employment, social status, or other personal status of the applicant.[10] In addition, the amendment gave clearer authorisation to the Minister for Judicial Affairs to provide more detailed guidance to the Legal Aid Committee on how to interpret the eligibility criteria for legal aid.

The aim of the amendment, as stated in the explanatory text accompanying the bill, was to clarify the rules on legal aid and to make the best use of funds. It is further stated that the section B provisions are very broad, and that it is not justifiable to use public funds to pay for people's lawsuits based on such a general provision. The bill was accompanied by a short annexe from the Ministry of Finance stating that the cost of legal aid would, in all likelihood, at least not continue to increase if the amendment was passed. Applications for legal aid had apparently increased from 315 in 1998 to over 500 in 2003 (General Committee of Alþingi, Majority Opinion).

While MPs from the ruling centre-right parties seemingly framed legal aid as something that should generally only be available based on low economic status, opposition MPs argued in defence of a wider provision. The minority in the General Committee, mostly comprising members of the Social Democratic Alliance, opposed the amendment on the grounds that it would, in the first place, limit the public's access to legal aid when they were seeking to defend their rights against the government, and state institutions; and in the second place, it would eliminate the possibility of legal aid in cases of great significance for the general public. The minority opinion also declared that the amendment went against the general public's sense of justice, and against legal aid developments in other democratic states.

The amendment was, however, passed and came into force on 11 February 2005. Subsequently, the Ministry for Judicial Affairs appointed a committee to examine the costs of legal aid in criminal and civil cases.[11] In March 2006, the committee produced a report with suggestions on how to decrease spending on public cases and public legal assistance. The number of applicants granted legal aid had increased by 61% between 2000 and 2005 and legal aid costs had increased by 106% during the same period. The cost of each legal aid case in Iceland in 2002 was the second highest out of 18 other European Countries. Only Denmark had higher costs.[12] The committee highlighted custody cases and tort cases, which are the biggest categories and ones where costs had increased the most between 2000 and 2005. In respect to custody cases, the increase was attributable to legislative changes to the Act in Respect of Children (no. 76/2003) where the main rule of joint custody had been adopted; the ministry no longer had authority to make decisions on custody and only the courts could decide custody disputes. Another factor explaining rising costs was an increase in experts' assessment reports. To cut costs, the committee recommended mandatory mediation in custody cases, before a court case was initiated.[13] Further cost-cutting measures recommended by the committee were the lowering of the income criteria for legal aid, and included more specific restrictions in the Legal Aid Committee's Regulations. As noted previously, public out-of-court legal aid is scarce in Iceland, while legal aid to pursue cases in court is available. This might also explain the relatively high cost of legal aid, as there is no financial incentive to resolve matters out of court (Magnússon 2005). The committee, however, did not recommend introducing legal aid for out-of-court cases as a means to cut costs in the long term.[14]

New regulations on the criteria for legal aid and the workings of the Legal Aid Committee (no. 45/2008) were set out in January 2008 fixing the annual pre-tax income criteria for legal aid at 1.6 million ISK (17,445 €) per single person and 2.5 million ISK (27,258 €) per couple. An additional 250,000 ISK (2726 €) was allowed for each dependent child.[15] In 2008, the income tax threshold for a single person was 1,191,004 ISK (12,986 €). In that year, the average annual income for men in Iceland was 5,255,000 ISK (57,295 €) and for women 3,738,000 ISK (40,755 €).

Apart from those made by the minority in Alþingi's General Committee, the main objections to these changes came from lawyers and the Icelandic Bar Association. Two Supreme Court lawyers expressed outrage at the new law and the regulations it brought in, claiming that the income criterion was so low that it was incompatible with the law, and contrary to the will of Alþingi (Guðjónsson 2008). Here it is important to bear in mind that, although the benchmark for the income criterion has invariably been the tax threshold, its impairment, as noted earlier, can give an inaccurate impression of people's financial capacity. The Icelandic Bar Association criticised these changes in an open letter to the government, suggesting that, instead of cutting costs, it should increase the budget to ensure the rule of law (The Icelandic Bar Association 2007). The Icelandic Bar Association also commissioned a report on legal aid that concluded it was doubtful that the extensive limitations on legal aid introduced by the amendment to the law met the requirements needed to ensure access to justice and the right to a fair trial as stipulated in article 70 of the Icelandic Constitution and article 6 of the European Convention on Human Rights. It also noted that it was not clear why Alþingi decided that citizens in certain types of cases had a right to legal aid irrespective of their economic status—which raised questions regarding the equality principle. According to the authors, it would be simpler to have more extensive legal aid provision and thus ensure equality between citizens (Jónsson and Harðardóttir 2008).

As noted at the beginning of this chapter, the restriction of access to legal aid, seemingly just to reduce costs, first by the 2005 legislation and subsequently by further legal aid regulations in January 2008, came at a time when the Icelandic economy was booming. The changes to legal aid are in line with the neo-liberal economic policy of the government according to which legal aid is viewed as a line in the state budget that needs to be kept in check, even if this means severely testing, if not breaching, the human rights principle of access to justice, enshrined in the constitution. At a time of considerable economic flexibility, a more measured approach could have developed a more comprehensive policy on legal aid. In the long term, introducing free out-of-court legal assistance, for example, might have decreased legal aid expenses overall.

In the Eye of the Economic Storm

After the economic collapse in October 2008, and the subsequent mass demonstrations against the government, in 2009, a new left-wing government was formed by the Social Democratic Alliance and the Left-Green Movement: the first left-wing government since World War Two. The left-wing parties took the reins of government in a severe economic depression. However, as early as 2010, the income criterion in the regulations was increased to its current level and in 2012, by an amendment to law no. 72/2012, the eligibility criteria for legal aid according to the first paragraph of Article 126 of the Law on Civil Procedure were again extended, with the reintroduction of section B.

The main argument for reintroducing section B came from the Economic Affairs and Trade Committee (EATC) of the Icelandic Parliament, stating that legal aid should be available to those debtors who might have a reason to initiate court cases against financial institutions that, on the basis of a decision by The Icelandic Competition Authority no. 4/2012 on 9 March 2012, had been allowed a degree of cooperation in the effort to expedite the reconstruction of debts of individuals and companies. While the Minister for Judicial Affairs emphasised that the main purpose of legal aid should be to support those who could not afford to cover the costs of court cases, the EATC reiterated the importance of increasing the access of the general public to the courts, irrespective of their financial status. By that time, a cross-party bill reinstating section B had been introduced in the three previous legislative assemblies. On these occasions, it had been emphasised that, firstly, the restrictions introduced in 2005 by the removal of section B severely limited the general public's ability to access justice in cases of considerable public or individual significance; and, secondly, they went against developments in legal aid in other democratic countries. The reintroduction of section B meant that legal aid became available in cases such as the following: claims for compensation for permanent invalidity, when invalidity is severe and the ability to earn a living is considerably reduced; cases concerning pension rights, employment rights or property rights; cases concerning compensation due to the loss of a provider; or cases to do with medical malpractice the right to privacy and other aspects of human rights.

However, in 2013, a centre-right government was voted back into office and currently a new government bill amending the law on legal aid has been prepared and was introduced to Alþingi in 2015–2016 but has, so far, not been enacted. In it, section B is removed once again, on the basis of the previous arguments, i.e., that it is not justifiable to pay for the lawsuits of individuals out of public funds under such a general provision, and that the main purpose of legal aid is to assist people of low economic status. The point is also made that disputes concerning the restructuring of loans have now mostly been resolved and therefore appropriate to re-evaluate the 2012 legal amendments.[16]

The question whether access to legal aid should be minimal or more extensive continues to be debate but without there being much by way of socio-legal research or a more comprehensive policy discussion on the general purposes and aims of legal aid for Icelandic society. On the face of it, the discussion seems to centre on the principle of access to justice and to divide along party lines, with the left wing mostly pushing for a more expansive understanding of access to justice, while the right wing mostly views legal aid as a budget concern. These divisions are thrown into relief when viewed against the backdrop of the extreme political and economic shifts that have characterised the politics and economy of Iceland in the last ten years. At the height of the economic boom the right-wing government restricted access to legal aid, while during the economic recession the left-wing government expanded it again. As we have seen, the return of a right-wing government has led to a bill reintroducing restrictions on access to legal aid.

Legal Aid Applicants and Recipients

Since the current legislation came into force in 1992, the majority of applications have concerned custody, compensation for physical injury, and cases where people have a legal right to state-funded legal aid (Gíslason 1994; Thoroddsen 2009; Ministry of the Interior 2014). While information on applications and legal aid grants has been published periodically, statistical information has varied according to the purpose of the publication, as can be seen in Table 6.1, which will be discussed in more detail below.

For the past 10 years, the Legal Aid Committee has processed between 438 and 599 applications a year and granted legal aid to between 292 and 397 applicants. The ratio of grants to applications has been 65–79% (Gíslason 1994; Ministry of Justice and Ecclesiastical Affairs 2006; Thoroddsen 2009; Ministry of the Interior 2013; Ministry of the Interior 2014). Statutory grants are those given to legal aid recipients who, by law, are entitled to state-funded legal aid. As already noted, such provisions can be found under various different laws.[17] When interpreting the statistics certain factors should be borne in mind. First, it is important to note that, as previously discussed, access to legal aid was restricted by law in 2005 and then again by regulation in 2008. In 2010, access to legal aid was widened again through regulation and further expanded by law in 2012. The year 2013 was the first whole year since 2005 when section B applications were submitted, and 30 applications were granted legal aid on that basis (Ministry of the Interior 2014). Secondly, statistical information for the years 2011–2013 was published in relation to the government's Gender Budgeting project, for the purposes of a gender analysis of applications and grants made. Therefore, information on grants made only exists if the applicants are individuals as indicated by the brackets in the Table 6.1.[18]

Table 6.1 Legal aid applications and grants (%) by year[a]

	1993	1994	2000	2001	2002	2003	2004	2005	2006	2007	2008	2011	2012	2013	2014
Applications	132	171							438	504	445	532 (518)	599 (588)	572	491
Statutory Grants	23	37							41	54	53	(65)	(51)		
Total no. of Grants	74	123	227	268	306	365	392	365	312	330	292	(365)	(397)		390
% of grants	56%	72%							71%	65%	66%	(70%)	(68%)		79%

[a]This table was created by collecting statistical information from the following sources: Gíslason 1994; Ministry of Justice and Ecclesiastical Affairs 2006; Thoroddsen 2009; Ministry of the Interior 2014. Statistical information for the year 2014 was provided by the Ministry of the Interior.

Gender Analysis

During 2011 and 2012, women and men on average submitted the same number of applications to the Legal Aid Committee: 51% submissions were by women and 49% by men. Women's applications were more often successful—76% of women's applications succeeded, as against 63% of men's. Women were more often granted legal aid than men on the basis of their low economic status, as stipulated in section A of the legislation. The reason for applying for legal aid is also partially gendered, as more women apply for legal aid in custody cases, while more men apply for legal aid in cases concerning compensation for physical injury. However, the amount granted to women is more often limited than that to men, as grants for custody cases are usually limited, while in cases of bodily injury, they are not. In 2011, the Legal Aid Committee received 17 applications from foreign nationals, ten women, and seven men. Of those 17 applications, 11 were awarded legal aid: seven women and four men (Ministry of the Interior 2013).

As mentioned above, on 1 January 2013 an amendment to the Act in Respect of Children made mediation in custody disputes mandatory before the initiation a court case. Applications concerning custody cases therefore decreased during that year, and those applications that were made were turned down. However, the number of other cases increased. As noted above, in 2008, the section B criteria were abolished but were reinstated in 2012. The first whole year when applications based on section B were submitted was 2013, and a total of 30 grants were awarded, divided equally between women and men (Ministry of the Interior 2014).

Legal Expenses Insurance

Legal expenses insurance (LEI) was introduced by one insurance company in Iceland in the late 1990s, after which the other main insurance companies started to provide similar policies. LEI is included in some home and family packages and the policy conditions are mostly similar. The main insurance companies typically offer four types of family insurance packages, of which only the most basic does not include LEI, which might suggest that low-income families are less likely to have cover. LEI does not generally cover out-of-court legal services, and the relatively long list of exemptions indicates that policy conditions are quite strict.[19]

Access to Free Legal Counselling

In Iceland, there is no general legislation that ensures that citizens have access to free legal counselling or out-of-court legal assistance. As previously mentioned, such provisions were included in two separate bills brought before Parliament in the 1980s, but neither of them came into force. Free legal counselling services are available through several members' organisations and voluntary organisations but free out-of-court legal assistance is rarely provided, the legal assistance given by unions being an important exception.

Women's organisations have offered women free legal assistance for a long time. The pioneer in providing free legal information and advice was Auður Auðuns (1911–1999), who was the first woman to graduate as a lawyer in Iceland, the first woman to become Mayor of Reykjavík, and the first to become a minister. In the period 1940–1960, Auður provided free legal aid through the Mothers' Support Committee (Mæðrastyrksnefnd), founded in 1928 by a number of women's organisations to support poor mothers (Rafnar 1981). These services are now provided by the Single Parents' Association. In 1984, Women's Counselling was founded during an active time for the women's movement in Iceland, which also resulted in the foundation of the Women's List, a feminist political party, the Women's Shelter and Stígamót, a counselling centre for survivors of rape and incest. At Women's Counselling, social workers and lawyers, including final year social work and law students, provide free counselling for women and now also for men. Women's Counselling is open two days a week for two hours (The Women's Counselling n.d.).

In terms of members' associations, The Single Parents' Association has provided free legal services to members since 1975 and those services are available on request during office hours (The Single Parents' Association n.d.). The Organisation of Disabled has offered free legal information to its members since 1975 and can pursue cases if they are considered likely to set a precedent for people with disabilities in general, or large numbers of people with disabilities (The Organisations of Disabled, n.d). Unions also offer their members free legal information and assistance in disputes between employee and employer. Union membership in Iceland was 86% in 2014 and has been at that level since at least 2003 (Statistics Iceland 2015b).

The Icelandic Bar Association has organised free legal information for the general public since 1993 through the Lögmannavaktin, which is now open once a week for an hour and a half (The Icelandic Bar Association, n.d.-b). Law student unions also provide free legal information to the general public. Orator, The Law Students' Association at the University of Iceland, has provided free legal information since 1980. The assistance is provided by telephone once a week for two and a half hours (The Law Students' Association at the University of Iceland, n.d.). Some law firms also offer free legal information and pro bono services, especially in relation to compensation cases.

Free legal counselling for immigrants is provided by the Icelandic Human Rights Centre (ICEHR) because of an agreement between the Ministry of Welfare and the ICEHR. The assistance is provided twice a week for six hours at a time (The Icelandic Human Rights Centre, n.d.).

Conclusion

In recent times, discussions on legal aid in Iceland can be characterised along the lines of right-wing vs left-wing politics and in narrow legalistic terms. Those to the right of the political spectrum have generally advocated for a more restricted access to legal aid, to be solely granted on the basis of low economic status, while those to the left of the political spectrum advocate for a broader access to legal aid for cases that are deemed to be of great significance for individuals or larger groups. So in Iceland, recent discussions on legal aid have taken place in the relative absence of socio-legal research and without the aim of developing a comprehensive policy on the topic. It is, therefore, difficult to discern how legal aid is conceptualised, understood, and used in Iceland. However, when viewing the development of the legal and policy frameworks, they seem to combine, to a greater or lesser extent, an understanding of legal aid as a form of charity, as a right, and as an individual responsibility.

In previous centuries, legal aid was understood mostly as charity, or support for the poor and needy. When the current law on public legal aid in civil cases came into force in 1992, access to the courts was understood as a right that should be available irrespective of economic status with the addition that cases of great public or individual significance should also be eligible for legal aid, although the latter criteria remain contested. However, given that there are no provisions for legal aid in the form of legal counselling or out-of-court legal assistance, and that such support is provided either by members' organisations or by the voluntary sector, albeit in some cases supported by public funds, it could be argued that legal aid has never fully been disassociated from charity.

While there is no official policy on the relationship between legal aid and LEI, legal aid applicants have to inform the Legal Aid Committee if they have such insurance, which implies that the applications of holders of such policies are rejected. However, given that such insurance is not mandatory, and that the policy conditions are strict, it cannot, on the face of it, be claimed that legal aid is conceptualised as an individual responsibility in Iceland, at least not yet. One could, though, argue that a very low income criterion for legal aid that has at times prevailed in Iceland, because the income criterion has not been firmly index-linked, does in effect give the signal that individuals need to make their own arrangements for legal aid through the purchase of insurance.

Notes

1. See for example article 54 of the Law on Public Procedure (no. 74/1974), and article 45 of the Law on Children (no. 9/1981).
2. Article 125, paragraph 2, states that the Minister shall appoint a committee of three lawyers—the Legal Aid Committee—for four years at a time to review and give recommendations on legal aid applications. One committee member is to be appointed based on recommendations from the Icelandic Bar Association and another on the basis of recommendation from the Icelandic Judges' Association. The third is appointed by the Minister.
3. Current regulation on the eligibility criteria for legal aid and the workings of the Legal Aid Committee is no. 45/2008 with amendments no. 1059/2010 and no. 616/2012.

4. The amount in Icelandic Kronor is converted to Euro on the basis of the exchange rate on 1 January 2010 (1 ISK = 0.0056218074 €) and rounded up to the nearest hundred.
5. Such provisions can be found in articles in the following laws: law on criminal procedure (no. 88/2008); the Child Protection Act (no. 80/2002); Laws on unions and labour disputes (no. 80/1938); adoption law (no. 130/1999); laws on obtaining advisory opinions from the European Free Trade Association (EFTA) Court on the clarification of the Agreement on the European Economic Area (no. 21/1994); laws on the Alþing ombudsman (no. 85/1997); and the Act in Respect of Children (no. 76/2003).
6. Information on the income tax threshold was obtained via email correspondence with the Internal Revenue, Tax Office Akureyri on 18 April 2016. The amount in Icelandic Kronor is converted to Euro based on the exchange rate on 1 January 2014 (1 ISK = 0.0063433743 €) and rounded up to the nearest hundred. I refer to the year 2014 so as to be able to compare it with average annual income statistics from Statistics Iceland, which does not have comparable statistics for 2015.
7. The amount in Icelandic Kronor is converted to Euro based on the exchange rate on 1 January 2014 (1 ISK = 0.0063433743 €) and rounded up to the nearest hundred. I refer to the year 2014, as Statistics Iceland does not have comparable statistics for 2015.
8. The Independence Party, a liberal conservative party seen as right-wing in Icelandic politics, and the Progressive Party, a centre-right liberal and agrarian party, were in government from 1995 to 2007.
9. Between 2005 and 2007 Iceland's GDP per capita was in line with Denmark's—19% above the European Union average (Svennebye 2008).
10. While the amendment imposed eligibility restrictions on the general provisions for legal aid, an exception was made to allow access to legal aid for those challenging decisions made by the Committee on Uninhabited Areas (Óbyggðanefnd), a public administration committee charged with determining the boundaries of private land, public land, and upland ranges.
11. The committee was comprised of five specialists: three lawyers and two economists, from the Ministry for Judicial Affairs and the Ministry of Finance.
12. Here the Committee is referring to the following survey: European Commission for the Efficiency of Justice (CEPEJ) (2005).
13. Mandatory mediation in custody cases was later enacted by an amendment to the Act in Respect of Children that came in to force in 2013.

14. The Committee also discussed cutting costs in public cases, and made recommendations on this, but that discussion is outside the scope of this article.
15. The amount in Icelandic Kronor is converted to Euro based on the exchange rate on 1 January 2008 (1 ISK = 0.0109030226 €) and rounded up to the nearest hundred.
16. The bill further suggests that applications for legal aid should no longer be submitted to the minister responsible for judicial affairs but to a District Commissioner (sýslumaður) whose decision can be appealed to the Legal Aid Committee. The Legal Aid Committee will be appointed as before except that, instead of the Minister for Judicial Affairs appointing one of the members of the committee, the appointment should be on the basis of a recommendation from the Icelandic Human Rights Centre (ICEHR).
17. Such provisions can be found in articles on the following laws: the law on Criminal Procedure (no. 88/2008); the Child Protection Act (no. 80/2002); laws on Unions and Labour Disputes (no. 80/1938); Adoption Law (no. 130/1999); laws on obtaining advisory opinions from the EFTA Court on the clarification of the Agreement on the European Economic Area (no. 21/1994); laws on the Alþing ombudsman (no. 85/1997); and the Act in Respect of Children (no. 76/2003).
18. Applications from other legal entities were submitted in cases where decisions made by the Committee on Uninhabited Areas (Óbyggðanefnd), a public administration committee charged with determining the boundaries of private land, public land, and upland ranges, were being challenged.
19. Information on LEI is based on correspondence with the main insurance companies, which include SJÓVÁ, Vátryggingafélag Íslands hf., Tryggingamiðstöðin, and Vörður.

References

Björnsson, Ó. (2005). Dæmdur málskostnaður. Sanngjarn eða sorglegur? *Lögmannablaðið, 11*(3).

European Commission for the Efficiency of Justice (CEPEJ). (2005). *European Judicial Systems 2002*. Council of Europe Publishing. Retrieved April 22, 2016, from https://wcd.coe.int/com.instranet.InstraServlet?command=com.instranet.CmdBlobGet&InstranetImage=1150243&SecMode=1&DocId=1009444&Usage=2

Eydal, G. B. (1973). Lögfræðiaðstoð án endurgjalds. *Tímarit lögfræðinga, 23*(4), 10–21.
Gíslason, A. (1994). Gjafsókn. *Úlfljótur, 47*(4), 429–446.
Guðjónsson, E. J. (2008, May 17). Þrengt að réttinum til gjafsóknar. *24 Stundir, 92*(4), 1.
Jónsson, J. (2005). Um málskostnaðarákvarðanir. *Lögmannablaðið, 11*(3).
Jónsson, A. Þ., & Harðardóttir, H. E. (2008). *Skýrsla um gjafsóknarmálefni*. Retrieved April 22, 2016, from http://www.lmfi.is/urskurdarnefnd/urskurdir/nr/4099/
Magnússon, S. T. (2005). Aðgangur að dómstólum á sviði einkamála. *Tímarit lögfræðinga, 55*(2), 133.
Ministry of Justice and Ecclesiastical Affairs. (2006 March). *Skýrsla nefndar um málskostnað í opinberum málum og opinbera réttaraðstoð*. Dóms- og kirkjumálaráðuneytið. Retrieved April 22, 2016, from https://www.innanrikisraduneyti.is/media/Skyrslur/DKM_malskostnadur.pdf
Ministry of the Interior. (2013) *Gjafsókn og önnur opinber réttaraðstoð*. Áfangaskýrsla II. Retrieved April 22, 2016, from https://www.fjarmalaraduneyti.is/media/skjal/irr_afang_2013.pdf
Ministry of the Interior. (2014). *Gjafsókn og önnur opinber réttaraðstoð*. Lokaskýrsla. Retrieved April 22, 2016, from https://www.fjarmalaraduneyti.is/media/rit2014/lokaskyrsla,-IRR-2014.pdf
Ólafsson, S. (2007). Skattastefna Íslendinga. In *Stjórnmál og stjórnsýsla, veftímarit, 3*(2). Stofnun stjórnsýslufræða og stjórnmála við Háskóla Íslands.
Ólafsson, S. (2010). Þandist ríkið út á árunum fyrir hrun? Umfang útgjalda hins opinbera 1990 til 2009 og stærð velferðarríkisins árið 2007. *Fréttabréf nr. 7/2010*. Þjóðmálastofnun Háskóla Íslands.
Rafnar, I. Þ. (1981) Réttarhjálp án endurgjalds. In *Auðarbók Auðuns*, pp. 111-122.
Sævarsson, J. A. (2005). Lögmenn og aðrir sérfræðingar. *Lögmannablaðið, 11*(3).
Statistics Iceland. (2015a). Income by sex and age 1990–2014. *Statistics Iceland*. Retrieved April 22, 2016, from http://px.hagstofa.is/pxen/pxweb/en/Samfelag/Samfelag__launogtekjur__4_tekjur__1_tekjur_skattframtol/TEK01001.px/table/tableViewLayout1/?rxid=8e92f24e-8471-49bc-a77b-345f5c8e460f
Statistics Iceland. (2015b). Trade union membership 2003–2014. *Statistics Iceland*. Retrieved April 22, 2016, from http://px.hagstofa.is/pxen/pxweb/en/Samfelag/Samfelag__vinnumarkadur__vinnumarkadur/VIN01007.px/?rxid=536f1855-c58f-42d8-ba40-bd6c6e58c27e
Svennebye, L. (2008). GDP per capita, consumption per capita and comparative price levels in Europe. Final results for 2005 and preliminary results for

2006 and 2007. *Eurostat, Statistics in focus* 112/2008. Retrieved April 22, 2016, from http://ec.europa.eu/eurostat/documents/3433488/5584112/KS-SF-08-112-EN.PDF/1525ad79-fd56-4e13-99fd-07d75cf2f832

The Icelandic Bar Association. (2007). Bréf LMFÍ til stjórnvalda: Útgjöld til réttaraðstoðar og málskostnaðar í opinberum málum. *Lögmannablaðið, 13*(1), p. 6.

The Icelandic Bar Association (n.d.-a). Lögmenn og þjónusta. *The Icelandic Bar Association*. Retrieved April 22, 2016, from http://www.lmfi.is/logmenn-og-thjonusta/hvad-kostar-thjonusta-logmanns/

The Icelandic Bar Association. (n.d.-b). *Lögmannavaktin*. Retrieved April 23, 2016, from http://www.lmfi.is/forsida/

The Icelandic Human Rights Centre. (n.d.). *Activities*. Retrived April 23, 2016, from http://www.humanrights.is/en/activities

The Law Students' Association at the University of Iceland (n.d.). *Lögfræðiaðstoð Orators*. Retrieved April 23, 2016, from http://www.humanrights.is/en/activities

The Organisations of Disabled. (n.d.). *Félags- og lögfræðiráðgjöf*. Retrieved April 23, 2016, from http://www.obi.is/is/radgjof-og-thjonusta/felags-og-logfraediradgjof

The Single Parents' Association. (n.d.). *Nýttu þér ráðgjöfina*. Retrieved April 23, 2016, from www.fef.is

The Women's Counselling. (n.d.). *Kvennaráðgjöfin*. Retrived April 23, 2016, from http://kvennaradgjofin.is/kvennradgjofin.html

Thoroddsen, Á. (2009). Fróðleikur um störf og afgreiðslur gjafsóknarnefndar. *Lögmannablaðið, 15*(1), 20.

Wade, R. H., & Sigurgeirsdottir, S. (2012). Iceland's rise, fall, stabilisation and beyond. *Cambridge Journal of Economics, 36*, 127–144.

Open Access This chapter is distributed under the terms of the Creative Commons Attribution 4.0 International License (http://creativecommons.org/licenses/by/4.0/), which permits use, duplication, adaptation, distribution, and reproduction in any medium or format, as long as you give appropriate credit to the original author(s) and the source, a link is provided to the Creative Commons license, and any changes made are indicated.

The images or other third party material in this book are included in the work's Creative Commons license, unless indicated otherwise in the credit line; if such material is not included in the work's Creative Commons license and the respective action is not permitted by statutory regulation, users will need to obtain permission from the license holder to duplicate, adapt or reproduce the material.

7

Juss-Buss [Law Bus]: A Student-run Legal Aid Clinic

Ole Hammerslev, Annette Olesen, and Olaf Halvorsen Rønning

Introduction

One of the strongest brands among alternative legal aid institutions in the Nordic countries is Juss-Buss [Law Bus], the legal clinic run by students of the Faculty of Law of the University of Oslo. Emerging from the radical student movements of the late 1960s and early 1970s and a climate of strong social commitment, law students and young lawyers—such as the Norwegian socio-legal pioneers Thomas Mathiesen, Kristian 'Kikki' Andenæs, and Jon

O. Hammerslev (✉)
Department of Law, University of Southern Denmark, Odense M, Denmark

Department of Criminology and Sociology of Law, University of Oslo, Oslo, Norway

A. Olesen
Department of Sociology and Social Work, Aalborg University, Denmark

O.H. Rønning
Department of Criminology and Sociology of Law, University of Oslo, Oslo, Norway

T. Johnsen—became interested in questions concerning access to legal assistance. They not only sought to gain knowledge about structural oppression in Norwegian society but also wanted to make oppressive structures visible, and to change them through so-called action research. Inspired by US trends in outreach legal aid, clinical legal education, and sociology of law (Mathiesen 2001; Capua 1975, 2001) the Norwegian scholars wanted more specifically to combine scientific knowledge with the establishment of legal aid infrastructures benefitting disadvantaged social groups (Hammerslev and Mathiesen 2013; Mathiesen 2011). They initiated a research project that revealed the legal problems of disadvantaged groups and showed there was unmet legal need in the population. The scholars concluded that unmet need was unevenly distributed, being greatest among the most disadvantaged. Current legal aid schemes were failing to alleviate this need. In addition, they found that, in most cases, the provision of legal aid did not improve the lives of the recipients (Eskeland and Finne 1973). Thus, legal aid needed to be provided in situations where there was found to be unmet need, and a concerted effort was required to improve the quality of life of clients. A legal aid outreach initiative was planned, originally just to supply legal information. In order to make it as accessible as possible, it was decided that the clinic should be mobile, which led to the idea of a 'juss-buss' [law bus]. Juss-Buss thus started as a research project in 1971. During the initial phase, the bus was the only office in use. From the very start, the purpose of Juss-Buss was twofold; it would provide legal aid to those in need, and also gather information on the need for legal aid in society, which could be utilised in research reports and in legal policy work (Capua and Juss-Buss 1978). The employees were law students and young lawyers, while the Institute of Sociology of Law, University of Oslo, created a post to help manage the initiative (Capua 2001, p. 12).

The first reports on Juss-Buss highlighted the fact that Juss-Buss clients lacked problem awareness, faced financial barriers, distrusted other public information schemes, and lacked access to affordable lawyers (this was particularly true of clients from rural areas), all of which, along with the clients' more immediate problems led to unmet legal need (Capua 2001). Furthermore, the reports showed that other people also lacked sufficient access to legal aid (Capua 1975). Later research on Juss-Buss based on a similar approach paints much the same picture (Andenæs 1975; Bull and Eidesen 1975; Edvardsen et al., 1975; Johnsen 1987, 1991, 1994, 1999; Juss-Buss 1996, 2001; Rønning & Juss-Buss 2011). Because of its particular way of combining education, legal aid, legal policy work, and research, Juss-Buss is unlike any other Nordic legal aid clinic.

This chapter examines the unique funding, staff recruitment, and case handling structures of Juss-Buss and how for decades it has maintained a strong tradition of legal aid and policy work. The aim of this chapter is, therefore, not to take a critical approach. First, there will be a description of the staff and funding of Juss-Buss, followed by consideration of how the case types and caseload mirror flaws in the welfare state. Second, the workplace organisation of the clinic, and the standardisation of its workflow will be examined, along with an analysis of its staff training, empowerment approach, and case handling structures, that focus explicitly on 'collective work' and outreach legal aid initiatives. Third, there will be a discussion of Juss-Buss' legal policy work, followed by some concluding remarks.[1]

Staff, Funding, and Case Types

We will now briefly describe Juss-Buss' personnel and funding resources. We will reflect on developments in the number and type of cases Juss-Buss handles, and relate the figures to changes in the welfare state.

Unlike many other legal aid institutions, such as, for example, Gadejuristen [The Street Lawyers] (see Chap. 8), that struggle for funding, and face budgetary cuts and the implementation of fixed fees (see Sommerlad and Sanderson 2013; Lied 2013), Juss-Buss has been relatively privileged: it has substantial funding, a strong base as a division in the Faculty of Law of the University of Oslo, and students queueing up to volunteer. The work of the Juss-Buss clinic is funded jointly by the Ministry of Justice, the Municipality of Oslo, and a number of charitable organisations. The annual budget is roughly 5 million NOK (526,315 €). In addition, the Faculty of Law and the University of Oslo provide Juss-Buss with offices, IT equipment, and supervisors. The legal basis for the clinic's licence to provide legal aid is the general legislation regarding lawyers and the provision of legal aid, in the Courts of Justice Act. Although licenced lawyers are the main providers of legal aid, the Supervisory Council for Legal Practice has been granted exceptional power to license special legal aid initiatives to provide legal aid. Having this licence, Juss-Buss can provide legal aid on condition that the clinic is supervised by the Faculty of Law, and has adequate quality control mechanisms.

The daily management of the clinic is carried out by a board, made up of student staff, and a student daily manager, all of whom are supervised by faculty members. The supervisors of the clinic do not take part in the quality control of the handling of individual cases but, by providing basic education and training of new staff members, they contribute to developing and modifying training schemes and quality control. The supervisors also offer support in cases of great complexity, or cases raising particularly difficult ethical questions.

Juss-Buss' personnel consists of around thirty law students, who voluntarily take a year off from their studies to work full-time on legal aid. They then work part-time for one semester. They get the equivalent of one semester's credits for the time they volunteer. The students are paid a small salary, comparable to the monthly student loan. The salary is by no means commensurate with the amount of work they do. In practice, therefore, much of Juss-Buss' work is based on voluntary activity.

Case Types Mirroring Flaws in the Welfare State

Juss-Buss provides most kinds of legal aid, apart from legal representation in court cases. Juss-Buss, for instance, writes administrative complaints, negotiates divorce settlements or employment disputes, and represents clients in conciliation council. Fig. 7.1 shows the number of cases Juss-Buss handled from 1990 to 2015.

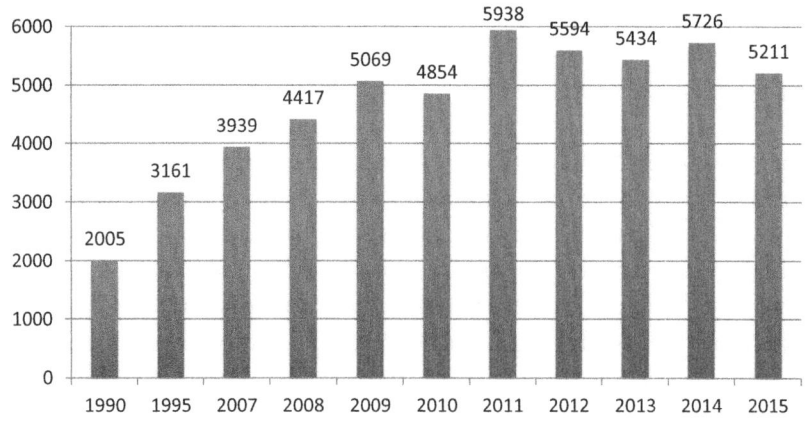

Fig. 7.1 Number of cases in selected years (Skårberg 2016)

The number of cases has more than doubled since 1990 but has been relatively stable since 2012. The increase in the number of cases immediately indicates that the need for legal aid increased significantly between 1990 and 2011. However, Skårberg (2016, p. 11) argues that the minor annual variations of cases in the later years do not reflect changes in client demands, but rather indicate developments in the administration of the clinic's outreach legal aid programmes.

Table 7.1 and Fig. 7.2 show Juss-Buss' caseload divided into the clinic's specific key legal disciplines. Most cases concern immigration law, and make up almost one fifth of the cases dealt with in recent years. These are mostly family immigration cases and expulsion cases, which are ineligible for legal aid under the public scheme. The second largest amount of cases involve labour law: most cases are related to unpaid wages and holiday pay, and unlawful dismissal. Most of these cases likewise do not qualify for legal aid under the public scheme. There is also considerable demand for advice on tenancy law, social law, and debt law.

The figures not only reflect Juss-Buss' internal prioritisations of social groups facing some of the most serious problems and vulnerable living situations, but also mirror what research on legal aid and welfare state ideology (see Chaps. 1 and 13) would interpret as flaws in the welfare state. It is possible to identify some social welfare changes and developments in how the caseload is distributed. For example, the increase in debt cases and labour cases has been related to the aftermath of the financial crisis (Arntzen 2009). Similarly the increasing number of cases concerning immigration law between 1990 and 2015 can be linked to parallel

Table 7.1 Number of cases in key legal disciplines, 1999–2015

	1999	2001	2003	2005	2007	2009	2011	2013	2015
Family	840	678	643	410	549	733	565	435	366
Tenancy	878	838	747	461	420	630	668	748	632
Social and national insurance	328	248	312	226	355	474	623	611	502
Debt	327	350	435	340	350	560	491	439	492
Prison	439	237	589	562	353	527	506	467	539
Labour	406	446	482	437	510	899	676	727	728
Immigration	339	439	454	590	740	913	1221	1007	986

Source: Skårberg 2016

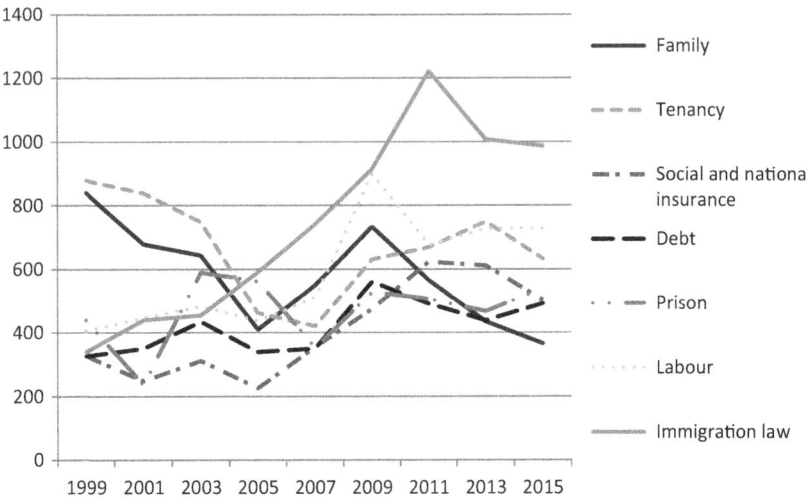

Fig. 7.2 Number of cases in key legal disciplines, 1999–2015 (Skårberg 2016)

developments in the flow of immigrants into Norway. Another parameter related to the increase of cases with an immigration law focus is the hardline foreign policy views that have emerged and gained ground during the same period. Thus, the welfare state does not assist the most disadvantaged citizens with their most basic problems, but civil society organisations have to handle problems the welfare state was set up and expected to handle. What makes the situation even more complex is the fact that Juss-Buss' client groups often have many interrelated legal problems, including claims against welfare state social services. Poor and alienated disadvantaged groups in need of welfare and support services end up in an unequal power struggle with the providers of welfare support—which goes against the values of the universal welfare state (see Olesen 2017).

Workplace Organisation and Standardisation of Workflow

Two factors have a significant influence on Juss-Buss' workplace organisation and code of practice for legal aid work. The first is that their licence to provide legal aid is conditional on quality control and supervision, which means they have to devote considerable resources to quality assurance. Quality control is therefore evident in Juss-Buss' organisation and standardisation of workflow, which is based on individual case handling followed by subsequent team processing of cases. The second factor that strongly influences the organisation of Juss-Buss is their target groups. Juss-Buss has always aimed to contact some of the most 'hard-to-reach' and disadvantaged social groups in society. Accordingly, they have adopted an empowering, client-centred approach to outreach legal aid, which also affects their workplace organization, and requires staff to know what the clients' lives are like; i.e., the staff needs to know how to interact with the specific client groups and how to work with them. In what follows, we will focus on how quality control and 'hard-to-reach' disadvantaged groups frame the training and professionalisation of the Juss-Buss staff, their empowerment approach, and their case handling structures. We will explicitly focus on 'collective work' and outreach legal aid initiatives.

Training

Juss-Buss staff training aims to give a basic introduction to the relevant fields of law, to how relevant legal institutions operate in practice, and to handling clients. Staff is also given basic training in ethics, case preparation, and case processing. The training period is usually short, and provides only brief introductions to the most important topics. Most of the necessary knowledge and skills must be acquired in the course of actual case handling and group work, as—to use the notion of Weber (1978)—a form of craft apprenticeship under the guidance of older students. The craft apprenticeship mentality is of pivotal importance, and forms the basis of Juss-Buss' case handling and client contact. Once a case has been taken on, the person responsible for it prepares the case, and presents it in a weekly group meeting in the form of a case summary, with suggestions on how it should be handled. The group meeting consists of six to eight students, including two or three experienced students who have completed their one-year full-time period at Juss-Buss, and now support and supervise the 'newbies'. In the group meetings, the participants comment on each case: the legal statements of facts, the process, administrative procedures, and possible solutions. Juss-Buss' standard procedure prescribes that all further developments in the case must be discussed at group meetings until the case is completed or closed (Johnsen 2003). A member of staff described how the group meetings were focused on giving feedback, even before he started working at Juss-Buss:

> 'At the job interview, we're asked how we would give and receive feedback on case handling. It makes you reflect from a very early stage on how you'll collaborate with others, and that reflection kinda continues, because we're constantly reminded about the importance of constructive feedback and being cooperative.' (Field notes, Olesen)

The group meetings could be related to Habermas' theory of communicative action, as communication and cooperative actions grounded in mutual dialogue, deliberation, and discussion (see Habermas 1984) serve as the core elements of the outcome of Juss-Buss' group meetings. In a year of full-time work, a Juss-Buss staff member handles between 200 and 250 individual cases, and through group meetings contributes towards around 1500 cases.

Translating the Law into Everyday Language

The law is a language of symbolic power (Goodrich 1990; Bourdieu 1987) that, among other ways, manifests itself in legal labelling, legal categorisation, different negotiation discourses, and control over meaning, and as an instrument and expression of domination (Conley et al. 1978; Goodrich 1990; see also Matoesian 1995; Newman 2013). Lawyers, judges, and legal aid workers, etc., should pay attention to their translation skills. Initially they must translate social problems into legal or non-legal issues (Felstiner et al. 1980/81; Olesen et al. 2017), and when handling a case, it is best if they translate the law into everyday language, to ensure that the clients understand and agree on the legal action being considered. If clients speak a foreign language, the legal aid worker might also have to consider getting an interpreter.

Interaction between clients and legal aid workers might be impeded by differences between the two parties regarding reality-views, vocabulary, and ways of communicating (Sarat and Felstiner 1997; Conley and O'Barr 1990). Attention to the kind of language one uses is therefore of vital importance when approaching disadvantaged social groups, who may lack communication and reading skills (Olesen et al. 2017). Consequently, one of Juss-Buss' key tasks, to which a great part of their craft apprenticeship is devoted, is translating legal language into client-friendly language. The Juss-Buss staff focuses not only on their spoken interaction with clients, carefully considering and discussing their choice of words, but also takes great pains to make written communication user-friendly. During the Juss-Buss group meetings that were observed the subject of styles of communication was brought up for discussion several times. The students commented on, and tried to improve, each other's oral and written presentations, to make them even clearer and easily comprehensible to their clients (Field notes, Olesen). The focus on language is not just about coping with different styles of speech, but also about being able to translate legal language into comprehensible terms. Juss-Buss adopts a further 'translation strategy' when they literally translate their booklets, videos, radio features, etc., into English and Arabic.

Referral Service for Clients

Along with their craft apprenticeship in learning how to translate the law into everyday language, Juss-Buss 'newbies' must also develop skills on the job that enable them to deal with clients in an approachable manner, offer support, or—in the best way possible—turn down a request for help. Since Juss-Buss' special legal aid licence determines and limits the services they offer, many clients contact Juss-Buss with legal or non-legal problems that they are not permitted to handle. Drawing on their experience of having to turn down many enquiries, Juss-Buss has developed a professional and standardised procedure for working as 'gatekeepers' dealing with client referrals:

Interviewee_1: 'We try to provide good referrals…'.
Interviewee_2: 'A rather large part of the job is actually doing that, referring [the client] to another person who's working mostly in the particular field that relates to the person's problem … there are always three people [from the Juss-buss staff] involved in the referral procedure. So, we'll say that we do not work on that specific issue and instead we'll come up with some ideas about who to contact, and then two other staff members must endorse these referrals'.
Interviewee_3: 'We put a lot of work into our referral service because we know that we receive a lot of requests we can't meet. So we try to provide a really good referral service, because we think that is helpful'.
Interviewer: 'And how do you do it? Do you have some kind of booklet?'
Interviewee_2: 'Yes … and each semester we bring it up to date.' (Interview notes, Olesen)

Juss-Buss has standardised the procedure of disseminating detailed information about where to seek specialist advice outside the domain of Juss-Buss legal aid. Their well-structured referral service for clients is seen as yet another initiative to ensure that the needs of disadvantaged social groups are met.

Apropos the discussion about Juss-Buss' craft apprenticeship, it is worth mentioning a general concern about contradictions in the professional work done by volunteers. As a result of the disparity between administrative and managerial standards on the one hand, and personal, impulsive work approaches based on free will on the other (la Cour and Højlund 2008) Juss-Buss could be categorised as a clinic positioned in an organisational mixture of highly-skilled working procedures and 'joint volunteering ownership'. However, this does not seem to be a problem for the professional volunteers involved in Juss-Buss. Instead, the data suggests the clinic to be founded on the rich tradition and fundamental principles of providing outreach legal aid, a tradition that determines the workplace organisation and frames the workflow. Even though Juss-Buss is heavily dependent on volunteers, their working procedures, supervision, and regular group meetings ensure the professional standardisation of their work. Despite this quality control and general supervision, however, the independence of the students working at Juss-Buss is in stark contrast to what happens in many legal clinics in the USA, where there is much closer supervision by faculty staff members or members of the Bar (see Chap. 11).

Outreach Initiatives: With the Aim to Empower and Influence the Political Agenda

In their attempt to reach the most disadvantaged citizens in society, Juss-Buss has from the very beginning implemented outreach approaches on many different levels in their legal aid programmes. The term 'outreach work' covers all activities targeting groups with justiciable problems who, for various reasons, do not seek legal advice (see Chaps. 8 and 9; Genn 1999; Genn and Paterson 2001). In the following, we will focus specifically on Juss-Buss' Prison Team, and examine whether their outreach legal aid approaches in prison actually invite people in need to 'troubles-talks' and through conversations provide a space for legal and non-legal problems to be voiced. Similar outreach projects are targeted at immigrant education centres, charitable organisations working with Romani people, migrant workers, and children care centres (Skårberg 2016). We will discuss some of Juss-Buss' wide-ranging attempts to inform, educate, and encourage people in need to take action and try to deal with their own problems, or seek legal advice. Juss-Buss' outreach legal aid initiatives include work to address inequalities embedded in policy, legal, and institutional frameworks, and to influence policy outcomes. Juss-Buss' legal policy work will be discussed in the closing section.

'Troubles-Talks'

Most Juss-Buss cases (84%) come from clients contacting Juss-Buss, either by telephone or in walk-in sessions at the Juss-Buss office; 14% of cases come (directly) through outreach sessions. However, many clients are encouraged to contact Juss-Buss after an outreach session, because the session itself may be considered an inopportune moment to conduct formal client interviews (Skårberg 2016). Outreach work thus has more impact than the figures indicate. This became clear in a conversation with a Prison Team member, who stressed how contact with a disadvantaged group, such as prisoners, is inextricably linked with outreach legal aid: '… we're convinced that our outreach work, the fact that we visit the prisons, is of great significance and value because only a handful of people call us, but if we come to them—reach out to them—it's easier for them to contact us', (Field notes, Olesen). Criminological studies support the view that some prisoners regard public authorities with distrust and hostility (Ricciardelli et al. 2015; Minke 2012; Olesen 2013), while legal aid research has shown that disadvantaged groups, regardless of their living situation and complex problems, may avoid taking legal action if they have previously had bad experiences with the police and/or legal institutions (Genn 1999; Carlin and Howard 1965; Sejr 1977). Thus, to improve prisoners' access to justice, the Juss-Buss Prison Team visits prisons in and around Oslo on a weekly basis. There are approximately 50 prison visits a year, and they give rise to around 650 cases concerning such issues as social security, debt, immigration, health care, and the terms of sentences (Skårberg 2016).

It is well-known that a large number of justiciable problems never make it to court, or enter any other legal institution. The dark figure of non-registered justiciable problems is also known as the 'tip-of-the-iceberg'

(Best and Andreasen 1977, p. 701) and '[the] "iceberg problem" in the administration of justice' (Barton and Mendlovitz 1960, p. 30; see also Miller and Sarat 1980/81; Coates and Penrod 1980/81). The infrastructure of legal aid support, therefore, plays an important role in efforts to fight social exclusion, and to ensure access to justice (Eidesen et al. 1975; Genn 1999; Pleasence et al. 2006). Juss-Buss' outreach legal aid prison programme could be seen as enhancing the infrastructure of legal aid support by contacting a disadvantaged group of prisoners, listening to their stories and trying to make them identify and act upon their justiciable problems. However, 'troubles-talks' are sensitive (Jefferson 1988), and call for a trusting relationship developed over time, and consistency from the case manager (Olesen et al. 2017). Since the initial interaction between a new client and a Juss-Buss staff member lasts on average for 15–20 minutes, and the caseload is divided between different staff members, depending on the legal disciplines relevant to the case, it can be difficult to take a client-centred, time-consuming and resource-demanding approach based on trust. For that reason, the Juss-Buss staff said, it was difficult to do outreach work with prisoners who did not meet them during their prison visits. A Prison Team member explained how the first encounter with a client during an outreach session normally went:

> '… usually they'll turn up and say "I need help with this, this is what I need help with". And then we'll look into that specific problem.' Another Prison Team member elaborates by saying '…the ones we meet are those who have decided to ask for help … and that's very much like "please just take it [the case/problem]!" "Help me now!" "I don't know how to cope with it!". 'But we might only see the tip of the iceberg.' (Interview notes, Olesen)

As reported by the Prison Team members, clients often specify their needs and the help they want to receive but, occasionally, some clients show up with a plastic bag of unopened letters from e.g., debt-collection agencies or public authorities, asking for help to deal with their vague and confused problems (Johnsen 2003).

Help to Self-Help

Because they realise that they cannot physically reach many of those who are in need of legal aid, a key element of Juss-Buss' outreach work, besides providing legal aid and information directly via outreach projects, is to raise legal awareness and rights consciousness—these are the terms used by Merry (2003)—among their target groups. To this end, Juss-Buss tries to establish grievance structures by empowering e.g., prisoners to reflect on their problems, voice them, and potentially take legal action. The aim is to make clients more aware of the availability of legal assistance, and the possibility of contacting Juss-Buss at a later stage, if they experience a need for legal aid. One of the ways Juss-Buss tries to establish and strengthen grievance structures among prisoners is by broadcasting information about prisoners' legal rights, and how specific justiciable problems can be dealt with, on the prison radio station 'Bandit Radio':

> '"Do you have the details of your debt? If not, you'll find a pamphlet with information on how to manage your debt and your contact prison officer must help you with this! If you do not get any help, call Juss-Buss…" [These slots] are aired between radio programmes, in various languages.' (Field notes, Olesen)

The radio slots are supported by helping access to the legal system by providing education, self-help programmes, and self-help materials. For less complex legal issues, self-help kits may be the most empowering and quickest problem-solving approach. For example, Juss-Buss has launched a self-help debt project providing prisoners with easily accessible step-by-step informational videos, forms and letter templates in plain language, to encourage them to take matters into their own hands (see e.g., Juss-Buss 2012).

The self-help approach differs significantly from trust-building 'troubles-talks' with disadvantaged people who are in need of face-to-face interaction and somebody to tell about their problems, before they can seek the help they need. However, educational self-help initiatives may establish easy understandable grievance structures, and procedures that enable the 'hard-to-reach' group to view their social problems in a legal context, and show them possible strategies to address them via Juss-Buss (see Hoffmann 2003).

Legal Policy Work

'I'm met with the smell of fresh paint when I come into the Juss-Buss office, and I soon notice a group of staff members lying on the floor, which is covered with large pieces of white fabric. Excitement and enthusiasm fill the room as the students write slogans on the banners in red paint. A young girl raises her head and says with a smile that they're getting ready for a march supporting the rights of refugees.' (Field notes, Olesen).

Juss-Buss' activist approach, combined with legal policy work, is of great importance in furthering their interest in change-making. A Juss-Buss staff member explains:

> 'We're very conscious that we have a strong legal aid inheritance. That's why we reacted so fiercely when the government suddenly decided that our appropriation could only be used on case handling, not on legal policy work. Juss-Buss has always stood on two legs, and the activist approach can't be removed without destroying the basic idea. So we protested, and used the media, and luckily we won, and the government backed down. We mainly based our protests on the fact that we could not be under the thumb of a party or a government. We do legal policy work, and work with a wide range of parties to promote what we consider best for our client group. And fortunately, they [the politicians] are very good at using us and listening to our opinions.' (Interview notes, Olesen)

Juss-Buss has always paid careful attention to case registration and to recording information about their client groups, to build up a unique stock of empirical knowledge about the lives and complex legal needs of 'hard-to-reach' groups. This accumulation of knowledge, underpinned by Juss-Buss' strong brand and network—which includes many former Juss-Buss staff members who now occupy high positions in public life—is mobilised to make sure their clients' voices are heard, and that their legal problems are in the news and on the political agenda. Juss-Buss' legal policy work is thus about informing debates and legislation that affect their client groups, about briefing politicians on the law in practice, and also, on real people's experiences, and about identifying and processing test cases. When Juss-Buss, after careful deliberation over their legal tactics, addresses specific test cases, the aim is not just to achieve a certain result in the individual case, but to get news coverage that lays bare society's social structures and legal barriers, in order to benefit their client groups by changing the law in a certain field. A side effect is to promote Juss-Buss as a pro-active brand in the area of the legal rights of disadvantaged groups.

Juss-Buss is not only active in Norway. It is also involved in various international legal aid projects. The main objective of these collaborations is to help establish, support, or develop similar legal aid clinics. Such projects have been launched in e.g., China, Vietnam, Poland, Lithuania, and Croatia.

Concluding Remarks

This chapter has shown how Juss-Buss was established in connection with action research projects conducted by visionary critical socio-legal scholars at the University of Oslo in the early 1970s. The outreach legal clinic was inspired by similar US outreach legal aid work and its governing principle was that it should both provide legal aid to disadvantaged groups, and collect information about the clients' legal needs and background for use in research and policy work to improve the life situations of the client groups.

Since its establishment, Juss-Buss has played an important role in providing outreach legal aid to disadvantaged groups that would otherwise struggle to name their legal problems, and claim their rights in core welfare areas where the welfare state has abdicated its social responsibility, and instead assumed the position of the opposing party.

Like other legal clinics, Juss-Buss relies on student volunteers, who obtain credits for their work. The high staff turnover has necessitated a form of training involving internal craft apprenticeship, through which the students not only learn how to meet and communicate with the client groups but also adapt to the strong culture and values of Juss-Buss, which include a commitment to do legal policy work.

An important aspect of Juss-Buss' work is outreach legal aid to prisoners. In outreach work, the staff aims to build trust in order to be able to start 'troubles-talks', and thus help transform prisoners' problems into legal terms. However, prisoners are hard to reach, so Juss-Buss also tries to establish grievance structures that inform, educate, and empower prisoners to voice their problems, use the Juss-Buss self-help-kits or seek help.

The other important task that Juss-Buss undertakes is legal policy work, and it is in a unique position to do so: First, they have a long tradition, and a strong brand supported by their position in the Faculty of Law of the University of Oslo; second, they have a strong network of former Juss-Buss students occupying important positions in the legal field; and finally, they have exceptional data covering the legal needs of different social groups and their complex legal challenges, and life situations of their client groups. In order to move beyond individual cases and improve the client groups' lives at a societal level, Juss-Buss tries to play an active role in setting the political agenda and influencing law making, to address the social problems of their client groups, together with the legal and structural causes of these problems.

Notes

1. The chapter is based on Olesen's and Hammerslev's observation studies and interviews and on Rønning's experiences as daily manager and legal aid worker in Juss-Buss.

References

Andenæs, K. (1975). Rettshjelp til norske sigøynere. In A. Eidesen, S. Eskeland, & T. Mathiesen (Eds.), *Rettshjelp og samfunnsstruktur* (pp. 118–152). Oslo: Pax.

Arntzen, S. B. (2009). *Årsrapport for Juss-Buss 2009* (Vol. 117). Oslo: Juss-buss, Institutt for kriminologi og rettssosiologi, Universitetet i Oslo.

Barton, A., & Mendlovitz, S. (1960). The experience of injustice as a research problem. *Journal of Legal Education, 13*, 24–39.

Best, A., & Andreasen, A. R. (1977). Consumer response to unsatisfactory purchases: A survey of perceiving defects, voicing complaints, and obtaining redress. *Law & Society Review, 11*(4), 701–742.

Bourdieu, P. (1987). The force of law: Toward a sociology of the juridical field. *The Hastings Law Journal, 38*, 805–853.

Bull, S., & Eidesen, A. (1975). Rettshjelp til herbergister. In A. Eidesen, S. Eskeland, & T. Mathiesen (Eds.), *Rettshjelp og samfunnsstruktur* (pp. 152–186). Oslo: UniPax.

Capua, G. D. (1975). Juss-Buss – Et rettshjelpstilbud for "vanlige folk"? In A. Eidesen, S. Eskeland, & T. Mathiesen (Eds.), *Rettshjelp og samfunnsstruktur* (pp. 72–94). Oslo: Pax.

Capua, G. D. (2001). *Om å legge ut på dypet*. Oslo: Institutt for kriminologi og rettssosiologi, Avdeling for rettssosiologi, Universitetet i Oslo.

Capua, G. D., & Juss-Buss. (1978). *Virksomheten i Juss-Buss i 1977/Gunnar de Capua* (Vol. 16). Oslo: Universitetet i Oslo, Inst.for rettssosiologi.

Carlin, J. E. & Howard, J. (1965). Legal representation and class justice. *U.C.L.A Law Review*, 12(2), pp. 381–437.

Coates, D., & Penrod, S. (1980/81). Social psychology and the emergence of disputes. *Law & Society Review*, 15(3/4), pp. 655–680.

Conley, J. M., & O'Barr, W. M. (1990). *Just words: Law, language, and power*. Chicago: Chicago University Press.

Conley, J. M., O'Barr, W. M., & Lind, E. A. (1978). The power of language: Presentational style in the courtroom. *Duke Law Journal, 78*, 1375–1399.

Edvardsen, O. B. E., Langbach, T., Svennebye, H., & Aakvaag, T. (1975). Rettshjelp til fremmedarbeidere i Norge. In A. Eidesen, S. Eskeland, & T. Mathiesen (Eds.), *Rettshjelp og samfunnsstruktur* (pp. 95–117). Oslo: Pax.

Eidesen, A., Eskeland, S., & Mathiesen, T. (1975). *Rettshjelp og samfunnsstruktur*. Oslo: Pax.

Eskeland, S., & Finne, J. (1973). *"Rettshjelp": En analyse og empirisk undersøkelse av tradisjonell rettshjelps muligheter og begrensningersærlig for folk som lever under vanskelige økonomiske eller sosiale kår*. Oslo: Pax.

Felstiner, W., Abel, R., & Sarat, A. (1980/81). The emergence and transformation of disputes: Naming, blaming, claiming. *Law & Society Review*, 15(3/4), pp. 631-654.

Genn, H. (1999). *Paths to justice: What people do and think about going to law*. Oxford: Hart Publishing.
Genn, H., & Paterson, A. (2001). *Paths to justice. Scotland: What people in Scotland think and do about going to law*. Oxford: Hart Publishing.
Goodrich, P. (1990). *Legal discourse studies in linguistics, Rhetoric and Legal Analysis*. Houndsmills: Palgrave Macmillan.
Habermas, J. (1984). *Theory of communicative action*. Boston: Beacon Press.
Hammerslev, O., & Mathiesen, T. (2013). Marxistisk retssociologi. In O. Hammerslev & M. R. Madsen (Eds.), *Klassisk og moderne retssociologi. Centrale temaer og tekster*. København: Hans Reitzels Forlag.
Hoffman, E. A. (2003). Legal consciousness and dispute resolution: Different disputing behavior at two similar taxicab companies. *Law & Social Inquiry, 28*(3), 691–716.
Jefferson, G. (1988). On the sequential organization of troubles-talk in ordinary conversation. *Social Problems, 35*(4), 418–441.
Johnsen, J. T. (1987). *Retten til juridisk bistand: en rettspolitisk studie*. Oslo: TANO.
Johnsen, J. T. (1991). *Juss-Buss and clinical legal education* (Vol. 51). Oslo: University of Oslo.
Johnsen, J. T. (1994). Nordic legal aid. (Sweden, Finland, Norway) (legal aid). *Maryland Journal of Contemporary Legal Issues, 5*(2), 301–331.
Johnsen, J. T. (1999). Progressive legal services in Norway? *International Journal of the Legal Profession, 6*(3), 261–310.
Johnsen, J. T. (2003). *Juss-buss – et fagkritisk eksperiment: idégrunnlag, arbeidsprinsipper og erfaringer: veiledning for medarbeidere i Juss-Buss*. Oslo: Juss-Buss.
Juss-Buss. (1996). *Juss-Buss 25 år: 1971–1996: jubileumsfestskrift*. Oslo: Juss-buss.
Juss-Buss. (2001). *Tvers igjennom lov til seier*. Oslo: Unipax.
Juss-Buss. (2012). *The Prisoner's handbook 2012. Juss-buss' guide to prison matters*. Olso: Juss-Buss.
la Cour, A., & Højlund, H. (2008). Voluntary social work as a paradox. *Acta Sociologica, 51*(1), 41–54.
Lied, C. (2013). *Gatejurister: Oppsøkende rettshjelp til folk med rusrelaterte problemer*. Oslo: Akademika forlag.
Mathiesen, T. (2001). Juss-Buss 30 år. In Juss-Buss (Ed.), *Tvers igjennom lov til seir* (pp. 16-19). Oslo: Pax Forlag.

Mathiesen, T. (2011). *Retten i samfunnet: en innføring i rettssosiologi* (6. utg). Oslo: Pax.

Matoesian, M. G. (1995). Language, law, and society: Policy implications of the Kennedy smith rape trial. *Law & Society Review, 29*(4), 669–702.

Merry, S. (2003). Rights talk and the experience of law: Implementing women's human rights to protection from violence. *Human Rights Quarterly, 25*(2), 343–381.

Miller, R. E., & Sarat, A. (1980/81). Grievances, claims, and disputes: Assessing the adversary culture. *Law & Society Review*, 15(3/4), pp. 525-566.

Minke, L. K. (2012). *Fængslets indre liv*. København: Jurist- og Økonomforbundets Forlag.

Newman, D. (2013). *Legal aid lawyers and the quest for justice*. Oxford: Hart Publishing.

Olesen, A. (2013). *Løsladt og gældsat*. København: Jurist- og Økonomforbundets Forlag.

Olesen, A. (2017). Released to the "battlefield" of the Danish welfare state: A battle between support and personal responsibility. In T. Ugelvik & P. S. Smith (Eds.), *Scandinavian penal history, culture and prison practice* (pp. 271–295). Palgrave Macmillan.

Olesen, A., Nielsen, S. P. P., & Hammerslev, O. (2017). Gadejura – kunsten at fremelske gadefolkets oplevelse af at bære rettigheder. In N. J. Clausen et al. (Eds.), *Festskrift til professor Hans Viggo Godsk Pedersen* (pp. 435–455). København: Jurist- og Økonomforbundets Forlag.

Pleasence, P., Buck, A., & Balmer, N. (2006). *Causes of action: Civil law and social justice*. London: Legal Services Research Centre.

Ricciardelli, R., Maier, K., & Hannah-Moffat, K. (2015). Strategic masculinities: Vulnerabilities, risk and the production of prison masculinities. *Theoretical Criminology, 19*(4), 491–513.

Rønning, O. H., & Juss-Buss (Eds.). (2011). *Med loven mot makta: Juss-Buss førti år*. Oslo: Novus.

Sarat, A., & Felstiner, W. L. F. (1997). *Divorce lawyers and their clients: Power and meaning in the legal process*. New York: Oxford University Press.

Sejr, L. E. (1977). *Retshjælp i et lokalområde*. Aarhus: Aarhus Universitet.

Skårberg, H. H. (2016). *Årsrapport for Juss-buss 2015*. Oslo: Juss-Buss stensilserie.

Sommerlad, H., & Sanderson, P. (2013). Social justice on the margins: The future of the not for profit sector as providers of legal advice in England and Wales. *Journal of Social Welfare and Family Law, 35*, 305–327.

Weber, M. (1978). *Economy and society.* Berkeley: University of California Press.

Open Access This chapter is distributed under the terms of the Creative Commons Attribution 4.0 International License (http://creativecommons.org/licenses/by/4.0/), which permits use, duplication, adaptation, distribution, and reproduction in any medium or format, as long as you give appropriate credit to the original author(s) and the source, a link is provided to the Creative Commons license, and any changes made are indicated.

The images or other third party material in this book are included in the work's Creative Commons license, unless indicated otherwise in the credit line; if such material is not included in the work's Creative Commons license and the respective action is not permitted by statutory regulation, users will need to obtain permission from the license holder to duplicate, adapt or reproduce the material.

8

Gadejuristen [The Street Lawyers]: Offering Legal Aid to Socially Marginalised People

Stine Piilgaard Porner Nielsen and Ole Hammerslev

Introduction

The streets of Copenhagen in the area behind the Central Station constitute the outdoor office of the *Gadejuristen*. Twice a week members of staff and volunteers bike around the streets of Copenhagen, transporting themselves and their supplies on a Christiania bike. The bike is parked; the staff open the bike cover, take out coffee, hot chocolate, disposable cups and biscuits. Packs of cigarettes and lighters are distributed among the staff to hand out on request and soon the first potential clients gather around the bike. Informal chat, the pouring of hot drinks and smoke from cigarettes fill the air – all part of a normal evening in the outdoor office of the *Gadejuristen* (field notes).

S.P.P. Nielsen (✉)
Department of Law, University of Southern Denmark, Odense M, Denmark

O. Hammerslev
Department of Law, University of Southern Denmark, Odense M, Denmark

Department of Criminology and Sociology of Law, University of Oslo, Oslo, Norway

The primary purpose of the welfare state is to compensate for events that may lead to the exclusion of citizens by offering support and help to those who are entitled to it (Appel Nissen 2007, p. 62; Bauman 2004, p. 66). However, a number of legal aid studies show that administrative deficiencies in the welfare system, and socially marginalised people's lack of knowledge of their rights to treatment or social benefits, may prevent their accessing welfare rights if they are not supported in the process (Lied 2011; Gadejuristen 2011). This chapter focuses on the organisation *Gadejuristen* (*The Street Lawyers*), which provides such legal aid to people who are among the most marginalised and most lacking in resources in Denmark, namely drug users, street sex workers, and homeless persons. *Gadejuristen* is an independent non-profit organisation established in 1999 as a response to what the founder, Nanna Gotfredsen, saw as inadequate treatment of socially marginalised people by public bodies such as the police and the welfare system. In an interview, Gotfredsen said:

> 'Some people were denied their rights – for instance, to treatment for drug use, or were not getting the benefit they were entitled to, because of maladministration. Having a lawyer to represent them increased their access to the rights they were entitled to, and this experience led to the establishment of the organisation and the practice of street lawyering.' (Our translation)

Gadejuristen started in Copenhagen where it still has its office and does most of its work but it also offers legal aid in other Danish cities. The aim of the organisation is to provide legal aid to the socially marginalised, and improve the daily lives of such people through policy work. To ensure these aims in the Danish welfare society the organisation focuses on two areas: at the individual level, it provides legal aid for the specific target group, partly through outreach legal aid, and, at the societal level, its work is policy oriented, and it seeks through knowledge dissemination, lobbyism, and education to improve the lives of their target group. In the organisation's view, the two levels are intertwined and equally important, as both contribute to improving the lives of the target group.[1]

Gadejuristen differs from other legal aid institutions in Denmark (see Chap. 5) in a number of ways: the organisation focuses on a specific target group, provides outreach legal aid, and assists its users throughout the legal process in terms of advice, representation, and in practical matters such as providing bus tickets, mobile phones, etc.[2] It also offers supplementary social and economic support to the target group and works to influence the political landscape. Against the backdrop of traditional understandings of legal aid, as defined in classic Nordic studies (see Chap. 1), the present chapter demonstrates how *Gadejuristen* interprets and delivers legal aid, and how the development of the Danish welfare state impacts the organisation's work. The case of *Gadejuristen* also illustrates how legal aid, for certain groups in society, is intertwined with social work, policy work and knowledge dissemination.

The only research existing on street lawyering in Denmark is Camilla Lied's Norwegian *Gatejurister. Oppsøkende rettshjelp til folk med rusrelaterte problemer* [The Street Lawyers. Outreach legal aid to people with drug related problems] of 2013, which is based on her University of Oslo doctoral thesis (2011). This compares *Gadejuristen* in Copenhagen with *Gatejuristen* in Oslo and examines the methods used in street lawyering, how *Gatejuristen* in Oslo and *Gadejuristen* in Copenhagen work with their target group, users, and public authorities, and how the users experience contact with the organisations. In 2011, a report was published by Copenhagen *Gadejuristen*, describing in detail the work of the organisation at the time.

Based on fieldwork and interviews with previous and present street lawyers, this chapter examines the work of *Gadejuristen* in the context of the Danish welfare state. The chapter has three parts and a conclusion. The first part outlines the organisation of *Gadejuristen,* focusing on the staff, the funding situation, and the number and type of cases dealt with. The second part examines the aid provided by *Gadejuristen* by investigating how the work on the streets is conducted, and how *Gadejuristen* navigate in the Welfare State and become a kind of mediator between their target group and the welfare state. The third part focuses on the effect of their political and societal approaches to socially marginalised people and how the organisation has adopted a street lawyer method of working. The chapter sums up its findings in a conclusion.

The Organisation of *Gadejuristen*

Staff, Funding, and Type of Cases

Gadejuristen represents socially marginalised people because of its founder's experience of street lawyering in the streets of Copenhagen in the 1990s. The recognition that socially marginalised people faced difficulties in accessing their welfare rights, and that legal representation remedied this, led to the establishment of the organisation in 1999 and the formulation of its objective: to improve the lives of the target group. The target group was defined as those with nowhere else to go, and who needed help the most: drug users, street sex workers, and homeless persons. This group typically lead chaotic lives, as a result of substance abuse, lack of housing, and/or the lack of networks and resources to navigate in the welfare system. *Gadejuristen* works to increase the target group's chances of inclusion in the welfare state by presenting their cases and supporting them in everyday life and in meetings with welfare state representatives, such as social workers and health staff.

When *Gadejuristen* was founded, it only had one full-time project leader. Since then, the number of people working with *Gadejuristen* has gradually increased, as has the number of volunteers. Today, the organisation has five lawyers and one social worker employed full-time and one law student part-time. The number of employees depends on external funding, which is related to the projects carried out by the organisation. Over the years, the organisation has initiated various projects catering for the target group, including The Parents' Network, in 2007, and The Street Level Project, in 2002. The Parents' Network enables parents with current or past drug use to access counselling and engage in informal social meetings, whereas The Street Level Network is an outreach project facilitated by volunteers who provide an alternative resource network for drug users. The support offered by the volunteers is tailored to the drug users' needs and demands, and is thus a flexible way of addressing the problems of the target group.[3] The two projects both provide a framework of support for the target group but differ in that the latter is directed to the entire target group whereas the former is targeted at parents. Between 25 and 40 volunteers work in the organisation—mostly law students but other professions, such as nurses and psychologists are also represented. The diversity in professional background is necessary to accommodate the complex problems of the users: nurses and psychologists may better understand the consequences of withdrawal symptoms and how to address them, whereas volunteers with a legal background are trained to identify problems that are of a legal nature, enabling them to advocate for the rights of the users. The organisation relies on the volunteers' work to be able to handle the increasing number of users and support them in their dealings with the social system. The different professional backgrounds of the staff and volunteers mirror the forms of aid *Gadejuristen* provides, and the complex needs of the target group. If the target group is to get the help they need, legal expertise must be supplemented by knowledge of the medical and psychological options available. Because multiple factors are often intertwined in the target group's problems, support needs to combine a number of areas of professional expertise, for example, knowledge about possible mental and physical treatment, knowledge about the workings of the welfare system, and knowledge about the law. Though the volunteers and staff have different professional backgrounds and, thus, also focus on different areas, it is the law that is central in the work of *Gadejuristen*, as the law is used as a tool to access the welfare system, for example, by pointing to unlawful administrative processes and identifying the rights of users. By applying the law and displaying detailed knowledge of how the welfare system functions, the organisation positions itself as a representative of the users.

Most legal aid institutions in Denmark receive money from the legal aid fund of the Department of Civil Affairs (Civilstyrelsen 2015). This is not the case, however, with *Gadejuristen*, which finances projects in various ways, mostly through fundraising, donations, and access to funds through cooperation with public authorities.[4] The organisation's outreach legal aid work, for example, is funded by the special fund for social areas,[5] and the Parents' Network, mentioned above, is funded by the so-called Tips and Lotto Fund, which earmarks funding for social purposes.[6]

Gadejuristen Cases

A report published by *Gadejuristen* indicates a steady rise in users, from 10 in 2005 to 400 in 2010, and argues that there is a continuing need for the support offered by the organisation (Gadejuristen 2011, p. 27). The organisation has existed since 1999 but between 2005 and 2010 the numbers of users dramatically increased, which indicates that users seek out the support of *Gadejuristen* in order to navigate in the welfare system (Fig. 8.1).

Typical cases dealt with by *Gadejuristen* are to do with financial issues, and problems related to housing and homelessness, the labour market, drug substitution, and in-patient treatment (*ibid.*, p. 10). *Gadejuristen* cases vary but a feature they often have in common is that different legal areas of expertise are involved at the same time, such as benefit rights, or rights to medical treatment. This is an indication of the complexity of the problems of the target group: they involve multiple legal areas and inter-related social problems, e.g., homelessness, drug use, and mental health issues. In order to support the target group, *Gadejuristen* thus needs to have comprehensive expertise in fields other than the legal, and in-depth knowledge of the lives of the target group, including familiarity with areas such as drug use and mental illness. Kristian Andenæs refers to this wide-ranging expertise as a professional requirement beyond legal professionalism, which is a necessary part of the street lawyer method

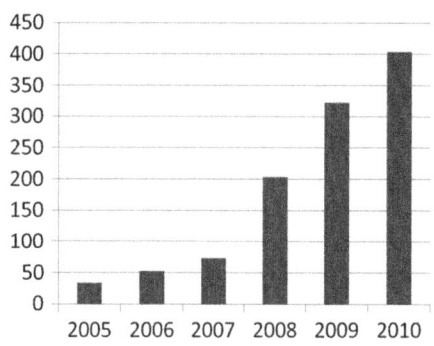

Fig. 8.1 Number of new users per year (Gadejuristen 2011, p. 27)

(*ibid.*, p. 21). This is elaborated further in the section on 'The Street Lawyer Method' below.

The increase in users, numbers of staff, and volunteers makes the organisation more visible on the streets, more available to potential users, and shows that there is an increasing need for the help provided by *Gadejuristen*. The complexity of the users' problems calls for detailed knowledge of various fields, and a professional understanding of how to navigate in these fields in order to ensure that the target group's needs are met. The following example elucidates how a detailed knowledge of legal administration and of rights to medical treatment enables *Gadejuristen* to act on behalf of the users: a man applied for in-patient treatment, i.e., treatment where the patient checks into the facility and remains there for the entire programme. He argued that if he did not have the treatment he would most likely die of his drug use. *Gadejuristen* helped him apply and waited for a ruling on the matter. When the letter arrived, it simply said: 'Decision: You cannot receive inpatient treatment.' *Gadejuristen* then contacted the responsible social worker and argued that the decision could only be interpreted as a ruling, and, as such, should be followed by the reason for the ruling and advice on how to appeal the ruling. *Gadejuristen* then helped formulate the appeal and based on the appeal the ruling was amended and the user was granted in-patient treatment (Gadejuristen 2011, p. 69).

The fact that *Gadejuristen* finances its work and projects by donations and fundraising means it has greater flexibility, and can go beyond traditional legal aid in a way that would not be possible if it had to conform to normal legal aid funds.

The Work of *Gadejuristen*

As mentioned in the introduction to this book, legal aid studies have shown that the visibility and accessibility of legal aid providers are important in establishing contact with and providing support to socially marginalised groups. From the beginning, *Gadejuristen* has been aware that it needs to create awareness of its services among the target group. Therefore, every Tuesday and Friday, *Gadejuristen* follows a specific route in the streets of Copenhagen with its Christiania bike which is a cargo bike with a large box in the front of the bike, loaded with coffee, snacks, and other goods for the target group. The route is in Vesterbro, where there are many socially marginalised people—as this is where shelters and facilities for drug users are available. *Gadejuristen* typically goes from its office to the hostel for homeless men 'Mændenes Hjem' in Istedgade, and then to Cafeen, which is a drop-in centre close to the drug use facilities. They stop where the target group and potential clients are able to drop by for a chat and a cup of coffee, served from the lid of the Christiana box, which functions as a table, or have a cigarette or get condoms and clean needles for intravenous drug use. With these basic items available on the street, an informal chat often begins around the bike. *Gadejuristen* staff and volunteers greet people by name, sometimes they get hugs which indicates familiarity and trust (field notes). The informal relationship between *Gadejuristen* and the people dropping by opens the way to dialogue about everyday life and its problems. One worker points out the difference between calling in at other legal aid offices, and talking to someone from Gadejuristen:

> 'The precondition to drop by there [at the traditional legal aid office] is that you are aware that you are suffering from something illegal, but then one needs to know one's rights or at least have an idea of them. And our users haven't got that … That [creating the awareness] is what happens in the encounters when we are having a cup of coffee.' (Our translation)

These informal talks enable *Gadejuristen* to systematically identify potential legal problems, which the target group may not be aware of, and so they are important steps towards providing users with the support they need. These informal talks and bike trips in the streets of Vesterbro go beyond traditional legal aid and are referred to as *extended legal aid*. Extended legal aid is a necessity due to the complexity of the target group's way of life and legal problems. It encompasses such things as informality, practical help in the form of covering expenses and providing cell phones, and the extra professional insights provided by the many volunteers and the staff.

As shown in the example above, *Gadejuristen* makes use of informal talks but also draws on traditional legal practice, as the organisation aims to serve the users' interests and handle their cases from beginning to end. In the case of in-patient treatment, *Gadejuristen*'s availability on the streets of Vesterbro made it visible to the target group, and the visibility is essential to establish contact, map out legal problems, and provide the necessary aid and support. The professional training of *Gadejuristen* staff enables them to identify and address irregular processes, as in the case involving the appeal on the ruling that failed to provide reasons for the denial of in-patient treatment. Professional knowledge of the appeal system thus provides the organisation with the necessary tools to represent users and their interests.

Gadejuristen goes beyond traditional legal aid, as relationships with users often continue after the legal needs have been met. This contrasts with target groups' usual encounters with the welfare system, in which they often encounter a number of different caseworkers. In the case of some users, encounters with the welfare system and previous experiences with public authorities have led to scepticism or even mistrust of the system. If several caseworkers are involved in users' cases, it can be difficult to establish trust and ensure continuity in the process. *Gadejuristen* is aware of this and engages in legal work on the target group's terms by meeting people in the streets in outreach work, recognising their legal needs as well as their physical and social needs. It also creates a high degree of accessibility by making itself available in the streets as well as in the *Gadejuristen* office, and by offering them cell phones to enable contact (field notes). By adopting these extended legal practices, *Gadejuristen* is able to build up trust relationships with the target group, and dismantle some of the structures found in the welfare system, by ensuring that it is easy to access help from the organisation's staff. This help is often multifaceted, and includes extra-legal aid, such as providing cell phones, covering the costs of travel to meetings with, for example, caseworkers, and establishing networks aimed at empowering the target group to handle their everyday lives. An example of such networks is the Parents' Network, described above, which over the years has helped parents with current or past drug use to experience themselves as being less stigmatised and more recognised, and thereby empowered in their parenting skills.[7]

By making themselves available on the target group's terms, providing them with basic items, giving them a hot cup of coffee, and through dialogue recognising and appreciating their situation: in short by showing users that they are quite aware of their needs and way of life, *Gadejuristen* works to build up trust relations with socially marginalised people. Informality opens the way to conversation, and this enables the staff and volunteers to identify potential legal problems. By articulating an 'us and them' relationship; 'us' representing the users and the organisation, 'them' being the welfare system, the organisation shows awareness of the scepticism and lack of trust felt by users towards the welfare system. The 'us and them' discourse stresses that *Gadejuristen* and the users are on the same page, and that both parties consider the welfare system as the opponent. Thus, the organisation aligns with the target group, indicating solidarity and representation on the target group's own terms. The target group's experience of being listened to, recognised, and supported empowers them to handle their everyday lives.

Navigating in the Welfare State: *Gadejuristen* as Mediators

Gadejuristen plays a central role for the target group as it works to address the shortcomings of the welfare system, which at times is unable to include socially marginalised people (Frivilligrådet 2010, p. 5). A move in welfare administration towards management models inspired by new public management has led to political scepticism about the efficiency of the welfare state (Appel Nissen 2007, p. 64), which is reflected in a focus on the individual citizen as being solely responsible for their own situation (Bauman 2004, p. 66). This development has led to an increase in the demands made by the welfare system on citizens trying to access it: for example, the demand that people should change their circumstances to fit in with the functioning of the welfare system. The founder of *Gadejuristen*, Nanna Gotfredsen, experiences that the welfare system also has a 'you scratch my back and I'll scratch yours' mentality that is manifested when, for example, citizens have their benefits cut off, due to their failure to conform to the expectations of the system (Gotfredsen 2004, p. 9). Citizens who are able to conform to these expectations and demands are recognised in the welfare system as responsible and are included, while those who fail to 'follow the rules of the game' may lose benefits or be excluded from other rights (Knudsen and Åkerstrøm Andersen 2013, p. 71).

The organisation of the welfare system may, in some cases, create obstacles to socially marginalised people's access to rights; social workers are often specialised in narrow fields, such as housing, benefits, or health treatment, but rarely in all of them (Lied 2011, p. 286). *Gadejuristen*, however, provide legal aid that takes account of the complexity and multifaceted aspects of the target group's problems, and is therefore able to represent users in the welfare system and ensure their access to rights by means of legal strategies. Users may face difficulties in getting to welfare offices because of their, at times, chaotic lives. The way they live makes it difficult for them to meet the requirements of the system, such as going to the social service office and waiting in line to attend meetings with a caseworker. *Gadejuristen* knows by experience that users may have withdrawal symptoms, and/or are be unable to turn up for a scheduled appointment which limits their ability to fulfil the requirements of the welfare system. When this is the case, the consequence may be that social security benefits are no longer paid and that people are left with no money at all. According to *Gadejuristen*, this systemic structure does not fit well with the target group's ability to navigate within the welfare system.

As previous research on legal aid shows, accessing rights is not only a matter of knowing your rights, it is also a matter of having the resources to pursue them with the appropriate legal strategies. Both these elements are challenging for *Gadejuristen*'s target group: they do not have the necessary knowledge of the law to formulate their health and social problems as legal problems, and because of their often chaotic lives, they do not have the resources to argue for their rights or pursue legal strategies (*ibid.*, p. 173). In short, the target group often do not have the resources to name, blame, and claim, which are pivotal in a legal process. Naming your rights is the ability to identify your problem as being of a legal nature, blaming involves knowing who is responsible for fulfilling the rights, and claiming rights is the ability to articulate this in a legal framework (Felstiner et al. 1980). The inability to name, blame, and claim leaves the target group in a vulnerable position where they are unable to recognise and fight for their rights. This is described by the leader of *Gadejuristen* when she notes that many socially marginalised people do not know their own rights:

> 'Often they do not even have the resources to find out about their rights. And if you do not know your rights, of course you would not realise when you do not have them.' (Gotfredsen 2004, p. 1, our translation).

Gadejuristen works by establishing contacts with their target group, re-formulating everyday problems as legal problems, when appropriate, and representing users in encounters with the welfare system. For example, an everyday problem could translate into a legal problem if a user faced eviction because they had not been able to pay their rent due to lack of benefit payments. In such case, *Gadejuristen* would investigate the user's entitlement to benefits, why he/she has not received them, and then take on the case, with the user's consent. In order to establish contact with the target group, and help them obtain their rights, *Gadejuristen* must function on different structural terms than those of the welfare system and other legal aid institutions. If the organisation is to ensure that the users' rights are upheld, a high level of accessibility is required, together with detailed knowledge of the kind of problems most often faced by the target group.

Socially marginalised people seeking to access their rights often need to communicate with various parts of the welfare system, e.g., the health system, the local municipality, or administrative institutions. This requires an ability to navigate in these systems, which are often structured by and for those who are not socially marginalised. They need, for example, to be able to attend meetings arranged by a social worker or give satisfactory reasons for cancelling them. Such things can be challenging for *Gadejuristen*'s users, as some have a limited ability to meet the requirements of the welfare system. This may lead to a labelling process where the target group is branded as 'not caring' or 'not trying' (Gotfredsen 2004, p. 7), though the issue is more often a matter of the discrepancy between the lifestyle of the target group and the structural functioning of the welfare system.

Gadejuristen's role in such circumstances is to represent its users, help them enter the system through legal representation, remind about them about meetings with welfare system representatives, and cover the travel expenses for attending the meetings. *Gadejuristen* is able to represent users because it has a detailed knowledge of their circumstances, as well as the legal knowledge necessary to navigate the welfare system. This means they have easier access to relevant actors in the system, for example, they may have a telephone number to reach a caseworker after working hours, as well as resources to operate in the field, due to their knowledge of the way the welfare system functions, and of the rights of the user. *Gadejuristen* often represent users with the welfare system as the opponent in order to help them engage with welfare agencies in their terms (Gadejuristen 2011, p. 126). *Gadejuristen* considers this way of working for and with users a necessity in order to ensure their access to rights:

> 'We want to go to that level where people are not able to find their way to legal aid … They [the target group] do not go to Stormgade,[8] they cannot draw a number and wait for two hours, then they have withdrawal symptoms. You have to organise legal aid so that they are actually able to use it.' (Our translation)

Though the welfare system was set up to help socially marginalised people, some users are left behind because they lack the resources to navigate the system; they therefore rely on the aid from *Gadejuristen*. It is not just *Gadejuristen*'s target group who sometimes lack sufficient legal knowledge; some caseworkers may lack the appropriate, up-to-date knowledge that is necessary to ensure users' access to rights (Lied 2011, p. 339). The lack of adequate legal knowledge leads to conflicts between *Gadejuristen* and caseworkers, who often have other considerations to bear in mind, such as budgetary constraints, that outweigh legal considerations (Rosholm 2009, p. 156; von Hielmcrone and Schultz 2007, p. 100) and a (too) great number of cases, which means that efficient casework is prioritised over detailed examination of each case (Wadskjær 2007, p. 91).

Since most of the staff is trained jurists, *Gadejuristen* presents different arguments from arguments which the staff in the welfare system may put forward. Their professional legal background becomes evident when *Gadejuristen* acknowledges that representing the target group may be easier when talking to a lawyer in the administration; it speeds up the process, as there is a shared language and understanding of the law between legal professionals. The law is thus a means to further *Gadejuristen*'s work and is applied when the organisation carries out legal policy work that aims to change unsound existing legislation and influence debates on new legislation (Gadejuristen 2011, p. 139). Legal knowledge puts *Gadejuristen* in a stronger position than their users, and many socially marginalised people find that it is not until *Gadejuristen* represents them that they are taken notice of by, for example, their caseworker. The difficulty of accessing justice means that the target group has to rely on the services of *Gadejuristen*. The unintended effect of this, however, is that users may feel offended by the fact that they are recognised when represented but undermined when they meet the social service system on their own (Lied 2011, p. 261).

The target group's difficulties in conforming to the ever-greater requirements and expectations of the welfare system leave them in a vulnerable position when trying to access and navigate the system. The systemic expectation of 'a willingness to change' may come up against their actual resources and living conditions. By working on their terms, *Gadejuristen* is able to represent the users' interests in encounters with the welfare system, and the detailed expertise of the organisation enhances its ability to address the shortcomings of the system, which may result from insufficient knowledge of the complexity of the lives of marginalised people.

The mismatch between how the welfare system functions and the life styles of the target group places *Gadejuristen* in a central role as mediators: staff and volunteers are able to reformulate what the users consider to be everyday problems into legal problems. *Gadejuristen*'s expertise is necessary for the process of naming, claiming and blaming to be carried out.

Working on a Societal Level

As mentioned, *Gadejuristen* provides legal aid on an individual level, in specific cases, and the organisation works at the societal level, as it represents the target group in public and in the media, arguing for improvements to their living conditions. Central to this is *Gadejuristen*'s work at the policy level on reducing drug-related harms (Lied 2011, p. 276). *Gadejuristen* draws on experience in the field, and research in related areas, and has established an advisory board composed of researchers and experts in the field. It also involves the target group to gain an understanding of their needs from a bottom-up perspective. The organisation stresses the importance of an evidence-based approach, and the need for dialogue with the parties involved: the authorities as well as the people living on the streets, so that drug-related harms can be addressed from multiple angles. Contact with researchers, experts, and the target group thus enables *Gadejuristen* to formulate ways to improve the living conditions of society's most marginalised people from the starting point of research and social recognition.

Since the establishment of *Gadejuristen* in 1999, dialogue and lobbying initiated by *Gadejuristen* have led to changes in the political discourse on drugs and to a less repressive approach on the part of the police which has improved the lives of the target group. One improvement resulting from their lobbying and dialogue is the ending of the so-called *ban zones*. In the 1990s, Vesterbro was divided into ban zones where drug users, homeless people, and street sex workers were prohibited from gathering or walking, because their presence, according to the police, was upsetting for the residents and citizens of the locality. The introduction of the ban zones was not accompanied by the provision of an alternative place for the socially marginalised people to go, and the ban thus led to an increasing number of fines of between 600 and 1000 DKK [80 € and 135 €] being imposed by the police, and then an increase in debt and imprisonment when they failed to pay the fines. *Gadejuristen* engaged in dialogue with the police, pointing out that the ban zones did not solve the problem, but merely caused stress among the organisation's target group and argued that the relationship between the police and the socially marginalised people was characterised by intolerance, fear, and repressive methods. Thus, *Gadejuristen* engaged with the police and argued on behalf of the target group that the ban zones did not result in nice, clean streets but damaged relations between the police and the target group. In 2012, the ban zones were dismantled as a result of the cooperation between the police and *Gadejuristen*.[9]

Gadejuristen does political legal work with the aim of improving the living conditions of the target group. This work focuses on two areas; first, it seeks to ensure that the practices of public authorities such as the police and caseworkers conform to existing legislation, and second, it seeks to change existing legislation when it is inadequate or unsound as regards the target group's needs (Gadejuristen 2011, p. 17).

The basis of *Gadejuristen*'s political work is an evidence- and research-based approach to understanding the situation of the target group. The organisation disseminates information through public meetings and the media, educates relevant actors, participates in the public debate through feature articles and discussion articles, and represents the causes of their users in public hearings (Lied 2011, p. 266). By disseminating information on a societal level, *Gadejuristen* hopes to make the lives of the people living on the streets better understood, and influence public and political opinion. The dissemination of information is thus prioritised by *Gadejuristen* as a way to nuance the debate and inspire political initiatives, which respect the autonomy of the target group and take their needs into account (Gadejuristen 2011, p. 33).

Gadejuristen frames itself as a *Hard Core Harm Reducer*, thus indicating that the organisation works to reduce drug-related harms. This is of relevance, as many of *Gadejuristen* users are involved in the drug scene and thus are affected by political initiatives and laws relating to that area (Gadejuristen 2011, p. 33). At the societal level, the legal approach of *Gadejuristen* is supplemented by research, cooperation with their advisory board, and dialogue with the actors involved—politicians, the target group, etc. The involvement of these different actors enables the organisation to take an evidence- and human rights-based approach to understand and articulate the needs of socially marginalised people, and disseminate information about them. Previous societal work has resulted in a less repressive approach to the target group on the part of the police to, and in political debate on drug use facilities. Moreover, by taking current research findings as its starting point, and drawing on the expertise of the advisory board, *Gadejuristen* is able to position itself as an authority in the field and thus well qualified to take part in discussions relating to harm reduction, socially marginalised people, and drug legislation.

Gadejuristen often invite politicians to participate in the street work to gain a better understanding of the target group. One of the main objectives in doing so is to address some current stereotypical political views of the drug scene and the needs of socially marginalised people. According to *Gadejuristen*, some politicians call the drug scene and drug use *the friendly enemy*. This means that the drug scene and drug use are portrayed as the reasons why the socially marginalised have problems handling everyday life and the welfare system. However, according to *Gadejuristen*, the target group often uses drugs as a means of coping with the actual problem, namely their complex living conditions (field notes). If politicians consider drugs to be the main concern, this may lead to unsound strategies that fail to consider the actual living conditions of socially marginalised people.

Working at the societal level with a focus on disseminating information, *Gadejuristen* has, to some extend, already improved the living conditions of the target group. This work continues with input from experts as well as users, in order to lobby for a better understanding of the situations of socially marginalised people and of how to address these within a sound legal and societal framework.

The Street Lawyer Method

Gadejuristen positions itself as a legal aid institution specifically targeting socially marginalised people. Making itself available on the terms of the target group and following an informal approach in street encounters are part of extended legal aid, and necessary to help a group of people in society who would otherwise face severe difficulties in navigating the welfare system (Lied 2011, p. 249). This characterises *the Street Lawyer method*, a term coined by Andenæs. He divides the method into three parts: a legal part, a professional part, and a practical part (Gadejuristen 2011, p. 132). The legal part of street lawyering consists of providing help through legal argumentation based on existing law. The professional part of street lawyering involves an interdisciplinarity that benefits the target group, by, for example, including specialised knowledge of the health issues of drug users. The practical part of street lawyering consists of practical support, such as covering users' transportation expenses and providing them with cell phones to enable them to make contact (*ibid.*). The three parts are seen in the following examples:

Based on their knowledge of the relevant law, *Gadejuristen* is able to re-formulate everyday problems as legal problems, thereby articulating the rights of the target group. Detailed knowledge of the drug scene enables the organisation to work at the policy level, and, for example, argue for the decriminalisation of drugs, as statistics show that this results in a reduction of drug-related harms. By way of practical support, *Gadejuristen* may cover the travel costs of getting to a meeting with a social worker, or provide cell phones in order to support users' access to social workers or other relevant actors.

As has been mentioned, *Gadejuristen*'s objectives are to improve the circumstances of the target group, reduce drug-related harm, and ensure the group's access to rights. As shown above, a variety of methods is adopted by *Gadejuristen* to meet these objectives: dialogue, judicial policy, recognition, and informal encounters, and these distinguish *Gadejuristen* from traditional legal aid institutions and traditional lawyers (Lied 2011, p. 136). Nonetheless, the organisation also makes use of traditional legal methods. They only represent the user with her/his consent; when they represent their users their users' interests are the primary concern, and they make use of legal methods, identifying and applying relevant legal sources when arguing a user's case (Gadejuristen 2011, p. 134). The organisation can, however, be distinguished from traditional lawyers by the informal approach taken to (potential) users and the 'us and them' discourse that places the emphasis on equality and recognition in the relationship between staff and users.

The informal approach involves the speedy verbal exchange of information due to the need for rapid solutions in difficult situations.

The welfare system is not flexible in the same way and lacks the ability to handle urgent cases: the informal approach that characterises extended legal aid enables *Gadejuristen* to identify potential legal problems and meet the, at times, urgent needs of the target group.

The working methods followed by *Gadejuristen*; the ability to respond quickly to cases thanks to informality and flexibility, the legal expertise, and practical support and empowerment of users, also help establish the trust between the organisation and its users that is crucial to mapping out problems and facilitating the legal process of identifying and enforcing rights. As mentioned, *Gadejuristen* adopts an 'us and them' discourse, identifying 'us' as the organisation and the user(s), and 'them' as the welfare system in all its various forms. The welfare system is often the adversary in the legal disputes dealt with by *Gadejuristen* (*ibid.*, p. 89), and the 'us and them' discourse establishes the trust needed to address the users' complex problems (*ibid.*, p. 286). Often the users' previous experiences of the welfare system have led to a feeling of lack of rights and lack of recognition. The social work done by the organisation helps establish the structures of trust that are necessary for socially marginalised people to become empowered and enabled to navigate the welfare system. Users' experiences of being rejected by the welfare system and of not knowing how to improve their situation, on the other hand, led to lack of trust in the welfare system and failure to improve their situations. *Gadejuristen* therefore strives to empower users by taking a recognition-based approach, both verbally and physically. Greetings by name, hugs, and compliments are typical tools used to build up self-esteem, improve the users' self-image (*ibid.*, p. 233), and help them handle their everyday lives.

Gadejuristen is able to meet its objectives by adopting the Street Lawyer method and by advocating for the rights of the target group at the policy level. The three different elements in the Street Lawyer method, together with the informality and flexibility characteristic of extended legal aid, constitute a holistic approach to the individual user. The focus on policy and social structures, on the other hand, is essential for *Gadejuristen*'s ability to address issues at the societal level, and this policy work is part of extended legal aid, though it is not targeted at a specific user but at the life situations of the target group as a whole. The ability to act flexibly and informally ensures a degree of speediness, which is pivotal in some users' situations; a promptness that the structures of the welfare system cannot always offer. *Gadejuristen* is thus able to compensate for some of the system's shortcomings by using the Street Lawyer method, and providing extended legal aid, while also working at the policy level.

Conclusion

The examination of the *Gadejuristen* organisation, its work and the way current legislation and the structure and functioning of the welfare system affect the non-governmental organisation's target group, makes it evident that *Gadejuristen* plays an essential part in ensuring the target group's access to their rights. Though the welfare state was established to compensate for society's shortcomings, its structure, and the way it functions, do not support many socially marginalised people's ability to navigate in the welfare system. *Gadejuristen* works at the individual level, focusing on the user's needs, and at the societal level, lobbying for new policies and laws, and changes in the practices of public institutions, in order to increase the target group's access to rights and improve the situation of socially marginalised people.

The complexity of the users' problems calls for detailed expertise in various fields and a professional understanding of how to operate in these fields, in order to ensure the target groups' needs are met. By adopting the Street Lawyer method and thus making itself available on the terms of the target group, *Gadejuristen* is able to earn the trust of its users. The articulation of an 'us and them' relationship and an informal approach based on dialogue, recognition and appreciation facilitate contact between *Gadejuristen* and the target group, enabling the organisation to formulate and translate the everyday problems of the users as legal problems. *Gadejuristen* thus functions as a representative of its users when claiming their rights in the welfare system. That fact that the way the welfare system functions is often incompatible with the circumstances of the target group, and that some case workers lack legal knowledge, gives the organisation a pivotal role: *Gadejuristen*'s expertise enables it to name, claim, and blame on behalf of its users.

Through lobbying and the dissemination of information at the societal level, *Gadejuristen* has to some extent managed to improve the living conditions of the target group. The organisation stresses the need for an evidence- and human rights-based approach, which is holistic in the sense that it involves all relevant actors. This approach is followed in the interests of achieving a better understanding of socially marginalised people's situations and how to address these. However, the societal and the individual levels are intertwined in the organisation's efforts to achieve its objective of improving the living conditions of the target group: the focus on the individual user enables *Gadejuristen* to represent her/his particular interests and thereby improve her/his situation.

As New Public Management has grown in the public sector, the ever-increasing demands made by the welfare system on citizens have become part of everyday life. However, it may be difficult for the target group to satisfy these requirements which leaves them unable to navigate in the welfare system and in a vulnerable position as regards accessing their rights. The shortcomings of the welfare system are addressed by *Gadejuristen* through the organisation's ability to formulate users' problems as legal problems, thus using the law as the primary tool to access the welfare system.

Notes

1. http://gadejuristen.dk/om-gadejuristen
2. *Gadejuristen* refers to the people making use of their services as 'users'. The term is therefore applied throughout the chapter.
3. http://gadejuristen.dk/netv%C3%A6rks-og-gadeplansprojektet
4. Regulations of *Gadejuristen*, section 8.
5. http://gadejuristen.dk/udg%C3%A5ende-retshj%C3%A6lp
6. http://gadejuristen.dk/for%C3%A6ldre-m%C3%B8dregruppe
7. http://gadejuristen.dk/for%C3%A6ldre-m%C3%B8dregruppe

8. Stormgade is the address of the office of Copenhagen Legal Aid, which offers free legal aid to citizens who drop by or telephone them (see Chap. 5).
9. http://www.gadejuristen.dk/forbudszonerne-er-nu-fortid

Bibliography

Appel Nissen, M. (2007). Magt og forandring i socialt arbejde. In M. Appel Nissen, K. Pringle, & L. Uggerhøj (Eds.), *Magt og forandring i socialt arbejde*. København: Akademisk Forlag.

Bauman, Z. (2004). *Forspildte liv*. København: Hans Reitzels Forlag.

Civilstyrelsen. (2015). *Beretning om tilskud til retshjælpsinstitutioner*. Available via: http://www.civilstyrelsen.dk/~/media/Fri%20Proces/Beretning_2015.ashx

Felstiner, W. L. F., Abel, R. L., & Sarat, A. (1980). The emergence and transformation of disputes: Naming, blaming, claiming. *Law & Society Review, 15*(3/4), 631–654.

Frivilligrådet. (2010). *Et stærkt velfærdssamfund skal skabes sammen med borgerne! Reformoplæg fra Frivilligrådet*. Available via: http://www.frivilligraadet.dk/sites/default/files/udgivelser/reformoplaeg_0.pdf

Gadejuristen. (2011). *Dokumentationsrapport*. Available via: http://gadejuristen.dk/sites/default/files/Gadejuristen%20Unders%C3%B8gelse%20af%20udsattes%20retshj%C3%A6lpsbehov%20V5%2016%20nov%202011_0.pdf

Gotfredsen, N. (2004). Gadejura. En nødløsning i en undtagelsestilstand. *Tid til respekt*. Dalager, S. and Jørgensen, P. S. (eds.) Socialpolitisk Forlag.

Knudsen, H., & Åkerstrøm Andersen, N. (2013). Hyperansvar: når personligt ansvar gøres til genstand for styring. *Dansk Sociologi*, 4/24.

Lied, C. (2011). *Irriterende til stede. Om gatejurister i Oslo og København*. Olso: Det juridiske fakultet.

Rosholm, M. (2009). Økonomiske mekanismers betydning for marginaliseringsprocesser på arbejdsmarkedet. In J. Elm Larsen & N. Mortensen (Eds.), *Udenfor eller Indenfor. Sociale marginaliseringsprocessers mangfoldighed*. København: Hans Reitzels Forlag.

von Hielmcrone, N., & Schultz, T. (2007). Større retssikkerhed i det sociale arbejde? In A. Nielsen, M. Appel, K. Pringle, & L. Uggerhøj (Eds.), *Magt og forandring i socialt arbejde*. København: Akademisk Forlag.

Wadskjær, H. (2007). Den sociale hjælpefunktion. In M. Appel Nielsen, K. Pringle, & L. Uggerhøj (Eds.), *Magt og forandring i socialt arbejde*. København: Akademisk Forlag.

Open Access This chapter is distributed under the terms of the Creative Commons Attribution 4.0 International License (http://creativecommons.org/licenses/by/4.0/), which permits use, duplication, adaptation, distribution, and reproduction in any medium or format, as long as you give appropriate credit to the original author(s) and the source, a link is provided to the Creative Commons license, and any changes made are indicated.

The images or other third party material in this book are included in the work's Creative Commons license, unless indicated otherwise in the credit line; if such material is not included in the work's Creative Commons license and the respective action is not permitted by statutory regulation, users will need to obtain permission from the license holder to duplicate, adapt or reproduce the material.

9

Ex-prisoners' Need for Legal Aid in Denmark

Annette Olesen

Introduction

This chapter examines and discusses the legal vacuum ex-prisoners face after being released from prison in Denmark, which makes them feel abandoned while facing their cross-legal and non-legal problems—a time when there is a high-risk of recidivism (Roxell 2009; Graunbøl et al. 2010). Legal aid studies have not only shown that lower-class individuals have complex problems, but also demonstrated that these disadvantaged groups are less likely to take their problems to the legal system and to take legal action (see e.g., Smith 1919; Carlin and Howard 1965; Abel-Smith et al. 1973; Eskeland and Finnes 1973; Eidesen et al. 1975; Sejr 1977; Lid 1981).[1] Within the rich Norwegian tradition of providing legal aid services and doing legal aid research critical voices have been raised. For example, Mathiesen (1975) has argued that legal aid offered to disadvantaged population groups seemed to meet a range of structural barriers in society. These structural barriers, however, did not limit or otherwise erode

A. Olesen (✉)
Department of Sociology and Social Work, Aalborg University, Denmark

the legal aid offers directed to the top of the social hierarchy; they only negatively affected the societal bottom (Mathiesen 1975, p. 189). Similarly, Eskeland questioned whether legal aid has the potential to act as a 'problem-solver' for all population groups or meet the needs of the disadvantaged (Eidesen et al. 1975, p. 10). According to the larger body of critical legal aid research, 'access to justice' is unequal as it depends on one's income level and social position in society.

If we change our focus slightly and study these critical legal aid research findings from a law *in* society perspective combined with a linguistic approach, it is possible to identify complex explanations of why disadvantaged citizens tend not to approach the legal system for assistance as part of a transformation process. In their 1981 study on the origin of legal cases, Felstiner et al. (1981) suggested that a problem has to undergo a transformation they called the *naming-blaming-claiming process* before the problem can be introduced to and enter the legal system. The naming transformation requires that the wronged party reflect on and voice his/her problem as a violation; the blaming transformation involves the wronged party identifying the party which caused the problem; and the claiming transformation requires the wronged party to confront the party which violated them, and ask the party to remedy the mistake. If the problem is not solved between the parties the conflict can form the basis of a legal case. The naming-blaming-claiming process is demanding, and the wronged party needs to face this transformation of the problem with sufficient mental, social, and linguistic resources to meet the legal system's unconscious expectations of collaboration and negotiation (Felstiner et al. 1981; see also Jefferson 1988; Pomerantz 1978; Newman 2013). Thus, the wronged party needs to be familiar with their legal rights and obligations to be able to name, blame, and claim the problem as a potential legal case. The naming-blaming-claiming process can provide us with knowledge about what happens before social problems are taken to the legal system and transformed into legal cases, and thereby also contribute to an understanding of the many challenges faced by potential but reluctant legal aid clients, which inhibit them from taking legal action.

This chapter's main focus and target group, ex-prisoners, like many of the poor population groups included in the International and Nordic legal aid research, are in need of support even before they have named, blamed, or claimed legal action, as they need encouragement to go through with the process of making a social problem into a legal issue (see e.g., Eskeland and Finne 1973; Eidesen et al. 1975; Sejr 1977). Outreaching legal aid is therefore an opportunity to supply legal assistance to ex-prisoners with specific and complex problems. 'Outreach' is a strategy employed by legal aid practitioners to assist these 'hard-to-reach' citizens in locations they frequent and feel at home in, and where they can develop an equal dialogue to identify potential problems that should be named, blamed, and claimed, and enter the legal system (Gotfredsen 2004; Lied 2011). However, outreaching legal aid raises yet another challenge because, even though ex-prisoners often have an immediate need for legal and non-legal support post-release (see e.g., Petersilia 2003; Leverentz 2014) we cannot pinpoint a common denominator for these citizens, apart from their former criminal offence. Ex-prisoners are, therefore, a challenging group to reach with legal aid, as once they have left prison they can no longer be located in any particular place or area.

This chapter examines ex-prisoners' need for legal aid and how legal aid could be organised, to fit in with their living conditions and the many hardships they face post-release in Denmark. First, the material based on a larger qualitative study of prison release in Denmark (Olesen 2013a) is outlined. Next, there is an outline of the existing, targeted legal support to ex-prisoners and a discussion of the ex-prisoners' complex and interrelated legal and non-legal problems. This is followed by an examination of the ex-prisoners' struggle to name their interrelated problems as legal issues and a discussion about how these interrelated problems cannot be considered as isolated rules; on the contrary, they must be dealt with as an intertwined web of various regulatory mechanisms that challenge general distinctions between legal domains and disciplines. After this discussion, the focus moves to the naming-blaming-claiming transformation process, and ex-prisoners' difficulties in approaching legal services for assistance are discussed. In relation to the ex-prisoners' struggle to name, blame, and claim their legal needs, the final section draws on observations and evaluations from various projects aiming to meet vulnerable citizens' need for legal support and discusses the challenges and opportunities involved in providing legal aid to ex-prisoners in Denmark.

Material and Methods

The chapter applies a theoretical and methodological argument combining perceptions from Bourdieusian reflexive sociology (Bourdieu 1977, 1990, 1996; Bourdieu and Wacquant 1992) and law *in* society research (Engel and Yngvesson 1984; Ewick and Silbey 1998; Silbey 1992, 2005). The study is based on face-to-face, in-depth, semi-structured interviews and follow-up interviews with reoffenders from Denmark with former pre-prison, in-prison, and post-prison experience. The participants are all men, aged 18 or older, and able to speak and comprehend Danish. Interviews took place over a 2.5-year period between June 2010 and November 2012, and the final sample includes 77 interviews with 41 reoffenders, a number of unstructured observations and e-mail correspondence, text messages, and telephone conversations with the reoffenders and some of their family members and friends. Of the 41 participants 38 were initially recruited from one open prison and one closed prison in Denmark. The remaining three participants were recruited through staff at a drop-in centre for ex-prisoners. The settings for the follow-up interviews were places where the participants felt most comfortable: their cars, homes, coffee bars, pubs, etc., all over Denmark. The recruitment strategy ensured a range of reoffenders; their ages ranged from 20 to 60 years (median = 34), 25 of them were in a permanent relationship or married, 18 had children, seven had ethnic minority backgrounds, 26 had spent part or all of their childhood in institutions or foster families or had been under special observation, 14 had not completed secondary school, 15 had never been officially employed, and 16 were connected to (semi)organised criminal groups or outlawed motorcycle gangs. The names of the interviewees have been replaced by pseudonyms. First-round interviews (n = 41) were concerned with reoffenders' pre-prison, in-prison, and post-prison experiences and living conditions. The initial semi-structured interview guide focused on reoffenders' experiences of, and interaction with, their (former) employers, landlords, teachers, with the police, the Tax Authority, bailiffs, social workers, job centres, family members, and friends, etc., to uncover the legal and non-legal effects of the social, mental, physical, and legal process of release. Participants who were released from prison within two years were asked after the interview to participate in one or more follow-up interviews during their re-entry into society. Second-round interviews (n = 21) were conducted shortly after release to provide first-hand insight into the newly released prisoners' particular experiences of, and approaches to, the many hardships they faced while trying to (re)establish everyday life in their local community. Third-round interviews (n = 10), fourth-round interviews (n = 4), and one fifth-round interview were conducted between approximately two months and two years post-release. These follow-up interviews elaborated on the previous interviews and covered how the ex-prisoners' plans for their life outside prison regarding housing, education, employment, finances, criminal activity, and social relations were put into action. Ex-prisoners were also encouraged to discuss the legal barriers they met in their criminal or law-abiding life post-prison, and to describe their need for legal aid. This analysis includes data from all parts of the interviews but focuses on direct questions regarding social, mental, and legal problems, and the reoffenders' need for legal support.

Lack of Legal Support for Ex-prisoners

Before the findings of this study are introduced, the situation of ex-prisoners in need of legal aid in Denmark will be briefly outlined. Scandinavian prison studies have shown that the majority of prisoners have complex legal, financial, social, mental, and addiction problems (Skardhamar 2002; Friestad and Hansen 2004; Kyvsgaard 1989, 1999; Clausen 2013; Nilsson 2002). However, unlike alcohol or drug addiction treatment, legal and financial problem-solving are not given high priority while the prisoners are serving their sentence. Their financial problems are met by a temporary reprieve deferring repayment of their debts, and their legal cases are usually placed on hold during incarceration (Ramsbøl and Rasmussen 2009; Ramsbøl 2003). The lack of action on prisoners' legal and financial problems and need for assistance means that, post-release, they meet a number of legal challenges they were spared from during incarceration but now have to confront in a challenging time period. Generally, the Danish Prison Service does not provide structured, goal-oriented legal assistance or debt counselling, even though one could argue that prison time seems like an obvious opportunity to help prisoners improve their living standard and obtain an overview of the many legal and financial hardships waiting on the outside: hardships that are often unknown to first-time offenders but considerable for reoffenders (Olesen 2013a). Consequently, newly released prisoners are seriously burdened with cross-legal and non-legal problems while trying to re-enter society.

Prisoners who serve their full time have neither demands nor support from the Supervision Authority, and they have to navigate the legal system on their own. Parolees, on the other hand, have to participate in regular meetings with the Supervision Authority, which has a dual role of control and support. However, in a qualitative study of the Danish Supervision Authority, Rönneling et al. (2011) found that probation officers felt their work was very time-consuming, with many conflicting deadlines. Because of this, the probation officers explained, they prioritised and allocated resources to the parolees, who they found to have the best potential to live a law-abiding life. This strategy ensured a certain success rate, which gave probation officers work motivation (Rönneling et al. 2011). If a Supervision Authority is short on financial and human resources, this challenges the important role of probation officers as 'problem noticers' that could help the parolee to name, blame, and claim some of their problems to the relevant legal institution. The importance of, and challenges to, the cross-sectoral collaboration between the Prison Service, Supervision Authority, and the Social Services in Denmark has resulted in a project called the 'Schedule of the Good Release', launched in 2010 and implemented nationwide (Ramsbøl and Rasmussen 2009; Ramsbøl 2003). The ambition to improve release is novel but the project consists exclusively of guidelines, without any codified obligations binding the authorities to comply with them (see also Olesen and Storgaard 2017 [forthcoming]). Therefore, neither prisoners released on parole, nor prisoners released after serving their full sentence are met with any 'legal readiness' or 'pre-release kit' to deal with the legal barriers they face while rejoining the society.

The Danish state has done nothing about offering legal aid to such specific groups as prisoners and ex-prisoners, and, consequently, a few non-profit organisations have launched various projects offering legal aid to prisoners and ex-prisoners. These private initiatives thus undertake the responsibility for rehabilitation that the state renounces, making criminal justice rely on the ability of private and community organisations to meet the legal needs of prisoners and ex-prisoners. However, the few legal aid organisations working with this group are dependent on private funds and funds from a special funding pool for the charitable social services, which makes their resources, and projects for their clients limited and discontinuous.

Ex-prisoners' Multifaceted Problems

This section reports findings on the ex-prisoners' perceptions and reactions to their living standards and post-prison experiences of re-entering society in a 'legal aid vacuum', highlighting the complex and interrelated problems they face. Findings identified the ex-prisoners' main concerns to be their need for income and housing while re-entering society. Furthermore, the findings showed how the ex-prisoners' lives were mostly characterised by multifaceted problems which were complex and interconnected. The problems most often raised by the interviewees concerned financial distress, debt, lack of education, few, if any, connections to the labour market, few, if any, pro-social relations, mental turmoil, health problems, and violent behaviour, together with drug and alcohol addiction. None of them faced only one, or a few, of these legal and non-legal problems—they all struggled with numerous problems (see also Friestad and Hansen 2004; Lid 1981, pp. 35–39). Their everyday difficulties were seldom pinpointed directly in our conversations but mostly discussed in connection with the local authorities' involvement in their problems. The ex-prisoners' unvoiced and indirect approach to their problems underlined their inability to name-blame-claim the problem and translate the social issue into a legal case. This section identifies how the two main legal concerns relating to income and housing were affected and problematised by the ex-prisoners' complex lives.

Need for an Income Combined with Complex Legal and Non-legal Problems Post-prison

A large body of criminological research has suggested employment to be one of the key factors for a successful re-entry into society (see e.g., Skardhamar and Telle 2012; Uggen 2000). However, conviction and serving prison sentences entailed many informal punishments (see e.g., Travis 2002, pp. 15–36; 2005, p. 64), which made it difficult for the ex-prisoners to meet the demands of the employment market. Every interviewee who had experience with official job-seeking described how they were challenged by their criminal records and gaps in their employment history, or by their history of no, or weak, employment and education. James, a middle-aged reoffender, voiced the general experience of job-seeking ex-prisoners: *'I kinda stopped believing in it … when you look at the job advertisements that all want students with long educations and no criminal records, which I can't compete with. I got some giant gaps in my CV.'*[2] Existing studies confirm these collateral consequences that have been shown to decrease even low-skilled employment opportunities for ex-prisoners (Pager 2003; Holzer et al. 2006; Raphael 2011; Visher et al. 2008; Holzer 1996, 2009).

The findings demonstrated that another common barrier post-prison that challenged the ex-prisoners' employment status was their lack of financial incentives to obtain official employment and receive a reported income, because of the threat of debt recovery by the Tax Authority. However, existing studies have argued that a relatively high income level decreased the risk of criminal relapse (Grogger 1998; Bernstein and Houston 2000), while indebtedness post-prison was considered a criminal risk factor (Harris et al. 2010; Olesen 2013a; Bannon et al. 2010; Pogrebin et al. 2014). Nevertheless, the Danish state has a right to recourse against criminal offenders to recover the necessary legal costs of their trial (Act no. 1308/2014, part 91).[3] This left the interviewees and the majority of released prisoners in Denmark heavily indebted to the state (Olesen 2013a, b, 2014; Recommendation no. 1547/2014). The ex-prisoners were supposed to repay their legal costs regardless of their income level, and without any actual opportunity for debt relief (Olesen 2013b). If the Tax Authority found that the ex-prisoners had no economic latitude the Tax Authority would give them a temporary reprieve. If, however, the Tax Authority, reckoned that the ex-prisoners had economic latitude, then they faced 'voluntary compulsion' to enter an instalment agreement, or the Tax Authority would withhold a portion of the ex-prisoners' monthly income before it was paid. Thus, the imposition of legal costs helped undermine the ex-prisoners' incentive to work (Olesen 2013a). Seeing no, or poor, opportunities to enter the labour market, and no immediate financial gain from obtaining a job, the vast majority of the newly released prisoners began their lives on the outside by going to the Social Services to seek social security benefit (see also Tranæs et al. 2008).[4] However, to avoid losing welfare entitlements, they came up against unemployment legislation that obligated them to perform verifiable individual job searches, job training, work-related activities, frequent meetings with caseworkers, etc.—legal obligations the ex-prisoners often struggled to satisfy because of anger management challenges and their various kinds of post-prison social phobia (see also Hochstetler et al. 2004).

Housing Need Combined with Complex Post-prison Legal and Non-legal Problems

Permanent housing has been identified as a factor protecting against criminal behaviour, like the abovementioned factors of income and employment (Williams et al. 2012; Gowan 2002; Bradley et al. 2001). The importance of housing was also reflected in the anxiety of most of the interviewees to secure accommodation pre-release. In Denmark, prisoners are generally released on parole after serving two thirds of their sentence, if they fulfil the requirements of having an address or temporary place to stay. In situations where the ex-prisoners had to rely on addresses of friends or families to meet the requirement of a temporary residence, they often faced the hidden challenge of legislation regarding housing benefit. The problem arose when the pre-parolee's release address was in receipt of housing benefit, because the extra tenant at the address would invalidate the original tenant's eligibility for housing benefit. A large number of the prisoners' acquaintances received housing benefit, which further complicated the prisoners' housing situation pre-release. Many of the interviewees, therefore, had to seek accommodation pre-release, and many said that they needed help and support to deal with this issue. However, according to the interviewees, the informal understanding between them and their contact person in prison was that there was an 'one-offer-policy' that made the prisoners feel they could not turn a housing offer down without risking their chance to secure the required address pre-parole. Applying for housing as a prisoner is challenging because they are often unable to apply through private agencies; on some occasions they also have to hand over responsibility for the negotiation on a house offer to their contact person in prison; they cannot always get permission to view a house, and have to decide without having full information. Existing studies support this finding, arguing that disadvantaged citizens that have named, blamed, and claimed their problem and entered the legal system often find they are excluded from the decision-making relating to their legal case, and that they are also ignorant of exactly what legal consequences the case handlers' choices will have on their living situation (see e.g., Newman 2013; Newman and Ugwudike 2014). Moreover, housing legislation reduces vulnerable prisoners' chances of getting housing because only a limited amount of council housing is offered to ex-prisoners because council housing policy aims to ensure multi-tenancy across heterogeneous resources. Complicating the prisoners' housing situation even further was the fact that the property on offer in the rental market seldom matched their expected financial situation post-release. The findings showed that, to become eligible for release on parole, many prisoners made compromises when seeking housing: that is, they faced a rent they could not afford post-release, or they had to move into tough neighbourhoods they did not wish to live in, or the move-in date did not remotely match their release date. These problems arose very often because the prisoners felt insecure due to lack of legal support, and this added to their fear of being homeless or losing their opportunity to be released on parole. Simon, a former drug addict, who had become clean in prison and might now get release on parole if he managed to meet the accommodation requirements, described some general considerations about the housing situation pre-release:

> 'They're throwing me in the ghetto every time, even though they know that's where the drugs are, that's where all the troubles are … I mean crime. They place you there cos that's where there's a flat available. It's not like they'll think "well, we better be careful, we better place him where it's a bit more quiet." They don't … They just have to offer me one flat then they're off the hook. "If that's not good enough for you, sort it out yourself."'

Like many of the other prisoners, Simon was worried about missing an opportunity for getting released on parole; at the same time, he also worried about ending up in the same environment that had driven him to drug use and criminal activities several times, and caused him to wind up in prison. Legal support for prisoners is important because prisoners without support mostly chose to accept housing offers in disadvantaged neighbourhoods, thinking they had no other choice. Nevertheless, they all expected their stay to be temporary and were surprised when they experienced how difficult it was to give their landlords notice, because their creditors levied distress on their deposit.[5] Once distress had been levied, the indebted ex-prisoners had no, or very few, options to secure a deposit for a new home because their financial vulnerability made it more or less impossible to take out a bank loan or make savings plans. Neither could the ex-prisoners apply to their local authority for a new residence deposit loan because they had generally already taken out such a loan without paying it back, and public loans for residence deposits are restricted to a maximum of one per citizen. Likewise, lack of economic latitude made it extremely challenging for most ex-prisoners to cover moving expenses and relocation costs, and the feeling of being 'chained' to an undesired home was common among the ex-prisoners. At first sight these challenges could be seen as personal and social problems but they all emerged from interrelated legal barriers developed before or during incarceration, and lack of legal support in prison made legal problems faced post-release appear even more widespread and central to the ex-prisoners' everyday lives (Olesen 2013a).

Debt and Criminal History Challenge Income and Housing

Previous findings have shown how pre-released and newly released prisoners' concerns about their income and housing were exacerbated by their multifaceted problems, which included a sanctioning unemployment policy practice and constrained housing policy practices that did not take into account this group's complicated lives and vulnerability. The lack of legal support for prisoners and ex-prisoners contributed to a feeling that they were facing these problems on their own, which led to their decisions determined by ignorance and distress. Furthermore, the findings suggested that the ex-prisoners' attempt to prioritise income and housing was made even more difficult when encounters with the police and bailiffs were taken into account. The ex-prisoners described how debt recovery made it detrimental to earn a reported wage. Liam (28), who had recently been released from prison, had never held official employment due to his debt for legal costs. He says he '… *mostly had unreported work and earned unreported money cos I just thought they* [the creditors] *could go to hell for all I care … it doesn't pay to work.*' The sum to be paid by indebted ex-prisoners is calculated by the Tax Authority based on a fixed disposable amount. The difference between the pay received and the fixed disposable amount is taken directly to cover the debt, which leaves the officially employed ex-prisoner with approximately the same income as a social security recipient. The vast majority of the interviewees, therefore, preferred to be paid informally or 'make' unofficial money (by committing crime) to avoid the Tax Authority's debt collection. However, an unreported income made any consumption or expenditure open to question, which triggered yet more problems. The ex-prisoners' spending patterns, criminal history, and public debt stemming from criminal matters aroused the police's suspicion about criminal activity, and the bailiffs' suspicion about default on debt payments. This suspicion meant that the ex-prisoners frequently faced home, car, and body searches by the police as well as visits from bailiffs (Olesen 2013a).

Whether or not the ex-prisoners were willing to meet the payment deadlines, the Tax Authority could always enforce such debt strategy actions as levying the debtor's bank account and registering an interest on the debtor's land or assets to secure (extra) debt payment (The Danish Guidance and Directions for Recovery 2010). Thus, ex-prisoners' everyday life was deeply affected by debt collection law and tax law, and their families were included in this tangled web of legal regulations that controlled even very private aspects of the lives of ex-prisoners and their families: household, savings, future investment plans, etc. The 'threat' of police searches and bailiff visits as part of debt collection actions challenged the ex-prisoners' rights to private property, ownership, and privacy in general, and contributed to the use of counterfeit ownership documents, fictive households, and unofficial addresses, which further complicated their everyday lives.

Many of the ex-prisoners said they felt alone and unsure how to tackle the debt recovery initiatives from the Tax Authority. The usual reaction was to call the Tax Authority; they would then be put on hold for hours before they finally got through to one of the Tax Authority's employees who '… *is careful not to say anything more than you can read on the web* [recalled in a sarcastic tone]. *She can't even give me a fucking answer? It's my life she's dealing with and I've been waiting for hours. But they don't care. As long as they can't be held to account for anything it's ok by them …*' As regards their debt recovery problems, ex-prisoners often mentioned that they could not get in contact with decision-making authorities within the Tax Authority and therefore felt unable to take control over their own lives. If, however, they did manage to transform their problems into a legal issue and present it to the right relevant people in the Tax Authority, lacking professional experience with debt negotiations, they often failed to negotiate a favourable instalment agreement before the Tax Authority had withheld a portion of their income, calculated on the basis of a (low) fixed disposable amount.[6] In situations such as these, the ex-prisoners needed legal assistance but seldom knew who to turn to or who to trust.

Intertwined Legal Aid Approach

The abovementioned examples of the ex-prisoners' multifaceted legal and non-legal challenges illustrate a need for targeted legal aid based on knowledge of their situation, social world view, and living standards. Based on this observation it is argued that to successfully deal with the problems of ex-prisoners (and those of many other social groups) necessitates an intertwined legal aid approach.[7] Looking at each of the ex-prisoners' legal problems in isolation would unquestionably draw a picture of a disadvantaged group: social workers specialising in social security legislation would, for example, advise the ex-prisoners on their social security issues and help them file for social security benefit and other subsidies; legal debt advisors would advise them to ask creditors for a reprieve, or help them seek debt relief; social workers specialising in social housing legislation would look for temporary accommodation and put the ex-prisoner's name down for a council flat or the like.[8] If we stick to this 'traditional' approach, where legal workers primarily pursue objective facts, it may give rise to a case within their legal domain (Mather et al. 1995, p. 289; Mather et al. 2001; Eekelaar et al. 2000; Melville and Laing 2008). However, if the cross-legal and non-legal problems and subjective experiential realities of the ex-prisoners' lives are ignored, potential solutions may come up short in bettering the ex-prisoners' living situation in the long term.

One example of the intertwined legal cluster of problems some of the interviewees faced post-prison challenged the traditional approach to legal case handling: Jayden, a 33-year-old with an impressively long criminal record, had just been released after serving his full prison sentence of 3.5 years. He was released to homelessness; he stayed temporarily at a friend's place and applied for social security benefits at the job centre to get money for an apartment deposit. He was told that he qualified for social security benefit but had to contact a bank to set up a particular bank account (Easy Account) because all payments from the public sector were paid into Easy Accounts. On visiting a number of banks, however, Jayden found that setting up an Easy Account required an address listed in the Danish National Register (DNR), which Jayden did not have. Therefore, he qualified for social security benefits but could not get them without an Easy Account and a DNR-address. Putting down a deposit for a home (DNR-address) became a great challenge for Jayden, and all ex-prisoners in a similar situation. Applying for a loan for a residence deposit in these situations could be a way to secure a DNR-address, but, as mentioned above, the data suggested that the interviewees' loan applications were usually turned down because they had already taken out such a loan without repaying it. Jayden's housing and income situation therefore remained unresolved. This example highlights two important points; first, it illustrates how a legal case cannot be adequately framed and proceeded in the absence of a thorough understanding of the history of the individual involved and of their overall living situation, which may contribute to their current difficulties or affect the way the case should be handled. Second, the example illuminates how distinctions between legal domains and disciplines are artificial, because laws are interrelated and cannot (in cases like Jayden's) be isolated from one another without serious consequences. Intertwined laws can, in fact, sometimes set off a sort of 'domino effect' in which a legal issue builds momentum for other issues (see also Pleasence et al. 2004). Such 'trigger' problems can put individuals at risk of social exclusion (Pleasence et al. 2006). Tailoring legal aid services and legal assistance to vulnerable clients by comparing the client's case with a contextually close-knit patchwork of cross-disciplinary intertwined laws, financial issues, social relations, and mental issues would contribute to a more holistic legal approach that would make the clients' difficulties less likely to resurface and produce similar recurring difficulties in the future (see also Olesen 2016b).

Difficulties in Transforming Multifaceted Needs into Legal Issues, and Applying for Help

The previous section included examples of how ex-prisoners with multifaceted problems struggled to name their wide-ranging needs for legal support. In this section, I will elaborate on the ex-prisoners' struggles to transform social problems into legal issues and will discuss the challenges and opportunities involved in providing legal aid to ex-prisoners in Denmark.

In two larger surveys of attitudes to the legal systems in England and Wales, and in Scotland, Genn (1999) and Genn and Paterson (2001) have shown that: 60% and 65% of the respondents who had experienced a non-trivial justiciable problem had obtained advice about resolving the problem; 32% and 36% had tried to handle the problem on their own, and 3% and 5% had failed to take any kind of action to deal with the problem (Genn 1999, pp. 67–68; Genn and Paterson 2001, pp. 85–87).[9] These studies showed that the legal institutions managed to reach out to a wider 'audience' in society, and that most of the citizens who had asked for advice had been met positively by the legal representatives. The population groups that preferred to deal with their non-trivial justiciable problem(s) on their own were, like the 'advice-seekers', a very diverse group and they therefore also developed many different self-help strategies. By contrast, Genn categorised the respondents failing to respond to any problem-solving methods as the 'lumpers', and she illustrated how this group was rather homogeneous and could be characterised as having a relatively low income and education level, while not differing significantly in sex or age (Genn 1999, p. 69). Furthermore, the 'lumpers' had more often experienced financial problems and met with unfair actions by the police. By comparing Genn's (1999) and Genn and Paterson's (2001) results with this study's findings, ex-prisoners can be identified as a very complex population group with a particular attitude to the legal system. Several of the interviewees had exhibited deviant behaviour from an early age, and thus encountered the police and the local authorities' psychological or educational rehabilitation programmes, etc. Frequent contact with the authorities had often continued during the interviewees' teenage years and increased in their adult life because of their appearances in court, prison sentences, periods of post-release supervision, visits to job centres, and involvement in local rehousing programmes, etc. These many experiences of being 'inside' the legal system had provided the interviewees with considerable insider-knowledge or quasi-legal awareness of how public legal institutions work and how to interact, and sometimes 'perform', to achieve conditions they considered to be the optimum (see also Olesen 2013a, pp. 50–54; Sandberg 2009). Lucas demonstrates this insider-knowledge when describing his different approaches to avoiding job activation:

Interviewee:	*'I've never joined any activation programmes, but if I had to I would wear my bullet-proof vest.'*
Interviewer:	*'You've never been activated?'*
Interviewee:	*'No I haven't … I always just cracked a lot of bullshit about being sick and so … Jah, well, I do look rather sick* (laughs). *I've come up with a lot of evasive explanations … My woman left me, which was crap and then someone from Social Services sat patting me on my back saying "he's had a tough life"* (laughs). *Stuff like that. Everything like that I could come up with.'*

Lucas stressed how the local authority's records attested to the many bad things he had experienced throughout his childhood, which may have affected his behaviour and way of thinking. However, Lucas takes advantage of his insider-knowledge of how the system works and seeks the social worker's sympathy and understanding to avoid the job activation requirement. The quote also illustrates how Lucas, like many of the other ex-prisoners, was capable of switching from being a victim to becoming a sly, threatening client showing latent violent behaviour by wearing a bullet-proof vest. Several of the interviewees recalled how their local authority records have supported and legitimised their 'performance' both as a victim and as an angry, threatening client. From this perspective, ex-prisoners could be studied as subjects who seek advice, but enter the legal system with a kind of embodied knowledge of how to perform and navigate within the system. However, the data showed that the ex-prisoners mainly asked for legal advice, or took legal action, in two particular situations: first, in crises where they had to act to obtain or sustain their rights to basic needs. They often ignored their problems and failed to name them or apply for help until they faced imminent eviction, welfare cuts, etc. In such crises they tended to approach their problems by frequently contacting their social worker, generally preferring to involve as many parties as possible (social workers from different departments, probation officers, organisations, etc.) in their case. The adoption of this 'aggressive tactic' is caused, among other things, by the ex-prisoners' lack of time (time is money) to wait for the case proceeding (see also Olesen 2013a, pp. 114–115)[10] and their mistrust of legal representatives, doubt about the fair handling of the case, and the outcome assessment. Like some of the ex-prisoners in this study, the 'lumpers' in Genn's studies also voiced their fear, powerlessness, and previous negative experiences of, and present destructive beliefs towards, the legal system (Genn 1999, pp. 70–71).[11] The second type of situation in which ex-prisoners would approach the legal system was when they had identified a legal loophole and, by taking legal action, could outsmart the system (see also Gustafson 2011). In these situations the ex-prisoners often used their insider-knowledge and quasi-legal awareness to target soft spots in the legal system. A reoffender called Tom, who owed approximately 2 million DKK [268,000 €] in public debt, demonstrated this approach when referring to his relationship with his defence lawyer during his time in detention:

Interviewee: *'…I had a defence lawyer who I told just to put everything on the bill. He came from Aarhus and he visited me on Zealand* [about three hours away by car]. *Last time I was detained for two years and he came once a week…'*

Interviewer: *'Why did you decide that this* [the legal case] *should be so costly?'*

Interviewee: *'… basically, I don't care. I don't have any plans to repay any of the money.*[12] *When I have served my sentence I have paid society back for my wrongdoing and I don't intend paying back more than that.'*

Another interviewee, who was also heavily indebted due to legal costs, spoke as follows about his attitude to the Danish state and the legal system post-prison: *'When I signed the divorce decree I wrote that we had not lived together for eight months even though it was a lie. But this way she* [the ex-wife] *got eight months of child support. I just did it to get as much money out of the public purse as possible. And afterwards we split the amount fifty-fifty … I still pay child support to my ex-wife even though the kids live with me. She might as well get the money because it doesn't affect my financial situation.'* [Actually, the Danish State pays child support to the ex-prisoner's ex-wife and the state therefore has the right to seek recourse from the ex-prisoner].

The findings suggest that ex-prisoners not only expect to achieve social or financial gain from their legal actions but also seek some sort of 'revenge' on the Danish state by increasing their public debt which they have no intention of repaying.[13] The two very different situations that mainly triggered requests for advice or legal action further highlight the ex-prisoner's complex, equivocal position of being both a victim and a sly, threatening client in the legal system.

Without neglecting the interviewees' different approaches to the legal system, their quasi-legal awareness, and insider-knowledge, I would, in the following, like to elaborate on those interviewees who wanted to get control over their lives and needed legal advice to find concrete solutions to their multifaceted problems. These ex-prisoners, despite their many previous experiences of the legal system, did not give an impression of being privileged when it came to naming, blaming, and claiming their problems to potential legal advisors in their quest for a sustainable improvement of their living standards. On the contrary, the findings suggested that, in more than one sense, it was a major challenge for the ex-prisoners first to identify and name-blame-claim a problem that was immense and intertwined with other problems, and second to ask for help, which conflicted with their self-understanding, and voice their need for help to local authority practitioners they often considered untrustworthy. Being more or less 'brought up' in the legal system or the Social Services, therefore, did not seem to improve the ex-prisoners' legal position in long-lasting ways.[14]

One problem that was generally difficult to grasp and therefore difficult to name, was the ex-prisoners' debt: '*When you're released you'll receive a pile of bills. For each month you've been in prison the amount of bills just increases and you then receive them all at once—there you go.*' Such debt was mostly a combination of public debt, private debt, and so-called 'street debt' (from illegal moneylenders) and ex-prisoners with an official address typically face an endless number of bills, demands, and reminders from their creditors post-prison. Despite the significant impact the debt had on the ex-prisoners' lives the interviews were full of remarks such as '*I've no idea how much I owe … actually I don't really remember how much money I owe, I lost track* [of the debt]*, I gave up counting them* [the creditors].' Debt had often become immense and incalculable. The ex-prisoners, who at some point had tried to face up to their debt problem, explained that it seemed incredibly difficult to take control of the problem and get an overview of their new bills, old bills, reminders, and reminders about reminders, etc. They were, moreover, challenged when it came to knowing the exact loan amount, because of the mounting interest. Debt consolidation was, however, related to yet another challenge regarding creditors' sale of unpaid debts to collection agencies. Instead of waiving the claim, the ex-prisoners' original creditors may sell their debt to debt-collection agencies (which may resell the debt to another debt-collection agency, and so on). In such cases, the debt became a commodity and the debt-collection agencies had the right to proceed against the ex-prisoners for the loan. Information about the assigned claim that should have been send to debtor may have got lost because of the debtor's incarceration, or lack of attention, or desire to open letters from debt-collection agencies. Thus, ex-prisoners' debt problems generally involved an unknown amount, and nameless, and sometime countless, creditors—amounts and creditors they could not check. The fact that they did not know who their creditors were increased the complexity of the ex-prisoners' debt position and made it harder for them to transform their specific problem into a legal issue and present it to legal advisors. Ex-prisoners were therefore often in need of legal aid to help them in the naming-blaming-claiming transformation process, and with addressing their legal issues relating to debt remission, debt relief, etc.

Trust and Seeking Comfort Amid Distrust and Discomfort

A 25-year-old reoffender called Jackson voiced his feelings about being referred to the local authority to ask for help:

Interviewee: *'Like everybody else I feel like a number in the system. You're just the next in the row … that's how I feel. I don't think they help you in any way. If you wanna get help you need to contact them and more or less beg for it.'*
Interviewer: *'And that's not your style?'*
Interviewee: *'No, not really … I'm not the type who asks for help. If people wanna talk to me they'll have to contact me. And if people wanna help me they have to contact … I can't do it myself … I mean I don't ask for anything.'*

Jackson's experiences with the local authorities is similar in many ways to the stories a lot of the interviewees told about prison: their feelings of impersonalisation; the unequal balance of power between them and the prison officers; the unwritten rules about minding their own business and avoiding situations where they could be turned down (see also Minke 2012; Ugelvik 2011). Jackson's statement could also be compared to one of Carlin and Howard's findings: they argued that lower-income individuals in particular are less likely to take legal action if they have been in contact with the courts (Carlin and Howard 1965, p. 425; see also Goudriaan et al. 2006). Genn has suggested that the experience of problem-solving in court or of tribunal adjudication is more stressful, more out of control, and less complete than resolving problems through agreement (Genn 1999). Distrust and discomfort could therefore also derive from the ex-prisoners' previous stressful experiences of the criminal court, bailiff's court, and/or of meetings with, and final settlements from, e.g., the State Administration. If we consider the feelings of discomfort and distrust voiced by Jackson when we look at how ex-prisoners try to transform their multifaceted problems into legal cases, it contributes to an understanding of ex-prisoners' negatively quasi-legal experiences from previous encounters with local authorities and their feeling of being left to their own devices (see also Ricciardelli et al. 2015). The reoffender called Caden summed up the approach to and difficulties with problem-solving and searching for legal assistance of many ex-prisoners: '*I like to handle my own problems you know but I can't really cope with the situation anymore.*' Logan, who struggled to qualify as an early retirement pensioner and was on a small budget, had the familiar 'hostility towards the system approach': '*They're so fucking annoying. I'm just sick of all this authority and government shit. I just wanna get it out of my system.*' What the ex-prisoners said about their relations with local authorities was generally two-faced because they would prefer to be financially, legally, and mentally independent of the system but, at the same time, they experienced the law and legal system as '… a web-like enclosure in which they are "caught"' (Sarat 1990, p. 345). Linking these findings to Genn's (1999) and Genn and Paterson's (2001) studies, the ex-prisoners must be considered a complex group with previous legal experiences that have provided them with insider-knowledge and quasi-legal awareness.

Their attitude to the legal system puts them in limbo: they will approach the legal system in situations that challenge them on their basic needs or give them an opportunity to take advantage of the system's loopholes. However, when it came to non-trivial justiciable problems and case handling with a more interrelated, long-term perspective, the ex-prisoners 'lumped', as they struggled to transform their multifaceted problems into legal issues and to ask local authority practitioners for help, because the ex-prisoners often found them untrustworthy. Taken together, the findings indicate that the ex-prisoners managed to ask for advice and to play the system when it came to 'performing' as a victim or as a sly, threatening client but failed to secure long-lasting stability in their turbulent lives.

New Legal Aid Initiative: Cross-functional Mentors Pre- and Post-release

The ex-prisoners' strained relationships with local authorities and legal institutions in general, and their difficulties in approaching legal services for assistance, could be a 'chicken and egg situation' because it is impossible to identify whether the ex-prisoners' distrust of these institutions has arisen from bad experiences with case work handling; whether it is a result of social, cultural, and language barriers to effective communication, or whether it is a mixture of the two. However, this study shows that the ex-prisoners need legal aid assistance to cope with their time-consuming multiplicity of legal and non-legal problems. Now, the question to be discussed is how the full amount of legal assistance they need can be provided to some of the most vulnerable and distrustful ex-prisoners.

If we accept that the appropriate provision of legal assistance for disadvantaged clients requires detailed knowledge of the legal issues, the clients' experience, their responses to these issues, and the outcome of these issues, this calls for a multi-agency approach. This subsection therefore moves on to a discussion about the challenges and possibilities of providing legal support to ex-prisoners with a cluster of legal and non-legal problems. The discussion draws on experiences and evaluations from different initiatives aiming to resolve a disparate client group's multiple problems when approaching inter-professional and multi-agency collaboration. One approach would be to identify the most appropriate gatekeeper that could refer clients to the most appropriate legal and non-legal systems. Melville and Laing (2010) have shown how family lawyers, despite their awareness of the clients' cross-legal and non-legal problems, and their specific training in directing clients to other legal or non-legal assistance, still avoided referring them to other services and generally found it difficult to place non-legal issues within a legal framework. Without abandoning the multi-agency approach Melville and Laing, however, concluded that lawyers may not be the most suitable gatekeeper of different legal and non-legal support services. On the basis of their findings, they addressed some important considerations about the gatekeepers' qualifications and professional background, and questioned whether there was a need for not just one gatekeeper but for multiple pathways (Melville and Laing 2010, p. 186; see also Melville and Laing 2008; Courmaerlos et al. 2006). These considerations were (unknowingly) challenged in the EXODUS (ex-offenders discharged under supervision) programme introducing inter-agency collaboration of core agencies catering for ex-prisoners at the same location in Southeast England (Wood et al. 2009). The programme provides a way to develop holistic post-prison services by putting the released prisoners at the centre of their support, and offering services around their needs. The EXODUS inter-agency collaboration was accompanied by a decreased reoffending rate, and the ex-prisoners involved were more satisfied with the support they received (Wood et al. 2009; see also Cinamon and Hoskins 2006; Robinson and Raynor 2006; Salmon 2004). Furthermore, Noone (2007) has shown how a similar 'Legal Aid Centre' (Banyule Community Health Centre) run in the socially disadvantaged neighbourhood of West Heidelberg, Australia, meet potential clients with a multi-disciplinary approach offering legal and non-legal services. The 'Legal Aid Centre' staff found that:

> 'Many people who contact the Legal Service are unsure whether their problem is a legal one and a major proportion of staff time is spent with people at this initial stage … The process of clarifying the actual problem,

identifying courses of action for the individual to choose from and other agencies for the person to contact for assistance takes up a lot of staff time. Many who contact the Legal Service are upset or distressed and do not know exactly what their problem is or where they should go for help.' (Noone 2007, pp. 98–99).

The 'Legal Aid Centre's' gatekeeper-function has shown to be beneficial in the clients' naming-blaming-claiming process, as more clients use the Centre as source of referral, follow through on the referral, and also take up the relevant referral (compared to community centres that do not have a multi-disciplinary approach) (Noone 2007, pp. 99–100). The different multi-agency and inter-agency collaborations are all novel,[15] but do not take the ex-prisoners' known distrust of, and unease with, the legal system into consideration. These mental barriers call for a mentor-mentee relationship that not only works as a gatekeeper to other legal and non-legal services but, actually, (1) identifies the client's underlying concerns ('problem noticer') and helps the ex-prisoners to address their long-term needs by supporting them through the naming-blaming-claiming transformation of the problem, and (2) provides a platform of cross-legal aid offers, based on an understanding of the ex-prisoners' history and living situation (Aarvold and Solvang 2008; Walsh 2004). One can further argue that the mentor-mentee relationship may provide a sense of community when translating legal language and challenging the lawyers' reification of the social problem in legal reasoning (Cain 1983; Travers 1997; Felstiner and Sarat 1997; Newman, 2013), while at the same time leaving space for client responsibility, independence, and empowerment.[16] This study's findings of ex-prisoners' multifaceted problems strengthen the case for a new legal aid initiative in Denmark. The ex-prisoners' need for extended legal aid support could, with advantage, begin in the form of outreach legal aid work in the prisons and during the high-risk period of release, while post-release it might continue as, or develop into, an organised (outreach) legal aid offer matching the ex-prisoners' social and practical need and everyday activities. To accommodate the ex-prisoners' multifaceted problems this flexible organisation of follow-up legal aid services could be provided by a cross-functional team of long-term mentors familiar with intertwined legal and non-legal post-prison problems. However, an important question as yet unanswered (and a question that goes beyond this study's findings and the aim of this chapter) is whether legal aid to ex-prisoners should be organised and offered by the Danish state or outsourced to legal aid offices, companies, charitable contributors, and/or non-profit organisations in the voluntary and private sectors.

Concluding Remarks

This article has shown that newly released prisoners faced multifaceted problems and urgently needed an income and stable housing post-prison. Furthermore, they had significant problems with naming-blaming-claiming their cross-legal and non-legal problems, and their precarious position called for more than guidance and referral to the legal system's various services. Thus, the most vulnerable ex-prisoners needed to get access to flexible legal aid services in order to (re)establish a crime-free life on the outside. The findings showed that to successfully provide ex-prisoners with legal support required an ability to consider their legal and non-legal problems as interrelated and closely related to their living situations. Moreover, the findings supported the view that the various legal areas that affected the lives of the ex-prisoners could not be considered as isolated rules; on the contrary, they must be dealt with as an intertwined web of various regulatory mechanisms challenging the usual distinctions between legal domains and disciplines.

This study's findings, and the very few Danish legal aid initiatives targeting ex-prisoners, point towards a need to develop a new kind of follow-up legal aid support through cross-functional mentoring teams that begins as outreach legal aid offers pre-release, and continues as organised (outreach) legal aid as long as needed post-release. Creating the right circumstances for trusting relationships to be built between ex-prisoners and mentoring teams with cross-functional qualifications and in-depth knowledge of the multiple barriers faced post-prison would support the ex-prisoners' naming-blaming-claiming processes and give rise to tailored casework meeting their specific needs. Developing the mentor-mentee relationship would prepare the pre-released to face their intertwined challenges in the high-risk period post-prison. However, if we fail as society to prepare a reasonable release, fail to meet the newly released prisoner with something other than informal punishment, and do not provide the necessary legal aid through the resettlement transition into society, we all contribute to recidivism and weakening community safety.

Notes

1. For an outline of legal aid research see Hammerslev 2016.
2. All quotes have been loosely translated into English.
3. The necessary costs include the expenses of their appointed defence lawyer, technical investigations such as DNA-tests and investigations to do with accounting data, etc.
4. For a discussion of the Danish state's contradictory legal approaches towards ex-prisoners see Olesen 2016a [forthcoming].
5. The data suggest that reoffenders' expectations, based on years of prison and post-prison experiences meant that they were aware of the challenging housing situation they faced post-release but, as first-time offenders, they had limited knowledge about the legal problems they were about to deal with.
6. Genn (1999) has shown that the majority of the 'self-helpers' who do not get legal advice do not successfully resolve their problems/achieve a resolution by agreement (Genn 1999, pp. 145-50).
7. See also the American Bar Association's task force on holistic lawyering (Moss 1992; Johnston 1994).
8. See also how Eekelaar et al. (2000) found that lawyers divided the legal issues of their clients to avoid the issues becoming too entangled (Eekelaar et al. 2000, pp. 112-113).
9. Genn's (1999) and Genn and Paterson's (2001) respondents who were dealing with money problems, consumer problems, benefit, or schooling problems were most likely to attempt to resolve their problems without obtaining advice, whereas respondents facing divorce or separation, or claiming compensation for an injury were more likely to seek advice.
10. Sarat has discussed welfare recipients' experiences of powerlessness and frustrations regarding red tape and waiting time (Sarat 1990).
11. The general negativity about legal processes is discussed in Genn and Paterson (2001, p. 93).

12. The Danish state pays the defendants' costs for, for example., defence lawyers, but the state has the right to seek recourse from defendants if they are found guilty (and have a disposable income to repay the debt).
13. This chapter does not report the results of analyses of client-lawyer interaction during detention or the clients' strategies for spending or saving money here but they are included in a larger work (Olesen 2013a).
14. For a discussion of empowerment and clientisation see e.g., Järvinen and Gubrium (2013); Bengtsson (2003).
15. For a discussion of the policy and law reform work regarding multidisciplinary legal work and lawyers as professionals as well as collaborators see Trubek and Farnham (2000).
16. See also Moorhead et al. (2003) for a discussion of the difficulties and possiblities relating to including the client's perspective in legal work.

References

Aarvold, R. H., & Solvang, I. L. (2008). *Fra innsatt til utsatt.* Oslo: Røde Kors.
Abel-Smith, B., Zander, M., & Brooke, R. (1973). *Legal problems and the citizen: A study in three London boroughs.* London: Heinemann.
Bannon, A., Nagrecha, M., & Diller, R. (2010). *Criminal justice debt: A barrier to reentry.* New York: Brennan Center for Justice at New York University School of Law.
Bengtsson, S. (2003). Overcoming goal displacement and power displacement in social service provision. *Scandinavian Journal of Disability Research, 5*(3), 262–280.
Bernstein, J., & Houston, E. (2000). *Crime and work.* Washington DC: Economic Policy Institute.
Bourdieu, P. (1977). *Outline of a theory of practice.* Cambridge: Cambridge University Press.
Bourdieu, P. (1990). *The logic of practice.* Cambridge: Polity Press.
Bourdieu, P. (1996). Understanding. *Theory, Culture and Society, 13*(2), 17–37.
Bourdieu, P., & Wacquant, L. J. D. (1992). *An invitation to reflexive sociology.* Chicago: University of Chicago Press.
Bradley, K. R. B., Richardson, O. N., & Slayter, E. (2001). *No place like home: Housing and the ex-prisoner.* Boston: Community Resources for Justice.
Cain, M. (1983). The general practice lawyer and the client. Towards a radical conception. In R. Dingwall & P. Lewis (Eds.), *The sociology of the professions. Lawyers, doctors and others* (pp. 106–130). London: Macmillan.

Carlin, J. E., & Howard, J. (1965). Legal representation and class justice. *U.C.L.A. Law Review, 12*(2), 381–437.

Cinamon, K., & Hoskins, J. (2006). The prolific and other priority offender initiative in practice. *The Journal of Community and Criminal Justice, 53*(2), 154–166.

Clausen, S. (2013). *Fængslet ta'r (stadig) de sidste*. København: Direktoratet for Kriminalforsorgen.

Coumarelos, C., Wei, Z., & Zhou, A. Z. (2006). *Justice made to measure: NSW legal needs survey in disadvantaged areas*. Sydney: Law and Justice Foundation of NSW.

Eekelaar, J., Maclean, M., & Beinart, S. (2000). *Family lawyers: The divorce work of solicitors*. Oxford: Hart Publishing.

Eidesen, A., Eskeland, S., & Mathiesen, T. (1975). *Rettshjelp og samfunnsstruktur*. Oslo: Pax.

Engel, D. M., & Yngvesson, B. (1984). Mapping difficult terrain: Legal culture, legal consciousness, and other hazards for the intrepid explorer. *Law & Policy, 6*(3), 299–307.

Eskeland, S., & Finne, J. (1973). *Rettshjelp*. Oslo: Pax.

Ewick, P., & Silbey, S. S. (1998). *The common place of law: Stories from everyday life*. Chicago: University of Chicago Press.

Felstiner, W. L. F., & Sarat, A. (1997). *Divorce lawyers and their clients: Power and meaning in the legal process*. New York: Oxford University Press.

Felstiner, W., Abel, R., & Sarat, A. (1981). The emergence and transformation of disputes: Naming, blaming, claiming. *Law & Society Review, 15*(3/4), 631–654.

Friestad, C., & Hansen, I. L. S. (2004). *Levekår blant innsatte*. Oslo: Fafo.

Genn, H. (1999). *Paths to justice: What people do and think about going to law*. Oxford: Hart Publishing.

Genn, H., & Paterson, A. (2001). *Paths to justice. Scotland: What people in Scotland think and do about going to law*. Oxford: Hart Publishing.

Gotfredsen, N. W. (2004). 'Gadejura – en nødløsning i en undtagelsestilstand. In S. Dalager & P. Schultz-Jørgensen (Eds.), *Tid til respekt*. Socialpolitisk Forlag: København.

Goudriaan, H., Wittebrood, S., & Nieuwbeerta, P. (2006). Neighbourhood characteristics and reporting crime: Effects of social cohesion, confidence in police effectiveness and socio-economic disadvantage. *British Journal of Criminology, 46*(4), 719–742.

Gowan, T. (2002). The Nexus. *Ethnography, 2/3*(4), 500–534.
Graunbøl, H. M., et al. (2010). *Retur*. Kriminalomsorgen: Oslo.
Grogger, J. (1998). Market wages and youth crime. *Journal of Labor Economics, 16*(4), 756–791.
Gustafson, K. (2011). *Cheating welfare*. New York: New York University Press.
Hammerslev, O. (2016). Retshjælpsforskning. In H. V. G. Pedersen (Ed.), *Juridiske emner ved Syddansk Universitet 2015*. København: Jurist- og Økonomforbundets Forlag.
Harris, A., Evans, H., & Beckett, K. (2010). Drawing blood from stones: Legal debt and social inequality in the contemporary United States. *American Journal of Sociology, 115*(6), 1753–1799.
Hochstetler, A., Murphy, D. S., & Simons, R. L. (2004). Damaged goods: Exploring predictors of distress in prison inmates. *Crime and Delinquency, 50*(3), 43–57.
Holzer, H. J. (1996). *What employers want: Job prospects for less-educated workers*. New York: Russell Sage Foundation.
Holzer, H. J. (2009). Collateral costs: Effects of incarceration on employment and earnings among young workers. In S. Raphael, M. A. Stoll, & S. D. Bushway (Eds.), *Do prisons make us safer?* (pp. 239–266). New York: Russell Sage Foundation.
Holzer, H. J., Raphael, S., & Stoll, M. A. (2006). Perceived criminality, criminal background checks and the racial hiring practices of employers. *Journal of Law and Economics, 49*(2), 451–480.
Järvinen, M. & Gubrium, J. (2013). *Turning troubles into problems: Clientization in human services*. London: Routledge.
Jefferson, G. (1988). On the sequential organization of troubles-talk in ordinary conversation. *Social Problems, 35*(4), 418–441.
Johnston, S. (1994). *Holistic lawyer seeks to help clients help themselves*. American Bar Association, *Bar Leader*, 19(5): pp. 38–39.
Kyvsgaard, B. (1989). *… og fængslet tager de sidste: om kriminalitet, straf og levevilkår*. København: Jurist- og Økonomforbundets Forlag.
Kyvsgaard, B. (1999). *Klientundersøgelsen*. København: Direktoratet for Kriminalforsorgen.
Leverentz, A. M. (2014). *The ex-prisoner's dilemma*. New Brunswick: Rutgers University Press.
Lid, B. (1981). *Fangers rettshjelpsbehov*. Stensilskrifter fra Institutt for Rettssosiologi. Oslo: Universitetet i Oslo.

Lied, C. (2011). *Irriterende til stede: om gatejuristar i Oslo og København*. Det juridiske fakultet, Oslo Universitet.

Mather, L., Maiman, R. J., & McEwen, C. A. (1995). The passenger decides on the destination and i decide on the route: Are divorce lawyers "expensive cab drivers". *International Journal of Law, Policy and the Family, 9*, 286–310.

Mather, L., McEwen, C. A., & Maiman, R. J. (2001). *Divorce lawyers at work: Varieties of professionalism in practice*. Oxford: Oxford University Press.

Mathiesen, T. (1975). Noen konlusjoner om rettshjelp, rettspolitikk og samfunnsstruktur. In A. Eidesen, S. Eskeland, & T. Mathiesen (Eds.), *Rettshjelp og samfunnsstruktur*. Pax.: Oslo.

Melville, A., & Laing, K. (2008). Personal action plans: Evaluating self-management initiatives in family law. *International Journal of Law in Context, 4*(2), 149–167.

Melville, A., & Laing, K. (2010). Closing the gate: Family lawyers as gatekeepers to a holistic service. *International Journal of Law in Context, 6*(2), 167–189.

Minke, L. K. (2012). *Fængslets indre liv*. København: Jurist- og Økonomforbundets Forlag.

Moorhead, R., Sherr, A., & Paterson, A. (2003). What clients know: Client perceptions and legal competence. *International Journal of the Legal Profession, 10*(1), 5–35.

Moss, D. C. (1992). The holistic lawyer. *ABA Journal, 78*(10), 38.

Newman, D. (2013). *Legal aid lawyers and the quest for justice*. Oxford: Hart Publishing.

Newman, D. C., & Ugwudike, P. (2014). Defence lawyers and probation officers: Offenders' allies or adversaries? *International Journal of the Legal Profession, 20*(2), 183–207.

Nilsson, A. (2002). *Fånge i marginalen: uppväxtvillkor, levnedsförhållanden och återfall i brott bland fångar*. Stockholm: Stockholms Universitet.

Noone, M.A. (2007). "They all come in the one door". The transformative potential of an integrated service model: A study of the West Heidelberg Community Legal' Service. In P. Pleasence & A. Buck (Eds.), *Transforming lives: Law and social process* (pp. 93–111). Legal Services Research. Norwich: The Stationery Office.

Olesen, A. (2013a). *Løsladt og gældsat*. København: Jurist- og Økonomforbundets Forlag.

Olesen, A. (2013b). Eftergivelse af gæld vedrørende sagsomkostninger i straffesager. In H. V. G. Pedersen (Ed.), *Juridiske emner ved Syddansk Universitet 2013* (pp. 327–344). København: Jurist- og Økonomforbundets Forlag.

Olesen, A. (2014). Retlige, retssikkerhedsmæssige og resocialiserende omkostninger ved sagsomkostninger i straffesager. *Nordisk Tidsskrift for Kriminalvidenskab, 101*(3), 248–270.

Olesen, A. (2016a) [forthcoming]. Released to the 'battlefield' of the Danish welfare state: A battle between support and personal responsibility. In P.S. Smith & T. Ugelvik (Eds.), *Embraced by the welfare state? Scandinavian penal history, culture and prison practice.* London: Palgrave Macmillan.

Olesen, A. (2016b). 'Retten – et sammenvævet lovkompleks. In H. V. G. Pedersen (Ed.), *Juridiske emner ved Syddansk Universitet 2015.* København: Jurist- og Økonomforbundets Forlag.

Olesen, A. & Storgaard, A. (2017) [forthcoming]. Released from prison in Denmark: Experiences versus ambitions. In R. Armstrong & I. Durnescu (Eds.), *Curtailed freedom: International perspectives of life on parole.* London: Palgrave Macmillan.

Pager, D. (2003). The mark of a criminal record. *American Journal of Sociology, 108*(5), 937–975.

Petersilia, J. (2003). *When prisoners come home.* Oxford: Oxford University Press.

Pleasence, P. et al. (2004). *Causes of action: Civil law and social justice.* Legal Services Commission. Norwich: The Stationery Office.

Pleasence, P., Buck, A. & Balmer, N. (2006). *Causes of action: Civil law and social justice.* Legal Services Research Centre. Norwich: The Stationery Office.

Pogrebin, M., et al. (2014). Employment isn't enough: Financial obstacles experienced by ex-prisoners during the reentry process. *Criminal Justice Review, 39*(4), 394–410.

Pomerantz, A. (1978). Attributions of responsibility: Blamings. *Sociology, 12*(1), 115–121.

Ramsbøl, H. (2003). *Kriminalforsorgens og de sociale myndigheders samarbejde.* Esbjerg: Formidlingscentret for socialt arbejde.

Ramsbøl, H., & Rasmussen, N. (2009). *Projekt God Løsladelse.* København: The National Board of Social Services.

Raphael, S. (2011). Incarceration and prisoner reentry in the United States. *The Annals of the American Academy of Political and Social Science, 635*(1), 192–215.

Ricciardelli, R., Maier, K., & Hannah-Moffat, K. (2015). Strategic masculinities: Vulnerabilities, risk and the production of prison masculinities. *Theoretical Criminology, 19*(4), 491–513.

Robinson, G., & Raynor, P. (2006). The future of rehabilitation: What role for the probation service? *Probation Journal, 53*(4), 334–346.

Rönneling, A., Sørensen, N., & Bak, P. C. (2011). *Undersøgelse af tilsynsvirksomheden*. København: The Danish Prison and Probation Service.
Roxell, L. (2009). *Tur och retur. Efter løsladelse*: 34–43. Rapport fra NSfK's 51.
Salmon, G. (2004). Multi-Agency Collaboration: The Challenges for CAMHS. *Child and Adolescent Mental Health, 9*(4), 156–161.
Sandberg, S. (2009). Gangster, victim or both? The interdiscursive construction of sameness and difference in self-presentations. *The British Journal of Sociology, 60*(3), 523–542.
Sarat, A. (1990). The law is all over: Power, resistance, and the legal consciousness of the welfare poor. *Yale Journal of Law and the Humanities, 2*, 343–379.
Sejr, L. (1977). *Retshjælp i et lokalområde: forskningsrapport*. Aarhus: Aarhus Universitet.
Silbey, S. S. (1992). Making a place for a cultural analysis of law. *Law & Social Inquiry, 17*, 39–48.
Silbey, S. S. (2005). After legal Consciousness. *Annual Review of Law and Social Science, 1*, 323–368.
Skardhamar, T. (2002). *Levekår og livssituasjon blant innsatte i norske fengsler*. Oslo: Institutt for kriminologi og rettssosiologi.
Skardhamar, T., & Telle, K. (2012). Post-release employment and recidivism in Norway. *Journal of Quantitative Criminology, 28*(4), 629–649.
SKAT. 2010. *Inddrivelsesvejledningen*. Copenhagen: Thomson Reuters Professional A/S [The Danish Guidance and Directions for Recovery 2010].
Smith, R.H. (1919). *Justice and the poor: A study of the present denial of justice to the poor and of the agencies making more equal their position before the law, with particular reference to legal aid work in the United States*. Issue 13. New York: Carnegie Foundation for the Advancement of Teaching.
Tranæs, T., et al. (2008). *Forbryderen og samfundet*. København: Gyldendal.
Travers, M. (1997). *The reality of law: Work and talk in a firm of criminal lawyers*. Aldershot: Dartmouth.
Travis, J. (2002). Invisible punishment: An instrument of social exclusion. In M. Chesney-Lind & M. Mauer (Eds.), *Invisible punishment: The collateral consequences of mass imprisonment* (pp. 15–36). New York: The New Press.
Travis, J. (2005). *But they all come back*. Washington, DC: Urban Institute Press.
Trubek, L., & Farnham, J. (2000). Social justice collaboratives: Multidisciplinary practices for people. *Clinical Law Review, 7*(1), 227–272.
Ugelvik, T. (2011). *Fangenes friheter*. Oslo: Universitetsforlaget.
Uggen, C. (2000). Work as a turning point in the life course of criminals: A duration model of age, employment, and recidivism. *American Sociological Review, 65*(4), 529–546.

Visher, C., Debus, S. & Yahner, J. (2008). *Employment after prison: A longitudinal study of releases in three states*. Research Brief. Urban Institute, Justice Policy Center.

Walsh, T. (2004). *Incorrections: Investigating prison release practice and policy in Queensland and its impact on community safety*. Faculty of Law QUT.

Williams, K., Poyser, J., & Hopkins, J. (2012). *Accommodation, homelessness and reoffending of prisoners: Results from the Surveying Prisoner Crime Reduction (SPCR) survey*. London: Ministry of Justice.

Wood, J., Kade, C., & Sidhu, M. (2009). What works for offenders and staff: Comparing two multi-agency approaches to offender resettlement. *Psychology, Crime & Law, 15*(7), 661–678.

Open Access This chapter is distributed under the terms of the Creative Commons Attribution 4.0 International License (http://creativecommons.org/licenses/by/4.0/), which permits use, duplication, adaptation, distribution, and reproduction in any medium or format, as long as you give appropriate credit to the original author(s) and the source, a link is provided to the Creative Commons license, and any changes made are indicated.

The images or other third party material in this book are included in the work's Creative Commons license, unless indicated otherwise in the credit line; if such material is not included in the work's Creative Commons license and the respective action is not permitted by statutory regulation, users will need to obtain permission from the license holder to duplicate, adapt or reproduce the material.

10

Nordic Legal Aid and 'Access to Justice' in Human Rights. A European Perspective

Jon T. Johnsen

Introduction

This chapter identifies some important features of the welfare perspective in Nordic legal aid schemes and compares them to a major European perspective, namely the 'access to justice' ideology of human rights.

Legal schemes have many characteristics that can be used for comparison. One important aspect is the legal provisions that control access to legal aid. Another is the empirical dimension: To what extent does actual delivery correspond to the legal criteria? Since empirical data suitable for European comparisons are scarce, my focus is mainly on the normative issues. However, it seems safe to assume that applications for legal aid that fall outside the legal entitlements are unlikely to be covered. International human rights bring in an important legal dimension through their access to justice provisions, which also contain standards for legal aid schemes that states must fulfil.

J.T. Johnsen (✉)
Department of Public and International Law, University of Oslo, Oslo, Norway

The chapter starts with a brief introduction to the welfare perspective and the extent to which the different sectors delivering legal services also offer non-commercial legal aid to people of limited means. The analysis sticks to the schemes organised by the legal aid acts in Finland and Norway. The next part compares the main normative framework for access to legal aid, focusing on problem criteria and poverty criteria and discusses the welfare ideas behind the entitlement criteria of the schemes. The following part first outlines the main ideas about legal aid in the 'access to justice' ideology of human rights. Then it turns to the main features of European Court of Human Rights' (ECtHR) case law on legal aid, and compares it to the welfare ideology of Nordic legal aid on problem and person criteria. The Council of Europe (CoE) supplements the case law of ECtHR with soft law on legal aid, which is summarised in the next part. This part also describes the initiative of the CoE to build a new institution—namely the European Commission for the Efficiency of Justice (CEPEJ)—that works to improve access to justice in Europe and focuses on its efforts to fulfil the soft law expectations concerning legal aid. The final part adds an empirical dimension to the analysis by using European statistics gathered and developed by CEPEJ to provide some basic information about the present state of the existing legal aid schemes in Europe. It makes a more detailed comparison of budgets and cases between the Nordic schemes and the other Western European schemes spending the most per inhabitant. Finally, conclusions are drawn on how the Nordic schemes meet welfare challenges, their performance in a European perspective and whether human rights can become a driver for legal aid reform in Europe.

Legal Aid Ideology in the Nordic Schemes

Welfare systems are meant to support people when they experience health problems, poverty, or unemployment, and to provide them with education according to their capacities. Governments can help by organising and providing welfare services themselves—for example, through public hospitals and schools—and by economic support by, for example, buying services for the needy from private providers or refunding the costs of using them (Berg and Christiansen 2014).

The Nordic countries have mainly put in place *universal* public schemes for health and education—including all groups in society—but have allowed supplementary private providers. However, the provision of some types of welfare services—like dentistry—is left mainly to the private sector. How do the legal aid schemes in the Northern countries conform to these ideas?

Nordic governments expect most people to buy the legal help they want in the legal services market. The main purpose of legal aid schemes is to provide people with legal services when they cannot otherwise afford to have their legal problems solved. Legal aid is meant to be a supplement to market delivery. Universal schemes have never been a realistic option for legal services.

In Nordic legal aid, we might distinguish between two main versions of legal services ideology (see Johnsen 1994, pp. 303–308; 2006, pp. 24–39).

Market ideology dates back to the end of autocracy and has been strongly supported by advocates and their organisations ever since. The modern version, as it has appeared in the legal aid debate since the 70s, views legal services as consumer goods, similar to other types of consumer services that ought to be distributed through the mechanism of the market. Actual consumption depends on the economic resources and priorities of the individual. Establishing a public delivery system interferes with the market. What can be accepted is a subsidy that addresses the basic legal needs of the weakest groups. How efficient and how generous such a subsidy system ought to be is a matter of policy.

Welfare ideology, by contrast, originated from the political ideology of the organised labour movement, and became integrated into its welfare thinking. Because ordinary and poor people could not master the complexity of the welfare regulations and bureaucracy, and appeared unable to assert their rights successfully, welfare law became less effective for the groups that were most in need of it. Legal services schemes became vehicles to improve the efficiency of the welfare apparatus. If judicare schemes appeared inadequate, government had to organise a public system that could deliver the legal service needed (Johnsen 1994, pp. 307–308; 2006, p. 37).

Nordic Delivery Models

The two dominant legal aid ideologies have impacted differently on the Nordic legal schemes. Delivery model alternatives to judicare appeared at the end of the nineteenth and beginning of the twentieth centuries. In all Nordic countries, voluntary legal clinics evolved, aimed at solving working class problems. When organised labour became a significant political power, these offices received public subsidies, and over time they became integral parts of the public legal services schemes. Salaried public offices were most significant in Sweden and Finland, and less so in Norway and Denmark. (Johnsen 1994, pp. 304–305).

In the remainder of the chapter, I limit my analysis to the schemes in Finland and Norway. Finland's legal aid is more different from Norway's than from the schemes in the other Nordic countries. Today, a nationwide network of public legal aid offices constitutes the backbone of Finnish legal aid, while Norway almost entirely relies on judicare (see Chaps. 2 and 4). By choosing the two extremes, we should also cover important features of the Danish and Swedish schemes.

We can distinguish between three main sectors of legal aid delivery in Finland and Norway (Johnsen 2008, 2009).

Commercial delivery or delivery for profit is the hallmark of the *market sector*. Law firms belong here. Market delivery, however, can be used in legal aid when paid for by someone other than the user. When governments pay all, or part of, the lawyers' costs, the expression 'judicare scheme' is commonly used.

Market delivery is perceived as a guarantee of lawyer independence—including in the field of legal aid. Lawyers are free to pick the commissions they want, without any loyalties to interests other than the client's, and potential clients are free to hire the lawyers they think best suited to the task. Lawyer independence—especially from government—has been a major argument in favour of judicare schemes put forward by advocates' associations. We might ask if insurance schemes that cover legal costs may also count as legal aid schemes. However, even if the user's costs are limited to the insurance premium, with an additional contribution to costs when the policy is used, insurance schemes are basically commercial enterprises. Companies offer such cover for profit. Nonetheless, the effects for the users are more or less to the same as judicare. Unions and other interest organisations often have similar schemes for covering legal costs for their members.

The *public sector* consists of public institutions that deliver legal services as one of their responsibilities. Governments do not buy legal services for the needy from private providers, but organise public offices and hire providers to staff them. Such entities can be law centres, public law offices, or defender offices; they may be integrated into welfare bureaucracy or other institutions of public administration, public corporations and foundations, public advice centres, ombudsmen etc. Such providers as public consumer offices, debt advisors, and student legal clinics can also be included in the public sector. These providers are usually salaried, which disconnects their economic interests from the cases they handle.

The *third sector* consists of an assortment of deliverers that do not fit into the two previous sectors. Their common characteristic is that they deliver non-commercial legal services to ordinary and poor people, and to vulnerable groups, as part of their activity. Examples are:

- Membership organisations—providers that are organisations within trade, labour, or other interest organisations that hire legal experts to advise their members on legal issues within the organisation's field of activity.
- Volunteer organisations—especially those targeting deprived or vulnerable groups and including interest organisations, NGOs, grassroots organisations and charities. Like membership organisations, they may offer legal service schemes free of charge to their target groups.

Unlike the situation in common law countries, third sector legal aid has received limited attention in Nordic legal aid research, although some information exists. Norwegian policy reports on legal aid have sometimes described legal aid delivery by a number of third sector organisations. An extensive comparative project on legal aid in Finland and Norway also carried out a provisional mapping of third sector delivery (Johnsen 2008).[1]

Findings indicate that third sector schemes provide a huge share of the total supply of non-commercial legal services in both Finland and Norway. They cover a far larger volume of legal service needs than the Finnish and Norwegian Legal Aid Acts (FLAA, NLAA), and both countries allocate significant public funds to them. (Johnsen 2009, pp. 5–6, p. 18 and more extensively in Johnsen 2008, pp. 25–29, 77–78.) Due to the lack of data, I will focus my analysis on the state funded schemes established by the FLAA and NLAA, with a few detours into third sector schemes when substantiated.[2]

Main Entitlement Criteria

Two main types of criteria are commonly used in public legal aid schemes for delimiting people's access to services. *Problem* criteria identify the type of legal issues that are covered under the scheme, while *poverty* criteria identify the means limits set for applicants to qualify; and whether contributions are a condition for grants. My question is how far has welfare ideology impacted on these main criteria in Finnish and Norwegian legal aid? I will focus on civil schemes and briefly comment on criminal schemes when substantiated.

Problem Criteria

Finland uses general, discretionary criteria for identifying the problems that qualify for legal aid under the civil scheme. All legal problems may qualify for legal aid unless certain specified exceptions apply (FLAA section 1). Norway uses a different technique and specifies in considerable detail the types of problems that qualify for civil legal aid. The NLAA makes a major distinction between litigation aid and aid for other legal problems. The list contains 11 specific categories for legal assistance outside the courts, and 15 for legal representation before the courts and certain other judicial bodies (NLAA sections 11, 12, 17). Other categories of problems are excluded from legal aid unless the circumstances are exceptional.

The Norwegian criteria focus on high frequency problems, without much evaluation of the individual welfare significance of the problem. Legal service needs, however, arise from problems with both high and low frequency in the population. A low frequency problem might also cause serious harm to the welfare of those affected (Johnsen 2008, pp. 42–43, Johnsen 2009, p. 9). The discretionary Finnish criteria provide markedly better possibilities for capturing all the different types of serious legal problems that exist in the target groups.

In a welfare perspective the Norwegian civil priorities show an urban bias. They focus on dissolution of marriage and cohabitation, compensation for personal injuries, loss of a breadwinner and criminal injuries, job dismissals, eviction, and complaints about denial of benefits. Family dissolution, living in rented accommodation, and working as an employee are far more common in urban areas than in rural ones, while legal problems connected with farming, fishing, forestry, and homeownership mainly fall outside the scheme. Several important minority problems are also outside the priorities of the NLAA.

Since the FLAA covers all sorts of legal problems, it overlaps both with the defender scheme and the victims' scheme, and with the third sector. Taken together, the criteria cover almost all serious welfare problems. On the other hand, the NLAA states that its schemes are subsidiary to other public and private schemes and only to be used if alternatives are lacking, NLAA section 5.[3] NLAA coverage is also less extensive. Although the third sector covers a varied selection of problems, it has not been harmonised with the NLAA schemes. This means that categories of problems exist that are not covered by any non-commercial scheme.

The main provisions for civil legal aid in Finland cover most legal problems that the target groups experience. Few serious problems are excluded. The Norwegian LAA scheme, by contrast, only includes selected parts of the legal problems people experience.

When it comes to criminal legal aid, the Norwegian defender scheme appears more liberal than the Finnish one, which depends on differences in the seriousness of the crime charged. In Norway, the use of a defender is obligatory and entitles the accused to legal aid whenever a criminal charge is decided in ordinary hearings, Norwegian Criminal Procedure Code (NCPC) section 96. In Finland, the minimum statutory penalty must be four months, Finnish Criminal Procedure Code (FCPC) Chap. 2. However, since the

FLAA covers all sorts of legal problems, criminal offences are also included for people who satisfy the poverty criteria.

Poverty Criteria

Since, in both countries, the main vehicle for providing legal services to the population is the market, a major welfare idea behind the LAA schemes is to support those who lack the buying power necessary for using the market efficiently. Both countries therefore use complex economic criteria, or means tests, to identify the target population, which makes precise comparisons difficult (see Chaps. 2 and 4) for comprehensive descriptions.

Means testing is not merely a question of someone's ability to bear costs. Depending on their level of poverty, people might be able to pay the full cost of simple advice and a contribution to the cost of a lengthy trial.

The two countries use different economic limits for free legal aid and for legal aid with contributions. At first sight, the Norwegian overall limits are the more generous. They do, however, involve different ways of calculating people's assets. Estimates continue to indicate that the Finnish limits are significantly more generous for households of two or more people, while they are approximately equal for single people.

In both countries the ceilings for free legal services are approximately half the upper limits for legal services requiring a contribution. Finland charges a basic contribution of 70 € from everyone above the contribution limit. In addition, progressive contributions from 20–75% of the costs apply, depending on the grantee's income. Finland does not put any limit on their percentage contributions.

Norway does not require progressive contributions. Grantees above the contribution limit are charged a basic contribution of about 100 € for non-litigation aid and 25% of the costs for litigation aid. The maximum litigation contribution is 627 €, irrespective of the actual costs. Although the ceilings for free legal services seem somewhat more generous in Finland than in Norway, Finnish contributions are significantly larger than those in Norway.

Finland uses means testing almost without exception. Norway omits a narrow selection of civil cases from means testing, and grants legal aid irrespective of the applicant's income and assets. One exception is cases involving serious interventions by the government into people's integrity—for example, by involuntary hospitalisation for health reasons or public child custody. Another exception is cases resulting from serious intrusions by other citizens, like compensation to crime victims. No contributions are payable in such cases.

The justification for these exceptions is not poverty and the inability to carry the costs. In the case of governmental interventions, the idea is that, although justified, no one who suffers loss of freedom or other essential integrity intervention ought to pay for the legal costs they incur. Similarly, when someone is the victim of criminal acts that cause serious bodily or mental harm or suffering, they ought not to have to pay the costs for using legal means to gain redress and rehabilitation.

In both countries, the main rule for civil litigation is that the losing party must cover the costs of the counterpart. On the other hand, both countries also except costs to the counterpart from coverage by legal aid (FLAA section 4, NLAA section 22). Finnish research shows that this cost risk deters poor and middle income people from litigation, irrespective of the merits of their case (Litmala 2006, pp. 166–188).

Welfare Ideology Behind the Finnish and Norwegian Schemes

How do Finland and Norway justify the present entitlement criteria for governmental legal aid and to what extent do they build on welfare ideology?[4]

Both Finland and Norway have introduced constitutional provisions that grant their citizens access to the courts or other independent judicial organs with matters that concern their legal rights and duties. The Finnish constitution, section 21 (Amendment of 11.6.1999/731), guarantees the public access and information about the case handling, the right to argue the case, the right to a reasoned decision, and to appeal. Other guarantees of a fair trial and fair public administration should be laid down by law. The Norwegian constitution, section 95, mainly ensures access to a fair and public trial by an independent and impartial court within a reasonable time, without further explication (Amendment of 27.5.2014/778).

Both constitutions emphasise equality before the law as an essential principle for legal aid policy. No one should suffer from legal losses due to lack of personal abilities or financial resources. The Finnish provisions on the objectives of the legal aid schemes, however, more distinctly express the government's obligation to establish adequate delivery systems than do those of Norway.

The Finnish motivation for its present legal aid act arises from the law's increasing complexity and the fact that access to competent legal counselling is regarded as an important guarantee of access to justice and fair trials. Equality before the law is threatened by rising legal costs, and a fair and efficient judicial system cannot allow people to suffer unreasonable economic risks when protecting and enforcing their legal rights. In the end, it is a governmental responsibility to see to it that the constitutional principle on equal access to the courts becomes a reality (Regerings proposition 82/2001, p. 5.).

Finland's welfare model includes both litigation aid and legal help outside the courts. The entitlement to legal assistance comprehends all professional services deemed necessary to solve the problem—including a duty to ensure that the provider system is adequate. Although access to the courts is the main constitutional concern, the FLAA has significantly broader approach. What matters is the seriousness of the legal problem, not whether the courts are the right institution for problem solving.

Finland's network of public law offices provide everyone entitled to it with actual assistance. They serve as the entrance into the legal aid system by deciding all applications for legal aid. They are located according to both geographic and population criteria. They ensure a reasonably even distribution of legal aid capacity throughout the country (Johnsen 2009, p. 18). For court cases, an additional judicare scheme exists that grantees can use instead of the public law office.

Such mechanisms are lacking in the Norwegian judicare schemes, although the motivation for the present schemes also emphasises equality before the law and the importance of legal services. Everyone ought to have access to the help they need, at an affordable price (Ot.prp. 35, pp. 36–38, St.meld. nr. 25, pp. 19–21, St.meld. nr. 26, p. 21).

Norway, however, has significantly more exceptions from this main principle than Finland. While the FLAA regards necessary legal aid as a citizen's right, its Norwegian counterpart defines access to legal aid as a welfare benefit restricted to legal problems of great personal or welfare importance to the applicant. Norway's focus on civil legal aid is more limited to access to the courts, and the government's obligation to provide legal services is mainly limited to the funding necessary to hire a lawyer in private practice. In most types of civil case, it is left to the grantee to find a lawyer willing to handle the case for the public fee.

The differences between Finland and Norway in their general approach to legal aid policy are marked. The welfare model dominates the government schemes in Finland, while Norway mainly uses judicare.

In Norway, welfare ideology is used to prioritise a limited range of problems as the 'most important' within a restrictive frame. Resources are spent on a universal scheme giving *everyone* legal aid without costs in particular cases, without asking if they can carry the costs themselves. The underlying idea differs from the welfare ideology behind legal aid that aims to help people who lack sufficient resources to obtain the legal services they need.

A policy that expands the cover for the poor and deprived better accords with the welfare ideology's aim of securing equal access to the justice system for all. For this, cover needs to be extended according to the Finnish problem criteria to all that qualify according to the poverty criteria, before limited resources are spent on more affluent groups. However, gaining political support for selective schemes that prioritise support to the poor is significantly more difficult than getting support for universal schemes, even when they become more costly. We can see the Norwegian model as a compromise between these two welfare ideologies.

The European Court of Human Rights' Case Law on 'Access to Justice'

Human rights include norms that provide legal protection for everyone—usually expressed in the concept of 'access to justice'. The right to legal aid is triggered when the individual lacks resources to pay for necessary legal services and this could be perceived as a European competitor to the Nordic welfare ideology. We shall explore how these two ideologies interact in legal aid. Before I make the comparison, I will outline the main human rights perspective on legal aid.

Main Features of the 'Access to Justice' Perspective

In the human rights context, 'access to justice' is perceived as a broad label with some ambiguity. Francesco Francioni distinguishes between three meanings:

Generally the concept is used to 'signify the possibility for the individual to bring a claim before a court and have a court adjudicate it'. A narrower meaning is 'to have his or her case heard and adjudicated in accordance with substantive standards of fairness and justice.' A third and even more specialised meaning is that 'access to justice can be used to describe the legal aid for the needy, in the absence of which judicial remedies would be available to those who dispose of the financial resources necessary to meet the, often prohibitive, costs of lawyers and the administration of justice' (Francioni 2007, p. 1).

In the human rights setting, legal aid is perceived as *one* of several vehicles for access to justice. It is part of a broader rule of law and access to justice obligation for governments. Others include accessible courts, simple procedures, alternative disoute resolution (ADR), conflict prevention measures, such as legal planning, educational measures to ensure that people themselves are legally competent, etc.

My analysis focuses especially on the legal aid element in the broad obligation, which is well expressed in the third of Francioni's definitions. When we try to elucidate its significance, however, the wider context should be kept in mind. The different policy measures available for promoting access to justice are to some degree interchangeable and the human rights obligations therefore have similar flexibility.

Globally, the UN Convention on Civil and Political Rights (CCPR) article 14 is the main provision for access to justice today and the UN is the main organisation for implementing it (International Covenant on Civil and Political Rights 1966). In Europe, the major provision for access to justice is the European Convention on Human Rights (ECHR) article 6, with the Council of Europe (CoE) as the prime promoter of the convention (European Convention of Human Rights and Fundamental Freedoms 1950). Since all member states of the CoE have also ratified the CCPR,[5] both Finland and Norway are obliged to enforce both CCPR, article 14, and ECHR, article 6, and Norway has also made them a part of domestic law that outranks national legislation (Menneskerettsloven 1999 sections 2 and 3).

Our focus is the European perspective. I shall concentrate on the CoE and the legal aid provisions of the ECHR. The CoE uses two major instruments in implementing them, namely the European Court of Human Rights (ECtHR) and the European Commission for the Efficiency of Justice (CEPEJ). Together with the European states, they form the most extensive enforcement system for 'access to justice' in the world.

The Obligation to Provide Legal Aid

Article 14 (1) of the CCPR and article 6 (1) of the ECHR entitle everyone to a fair hearing in both criminal and civil cases. An accused person is explicitly entitled to legal aid 'where the interests of justice so require' as a 'minimum guarantee'. The wording appears discretionary and leaves many issues open to interpretation.

Since the articles demand fair trials for both criminal charges and other 'suits of law', the 'interests of justice'-standard for legal aid cannot be limited to criminal cases. They must be understood as specifications of the general principle of the right to a fair trial. States must also provide legal aid in civil cases, when it is deemed necessary to make the right to a fair trial effective.

The wording of ECHR article 6 only covers 'civil rights and obligations' and 'criminal charges'. It does not mention rights and duties regulated by administrative law. However, the ECtHR has gradually expanded the scope of article 6. CCPR article 14 will anyhow oblige European governments to provide legal aid in all 'suits at law' irrespective of the type of law involved.

The entitlement to legal aid has been brought before the ECtHR in a number of cases. I will comment on three that relate to the problem and person criteria, because they contain important requirements for national legal aid schemes. *Airy v Ireland,* of 1979, relates to civil legal aid, but has a bearing on criminal aid too (Application No. 6289/73). Airy was a low-paid worker and a homemaker with four children; at times, she was on unemployment benefit. She wanted a judicial separation from her husband, only obtainable at the Irish High Court, but could not afford to pay for legal representation. Legal aid was not available. The ECtHR accepted that self-representation in the High Court would not be effective, due to the character of the substantive matter, the complexity of the proceedings and Airy's personal capacity. (§ 20–28).

The decision set the precedent, which obliges governments to provide sufficient funding for legal aid according to the following discretionary criteria:

- importance of the case to the individual (applicant);
- complexity of the case and the individual's capacity to represent himself;
- costs and the individual's capacity to carry them.

The Airy principles have been confirmed in several judgements. A violation will be established by ECtHR if costs act as an actual barrier to access to court.

The Airy criteria of the ECtHR do not distinguish between different types of legal claims. Some states—like Norway—limit the scope of their schemes either by excluding certain types of legal problems, or by restricting them to selected categories. According to article 6, legal aid must be provided 'when the interests of justice so require'. We might therefore ask if this minimum requirement is compatible with restrictions on the types of problems that are covered. The main criterion is the problem's importance to the individual, not the legal category. The ECtHR decision in *Steel and Morris v UK,* of 2005, further develops the Airy principles (Application No. 64186/0):

Steel—a part-time bar worker—and Morris—a postal worker—had joined London Greenpeace (unconnected with Greenpeace International), a small group promoting environmental issues. The group published a leaflet accusing McDonald's of contributing to 'the starvation of the third world' by 'hungering' for profit, economic imperialism, gross misuse of resources, destroying rainforests, producing unhealthy food using a lot of chemicals, exploiting children as consumers, inhuman slaughtering of animals used in hamburger production, and exploiting young unskilled workers as staff. McDonald's sued the applicants for slander.

The proceedings became one of the most extensive in English history. The judgments alone filled more than 1100 pages (§ 65). Although the applicants fulfilled the means test, defamation proceedings were outside of the problem criteria of the legal aid scheme in England. They were effectively left to represent themselves, while McDonald's used a team of experienced lawyers. (§ 58, 68).

ECtHR found that in a matter of such complexity, neither the sporadic help from volunteer lawyers nor extensive assistance from the judge, could form 'any substitute for competent and sustained representation by an experienced lawyer familiar with the case and with the law of libel …' The disparity between the levels of representation 'was of such a degree that it could not have failed … to have given rise to unfairness, despite the best efforts of the judges at first instance and on appeal' (§ 69). The Court concluded that the denial of legal aid was a violation of ECHR Article 6 (1) (§ 72). The UK argued in vain that 'states did not have unlimited resources to fund legal aid systems, and imposing restrictions on eligibility for legal aid in certain types of low priority civil cases was therefore legitimate, if such restrictions were not arbitrary' (§ 53). The Court accepted that a defamation action might generally be of lesser importance to vital personal interests than a claim for legal separation, as in Airy. However, defamation issues had to be considered according to the Airy criteria too. Therefore, legal aid schemes cannot exempt selected categories of problems from legal aid irrespective of their importance to the individual.

The 'access to justice'-approach to legal aid focuses on access to courts and similar judicial institutions. The human rights obligations on governments to provide legal aid are therefore mainly limited to what is necessary for proper enjoyment of them. To what extent do human rights oblige states to provide legal assistance outside the courts?

Many disputes that end in court might well have been resolved in other ways, had the parties had access to legal advice at an early stage, be it by abandoning the claim, settlement, conciliation, mediation, arbitration, etc. We also know that effective use of the right to a fair trial presupposes that the decision on whether to go to court is an informed one. Most people need expert advice on whether to sue, or dispute a claim in court.

In *Golder v UK (Series A No. 18, 1975)*, a prisoner wanted legal advice on whether to sue a guard for defamation. The prison would not allow him to write to a lawyer. The majority of the ECtHR stated that entitlement to a fair trial also included the right to make an informed decision on whether or not to use this entitlement. If a person lacks sufficient means for necessary counselling, legal aid might become a prerequisite for effective access to the court. However, since the main aim of Article 6 is to restrict access to court to claims with merits, governments' obligation to provide access to pre-trial legal counselling might be shaped to achieve this end.

To sum up, states can ensure access to justice for their citizens by various means.[6] The practical impacts of governments' human rights obligation to provide legal aid therefore depend on the structure of their judicial systems. If one state—such as Ireland—practises complex and restrictive rules for divorce that demand that the irreversible breakdown of the marriage is established, and if divorces are available only through complex court proceedings, then the individual need for legal aid can be considerable among poor people who want to divorce. If other states—such as Finland and Norway—have no-fault divorce based on the request of one of the parties, and process divorce administratively, then brief legal advice might suffice in most cases. Liberal states, however, might see far more divorces than do restrictive ones, and might have to establish schemes capable of handling such cases for large numbers of people.

10 Nordic Legal Aid and 'Access to Justice' in Human Rights....

Access also must work in practice. The ECtHR judgments therefore contain important requirements for national legal aid schemes. The wording of neither the ECHR nor the CCPR allows for any leeway for the member states if they deviate from the 'when the interests of justice so require'-standard by adopting inadequate legal aid schemes. The ECtHR has repeatedly said 'Article 6 (1) of the Convention imposes on the Contracting States the duty to organize their judicial systems so that they can meet its requirements.'[7] States cannot set priorities that conflict with the case law of ECtHR.

Access to the courts is meant to be effective for all citizens, irrespective of the type of legal problem, or of their economic situation. However, the ECtHR applies the Airy criteria to the actual circumstances of the complaint. Violations are always established in relation to individuals; systems are not considered as such.

The following will estimate the *potential* for violations, not actual breaches. The ascertainment of actual violation presupposes a complaint, and most violations are, for many reasons, never forwarded to the ECtHR. I will ask to what extent the present schemes in Finland and Norway are organised in such a way that violations are avoided. I will end with some reflections on how far the Nordic welfare models correspond to 'access to justice' and how far the market model and the welfare model on one hand, and the 'access to justice' model on the other, have impacted on each other.

Comparisons to Nordic Legal Aid

Since the main provisions for civil legal aid in Finland cover most legal problems that the target groups experience, I think the scheme conforms well to the *Airy's* problem criteria. All types of problems that have a certain degree of seriousness will qualify. Norwegian problem criteria seem far more problematic. They only include selected areas of need for services. The 'when justice so requires'-standard demands an individual assessment of the particular circumstances of each case—including low or non-priority problem areas. It follows from *Steel and Morris* that states cannot totally exclude certain categories of problems in the way Norway does.

The Finnish *criminal* scheme included in the criminal procedure code appears significantly more restrictive than its Norwegian counterpart. I am not very familiar with the Finnish criminal code, but I would suspect that using a *minimum* statutory punishment of four months as the main criterion will open the way to quite severe punishment being imposed in the absence of a defender, which seems problematic viewed in the light of the Airy criteria. However, access to a defender when the accused also is covered by the FLAA seems comparable to that in Norway, since the FLAA supplements the defender scheme in the Finnish criminal procedure code. However, the exceptions in the Norwegian scheme might also conflict with the Airy criteria under certain circumstances.

The economic ceilings are fixed sums in both countries, which mean that the poverty criteria vary with inflation and general shifts in household economies, unless they are updated. Both countries have been unwilling to use automatic adjustment techniques—such as those used for social insurance and pension schemes—to ensure that the poverty criterion is kept reasonably stable. Adjustments thus depend on policy considerations.

The 'access to justice' principle, however, relates to the actual costs in a particular case. The ECtHR asks if they constitute an unjust barrier to litigation. If they do, public subsidies are justified to the extent necessary to remove the barrier. Legal aid cannot therefore be limited to the poor. If costs become exorbitant, as in *Steel and Morris*, middle-income and even high-income people might also be in need of public support.

For people of some means, the human rights consequence is—as spelled out in *Steel and Morris*—that they can claim access to legal aid if trial costs exceed what they can reasonably be expected to pay. Human rights do not lay down a right to *free* trials, but costs must be adjusted to the economic capacity of the individual. A legal aid system that demands that middle-income people pay affordable legal aid costs themselves will not conflict with human rights if this protects against exorbitant costs. For the better-off, contributions might therefore be significant. However, since both Norway and Finland have upper income limits for cover, their schemes do not fully conform to human rights requirements.

Similarly, schemes that use percentage contributions without any ceiling, might also conflict with Article 6 if costs become high. In *Steel and*

Morris even a 10% contribution to the costs would probably have ruined both applicants. Norway sets a limit of 627 € on its current percentage contribution requirements, while in Finland there is no upper ceiling.

Norway also exempts certain types of cases involving loss of freedom and redress for victims of criminal acts from both all means testing and all contributions. In these case categories everyone has free access to the courts, which obviously does not conflict with *Steel and Morris*. Finland, on the other hand, has income limits and levies contributions in these categories too.

If a court orders a legal aid grantee to pay the litigation costs of the other party, they are not covered by legal aid, neither in Finland nor in Norway. Therefore, the economic consequences of going to court can become unpredictable. The total costs for the individual should be reasonable. Access to justice should not expose people to cost risks that make it possible for wealthy and ruthless opponents to intimidate poor litigants by threatening to ruin them.

Although England does not award costs to the winning party, I think *Steel and Morris* has a bearing on this issue too. The ECtHR pointed to the size of the damages claim and said it would have ruined both Steel and Morris. Since McDonald's trial costs were estimated to be more than £10 million, if Steel and Morris had had to pay them it would have been devastating for them. It seems a safe inference that the ECtHR will include trial costs when it considers governments' obligation to guarantee access to justice.[8]

It seems that keeping the costs of the opposing party outside legal aid schemes amounts to a contradiction. If contributions are set on the basis of the costs that it seems reasonable to expect the grantee to bear, additional costs are bound to cause unreasonable harm. Rules that oblige a losing party to also pay the costs of the winner should be taken into account when the individual's need for legal aid to bear trial costs is considered. Neither of the two schemes fulfils such demands at present.

The 'access to justice'-approach to legal aid focuses on access to the courts and similar judicial institutions. The human rights obligations for governments to provide legal aid is therefore mainly limited to what is necessary for proper enjoyment of these rights. Providing legal aid outside the courts is mainly left to national policies. However, when legal assistance appears necessary for an informed decision on whether to use the courts, the 'access to justice'-obligation might mean governments have to provide pretrial aid. The problem criteria in the Finnish legal aid act apply to all sorts of legal problems, whether civil or criminal, or whether relating to court cases or to problems outside court. I therefore think the problem criteria in the Finnish scheme fulfil the human rights demands for pretrial legal aid.

As mentioned, Norway has separate problem criteria for civil legal aid in court cases and those in other cases, although the two generally overlap. Problems that fall outside the defined categories are generally not covered, which might conflict with the human rights demands, including at the pretrial stage.

The defender schemes in the criminal procedure codes in both countries mainly cover preparation and representation at the trial stage. They do not generally include assistance when the case is under investigation by the police or prosecution unless the suspect is in custody. Unlike its Finnish counterpart, the Norwegian legal aid act does not supplement the defender scheme either at the trial or at the pretrial stage. The deficits in the poverty criteria also apply at the pretrial stage in both Finland and Norway. It is, however, less probable that pretrial costs will become exorbitant.

To sum up, the main human rights provisions on access to justice appear in both the Finnish and the Norwegian constitutions. Entitlement in both countries more or less satisfies the access to justice demand, but does not fully correspond to the demands that follow from the case law of the ECtHR. The Finnish problem criteria seem well in line with the human rights demands, including those for pretrial aid, while the Norwegian schemes exclude important welfare problems from coverage, both at the pretrial and trial stage. Poverty criteria are most generous in Norway. However, none of the schemes cover costly civil trials for the more affluent part of the population—not even when costs become exorbitant. Neither do they cover trial costs awarded to the other party that the court obliges the grantee to pay.

We might note some differences between welfare ideology and access to justice. Human rights protect every human being, whether rich or poor. Welfare benefits are mainly limited to the poorer part of the population, unless the scheme is universal, which legal aid is not in any Nordic country, except for a few case categories in Norway.

As we can see from the differences between Finland and Norway, welfare ideology might be used to justify both a narrow delimitation of problems covered under the scheme, as in Norway, or a broad approach covering virtually any legal problem with potentially serious consequences, as in Finland. On the other hand, welfare ideology has resulted in legal assistance schemes for non-court problems in both countries with legal delimitations similar to the schemes for trials, which fall outside the access to justice demands.

The European Commission for the Efficiency of Justice (CEPEJ): A New Instrument for Improving Legal Aid?

The CoE's Soft Law on Legal Aid

The ECtHR's case law constitutes the minimum rights that governments must not violate. States are, however, free to establish better systems, and the CoE often encourages such developments by issuing resolutions and recommendations calling on governments to develop legal aid schemes. They are meant as political incentives to improve human rights, not as binding obligations. If member states adhere to them in practice, over the years they can become part of customary law or be included in the treaty through amendments and dynamic interpretations. Taken together they constitute a very ambitious programme for developing legal aid in Europe, and I will now summarise their main contents:

The CoE recommends that governments of member states should grant legal aid to all their citizens, and to all residents, on an equal footing with citizens (Resolution 76 (5) on legal aid in civil, commercial, and administrative matters 1976).

Economic obstacles to legal proceedings ought to be eliminated, and an appropriate system of legal aid will contribute to such aim. Access to legal advice for the economically weak is also important in the elimination of barriers to access to justice. The resolution has an appendix spelling out the principles for the means test and contribution system, the merits test, availability, the sort of legal services a proper legal aid system ought to deliver, and a complaint system; it says the financial responsibility for this should be borne by governments (Resolution 78 (8) on legal aid and advice 1978).

Governments should promote action to make the legal profession aware of the problems of the very poor, should promote legal advice services for them, carry the costs, and set up advice centres in underprivileged areas. States should facilitate access to ADR for the very poor, and extend legal aid to such methods of conflict solution. They should also extend legal aid for the very poor to all judicial bodies and proceedings, be they civil, criminal, commercial, administrative, or welfare, and give aid to aliens and stateless people resident in the territory of the member state in which the proceedings take place. Legal aid before judicial bodies should be refused only because claims appear inadmissible or manifestly ill founded, or because the application does not satisfy the standard of being 'in the interests of justice'. States are advised to simplify their procedures for granting legal aid to the very poor, and to consider enabling NGOs to provide representation before both national tribunals and international judicial bodies such as the European Commission and the ECtHR (Recommendation No R (93) 1 on effective access to the law and to justice for the very poor 1993).

States should encourage lawyers to provide legal services to economically disadvantaged people, and ensure that effective legal services are available to them, particularly if they are deprived of their liberty (Recommendation 21 on the freedom of exercise of the profession of lawyers 2000).

Governments should provide the text of the law, both as enacted and as consolidated, in an electronic form readily available to the public. Simple text access to the law database should be free of charge for the public, and governments should make the electronic base available to the private sector for further adaptation and dissemination (Recommendation 3 on the delivery of court and other legal services to the citizen through the use of new technologies 2001).

The resolutions and recommendations adopted by the committee of ministers show that legal aid has been a matter of concern for the CoE for many years, and that European governments have received ample encouragement to develop their schemes.

However, 'access to justice' —including legal aid—increasingly became a challenge to the CoE. Recommendations and resolutions did not appear sufficient, and the CoE recognised the need for a general overhaul of the judicial systems of the member states to ensure that they worked in accordance with both the Court's interpretations of the ECHR, and the CoE's soft law. To carry out the task, the CoE established the European Commission for the Efficiency of Justice (CEPEJ) in 2002.

The CEPEJ's Main Challenges Concerning Legal Aid

The CEPEJ became operational in 2003 as a human rights body specifically designed to improve access to justice in Europe (Resolution 12 establishing the European Commission for the efficiency of justice 2002). It is governed by a plenary with representatives from all member states that meet twice a year.

The CEPEJ focuses solely on policy-making arising from the 'access to justice' provisions in ECHR—especially article 6. It is probably the only human rights body in the world today that has access to justice as its prime and only concern. The CoE especially sought improvements in legal aid, for both civil and criminal cases, and at both the pretrial and trial stage (Resolution (2002) 12 I.1.i.). Obviously the CoE's soft law on legal aid constituted an important platform for the CEPEJ's work.

Pursuant to the resolution, CEPEJ should develop indicators, collect and analyse data, and define measures and means of evaluation. It might also produce statistical reports, best practice surveys, guidelines and action plans, and collect opinions and general comments, to improve access to justice. The CoE encouraged the CEPEJ to collaborate with research groups and invite qualified people, specialists, and NGOs to take part in exchanges, and to arrange hearings and create networks of professionals working in the justice area (Resolution 12 (2002) article

2 and 3 CEPEJ/GENERAL 2003, pp. 5–6). A great variety of tools was recommended for legal aid analysis and other access to justice purposes.

Improvements require voluntary acceptance and collaboration from the member states. The main task is to produce viable reform ideas, communicate them to governments, interest groups and the public, and assume that the states will adopt them voluntarily. In accordance with human rights thinking, the CEPEJ is a vehicle for general improvements in access to justice, and one that has legal aid schemes as a distinct part of its mandate. Such a broad range of policy commitments has the potential to produce far-reaching and innovative reforms for legal aid.

Yet legal aid has not been a priority in later CEPEJ programmes, and, although the potential of CEPEJ for an activist role in developing European legal aid seems significant, it has remained mainly unused so far.

Nonetheless, the judicial statistics of the CEPEJ do include legal aid. The methodological challenges are, or course, considerable, and the reliability of some statistics might be questioned, see CEPEJ EVAL (2014), pp. 6–12 for a description of the design of the study. However, I still think the data show significant differences between legal aid schemes in Europe.

Although rudimentary, they have improved over the years, and I will devote the next part of my chapter to analysing the main findings on legal aid in Europe.

What Does the European Judicial Survey Tell Us About the Performance of European Legal Aid?

In the following, I will give a brief overview of some findings, then I will make a more thorough—although not very sophisticated—comparison between the Nordic schemes and other European schemes that, judged by their cost, are among the top 25% of the existing schemes in Europe.

The Overall Picture

All 45 of the 47 members (Lichtenstein and San Marino are missing) stated that they provide legal representation in both criminal and civil court cases (CEPEJ EVAL 2014, 8 and Table 3.1, p. 70). They do not tell how extensive the provision was. (CEPEJ EVAL 2014, Q 16 and Q 21, pp. 488–481).

Legal aid expenditure also varied enormously among the states that could provide figures. While Azerbaijan spent 0·05 € and Hungary 0·09 € per inhabitant, Germany spent 4·3 € and France 5·6 €. At the top we find Northern Ireland with 50·7 € and Norway with 53·6 € (CEPEJ EVAL 2014, Fig. 3.4, p. 76) —more than ten thousand times the expenditure per inhabitant in Azerbaijan, and more than ten times the expenditure in Germany.

A listing of the total 2012 public expenditure on courts also shows huge variations. The republic of Moldovia spent the least, with 2·7 € per inhabitant, Azerbaijan 6·4 € and Hungary 32·9 €. The figure for Northern Ireland was 40·5 € and for Norway it was 46·3 €, while Germany spent 103·5 €. The largest spender was Switzerland, with 122·1 €. Data was given by 37 countries. (CEPEJ EVAL 2014, Fig. 2.5, p. 31).

These findings show that states have very different priorities as regards court and legal aid costs. In most countries, the legal aid budget made up only a very small share of the court budget, while Norway and the three UK jurisdictions, Northern Ireland, England and Wales, and Scotland spent more on legal aid than on courts.[9] Spending per inhabitant on courts by jurisdictions in Southern and South Eastern Europe, which seemingly have the greatest problems with speed and backlogs, is not very different from that of the Northern and Western European jurisdictions, but they spend comparatively very little on legal aid (CEPEJ EVAL 2014 Fig. 2.5, p. 31 and Fig. 2.15, p. 47).

The number of legal aid grants also varies significantly. Azerbaijan provided 6·5 grants per 10,000 inhabitants and Armenia 10·9, while Finland reported 144, Northern Ireland 314 and the Netherlands 326. (CEPEJ EVAL 2014, Table 3.5, p. 77).[10] The Netherlands gave 50 times as many grants per 10,000 inhabitants as Azerbaijan did.

Nordic Legal Aid in the European Setting

When we compare the legal aid expenditure of the Nordic states with that of other European states, both all the Nordic states end up in the top 25%. All the other states in the top quarter are located in Northern and Western Europe too.

Table 10.1 shows the legal aid budget:

Norway is the biggest legal aid spender in Europe, followed by the Northern Ireland. There is a significant gap between these countries and the other Nordic states. Norway spends twice as much as Sweden per inhabitant, three times as much as Denmark, and four times as much as Finland.

The English-speaking countries, or 'common law' countries, constitute the group with the largest budgets in Europe, with the Nordic countries in second place. The Netherlands and Switzerland also are among the countries with the highest budgets per capita (Table 10.2).

Even states that spend the most on legal aid seem reluctant to report data that can be used to further analyse the huge differences in costs and provision. The picture for the rest of Europe is similar. Only 26 of 46 countries have provided one figure or more.

Still, we can see that the Netherlands handles three times as many court cases per 10,000 inhabitants as Norway, at a cost per case of only

Table 10.1 Legal aid budget per inhabitant, from the top 11 countries, in 2012

Country/ranking	Budget per inhabitant (€) 2012
1 Norway	53·6
2 Northern Ireland	50·7
3 England and Wales	41·2
4 Scotland	33·7
5 Netherlands	28·8
6 Sweden	24·8
7 Ireland	18·1
8 Denmark	14·9
9 Switzerland	13·5
10 Finland	12·5
11 Iceland	11·1

44 of the 47 states gave data. Table 1 contains the top 25% of the 44
CEPEJ EVAL (2014) Fig. 3.4 p. 76

Table 10.2 Legal aid cases and costs per case

Country/ranking	Court cases per 10,000 inhabitants.	All cases per 10,000 inhabitants.	Costs per legal aid case. Court cases. (€)	Costs per legal aid case. All cases. (€)
1 Norway	90·4	128·1	5639	4180
2 Northern Ireland	314·8	–	–	–
3 England and Wales	125·3	–	–	–
5 Netherlands	290	326·0	863	–
7 Ireland	131·9	–	1373	–
10 Finland	79·7	143·8	887	–

No figures: 4 Scotland, 6 Sweden, 8 Denmark, 9 Switzerland, 11 Iceland. Ranking from Table 10.1. States that did not give any of the four figures asked for, have been left out
CEPEJ EVAL 2014 Table 3.5 p. 77

15% of Norway's. Finland's cost per court case is similar to that of the Netherlands, while Ireland's cost per case is 24% of Norway's.

The 2008 comparative study of Finland and Norway found that Norway spent more than twice as much per case on civil legal aid outside the courts (1000 € as against 425 €) and more than three times as much per court case as Finland (4750 € as against 1500 €). The average time spent on non-court cases in Finnish legal aid offices was estimated at 4–5 hours, and 9 hours in Norway. Time spent on civil court cases handled by private lawyers in Finland was estimated at 10 hours, compared with 50 hours in Norway, and the average time spent on court cases in the Finnish public legal aid offices was even lower (Johnsen 2009, p. 17).

Some of the differences might be explained by differences in case structure—especially the significant number of cost-free categories of legal aid cases in Norway—and by differences in the fees charged by private lawyers, and also by the somewhat lower time costs in the Finnish public legal aid offices. The major explanation, however, seems to be that most comparable categories of cases are dealt with faster and more economically in Finland than in Norway (Johnsen 2009, p. 17). The strong element of public legal aid offices in Finland's legal aid seems a major factor influencing judicare lawyers' time use since the public lawyers solve legal aid cases significantly faster than the judicare lawyers (Johnsen 2008, pp. 94–95).

The CEPEJ's Evaluation of European Legal Aid Schemes

CEPEJ EVAL (2014) also evaluates some of its findings about legal aid. The report welcomes the fact that:

> '(A) all the member states provide legal aid both in criminal law and civil law fields, which is welcome when considering the requirements and the spirit of the European Convention on Human Rights and of the case law of the Court.' The report remarks that '[O]utside the criminal law field, legal aid can be granted more or less according to the type of case concerned.' (CEPEJ EVAL 2014, p. 88)

We read that the report does not set out to give a precise evaluation of the fulfilment of the problem criteria in the ECHR and the case law of the ECtHR from the data gathered. Person criteria are not mentioned at all. The CEPEJ's evaluation builds on a question in the European Survey that only asks whether legal aid *concerns* criminal, civil, or other matters (CEPEJ EVAL 2014, Q.20, p. 488). It does not ask how extensive the aid is—for example, whether all criminal cases are covered, or only the most serious ones. As shown in the citation above, the report therefore admits that the problem coverage in civil cases varies significantly. Such exclusions will usually be made by removing certain types of problem, as we have seen in Norway, Ireland (*Airy*), and England (*Steel and Morris*) and might well conflict with the case law of the ECtHR.

The report does, however, rank the European schemes in four groups of generosity, using the number of cases and spending per case as criteria. Norway, and to a lesser extent, the Netherlands and Ireland belong to the top group with the most generous schemes, while Finland is placed in the second group.[11]

As shown in the comparison of Norway with Finland, spending appears to be an unreliable predictor of actual coverage. Taking into account the quite complex Airy criteria described above, I think it more to the point to conclude that, in most areas, the Finnish scheme is significantly more generous than its Norwegian counterpart. The obvious exception is the few case categories in the Norwegian scheme where everyone has free access to legal assistance both outside the courts and in court cases.

Conclusion

Although Finland and Norway both use welfare ideology to legitimate their legal aid schemes, the analysis shows significant differences. Finland uses universal problem criteria, while Norway is selective, focusing on a limited selection of legal problems regarded as being statistically the most detrimental to people's welfare. Both countries exclude the most affluent part of the population from coverage and require contributions, although Norway excludes from means testing a small selection of problems relating to loss of freedom due to governmental intervention, and harm due to the criminal acts of other citizens.

None of the schemes cover all costs. If a legal aid grantee loses his case and the court order him to pay the opposing party's cost, they are not covered by any of the schemes, which might make the full cost risk difficult to predict and deter poor people from going to court even when they qualify for legal aid.

Delivery is most efficient in Finland, due to the extensive network of public law offices and their central role in managing the legal aid system. Norway's civil scheme lacks efficient mechanisms to check if the available judicare capacity is sufficient for most case categories. For efficiency reasons, Norway allows the judicare lawyer in question to grant up to 10 hours of aid. Those decisions are made on the basis of the capacity and interests of the individual lawyer. They cannot ensure a rational overall use of the available capacity for legal aid, and may be a significant cost driver. The Norwegian system probably makes strict, mechanical rules on entitlement to legal aid a necessity. Finland's legal aid policy appears more holistic than Norway's since it puts more emphasis on integration and coordination of the different sectors and suppliers (Johnsen 2008, pp. 94–99; Johnsen 2009, pp. 19–21).

Both Finland and Norway have developed schemes for legal assistance for non-court problems. Welfare ideology is a major motivation. Establishing welfare states has meant a variety of new rights and obligations, and also new bureaucracies that must function properly to fulfil governments' obligations. Legal aid is also important in dealing directly with malfunctions in public administration without going to court.

Non-LAA schemes provide a major share of the total supply of non-commercial legal services in both Finland and Norway. They cover a far larger volume of service needs than the general legal aid schemes and both countries allocate significant public funds to them. I would expect third sector schemes to be important in other European countries too.

The existence of a large third sector in both countries is also an important indicator that governmental non-court advice schemes are seriously inadequate, although there is no reliable mapping. Finland is aware of the challenge and has developed a countrywide telephone service from the public law offices.

Since human rights are meant to be effective for everyone, empirical analyses are important for a reliable picture. However, such comparisons are almost impossible today, due both to the complexity of the issue and the lack of research. Only rough and uncertain assumptions can be made.

The data on European legal aid schemes gathered by the CEPEJ are rough and basic. Although the scope for error is considerable, one cannot escape the assumption that the enormous variation in legal aid funding among European countries also means that the legal aid offered to the poorer part of the population differs significantly both in volume and quality.

Nordic legal aid schemes seem better developed than those of most other European countries. Finland's legal aid is more universal overall, and makes significantly more use of public delivery than Norway. From a European perspective both these features are unique.

Together with the English-speaking countries, the Netherlands, and Switzerland, the Nordic countries seem to constitute the top fourth of European schemes when it comes to coverage, while countries in Southern and Eastern Europe spend significantly less. On the other hand, we do not find similar differences in spending on courts. Data are, however, quite rudimentary.

One possible theory is that differences in legal cultures explain some of the findings. Common law countries have traditionally favoured adversarial proceedings, while Roman law countries have relied on the inquisitorial method. A fair adversarial proceeding demands significantly more input from the parties than systems that put the judge in charge of collecting and analysing the evidence. Efficient legal aid schemes seem far more crucial to adversarial proceedings than to inquisitorial schemes if trials are to be fair. However, further research is needed to draw conclusions.

Are welfare ideology and access to justice competing ideologies for legitimating legal aid schemes? Welfare ideology focuses on the structure of people's needs, problems, and well-being, and asks how legal expertise can best contribute to solving them. The access to justice perspective is mainly concerned with people's right and capacity to use a specific institution—namely the courts—for problem solving, and puts less emphasis on whether the courts can provide them with viable solutions to their problems in an efficient way. In a nutshell: welfare ideology takes an instrumental approach, while access to justice is institutional. The welfare meaning of access to justice therefore depends on the substantive content of people's rights, and the existence of non-implemented rights that can be made operational through better access to the courts.

The poorer states in Europe prioritise criminal legal aid over civil aid. Although fines and prison sentences obviously impact negatively on people's welfare, such protection is not at the heart of welfare ideology. Welfare rights are meant to improve the quality of people's lives, not to protect them from unreasonable punishment by the state. Welfare states have so far seemed more inclined to view legal aid and advice outside court as a better method to impact welfare bureaucracies than putting pressure on them through the courts. 'Access to justice', as expressed in the human rights doctrine, has the potential to become a driver for progressive change in the Nordic schemes, as well as in other European schemes. The case law of the ECtHR contains important decisions on legal aid and is an obvious driver for the reform of legal aid in Europe. Finland and Norway, for example, have incorporated the access to justice provisions in human rights treaties into their constitutions. However, closer analysis reveals that the implementation in national law has flaws that might need correction.

It is highly likely that, in the European countries with the poorest funding, we will find widespread violations of the Article 6 entitlement to legal aid, which demonstrates that the human rights obligations of many European states demand reforms in their legal aid schemes. CEPEJ also lists a number of legal aid reforms in progress in the member states (CEPEJ EVAL 2014, p. 89).

The mandate of the CEPEJ still has the potential to ensure more effort is put into improving European legal aid. The ECtHR has repeatedly stated that 'Article 6 (1) of the Convention imposes on the Contracting States the duty to organize their judicial systems so that they can meet its requirements.' Member states have the freedom to choose different strategies to fulfil their obligations to develop access to justice. They could consider the option of providing legal aid by reorganising the judicial system in a way that diminishes the need for legal assistance. They could simplify both substantive and adjudicative law, and better educate citizens in legal matters, or develop 'do-it-yourself'-systems that might diminish the need for professional legal counselling and representation. Many matters might be resolved faster and more inexpensively through ADR. Such strategies might become options for governments to improve their legal aid schemes. At all events states must act, and the outcomes must satisfy their human rights obligations.

Notes

Johnsen 2008 builds on two national research projects. The Norwegian research was conducted by Statskonsult and published in Statskonsult 2008. The Finnish study was carried out by the National Research Institute of Legal Policy (OPTULA). It was published in Henriikka Rostii & Johanna Niemi & Marjukka Lasola 2008. Additional materials were used when substantiated, see: *Regan & Johnsen, Jon T. 2007* and Johnsen & Regan 2008. Both the Norwegian and the Finnish Ministry of Justice supported the project and, upon request, they provided the comparative research project with all data and materials that they possessed.

1. Norway: rettshjelpsloven 1980, straffeprosessloven 1981, Finland: Rättshjälpslag 2002, Lag om statliga rättshjälpsbyråer 2002, and Lag om rättegång i brottmål 1997. Finnish legislation is issued in both in Finnish

and Swedish. I read Swedish, but not Finnish, and therefore use the Swedish versions for references and citations.
2. Both Finland and Norway exclude problems covered by legal expense insurance from legal aid.
3. My comparison builds upon the public documents establishing the present LAA schemes
4. See http://search.un.org/original/?tpl=un&search_group=untc&lang=en&query=CCPR. Visited 20 March 2016. 179 nations had joined CCPR. (181 if Scotland and Northern Ireland are counted separately as in the CEPEJ statistics.)
5. Usually labelled 'margin of appreciation'.
6. See, for example, *Hadjinis* v *Greece* (Judgment of 28 April 2005).
7. The UN Human Rights Committee, in a communication concerning CCPR article 14, said that Norwegian Sami seeking court protection for their reindeer herding rights, and risking the high costs of the opposing party, might qualify for legal aid (Joseph and Schultz 2004, pp. 397–398. They refer to 1991 UN doc. CCPR/C/79/Add 112). The Committee expressed a similar opinion in a communication concerning Finnish Sami seeking court protection for their rights according to CCPR article 27. A strict obligation to pay the opponent's costs if they lost the case, with no discretionary power for the court to modify it, might deter them from accessing the court and violate CCPR article 14 (Joseph and Schultz 2004, pp. 398–399 (*Äärelä and Näkkäläjärvi v Finland* Communications 779/97)).
8. CEPEJ EVAL 2014 gives separate statistics for the three UK jurisdictions England and Wales, Northern Ireland, and Scotland
9. 17 states did not give any figures on the number of applications granted.
10. The other Nordic schemes have not been ranked in the CEPEJ report, doubtless because of lack of data.

References

Berg, O. T., & Christensen, J. (2014). Velferdsstat. In *Store norske leksikon*. Collected 12 March 2016 from https://snl.no/velferdsstat

Francioni, F. (2007). The rights of access to justice under customary international law. In F. Francioni (Ed.), *Access to justice as a human right* (pp. 1–56). Oxford: Oxford University Press.

Johnsen, J. T. (1994). Nordic legal aid. *Maryland Journal of Contemporary Legal Issues, 5*(2), 301–331.

Johnsen, J. T. (2006). How has the complexity of the law and the market for legal expertise impacted on the development of legal aid in Norway? *International Journal of the Legal Profession, 13*(1), 19–39.

Johnsen, J. T. (2008). *Hva kan vi lære av finsk rettshjelp? En sammenlikning av rettshjelpordningene i Norge og Finland.* Oslo: Justis- og politidepartementet 2009. Appendix to St.meld 26 (2008–2009) Om offentleg rettshjelp. Rett til hjelp. Justisdepartementet.

Johnsen, J. T. (2009). *Might Norway learn from Finnish legal aid? A comparison of legal aid in Norway and Finland.* Summary Report from Johnsen 2008. Paper to "Delivering Effective Legal Aid Services Across Diverse Communities" ILAG Conference Wellington New Zealand 2009-04-01–2009-04-03.

Johnsen, J. T., & Regan, F. (2008). How to use an international "best policy"-model in the analysis and improvement of Finnish legal aid. In C. H. van Rhee & A. Uzelac (Eds.), *Civil justice between efficiency and quality: From Ius commune to the CEPEJ* (pp. 151–188). Intersentia: Antwerp-Oxford-Portland.

Joseph, S., & Schultz, J. (2004). *The international covenant on civil and political rights.* Oxford: Oxford University Press.

Litmala, M. (2006). Evaluating the practical effects of the Finnish reform of legal aid. 6th International LSRC Conference 2006, pp. 166–88.

Regan, F., & Johnsen, J. T. (2007). Are Finland's recent legal services policy reforms swimming against the tide of international reforms? *Civil Justice Quarterly, 26*, 341–357.

Rostii, H., Niemi, J., & Lasola, M. (2008). *Legal Aid and Services in Finland.* National Research Institute of Legal Policy Report 237.

Statskonsult 2008 Kartlegging av rådgivnings- og konfliktløsningstilbudet i Norge DIFI-report 2008:1.

Legislation and Other Legislative Documents

Finland:

Rättshjälpslag 5.4.2002/257 (FLAA).
Lag om statliga rättshjälpsbyråer 5.4.2002/258.
Lag om rättegång i brottmål 11.7.1997/689 (FCPC).
Regeringens proposition till Riksdagen med förslag till rättshjälpslag och vissa lagar som har samband med den, RP 82/2001 rd, p. 5.

Norway:

Lov 13. juni 1980 nr 35 om fri rettshjelp (NLAA).
Lov 22. mai 1981 nr 25 om rettergangsmåten i straffesaker (NCPC).
Lov 21.mai 1999 nr.30 om styrking av menneskerettighetenes stilling i norsk rett (Menneskerettsloven).
Ot. Prp. 35(1979–80).
St.meld. nr. 25 (1999–2000) Om fri rettshjelp.
St.meld. nr. 26 (2008–2009) Om offentleg rettshjelp. Rett til hjelp.

Council of Europe/CEPEJ:

Convention for the Protection of Human Rights and Fundamental Freedoms (ECHR)
European Commission for the Efficiency of Justice 2014 European judicial systems. Efficiency and quality of justice. Edition 2014 (2012 data). CEPEJ. Council of Europe. Strasbourg (CEPEJ EVAL 2014).
Resolution 76 (5) on legal aid in civil, commercial and administrative matters. Adopted by the committee of ministers on 18 February 1976 at the 254th meeting of the Ministers' deputies. Council of Europe. European commission for the efficiency of Justice Relevant Council of Europe Resolutions and Recommendations in the field of efficiency and fairness of justice. CEPEJ 2003 7 Rev. 5.
Resolution 78 (8) on legal aid and advice. Adopted by the committee of ministers on 2 March 1978 at the 284th meeting of the Ministers' deputies. Council of Europe. European Commission for the efficiency of Justice Relevant Council of Europe Resolutions and Recommendations in the field of efficiency and fairness of justice. CEPEJ (2003) 7 Rev 6–8.
Recommendation No R (93) 1 on effective access to the law and to justice for the very poor. Adopted by the committee of ministers on 8 January 1993 at the 484th meeting of the Ministers' deputies. Council of Europe. European Commission for the efficiency of Justice Relevant Council of Europe Resolutions and Recommendations in the field of efficiency and fairness of justice. CEPEJ (2003) 7 Rev. pp. 27–29.
Recommendation (2000) 21 on the freedom of exercise of the profession of lawyers. Adopted by the Committee of Ministers on 25 October 2000 at the 727th Meeting of the Ministers' Deputies.

Recommendation (2001) 3 on the delivery of court and other legal services to the citizen through the use of new technologies. Adopted by the committee of ministers on 28 February 2001 at the 743th meeting of the Ministers' deputies. Council of Europe. European Commission for the efficiency of Justice Relevant Council of Europe Resolutions and Recommendations in the field of efficiency and fairness of justice. CEPEJ (2003) 7 Rev. pp. 84–89.

Resolution (Res. (2002)12) establishing the European Commission for the efficiency of justice (CEPEJ). Adopted by the committee of ministers on 18 September 2002 at the 808th meeting of the Ministers' deputies and amended on 19 March at the 832nd meeting of the Ministers' deputies. Council of Europe. CEPEJ/GENERAL (2003) p. 1.

United Nations Intenternational Convention of Civil and Political Rights (CCPR)

Open Access This chapter is distributed under the terms of the Creative Commons Attribution 4.0 International License (http://creativecommons.org/licenses/by/4.0/), which permits use, duplication, adaptation, distribution, and reproduction in any medium or format, as long as you give appropriate credit to the original author(s) and the source, a link is provided to the Creative Commons license, and any changes made are indicated.

The images or other third party material in this book are included in the work's Creative Commons license, unless indicated otherwise in the credit line; if such material is not included in the work's Creative Commons license and the respective action is not permitted by statutory regulation, users will need to obtain permission from the license holder to duplicate, adapt or reproduce the material.

11

Legal Aid and Clinical Legal Education in Europe and the USA: Are They Compatible?

Richard J. Wilson

Introduction

Clinical legal education has made enormous global advances in the past few decades, primarily as a means of providing students with supervised experience in the practice of law as a formal part of the law school curriculum. Nowhere has this phenomenon grown more rapidly, and in some ways, more surprisingly, than in Western Europe. Europe combines a tradition of the magisterial lecture, a method for which partisans have advocated since the Middle Ages, with a period of practical training after law school, designed to accomplish many of the goals of a clinical experience in school. European professors are not generally practitioners of law. Yet the phenomenon grows apace everywhere, Europe being no exception.

This chapter will examine the growth of clinical legal education in one particular historical context in Europe and the USA: that of clinics

R.J. Wilson (✉)
Washington College of Law, American University, Washington, DC, USA

providing systematic legal aid services in civil matters to those who cannot afford counsel. It will begin with some basic definitional issues regarding what is 'clinical' in the US legal academy, as well as some basic parameters of the legal aid paradigm. The second part of the chapter will compare and contrast the historical development of clinics in the USA with those in Central and Western Europe. The US experience will give particular focus to the decade of the 1980s, during the presidency of Ronald Reagan, a crisis period for civil legal aid on a national scale, while clinical legal education was growing dramatically as an alternative pedagogy within law schools. The European experience will give particular attention to events in Central Europe after the fall of the Soviet Union, with a focus on Poland as one jurisdiction that provides legal aid through clinics. A more recent look at clinics shows a shift in both more recent experience in US law schools, and a diversity of models for clinical work in newer programmes in Western Europe. Several examples will be noted in a final section. Having provided that basis for comparison, the chapter will conclude by asking the none-too-rhetorical question of whether law school clinics should be a major provider of legal aid in any national scheme. At this stage in the European experience, it is defensible to argue the 'let a hundred flowers bloom' theory of clinical education, as experimentation and academic, local, or national conditions may dictate particular models for particular times.

Definitions: Clinical Legal Education and Legal Aid

Clinical Education

Some suggest that clinical legal education is part of a range of experiential learning methods that can be utilised in the law school curriculum, including them among such models as externships, which provide an out-placement of students in a law office, usually with an accompanying seminar for credit in the law school, or simulation-based courses that provide students with fact-based legal problem solving situations (Milstein 2001). In the context of this chapter, I use a somewhat more specific definition of clinical legal education, though without some elements that I have emphasised elsewhere. The most relevant elements in this context are three: (1) the provision of legal advice or services to actual clients, whether in court or not, by law students; (2) clients of the clinic are persons without the resources to retain counsel, or persons or groups in underserved or marginal communities; and (3) all student work is reviewed closely by, regularly supervised by, and may be vouched for by, a member of the bar, hopefully a member of the faculty of the school where the clinic is located. An ideal clinical experience has two additional elements, some of which require time and effort within the law school: (4) the participation of law students is given academic credit within the institution in which the student is enrolled and is an integrated part of the course of study in law school; and (5) the student is prepared for interactions with clients by either a preparatory or a parallel course of study that focuses on the doctrine, skills, ethics, and values of professional practice in the law. The most robust and effective clinics combine all five elements (Bryant et al. 2014).

Legal Aid and 'Legal Services'

Legal aid, as a term of art, means different things in the historical and constitutional context of the USA than it does in most other parts of the world. Legal aid in the USA generically refers to the provision of legal services for indigent persons who cannot afford to retain counsel, but its scope and structures are radically different from continental Europe in practice, distinguishing sharply between services provided in criminal versus civil cases.

In the criminal law context, the origins of defence of the indigent poor (who are the overwhelming majority of all persons charged with any crime anywhere) primarily lie with the US Supreme Court's 1963 decision in *Gideon v. Wainwright*, holding that an indigent person charged with a felony offence in state court, where the overwhelming number of criminal prosecutions occur, is entitled, under the Sixth Amendment to the US Constitution, to counsel at state expense (*Gideon* 1963). *Gideon* and related cases before and after it, at both the federal and state levels, have mandated systemic structures to provide access to a lawyer, both at trial and on appeal, for all of those indigent criminal accused sent to jail. The three major systems used today in the USA for legal aid in criminal matters include staffed public defender offices, contracts for services by law firms, and lists of individual counsel assigned by trial court judges. All are compensated by the state, but may be paid by federal, state, or local budgets (Mounts and Wilson 1986, p. 197). The constitutional right to counsel does not extend to discretionary appeals or prisoners under sentence.

Legal aid in all other contexts—civil, administrative, immigration, etc.—is through funds appropriated by the national, state, and local legislatures or raised by legal aid programs to meet their budgetary needs. There is no federal constitutional right to counsel in US civil cases. Funding for civil legal aid programmes comes largely from federal or state appropriations of funds by statute or court rule. The biggest single programme in the USA is the federal Legal Services Corporation (LSC), founded in 1974 during the administration of Richard Nixon. Although state and local funding is now almost double that of LSC's budget, the LSC remains the largest single provider of civil and related legal services for the poor. In addition to guidelines limiting representation to those with poverty-level incomes, the LSC is burdened by dozens of restrictions limiting access to certain populations such as immigrants, and limitations on certain client groups, such as undocumented immigrants, and certain types of advocacy, such as legislative lobbying and class actions (Houseman and Perle 2013, pp. 34–40). As used throughout this chapter, the term 'legal services', taken from the name of the principal entity funding such services, refers to civil legal aid matters only, not to legal aid in criminal matters.

As is discussed throughout this volume, legal aid schemes in Europe generally, and the Nordic region specifically, are mostly state-administered programmes with budgets to provide legal services to the poor in both criminal and civil legal matters, often without income or asset limits on clients to be served. In recent years in Europe, insurance for legal issues can defray costs of legal aid for many, while legal insurance is virtually unknown in the USA. In the context of this chapter, I am discussing only civil legal aid in the USA, while referring comprehensively to all legal aid in Europe.

Legal Aid and Clinics in the USA: The Reagan Assault on Legal Services

The Earliest US Clinics: Europe's Surprising Role

The early history of clinical legal education in the USA is deeply and inextricably linked to the provision of legal aid for the poor. Scholars have noted what they call the 'legal aid origins' of clinical legal education, not only in the USA but in many other countries as well, including Australia, India, and South Africa (Bloch and Noone 2011, p. 153). Within the USA, they mention the establishment, in the 1920s, of student-directed 'legal aid societies', often voluntary, at the law schools at Yale, the University of Southern California, and the University of Chicago. These programmes were established, first and foremost, to provide legal services to those who would not otherwise have access to a lawyer or the courts (*Ibid.*, p. 157). While these efforts are noteworthy, my own research has discovered roots much earlier, in the late nineteenth century, and with a surprising connection to Europe.

Arthur von Briesen, a private lawyer who led the early legal aid movement in New York City, became the first President of the New York Legal Aid Society. The Society, founded in 1876, is the oldest and largest not-for-profit legal aid programme in the USA. Even in its earliest days, it sought ways to expand the scope of its services. Von Briesen, who assumed leadership in 1890 of what had been largely a programme serving the German immigrant community in New York City, travelled abroad on a study tour. He returned with news of a grand experiment in Copenhagen, Denmark. There he found a programme called *Studentersamfundets Retshjælp for Ubemidlede*, translated as 'The Student Association for Securing Legal Aid for the Poor', but known popularly as the Legal Aid Society (von Briesen 1907). Another early legal aid activist lawyer, Reginald Heber Smith, in his own contemporary work, supplements the observations of von Briesen, noting that the Copenhagen Society was founded by the University of Copenhagen in 1885 (Smith 1919, p. 227). Von Briesen writes that the Society received national, city, and university financial support for its operations. The programme was simple and direct in providing legal services to the needy. It was housed in a building with seven rooms. Each night of the week, except Sundays, seven different prominent lawyers and judges, all graduates of the university, sat in the rooms, doing intakes on cases. These 42 lawyers were joined by one law student per room per night, assigned from the University of Copenhagen law faculty, a total of 42 law students every semester. One paid staff lawyer, together with a paid clerk, completed whatever work needed to be done if a case could not be resolved in the first encounter. Students assisted with interviewing and research, with some drafting. Any case that went to court was done by a practising lawyer, often with the student seated at his side. During the year 1906, according to von Briesen, the programme did an extraordinary 25,782 intakes, resulting in some 7000 files being opened. Of the opened files, 114 cases were settled and 88 brought to trial, and 61 trials achieved results favourable to Society clients. Von Briesen comments that the confidence of clients in these lawyers and students 'is naturally very great; their decisions are taken without a murmur and terminate what otherwise might become much needless controversy.' (von Briesen 1907, p. 26) To my knowledge, this is the first known programme of clinical instruction in the world, and its roots are in Europe, not the USA.

Von Briesen was interested in the structure of the Society, primarily, because of its ability to extend the scope of legal services to the poor, so he documented neither the origins of the programme nor whether it provided students with credit for their participation, but he did suggest pedagogical value through the law students' 'actual contact with litigants and their skilled advisers', as well as 'a great variety of questions, some of considerable intricacy, the solution of which will be of more value to the students even than to the party who deems himself aggrieved.' (*Ibid.*, pp. 26–27).

The Copenhagen model, and other domestic proposals, gained some attention in the USA, and led to what might be called the earliest of clinical models in the USA, denominated generally as the 'legal aid clinic' and taking its name from medical practice in a clinical setting (Bradway 1933). In an era in which there was no national programme of legal aid services, some called for clinics in law schools to take on a significant role in providing assistance in legal aid cases as a means to train law students for practice. The impulse behind these efforts was a noble one focused on the professional training of law students for practice: as Smith notes in his early work, there is 'a gap in the present method of training lawyers. The law schools do not teach practice. The law offices do not teach practice. The student is left to pick up his information about the conduct and procedure of cases in any way and in any place that he can manage to find it.' (Smith 1919, p. 230).

John Bradway, who ran the Duke University Legal Aid Clinic in Durham, North Carolina for 28 years, from 1931 to 1959, was an eager proselytiser for legal aid clinics. In the dozens of articles he wrote on legal aid clinics for law schools and the popular press, including the one cited here, he never raised any concern about excessive case- or workloads for students in clinics. His concern for clients and the integrity of their cases was expressed instead in his insistence that students be adequately and closely supervised by a practicing lawyer. Writing in 1936, Bradway and the prominent lawyer Reginald Heber Smith documented the growth of legal aid work in the USA from its origins (Smith and Bradway 1936). They offer a full chapter on the earliest relationships between law schools and legal aid, documenting the work of legal aid clinics in law schools between 1893 and 1916. Their introductory overview of the work is instructive:

> 'The legal aid clinic is the outgrowth of certain needs common to the legal-aid movement and to legal education. Each group exploring the boundaries of its own field found in the interstitial area possibilities for mutual development.' (*Ibid.*, p. 156)

Certainly this was true then. The remainder of this chapter explores more recent history, when the social and pedagogical missions of clinics become more contested, and one mission might prevail at the cost of the other.

The Second Wave: Social Activism in the 60s and Beyond

Later writings on the topic document the now-conventional story that the US clinical movement finds its greatest period of dynamism and expansion in the social movements of the turbulent 1960s and 1970s. Barry and co-authors appropriately call this phase the 'second wave' of clinical legal education, following the first wave in the early twentieth century, discussed above (Barry et al. 2000, p. 12). The second wave covers the period from the 1960s up to the late 1990s. According to the authors, new clinics during this period were designed almost exclusively to respond to a demand by law students for relevance in their training, as well as a desire to use the law as an instrument of social change, primarily through the provision of legal services to the poor, who would otherwise not have access to the legal system or justice itself (*Ibid.*, pp. 12–14). The authors note that new clinics during that time also served deeper social goals. Clinical courses 'expose students not only to lawyering skills but also the essential values of the legal profession: provision of competent representation; promotion of justice, fairness, and morality; continuing improvement of the profession; and professional self-development.' (*Ibid.*, p. 13).

Crisis: Reagan's Attacks on Legal Services via Clinics

Although the social justice motif was strong in early clinics, few US clinics aspired to seriously fill the yawning need for more legal aid in civil matters. Instead of high-profile 'impact litigation' or massive numbers of cases, clinics during this period leaned towards the use of simulation to introduce lawyering skills and the small-case model, with low numbers of clients and slowly unfolding litigation that provided students with many opportunities for reflection and change in case theory or direction as cases developed over time before an actual court hearing (Schrag and Meltsner 1998, p. 18, 40). Clinics received a boost in support through Ford Foundation grants that allowed virtually any law school that wanted a clinic to have one, so long as the school was willing to match foundation funding. Ford's Council on Legal Education for Professional Responsibility (CLEPR) programme dispensed over $11 million during the 1970s, then 'vanished, as planned.' During that time period, more than half of US law schools had received CLEPR funding for their clinical programs. By the end of the 1980s, 98% of accredited law schools offered clinical legal education of some kind, in no small measure due to the seed-money efforts of the CLEPR movement (Schrag and Meltsner 1998, pp. 5–7).

The 1960s and 1970s were also a time of enormous development of civil legal services for the poor in the USA. Again, the Ford Foundation funded a small number of legal services offices that became a model for the first federally-funded legal services programme. In 1965, the US Office of Economic Opportunity (OEO) created a Legal Services Programme that grew to over $70 million a year, in 1974, through grants to local non-profit groups of lawyers to provide civil legal services (Rhudy 1994, pp. 231–232). These programmes, largely independent, literally transformed US poverty law practice, with dozens of stunning victories in the US Supreme Court on behalf of poor people throughout the nation. The welfare rights movement, in no small measure, owed its success to these OEO-funding programs (Lawrence 1990; Davis 1995). In fact, many suggest that the early successes of the programme were what led to the right-wing political backlash against legal aid in the following decades. OEO Legal Services was replaced by the national Legal Services Corporation (LSC), established in 1974 during the presidency of the ill-fated Richard M. Nixon, the only US president to resign the office.

Legal clinics did play a role in legal aid delivery in civil matters. As early as 1978, a report from the federal General Accounting Office on the operations of the recently created LSC indicated that about 30% of all grantees reporting in their survey used law students 'as a resource.' This included using students as programme paralegals and supplemental staff, not necessarily through clinical programmes, although the same report documents a single law-school-based clinic with a staff of five lawyers who devoted 30% of their budget to civil legal services, and seven law schools 'with programmes which provide legal services to the poor.' (US General Accounting Office 1978, pp. 10–11)

Ronald Reagan became president of the USA in 1981, having served as governor of California from 1967 to 1975. He arrived in Washington as a new conservative voice, which included strong negative attitudes about government expenditures on legal aid for the poor. During the time of his governorship, his administration had clashed deeply with California Rural Legal Assistance (CRLA), a state-wide legal aid programme funded as part of the OEO Legal Services Program mentioned above. He lost repeatedly. The CRLA scored a series of court victories on behalf of *braceros*, temporary Mexican workers imported to assist big agribusiness in California. When the press painted Reagan in an embarrassing light, he vowed revenge against the programme and others of its ilk, and took it by repeated attempts, all unsuccessful, to prevent funding from OEO to CRLA (Bennett and Reynoso 1972).

The newly elected President Reagan reignited his antagonism to legal aid immediately after his arrival in Washington in 1981. His first federal budget provided for zero funding for the LSC, which, at the time, was operating with a budget of $321 million nationwide. When Congress, and strong supporters, particularly the voluntary, but politically powerful, American Bar Association (ABA), rallied to assure adequate funding for the LSC in the budget, and Reagan didn't have the votes to deny all funding, he shifted his strategy to one of slowly strangling the Corporation through indirection. He named members of the national board of directors who were hostile to the programme. He managed to significantly cut the LSC budget, by a third from 1981 to 1982, resulting in the loss of 1773 lawyers and 2860 other staff in a single year. Many of these lawyers were the most experienced and seasoned veterans of the programme. Three hundred field offices were closed, and 17 national backup centres, which provided essential technical expertise to the field, were threatened with closure (and eventually did close) (Abel 1985, pp. 547–548).

In the spring of 1981, President Reagan's old friend and colleague from the California years, Attorney General Ed Meese, proposed that the legal needs of the poor could be met by law students working in law school clinical programmes. In a commencement speech at the law school of the University of Delaware, Meese suggested an 'expansion' of clinical programmes to establish 'neighbourhood law offices for the poor', working under the supervision of lawyers who would donate time to supervise the work. In a press conference preceding the address, he noted that most legal aid matters were 'relatively simple legal cases – landlord cases, divorce cases, creditor-debtor cases, that sort of thing.' Such matters were the kind of thing staff lawyers had done, he asserted, and the LSC lawyers themselves 'are usually lawyers in their first few years of practice, too, and they don't have as adequate supervision as you would have in the programme I'm going to outline.' (Stuckey 2005, p. 12) Whether straightforward or cynically calculating, the Meese speech and subsequent actions within LSC to fund legal aid programmes in law school clinics were seen as part of the Reagan strategy to cut legal aid funding or water down services. A national newsletter circulated to law school clinics by the Association of American Law Schools (AALS) noted, in November of 1983, that the LSC was funding a pilot law school clinic project 'to supplement services offered by existing legal services programmes.' Eight to twelve accredited law schools would be awarded grants between $50,000 and $100,000 over 18 months. The newly appointed president of the LSC, a corporate lawyer with no prior experience in poverty law, called the grants an opportunity to tap into the 'well-spring of talent and dedication' of law students to work on behalf of the poor (LSC Announces New Clinical Program, Nov. 1983).

Reaction from the clinical teaching community was immediate and almost completely hostile. A short essay in a clinical community newsletter, written by a clinical teacher from the University of Maryland, urged clinics not to apply for the proposed grants (Capowski 1984, pp. 24–25). Capowski gave four reasons not to do so. First, he argued, funding for legal aid should go to 'the most efficient providers of legal services for the poor.' Dollars taken by clinics would result in further cuts to already severely underfunded staff programmes. Second, clinics, by their nature, 'require significant supervision and low student caseloads.' They are inherently 'ineffective in reaching large numbers of clients.' Third, taking grants might create conflicts of interest for clinics seeking to engage in law reform activities, which are inimical to Congressional restrictions imposed on all LSC grantees. Finally, because the current direction of the LSC was toward abolition of the staff model in favour of private bar delivery, any funding of clinics was disingenuous, and would end all too soon.

However, clinics were still experiencing the growth phase of their adolescence, and law schools were often reluctant to fund what was seen as an expensive addition to a law school's curriculum. The LSC funding proposal was tempting to some schools. In June of 1984, the AALS Newsletter announced that nine law schools had received LSC grants between $65,000 and $95,000, selected from 57 'high-quality grant proposals.' The primary function of the grants, according to the LSC Washington office under control of Reagan appointees, was to 'test' whether clinics can be 'an efficient and effective means of augmenting the work of existing legal aid programmes.' Other goals of the programme were said to be to enhance the education of law students and to create a future group of lawyers interested in providing legal services to the poor (LSC Announces Grants, June 1984, pp. 7–8).

The issue continued to churn through the clinical teaching community. One more newsletter entry, in November of 1987, indicates that the LSC made grants totalling over one million dollars for the 1987–1988 academic year. The grants went to 27 law schools and ranged from a low of $26,615 to a high of $50,000. The newsletter notes the 'lack of consensus' among members of a Committee on Legal Services of the clinical community, as to whether law schools should, or should not, accept grant funding (Committee on Legal Services Nov. 1987, p. 4). In a 1990 publication from the generally conservative American Enterprise Institute, the LSC's coordinator of the law school clinic grants wrote. His data conform generally with the dates and amounts recorded here, and then he notes that only 'two-tenths of 1 percent of the resources of the corporation have gone into this programme, even though we have a total pool of 176 law schools accredited by the American Bar Association. So we are not dedicating huge resources to the project.' Later in the same presentation, he notes that in the 18 months during which the grant operated with the grantee schools, 5500 cases were completed; while another 2000 were pending. Client surveys of satisfaction were very high, with 81% satisfied with the outcome and 92% satisfied with the quality of service. Students in the programme also showed a significantly greater likelihood of providing pro bono services in the future (Moses 1990, p. 169, 171). I found no other evidence that additional funding was provided to clinics from the LSC.

The small percentage of grant funding for clinics, together with active resistance from the clinical community, seem to have fended off any further efforts by the Reagan administration to shift from staffed legal services offices to clinics. A 2015 survey bears this out. It indicates that clinics now play a minimal role in the delivery of legal aid in the USA; law school clinics account for less than 2% of all clients served (Houseman 2015, p. 26). For historical reasons, then, it is very unlikely one will see any law school clinic in the USA that provides a significant portion of the legal aid services in any locality.

Early Legal Clinics in Central Europe: Poland's Clinical Links to Legal Aid

Post-Soviet Rapid Expansion of Clinics

Clinical legal education emerged in Europe with a much different trajectory than that of the USA. It began in earnest in Central Europe with the fall of the Soviet Union, which formally dissolved in 1991. The instability and reform impulses of the post-Soviet period created space for innovation within traditional law schools. The first clinic to see real clients in the post-Soviet era of Central Europe came into being at Palacky University in Olomouc, Czech Republic, in 1995, with support from the Ford Foundation. A later review of the clinic notes that it 'stagnated both in number of students and in quality of education,' in part owing to financing difficulties and lack of faculty involvement. With renewed funding from European and national sources, the clinics at Palacky revived and grew to five, as of 2006 (Bryxová et al. 2006, p. 150). The first clinic in Russia began to operate with a full complement of students in February of 1996, as a result of a sister-state relationship begun as early as 1994 between Vermont Law School in the USA and Petrozavodsk State University, in the Karelia region of Russia (May 1997). Throughout the 90s and first decade of the new century, clinical legal education programmes based in universities grew in number and academic standing. In part, this was due to funding support from international donors, public, and private (Wilson 2004). In addition, the Bologna Process, begun in 1999, provided an impulse for European higher education reform; it also played an important role in creating space for innovations such as legal clinics (Terry 2008).

The Polish Case

Poland, perhaps uniquely to the region, began on a small scale but then pursued an aggressive path toward the adoption of clinics on a nationwide basis, with much of the emphasis of clinical work focused on access to justice, the social mission of clinics, and legal aid services that the state was not providing. The first clinic in Poland was at the Jagiellonian University in Krakow, where a Human Rights Clinic began operating in the fall of 1997 (Rekosh 2008, p. 98). Shortly after its founding, the Human Rights Clinic received an influential grant from the UN High Commissioner on Refugees (UNHCR) to provide representation to asylum seekers and other refugees (Wortham 2006, p. 622). That grant, in turn, gave rise to intense efforts by UNHCR to fund clinical legal education as a means of providing legal aid to refugees in the new accession countries of the European Union. Although relatively short-lived, the collective projects gave rise to at least 23 refugee law clinics in 11 countries in the region, as well as an annual asylum law moot court competition and other on-line resources, all of which were a form of legal assistance to persons in need who would otherwise not have been served by the legal system (Konstantinov 2004, slide 16).

Clinics spread quickly in Poland. After the start of the Jagiellonian clinic, Warsaw University quickly followed in 1998, and Białystok University began a tax clinic in 1997 that later developed into a larger clinical programme. Students enrol in clinics in their fourth and fifth years of study, after three years of theoretical classroom work, making it part of their Masters studies (Skrodzka et al. 2008, pp. 58–59, p. 71). Since their early beginnings, clinics have spread throughout the country, with 25 clinics in 16 cities as of the 2012–2013 academic year (FUPP 2015). Clinics have been established in every public university in the country, and in virtually all of the private universities. As their national reach has grown, their focus has moved to one of provision of legal aid services to the poor.

The Polish Legal Clinics Foundation (FUPP) as Unifying Influence

A strong influence in the spread of clinics in Poland was the creation, in 2002, of a national entity with its focus exclusively on clinical legal education, the Polish Legal Clinics Foundation, or FUPP, as it is known by its Polish acronym. FUPP went into operation quite quickly, with the goals of strengthening the structure of clinical education and providing a national platform for training, support, and standards in the operations of clinics. FUPP has since become not only a national role-player in legal education but a patron for international relationships of Polish clinics with others on a worldwide basis. Today, every clinic that comes into existence in Poland strives to meet the minimum national standards established by FUPP for all clinics; the organisation plays a role not only in the approval of clinics but also in their financing and relationships with the national government. As a result, almost all of the clinics in Poland are included within the curriculum of study for a law degree, and office costs and professors' salaries are paid by the universities; very few of the costs of clinics are borne by the government (FUPP 2015). Because of its strong relationship with the national ombudsman of Poland, FUPP also plays a key role in the development of laws and regulations on access to legal aid, as well as in the provision of pro bono legal services throughout the nation. It sponsors frequent national clinical conferences and workshops, and has developed a voluminous manual on clinics, now available in English, Russian, and Chinese. The foundation has also published a number of texts on clinical legal education at the national level.

The foundation documents the work performed by clinics throughout Poland. From the data available, it is clear that clinics within the FUPP network see their mission as twofold. First, clinics fill an educational goal of teaching practice skills and ethics to massive numbers of law students who participate in the programmes through work with real clients. Second, clinics fulfil a social goal of providing legal services to poor and otherwise unrepresented people. Statistics show that during 2012–2013, almost 2000 students and some 250 teacher-supervisors participated in clinics. This represents a steady increase in student and faculty participation in the programmes over the life of FUPP. During a nine-month period between 2012 and mid-2013, some 11,100 cases were reviewed in legal clinics, about 30% of which dealt with civil law matters. Other significant areas of student work include criminal cases, family matters, and labour and unemployment issues (FUPP 2015). One authority estimated, more than a decade ago, in 2003, that clinics provided about 30% of all legal aid services at that time, with the rest being provided by lawyers and non-governmental legal services organizations (Bojarski 2005, p. 27). Given that the caseload of clinics has more than doubled since that year, it can be assumed that legal clinics may be the most significant providers of legal aid to the poor in the country.

One concern about providing such a large array of services is the potential clash of the pedagogical and social missions of clinics. If too many cases are handled by novice lawyers-to-be, neither the clients nor the students are well-served, and speedy, pro-forma representation can result in real damage to the claims of clients, each of whom brings a unique story. There must be a learning space in which students can acquire both the doctrinal and lawyering skills necessary to provide effective representation in any real legal matter. Polish clinics purport to mitigate these concerns in two ways. First, the strong faculty participation in the programme ensures that student supervision and oversight is close, and caseloads are limited. The average student-to-faculty ratio for supervision purposes is now around seven to one, comparable to most clinics in the USA and much lower than many clinics in the region. Second, legal aid representation is largely limited to non-court matters and advice or referral. Some 86% of all cases are resolved with one to two visits to the clinic, and within two months. Students are expected to work with at least two clients during an academic year, and most students resolve about six cases per year (Czernicki 2015; FUPP 2015). Efficiency is a goal, but not at the expense of pedagogical soundness.

Poland is unique in many ways with regard to its fast-growing clinical offerings. First, it developed a totally indigenous clinical movement, unique in itself, but drawing from the prior experience of others. Interestingly, it took its model not so much from contemporary US structures but from other strong clinical programmes around the world, particularly that of South Africa, which gave Poland a programme strongly grounded in legal aid work, but also a structural model for its national accrediting agency, the FUPP, drawing on South Africa's Association of University Legal Aid Institutions (AULAI). AULAI plays a strong role in South Africa in the structures and funding of clinics, with an endowment from the Ford Foundation to strengthen clinic funding (McQuoid-Mason 2008, p. 9). In describing the wide variety of clinical programmes in South Africa, McQuoid-Mason draws sharp distinctions between what he calls 'state-funded law clinics', and those he calls 'independent law clinics'. The former group of clinics provides legal aid services. However, those clinics also offer a service for students that is unique in the world, at least in my experience. As a result of law changes in 1993, prospective lawyers can complete their required articles of clerkship, or practical training after law school, through legal aid service in a clinic. In return, the government funds those clinics to provide legal aid services. As of 2000, 20 clinics functioned in this way, although government support was quite minimal—no more than $72,000 per year for their operations. It is the independent law clinics that receive support from the AULAI Trust (McQuoid-Mason 2000, pp. 123–124, p. 129). Recent scholarship from South Africa has been critical of the role of clinics there in providing only legal aid services, claiming that such clinics dilute a clinic's purely pedagogical mission. A recent article collects critiques of the legal aid clinic model from Australia, UK, the USA, and India, as well as from South Africa itself (DuPlessis and Dass 2013, pp. 397–400). McQuoid-Mason himself puts the matter quite succinctly:

> The greatest challenge for general practice [legal aid] clinics is how to limit the numbers of clients so that the clinics do not become overwhelmed. If the number of clients exceeds the capacity of the clinic both the clients and the clinic will suffer. The clients will suffer because they will not receive proper advice and service. The clinic will suffer because its reputation will be harmed and its staff and students demoralised. Intakes need to be limited and clients referred to other agencies once the clinic reaches its capacity. (McQuoid-Mason 2008, p. 6)

A second strength of the Polish clinic system is that it is the only country in the Central and East European region to provide a significant portion of the nation's legal aid services through clinics, although students themselves never appear in court. However, legal aid is not the only mission of clinics, as is evidenced by the early clinics that provided legal services in human rights and other areas. A third unique aspect is that, while many other countries from the former Soviet bloc have nationwide clinical education associations, none has the certifying powers of the Polish FUPP. Poland is not unique in its struggle to provide legal aid systematically, a challenge for all of Europe and the world. Major reform appears to be on the horizon. Poland is about to adopt a comprehensive new programme of staffed legal aid offices in 2016, which may affect the reach and involvement of clinics in such services (Czernicki 2015).

The Aftermath: Let a Hundred Flowers Bloom Throughout Europe and the USA

Recent developments in Western Continental Europe and the USA indicate that clinics are thriving and growing apace. In the USA, virtually every one of the nation's 198 accredited law schools has more than one clinic: a national survey for 2013–2014 indicates that the average number of different subject-matter clinics at each school is seven, with nearly a quarter of the clinics working in the areas of criminal defence, immigration, children and the law, and mediation, or other alternative dispute resolution methods. An average of from 51% to 55% of all law students in the USA participate in a clinic, with a median enrolment in individual clinics of from nine to twelve students. Faculty supervision in clinics is also gaining greater stability. In the relevant time period, nearly 44% of all clinic faculty were either tenured or tenure-track employees. Another 75% of all faculty employees are on presumptively renewable full-time contracts. Student-teacher ratios are generally stable at between 6 to 1, and 8 to 1, in order to assure adequate supervision. Virtually all clinics receive academic credit for both fieldwork and seminar components, although the average clinic experience is only one semester of the six semesters of legal study, and is generally part of a larger class load for full-time students.

There is no hard data today giving estimates of the sources of funding for US law school clinics. Very little comes from state or federal sources. The last such data I have found comes from a report by the American Bar Association for the years 1991–1992. According to that report, 68.4% of funding, the majority came from the law school or university budget (hard money). Another 12% came from state sources that no longer contribute today: federal grants under Title IX, which formerly provided seed money grants for clinics, and the LSC, discussed above. Another 8% came from foundation grants, with only 3.8% coming from other state agency funding. A small remaining percentage of funding came from lawyers' fees and earmarked alumni donations (American Bar Association 1992, p. 250). The more recent national survey of clinical legal education only suggests budgetary issues by identifying the lack of hard money (money within the law school's own budget) as the most significant challenge facing in-house clinics (Kuehn and Santacroce 2015, p. 14). Given the number of law schools and clinics, it should not be surprising that the survey estimates that clinics gave over 3.4 million hours of pro bono civil legal services during the 2012–2013 academic year, or just over 3300 hours per clinic. Clinics are estimated to have provided free civil legal services to over 70,000 individuals during that year (Kuehn and Santacroce 2015). Thus, although clinics in the USA are not generally linked to legal aid programmes, their contribution to civil justice in the USA is significant.

Six years ago, I wrote an article arguing that continental Western Europe was what I called 'the last holdout' in accepting clinical legal education. I argued that there were many possible explanations for that phenomenon, noting that clinics have thrived in the USA and the rest of the common law world, and they are a commonplace throughout Latin America, Asia, and Central and Eastern Europe. I then counted less than 10 clinics in all of continental Western Europe (Wilson 2009). Again, in 2012, after acquiring new comparative data, I concluded that 'clinical legal education is conspicuous by its absence in Western European countries.' (Wilson 2012, p. 71) Now, only four years later, I believe that my conclusions no longer hold true. Based on some rapidly evolving data on the ground, and on some empirical data, I believe Western Europe is joining the international chorus singing the virtues of clinical legal education as part of the law school curriculum. Although many of the clinics did not begin operations until after 2011, one survey identifies 51 clinics in Western Europe, in the following countries: Austria, Belgium, France, Germany (which has 24, the most), Italy, the Netherlands, Norway, and Spain. There may well be more that have not yet been documented. Europe now also has its own regional clinical organisation, the European Network for Clinical Legal Education, or ENCLE, with a rapidly growing list of participating institutions across the continent.

While no systematic information is available as to the nature of the work performed by these clinics, or the sources of their funding, my strong impression is that, in general, European clinics have not been organised on the Polish model, primarily as a means to provide legal services to the poor. In fact, most of the countries in question have robust legal aid programmes provided by the private bar or NGO groups. One notable exception is the Juss-Buss programme in Oslo (see Chap. 2 above), and a very impressive programme in action, as I can attest from a personal visit to its operations in 2012. Otherwise, the range of clinical offerings is quite diverse: asylum and immigration, business law, environmental law, international human rights, or multiple subject matters, to name but a few. This broad range of offerings reflects a general sense that clinic content is governed by local conditions, and such local conditions often include the interests and abilities of the teachers and students involved in the clinic, as well as the general local legal culture, both inside and outside of the university. Clinics can provide valuable legal services to the poor in civil matters but great caution should be taken, as has been the case in Poland, to ensure that there is adequate supervision of student work-product, as well as appropriate limited caseloads per student over the time of enrolment, in order to provide maximum pedagogical opportunities while providing much-needed legal services to the community.

References

Abel, R. L. (1985). Law without politics: Legal aid under advanced capitalism. *UCLA Law Review, 32*, 474.

American Bar Association. (1992). *Legal education and professional development: An educational continuum.* Report of the task force on law schools and the profession: Narrowing the gap.

Barry, M., Dubin, J., & Joy, P. (2000). Clinical education for this millennium: The third wave. *Clinical Law Review, 7*, 1.

Bennett, M., & Reynoso, C. (1972). California rural legal assistance (CRLA): Survival of a poverty law practice. *Chicano Law Review, 1*, 1.

Bloch, F. S., & Noone, M. A. (2011). Legal aid origins of clinical legal education. In F. S. Bloch (Ed.), *The global clinical movement: Educating lawyers for social justice.* New York/Oxford: Oxford University Press.

Bojarski, Ł. (2005). The social aspect of legal clinics. In *The legal clinic: The idea, organization, methodology* (pp. 19–26). Warsaw: The Legal Clinics Foundation.

Bradway, J. S. (1933). Legal aid clinics: Their purpose and their value to the bar. *The [California] State Bar Journal, 8*, 261–264. California.

Bryant, S., Milstein, E. S., & Shalleck, A. C. (2014). *Transforming the education of lawyers: The theory and practice of clinical pedagogy*. Durham: Carolina Academic Press.

Bryxová, V., et al. (2006). Introducing legal clinics in Olomouc, Czech Republic. *International Journal of Clinical Legal Education, 9*, 149–150.

Capowski, J. J. (1984). Legal services corporation grants for clinical education. In Association of American Law Schools section on Clinical Legal Education. *Newsletter*, March 1984.

Committee on Legal Services. (1987). In AALS section on Clinical Legal Education. *Newsletter*, 4 November.

Czernicki, F. (2015, October 21–22). President of the polish legal clinics foundation (email exchange with the author).

Davis, M. F. (1995). *Brutal need: Lawyers and the welfare rights movement. 1960–1973*. New Haven: Yale University Press.

DuPlessis, M. A., & Dass, D. (2013). Defining the role of the university law clinician. *South African Law Journal, 130*, 390.

FUPP. (2015). *Legal clinics in Poland: 2003–2013*. PowerPoint available at http://www.fupp.org.pl/en/. Visited on 22 October 2015.

Gideon v. Wainwright. (1963). 372 U.S. 335.

Houseman, A. W. (2015, May 14). *Civil legal aid in the United States: An update for 2015*. Washington: Center for Law and Social Policy (CLASP).

Houseman, A. W., & Perle, L. E. (2013). *Securing equal justice for all: A brief history of civil legal assistance in the United States*. Washington: Center for Law and Social Policy (CLASP).

Kuehn, R. R., & Santacroce, D. A. (2015). *Survey of applied legal education*. 2013–14. Center for the Study of Applied Legal Education, University of Michigan.

Konstantinov, B. (2004, June 5–6). *Developing refugee law clinics in Europe's transitioning countries* (PowerPoint presentation).

Lawrence, S. E. (1990). *The poor in court: The legal services program and supreme court decision making*. Princeton: Princeton University Press.

LSC Announces Grants. (1984). In AALS section on Clinical Legal Education. *Newsletter*, 7 June 7.

LSC Announces New Clinical Program. (1983). In AALS section on Clinical Legal Education. *Newsletter*, 4 November.

May, J. C. (1997). Creating Russia's first law school legal clinic. *The Vermont Bar Journal & Law Digest, 23*, 43.

McQuoid-Mason, D. (2000). Essay on the delivery of legal aid services in South Africa. *Fordham International Law Journal, 24*, 111.

McQuoid-Mason, D. (2008). Law clinics at African universities: An overview of the service delivery component with passing references to experiences in South and South-East Asia. *Journal for Juridical Science*, (Special Issue 1).

Milstein, E. S. (2001). Clinical legal education in the United States: In-house clinics, externships, and simulations. *Journal of Legal Education, 51*, 375.

Moses, C. T. (1990). The law school clinic program. In D. J. Besharov (Ed.), *Legal services for the poor: Time for reform* (p. 168). Washington, DC: American Enterprise Institute.

Mounts, S. E., & Wilson, R. J. (1986). Systems for providing indigent defense: An introduction. *New York University Review of Law & Social Change, 14*, 193.

Rekosh, E. (2008). Constructing public interest law: Transnational collaboration and exchange in central and Eastern Europe. *UCLA Journal for International Law & Foreign Affairs, 55*, 80–82.

Rhudy, R. J. (1994). Comparing legal services to the poor in the United States with other western countries. *Maryland Journal of Contemporary Legal Issues, 5*, 223–246.

Schrag, P. G., & Meltsner, M. (1998). *Reflections on clinical legal education*. Boston: Northeastern University Press.

Skrodzka, M., Chia, J., & Bruce-Jones, E. (2008). The next step forward—The development of clinical legal education in Poland through a clinical pilot program in Białystok. *Columbia Journal of East European Law, 2*(1), 56–93.

Smith, R. H. (1919). *Justice and the poor*. New York: Arno Press.

Smith, R. H., & Bradway, J. S. (1936). *Growth of legal aid work in the United States*. US Department of Labor, Bureau of Labor Statistics.

Stuckey, R. (2005, October 7). *The history of the KBG and the Gang of Eight (1979–1993)* (Draft, on file with the author).

Terry, L. S. (2008). The bologna process and its impact in Europe: It's so much more than degree changes. *Vanderbilt Journal of Transnational Law, 41*(107), 113–114.

United States General Accounting Office. (1978). *Free legal services for the poor – Increased coordination, community legal education, and outreach needed.* Report to the Congress by the Comptroller General of the United States.

von Briesen, A. (1907). The Copenhagen legal aid society. *Legal Aid Review, 5,* 25.

Wilson, R. J. (2004). Training for justice: The global reach of clinical legal education. *Penn State International Law Review, 22,* 421.

Wilson, R. J. (2009). Western Europe: Last holdout in the worldwide acceptance of clinical legal education. *German Law Review, 10,* 823.

Wilson, R. J. (2012). The role of practice in legal education. In *General reports of the XVIIIth congress of the international academy of comparative law* (p. 57).

Wortham, L. (2006). Aiding clinical education abroad: What can be gained and the learning curve on how to do so effectively. *Clinical Law Review, 12,* 615.

Open Access This chapter is distributed under the terms of the Creative Commons Attribution 4.0 International License (http://creativecommons.org/licenses/by/4.0/), which permits use, duplication, adaptation, distribution, and reproduction in any medium or format, as long as you give appropriate credit to the original author(s) and the source, a link is provided to the Creative Commons license, and any changes made are indicated.

The images or other third party material in this book are included in the work's Creative Commons license, unless indicated otherwise in the credit line; if such material is not included in the work's Creative Commons license and the respective action is not permitted by statutory regulation, users will need to obtain permission from the license holder to duplicate, adapt or reproduce the material.

12

Juridification, Marginalised Persons and Competence to Mobilise the Law

Knut Papendorf

Introduction

Access to the law for marginalised, disadvantaged or, in this context, what may be termed law-dissociated groups, and their capacity to mobilise the law, are central to research on legal aid. Experienced lawyers assert that 'being right is insufficient, one must also be granted rights.' This is a recurring theme amongst experienced lawyers with a legal aid portfolio, i.e., a practice used by 'non-paying clients dependent on either free legal advice or finding a lawyer willing to work nearly for free.' If clients fail to get such advice, they often do not take their disputes further, because of the not insignificant economic risks involved in a suit. This cements the asymmetry that already exists between private actors on the one side and the public authorities on the other. These lawyers describe their clients as being in a *situation of double powerlessness*, which arises from their lack of competence and economic opportunities (Papendorf 2012, p. 138).

K. Papendorf (✉)
Department of Criminology and Sociology of Law, University of Oslo, Oslo, Norway

This claim will be discussed below in the context of the more general judicial development represented by the extensive juridification of society. In Norway (and the other Scandinavian countries) there is a tradition of setting in train an extensive research effort every 20–30 years in order to analyse power relations and the state of democracy in the various countries. The most recent such research effort in Norway—carried out by the Research Group on Power and Democracy[1] (1998–2003)—has indeed renewed this debate on juridification. Øyvind Østerud, the head of this research group, has identified juridification as a problem for democracy. According to Østerud (2006, p. 112f),[2] a combination of rights legislation, government directives, and municipal budget scarcity may produce unintended redistribution: 'When means are scarce, it becomes crucial to have the support of resources and strong spokesmen.'

The work of the research group and its final report in particular, has undoubtedly led to a new consideration of juridification, its underlying notions and consequences for the rule of law—and more concrete questions concerning access to the law. One may ask whether access to the law for particularly law-dissociated members of society has deteriorated or improved as juridification takes place. The research group's analysis includes evidence for both possible views. This makes an interesting starting point for a more thorough examination of the views of the research group on juridification and its consequences for access to the law for law-dissociated groups in society. Juridification must itself be seen in a wider context, namely the debate on the limitations of modern law from an administrative perspective which, again, has consequences for the capacity to mobilise the law.

The Norwegian Research Group on Power and Democracy, which resulted from the parliamentary decision of December 1997, worked from 1998 until 2003. The first item of the research group's mandate is described as follows:

> The main theme is principles of the Norwegian democracy and changes in these … The starting point is the Norwegian social model built on representative democracy … Important conditions for representative democracy include that the individual having a voice, and there being local and central government bodies which are representative and have legitimacy and authority. (Østerud et al. 2003, p. 3)

A major conclusion of the research group's final report is that democracy is withering, partly as a result of juridification: ever greater parts of society are regulated by laws and directives, thus increasing the decision-making capacities of judicial bodies at the expense of politics and government (NOU 2003, p. 19).

First of all, the research group points out a new pattern of welfare distribution on the basis of what they see as parliament's increased use of rights legislation within the areas of health, welfare, and education. What was previously decided by, among other things, municipal political debate is now determined by interpreting rights legislation. They argue that the power of jurists, particularly that of lawyers and the courts, has increased (NOU 2003, p. 19, 31). Second, they describe increasing juridification associated with supranationalisation: the implementation of the EEA-agreement, international human rights, and internationalisation of commercial and contract law lead to 'the diminution of elected bodies' space for action. The power of interpretation and balancing of contradictory rights is transferred to the judicial system and courts. (*ibid.*, p. 14)

In what follows, I will primarily concentrate on the first—national—perspective, examining the different forms of juridification as regards three social actors: the legislator, administration, and judiciary. Then the research group's view on juridification will be concretised and the positive and negative conceptual content of juridification will be presented. Thereafter, Habermas' concept of juridification and his legal policy proposals will be discussed in the light of Norwegian research on legal aid. Next, I will look at how Weber's formal legal rationality developed into the procedural rules of the welfare state and its consequences for those seeking justice. The article ends with a conclusion in relation to mobilising the law.

The Theory of Juridification and Law-Dissociated Seekers of Justice

As a first step, I will clarify the concept of juridification.[3] Three different forms of juridification can be seen in three different producers or social actors. The first is the legislator, who contributes to juridification by an increased production of laws. This form of juridification is called *legislative growth*, which can be seen not only in the actual growth of the scope of legislation (quantitative juridification), but also in its increased detail and specialisation, which includes the outsourcing of some areas of legal regulation (the qualitative aspects of juridification). Power thus lies with the legislator, who is able to take decisions regarding political goal setting.

The second form of juridification is administrative, with the production of sub-legal law decrees, circulars, resolutions, etc. *Bureaucratisation*, then, means the 'law' created by the administration. According to Max Weber's ideal type of a legal-bureaucratic leadership, all such administrative actions must be traceable back to a legal basis. The starting point here is Max Weber's classic differentiation between 'formal' and 'material' legal rationality. Formal legal rationality is marked by precisely formulated conditions and legal rules applied according to clearly defined principles, and predictable decisions are expected. Weber regarded the modern European law of his time as 'formal rational'. The exercise of formal rationality is thus associated with the modern era's rationalisation processes by, amongst other things, giving rise to a legal profession, a legal system, legal doctrines, and so on.

The reality of administrative action has, over time, departed to a significant degree from this ideal: today it is primarily characterised by the enforcement of rules by non-jurists or non-judicial rule-appliers. This produces different, often incompatible, legal cultures as regards the application of the law (Mathiesen 2005, p. 231ff.). Moreover, modern interventionist law often features open means-end programmes (often general clauses) rather than precisely programmed conditional programmes. These give wide scope to the administration.

The third form of juridification takes place through *judicialisation*, which describes the production by the judiciary, via its legal practices, of norms with governing potential.

In legal discussion of the concept of juridification, as I have already indicated, growth is the phenomenon most often identified. Flexibilisation is considered as a strategy to deal with supposed overmanaging. Thus there are discussions about decentralising management tasks, switching from detailed rules to framework regulations, as well as using general clauses and indeterminate legal concepts (flexibilisation in a narrower sense). But, what qualitative changes in the legal structure has this juridification entailed? Gunther Teubner suggests problematising the processes of juridification in terms of the particular conditions of the interventionist state. He investigates how these processes correspond to social areas with different political and social structures (Teubner 1985, p. 295). Such an expanded, not exclusively, juridic perspective focuses on, and calls for, 'alternatives to court'. Nils Christie (1977) can be mentioned as a proponent of such thinking. In his trailblazing article written in 1977 *Konflikt som eiendom* [Conflict as property] he traces how juridification can be seen as a process whereby human conflicts are torn from their living context through formalisation; conflict is denatured through its legal treatment. Christie speaks of 'conflict theft'—which prevents those actually involved in the conflict from resolving it. His conclusion is that the conflict should be given back to the actual parties involved in it.

In the final book by the research group, we find several definitions clarifying their interpretation of juridification, and its consequences for democracy:

> Social and cultural problems are increasingly formulated as legal claims. Ever more areas of social life have become subject to legal regulation, and the regulations are in many areas more detailed … Juridification is expressed at different levels, nationally and internationally. Since the 1990s a number of laws has been passed in Norway establishing rights to health services, welfare and education; equality rights and the rights of cultural minorities have been expanded … Juridification means that more areas and more details of social life are regulated by laws and directives, that the power of courts and other legal institutions to make decisions increases at the expense of political and administrative bodies, and that interests are increasingly formulated as legal claims. (Østerud et al. 2003, p. 33, 116)

In other words, the research group identifies both quantitative and qualitative growth in juridification through the establishment of rights in various areas of welfare. This happens nationally and internationally. According to the analysis of the research group, what is positive in this development, namely the fact that citizens have been granted rights and services, comes at a heavy cost to the democratic system.

Because of developments in the law, the centre of gravity has shifted away from citizens organising to influence political decisions, to the individual user/ consumer of the legal apparatus available when interests are to be claimed. This is one of the central arguments of the research group: that the power of elected bodies is transferred to rights-holders and the courts and that local democracy is therefore weakened (*ibid.*, p. 33). This being a central claim of the research group, I will give several key quotes from their report:

> Many of the general welfare rights are to be implemented at the municipal level. Even though many of the laws are imprecise in their allocation of rights, they limit the scope for local autonomy. (*ibid.*, p. 33)

To expand on the research group's claim regarding the weakened state of local democracy due to juridification: the problem for local democracy does not lie solely in the establishment of rights, but also arises from the fact that these rights involve a strain on municipal budgets, so that 'not all rightful claims can be fully satisfied at the same time' (*ibid.*, p. 33). Here lies a great potential for unequal access to the new rights, which according to the research group, is linked to people's individual situations and their ability to mobilize their rights:

> Thus new and unintended forms of inequality arise, where opportunities for pursuing one's case through the mass media and courts may be decisive. Juridification creates a growth in the market for legal services, while the welfare and care professions are squeezed between growing demand and insufficient budgets. (*ibid.*, 33)

In the researchers' analysis, it is local democracy (including the welfare and care professions) which is the 'loser' from growing juridification. If this analysis is extended to access to justice itself, to take an actor perspective, then the 'loser' is precisely the person who is wholly unable to pursue his or her case, or who can only do so to a limited extent—namely people who are disadvantaged, marginalised, or law-dissociated. There are, however, several 'winners'. In the case of Norway, these include actors

12 Juridification, Marginalised Persons and Competence... 293

involved in the legal system (and other supervisory bodies)—judges, lawyers, and jurists:

> This implies that the courts or court-like bodies are increasingly influential at the expense of the legislative branch, and that the separation between legislation and the interpretation of the law is being blurred … In the case of conflict, the regulations have to be interpreted, and different rules are weighed against each other. In this way too courts and other parts of the legal system increase their power and authority. (*ibid.*, p. 33, 116)

The courts and court-like actors are not the only winners. There is more to the concept of juridification, and this is the power of the legal model (Brinkmann 1982): 'The concept of juridification implies that legal language and decision-making methods have annexed other areas, such as the political or pedagogical' (*ibid.*). This development is not happening only at the national level. The research group was also deeply concerned about the continuing constraining effects of international developments:

> When, in ever more areas of life and society, rights are conferred through a constitution or through the incorporation of international treaties, the scope for action of elected bodies is reduced … The EEA-agreement means Norway is bound by the EU's directives and regulations in all areas covered by the agreement. Through supranational court interpretations of treaty clauses and common law, Parliament's ability to draft independent legislation declines in more and more new areas. (*ibid.*, p. 21, 33)

In other words, the group's central argument on the shift of power to the courts focuses on international legal developments as represented by supranational courts such as the European Court of Human Rights or the European Court of Justice (ECJ) and European Free Trade Association (EFTA) courts; international treaties such as the EEA-agreement or World Trade Organisation (WTO) regulations and human rights conventions.

Juridification here, then, has been loaded with a *negative conceptual content*. However, one of the group's core researchers, Hege Skjeie, expressed a separate, dissenting opinion, maintaining that rights may contribute to strengthening the democratic process. Her central argument is that various human rights, and other social rights, can help ensure that groups with less economic and social power have an equal opportunity for democratic participation. She lays particular emphasis on the 'significance in terms of gender politics of rights policies and rights doctrines', which provide 'opportunities for individual and collective empowerment' (NOU 2003, p. 19, 75). This is very interesting from a legal policy perspective as it suggests a great potential for improving the legal opportunities of marginalised groups. So here, juridification has a *positive connotation*, one also to be found in the view taken by Rüdiger Voigt in the 1980s. Voigt recognises the potential both to increase and to limit freedom of juridification, in the individual and structural planes:

> Does juridification always mean a curtailment of liberty for the individual, or is it possible in at least certain policy areas to say that we are dealing rather with a tendency to ensure individual liberty (for instance, by ensuring social rights)? And is the curtailment of political scope for action (for instance, through depoliticisation) necessarily a consequence of juridification, or in certain circumstances can it contribute to expanding the scope for reform politics? (Voigt 1980, p. 10, my translation)

This question has also been raised by Detlef Schulze (2005), who asks whether 'the man in the street' himself contributes to processes of juridification. He questions the thesis that the juridical perspective and everyday life are separate areas only superficially linked to each other, suggesting that, in certain situations, it is precisely 'the man in the street' who may independently demand 'juridification'. He calls this positive, or partly emancipatory, form of juridification *performative* juridification, as opposed to its restricting *deformative* twin.

The research group's view that juridification has had negative consequences for the Norwegian democratic system has been criticised. For reasons of space, this critique cannot be fully explored here, but some of the points of contention will now be briefly mentioned.[4] Andenæs (2006, p. 587ff.) is sceptical about the courts' alleged growth in power, and, among other things, points out the stability of the number of cases heard in the period from 1950 until today. Moreover, the great increase in the number of jurists in Norway (1815: 329; 1960: 6600; 2002: 14,000) does not demonstrate a transfer of power from politicians to others, but is rather a sign of a more complex and confused legal situation resulting from globalisation. Blicher and Molander (2006, p. 601ff.) criticise the research group on the grounds that they do not treat juridification in a 'sufficiently differentiated fashion and thereby close the discussion on juridification, in both descriptive and normative terms.' Feiring criticises the research group's thesis on juridification in relation to welfare policy for taking a mainly quantitative perspective. Rights will only be able to limit political freedom of action if they are strong, and also provide strong rights protection (Feiring 2006, p. 577). All in all, the research group paints a 'pessimistic picture of the future of democracy'. As has been mentioned, this is linked to the negative conceptual connotations of their view of juridification. Their analysis is in line with the dominant message of the critical debates on juridification in Germany in the 1980s, which can be understood as a reaction to the disappointing results of the eagerness for social-democratic reform in the 1970s. Besides quantitative and qualitative claims regarding the growth in legislation, claims were also made in these debates that it was bringing about large-scale regulation of the last remaining autonomous areas of human action, along with judicialisation and a de-democratisation of politics through the continual increase in the use of the courts.

Habermas' Concept of Juridification and Legal Policy Proposals as Seen by Norwegian Legal Aid Research

Jürgen Habermas took this debate further, and sharpened it by claiming that there is an ongoing 'colonisation of the lifeworld' (Habermas 1981, p. 522f.; 1987, p. 356ff.). He argues this results from an eagerness for legal regulation, which also gets directed at remaining non-regulated and intimate areas. Here, too, juridification takes on deeply negative connotations.

Kirchheimer had, as we have seen, narrowed the juridification concept to apply to the phenomenon of the Weimar Republic and, thematically, to (labour) law and politics. Further, developing this thematic concept, Habermas generalises the notion of juridification in two ways. First of all, he disengages the concept from the historical association with the Weimar Republic. He then uses it in an expanded perspective to analyse the relation of law to politics, and to identify legal expansion processes in a number of partial social systems, such as economic and education systems. The problems of the welfare state in relation to the expansion of the law are identified as a 'colonisation of the lifeworld' (Habermas 1981, vol. 2, p. 522ff.; 1987, p. 356ff.). Habermas identifies four phases of juridification: the first determines the shape of the bourgeois state in the era of absolutism in Western Europe. The second leads to constitutional government such as the monarchy in Germany in the 1800s. The third produces the democratic constitutional government seen in Europe and North America after the French Revolution. The last phase shapes the social and democratic constitutional government that arose from the struggle of the European labour movement during the 1900s.

This last phase has a liberty-granting character, from the perspective of both citizen and the democratic legislator. Habermas does not, however, consider this to apply to all social governmental regulations. Governmental welfare policy is marked by ambivalence between guaranteeing and denying liberty (*ibid.*, p. 531, 361). In the field of governmental welfare policy Habermas discusses this idea under the heading 'juridification and bureaucratisation as the boundaries of welfare policy'. In the case of legal rights to sickness or old age benefits, these represent progress compared with poor relief, but on the other hand those entitled to social security pay a high price in terms of the encroachment on their lifeworlds. 'These costs ensue from the bureaucratic implementation and monetary redemption of welfare entitlements' (*ibid.*, p. 362). This is linked with the legal necessity to lay down rights for individual claims under carefully specified general conditions. The individualised regulation of old age pensions can have negative consequences for holders of the rights and their relation to their own local communities; for instance, it may affect the willingness of the surroundings to give additional assistance. The specification of legal conditions is once again associated with a significant compulsion to redefine everyday situations. Finally the problem-solving of the administration is peculiar in the sense that it abstracts human beings from the situation, to subsume them under the rule and treat them administratively. In other words, the administration must be selective.

Kjersti Ericsson has described this problem in relation to the child welfare services, as an example of the juridification of social work. She writes:

> 'Child welfare services have to evaluate concrete family relations and protect the good of the individual child. As a public body the service must at the same time function according to the principles of justice and the rule of law … But it is problematic if juridical language becomes norm-creating for the way child welfare problems should be handled and understood.' (Ericsson 1998, p. 187).

According to Ericsson, the problematic lies precisely in that transition point where jurisprudence goes from representing 'gateways' to delivering a rule-bound, systematised thinking that becomes a dominant 'pattern of understanding'—one that 'phenomenalises' the lives of children in the operationalisation of juridical thinking, without recognising the unique and many-faceted nature of the context they are in. Ericsson's analysis also provides a good example of the functional limits of the law, where certain juridification processes relating to alternative problem-solving structures—'everyday meetings between social worker and client' (*ibid.*, p. 193)—turn out to be inadequate because they require too much of the governing capacity of the law (Teubner 1985, p. 292).

The fundamental basis of the juridification debates, in relation to the limits of governmental steering policy and the function of the law, has, in recent years, become less dominant in the German debate. This is particularly true for Habermas, who has clearly changed his opinion. In his 1992 book 'Faktizität und Geltung' ('Between Facts and Norms', English transl. 1996 from Habermas 1992), he dissociates himself from the view that juridification has a generally problematic—socially disintegrative—structure in the field of social law (Habermas 1992, p. 502 fn. 47): According to this thesis, the governmental promise of serving social integration by appropriate juridification efforts would, in fact, lead to the disintegration of the life relations replaced by legal social integration (Habermas 1985 II, p. 534). This thesis is one no longer espoused by Habermas.

In 'Faktizität und Geltung' (Habermas 1992), there are also interesting discussions of legal policy and the sociology of law on the possibilities and limitations of disadvantaged groups in relation to legal strategies. Habermas' point of departure is that the complexity of the law means that the user needs a high level of competency, which is usually lacking.

The law can only be effective if users are sufficiently informed and able to concretise their rights:

> 'The competence to mobilize the law already depends in general on formal education, social background, and other variables (such as gender, age, previous courtroom experience, and the kind of social relationship affected by the conflict). But the access barriers are even higher for utilizing materialized law, which requires laypersons to dissect their everyday problems (regarding work, leisure and consumption, housing, illness, etc.) into highly specialized legal constructions that are abstractly related to real-life contexts.' (Habermas 1996, p. 411)

Habermas calls for a compensatory legal protection policy that 'strengthens vulnerable clients' legal knowledge, their capacity to perceive and articulate problems, their readiness for conflict and, in general, their ability to assert themselves' (*ibid.*). Habermas expects a strengthening of the countervailing power of social interests, both in the form of conventional measures such as legal protection insurance, free legal aid and 'collective modes of implementing the law' (*ibid.*). Among these are community complaints and class-action lawsuits, and the provision of ombudspersons and other conflict resolution measures. However, it is important, if one remembers his starting point, that the client should not be completely disempowered or forced into the role of the passive recipient of legal aid. According to Habermas, this can only be counteracted:

> 'if collective legal protection, besides relieving the strain on individuals through competent representation, also involves them in the organized perception, articulation, and assertion of their own interests. If the above

proposals are not to further exacerbate the loss of voice in the welfare state, then affected citizens must experience the organization of legal protection as a political process, and they themselves must be able to take part in the construction of countervailing power and the articulation of social interests.' (*ibid.*)

Legal aid is thus politicised, and attributed with the potential to be a countervailing power, if the actual aid recipient is involved in the process of formulating policy.

At this point it is important to rehearse some of the central findings of Norwegian legal aid research, to provide empirical illustration of the theoretical statements of Habermas. First, there was the discovery of a great unmet need for legal aid, particularly amongst disadvantaged groups. Second, the social distribution of the unmet need for legal aid was skewed. There was a very strong correlation between lack of education and the need for legal aid. Third, it was shown there had to be a strong 'proactive' element to legal aid, in order to uncover people's problems. Fourth, the best and most proactive legal aid was always confronted by a fundamental limitation: particular problems may be solvable, but not the actual foundation of the problems: poverty itself could not be changed. As the authors of a classic 1971 legal aid study put it, this is '… an expression of how it is when some are poor and some are rich, a condition by and large in accordance with prevailing law … Their fundamental problem is to escape poverty.' (Eskeland and Finne 1973, p. 214) This analysis cannot be challenged even now that Norway has a system of free legal aid, as it is less 'free' than its name suggests. The system has access barriers, and only those with low incomes and little wealth are entitled to free legal aid. The system is also excess-based and does not apply to cases in many areas, such as those against the public administration (see Chap. 2 above). In 2005, when the Oslo Office for free legal aid, then the only one in the country, was evaluated, researchers found almost 50% of requests did not fall within the scope of the law for free legal aid (Andenæs et al. 2005, p. 31). It took a long time to convince politicians that the report's findings were meant as a criticism, not of how the office was working, but of the serious defects of the Legal Aid Act.

The Development from Weber's Formal Rationality to the Procedural Rules of the Welfare State and the Consequences for Those Seeking Justice

As Habermas has shown, juridification must be viewed in a wider historical context, to see how the law changes character and function in step with general societal changes. As we have seen, he identifies four juridification thrusts that show how 'modern' law has responded to global societal changes. Continuing this line of thinking, on the basis of a problem analysis of juridification and its limits of operation, Teubner makes two inferences he sees as substantial. The first of these is that one should concentrate on social state juridification, where the law as a governing tool has an intervening and compensatory function. In such circumstances, a proliferation of norms is not so much a problem for the law, as for the welfare or interventionist state. The second consequence is that because of the complete differentiation of different life areas in a legal form, there can be no talk about developing a strategy based on deregulation or dejuridification. The welfare state's spur to juridification must be accepted as a historical fact, without losing sight of its 'dysfunctional consequences' (Teubner 1985).

The question becomes how the law itself changes in the particular welfare state juridification. Earlier, I have mentioned Max Weber's differentiation between a formal and a material legal rationality. Weber argues that formal rationality is threatened by unmodern material rationality such as 'ethical imperatives, utilitarian or other prescriptions or political purposes', which go against formal rationality's logical abstraction (Weber 1967, p. 125). The internal quality of the legal culture will therefore suffer 'if sociological and economic or ethical considerations are utilised instead of juridical concepts' (*ibid.*, p. 346). In the age of Weber, such material tendencies in law appeared particularly as social demands in democracy. Although these tendencies in Weber's age can be considered marginal, a materialisation of formal law represents the 'dominant development trend', after Teubner (1985), in welfare law juridification.

A significant structural factor in welfare law juridification is its focus on the purpose of the law. Formal law's rule orientation is in favour of an instrumental orientation in retreat. Nonet and Selznick describe this development as 'sovereignty of purpose' (1978, p. 78ff.). As an answer to formal law's internal crisis, this responsive law is more open and flexible, and more able to respond to the needs of particular circumstances. It is the autonomous processes in law itself that inevitably produce dogmatic structures and forms of argumentation, as well as conflict resolution methods and participation models. These characteristics develop a dynamic whereby formal law is destroyed and reconstructed through incorporation of the new—responsive—law's attention to needs, sociological orientation, and political participation (Nonet and Selznick 1978). This is precisely what Weber identified as the 'materialisation' of the law.

Teubner calls the interventionist welfare state's new legal form 'regulatory law', and describes it thus:

> 'In its function it is geared to the guidance requirements of the social state, in its legitimation the social results of its controlling and compensating regulations are predominant. In its structure it tends to be particularistic, purpose oriented and dependent on assistance from the social sciences.' (Teubner 1987, p. 19)

As the last step in his analysis, Teubner discusses whether regulatory law has now reached its limits. As we have seen, Weber pointed out two contradictory developmental tendencies in law. One is continued specialisation and professionalisation in the legal system that extends its formal aspects. The other is determined by the 'material' demands of the social state. From a systems theory, Luhmann-inspired perspective, this is about a conflict between, on the one hand, the function of the law, which requires specialisation in order to react to the expectations of society, and on the other hand, the regulatory output of the law demanded by the systems in their surroundings.

According to Luhmann, the legal system's 'formalisation' will increase to such a degree of autonomy that one may speak of autopoietic self-reference. As is well known, Luhmann underwent a so-called paradigmatic shift (autopoietic turn) around 1980. General systems (such as politics, the law, the economy, science, the mass media, religion, etc.) were no longer exclusively characterised as system-environment-difference, but as so-called self-reference or autopoiesis. By this, Luhmann means a state of affairs where the selection mechanisms necessary for the formation of a system become ever more complicated. Systems become more and more normatively closed, refer to themselves, and organise everything on the basis of themselves. This is what is meant by self-reference or autopoiesis. For Luhmann, the necessity to reproduce themselves constitutes the central factor in the development of systems. From this viewpoint, the legal system is understood as a closed system, constantly preoccupied with its own autonomy and the reproduction of autopoiesis:

> 'Their characteristics are: that they themselves produce and delimit the operative unity of their elements (i.e. for our area: legally relevant events and decisions) through the operation of their elements and that it is precisely this autopoietic process that lends its own unity to the system.' (Luhmann 2014, p. 281f)

For the law, this means, among other things, that such a system produces, and reproduces itself. The law supports its validity solely by normativity and thereby disconnects all extra-judicial circumstances such as politics, morals, and science from natural law justifications (Calliess 2006, p. 64). At the same time, the law's growing formalisation increases its materialisation. This is related to its specialisation within the system, where it keeps forming norms and procedures, which, in turn, may be used for social state governing purposes. Teubner formulates it in this paradoxical fashion: 'Law, by being posited as autonomous in its function—formality—becomes increasingly dependent on the demands for performance from its social environment—materiality.' (Teubner 1987, p. 20) Put another way, when it is instrumentalised for welfare state purposes, modern, autonomous, highly formalised, and professional law becomes subject to specific demands both from the political system and from the areas of life which are to be regulated. In this conflictual relationship, between increasing autonomy and increasing dependence,

Teubner sees modern juridification's necessity and problematics (*ibid.*, p. 315).

Thus, as Luhmann and Teubner see it, the problem for modern law lies in the contradiction between the growing autonomy of systems and the parallel increase in dependence. Once different systems such as the economy, the law and politics are so strongly characterised by self-reference, they are no longer accessible to each other. So, for example, politics makes binding decisions within its own sphere of power, while the law relates exclusively to its demands for normativity in the same way that the economic system relates to demands for competition and the money economy. External demands are only recognised by systems if they satisfy the systems' internal logic and selection criteria.

> 'In terms of environmental influences on law, this means that even the most powerful social and political pressures are only perceived and processed in the legal system to the extent that they appear on the inner 'screens' of legal reality constructions'. (Teubner 1987, p. 20)

From a steering perspective the effect of the regulatory or interventionist law must be assessed as neutral, within the limits of the individual system's self-reference. This relation is described by Teubner as a regulatory trilemma: 'Every regulatory intervention which goes beyond these limits is either irrelevant or produces disintegrating effects on the social area of life or else disintegrating effects on regulatory law itself.' (Teubner 1987, p. 21)

The situation is now even more complicated, as juridification processes constitute not only a relation between the legal system and the area of social life to be regulated, but also a relation to the political system. Thus juridification must go through a complicated process of many-faceted political steering decisions, followed by legal operationalisation and applications, and finally implementation. Many problems may arise, due to the insufficient 'structural coupling of politics, law and the area of social life' (Teubner, *ibid.*).

What Teubner doubts is whether the law and politics are at all capable of ensuring the integration Durkheim expected to result from organic solidarity—given the problematic framework we have discussed and the systems' often disintegrating and hence incompatible internal logic. Politics and the law seek a solution by not attempting to standardise social conduct directly, but rather governing it more indirectly through legislation. This can be seen in the introduction of legal procedural elements in the law following a formal legal starting point. Proceduralisation (Röhl and Machura 1997) is a collective concept describing the role of the law in promoting the establishment of social systems that can learn on the way and can be controlled (Teubner 1987). Such procedural rules or legal frames declare which groups are to be brought in to solve the problem in question. Control must happen in the particular field requiring regulation, through persons located there.

I want to conclude by looking at the example of the Norwegian extra-judicial conflict resolution system for consumers. This can be viewed as an example of 'hybrid regulation forms, where the public, industry and consumers meet together to administer, interpret and shape current legal practice' (Stø et al. 2007, p. 11). The purpose of these forms of procedural regulation is both to ease the burden on the courts, and to effectivise and legitimise the execution of the law 'by affected parties themselves finding amicable solutions and interpreting the relevant law' (*ibid.*). This self-regulation of industry and consumers is inspired by the state's acknowledgment that it is unable to regulate everything itself: 'In the real world the state often lacks sufficient knowledge and/or instruments of power and is dependent upon the cooperation of the regulated to be able to regulate and rule society' (*ibid.*). This modern form of conflict resolution by procedural or hybrid forms of regulation has resulted in most consumer complaints being solved by the Consumer Dispute Board [*Forbrukertvistutvalget*]—which handles consumer complaints in the areas of the Consumer Purchase Act, Tradesman Services Act, and the Return of Purchases Act, and a number (22 in total) of voluntary, sector-specific claims boards such as the Banking Complaints Board, Dwellings Dispute Board, Insurance Complaints Board, Complaints Board for Car Hire Services, Parking Complaints Board, and so on (*ibid.*, p. 20).

But proceduralisation cannot stop weak rights being ineffective—in this case, the rights of consumers—when they cannot compete with the legal position of the opposing side. The practices of the Insurance Complaints Office (ICO), which opened in 1971, will illustrate this point. The office is also the secretariat of the Insurance Complaints Board. The ICO provides free legal aid to insurance customers making complaints, through an agreement between the Norwegian Financial Services Association, the Consumer Council, and the Confederation of Norwegian Enterprise. The office is financed by the insurance industry, on a per incident basis, in relation to the numbers of cases reported to the ICO. The individual boards are chaired by an independent jurist. The boards also include two representatives from the Consumer Council and two from the insurance industry. The evaluation report of the Norwegian extra-judicial dispute resolution system, quoted above, concludes that 'the system works well in the main' (Stø et al. 2007, p. 79), but problems regarding the neutrality and independence of the systems are pointed out.

A general problem with such forms of regulations can occur when private actors are involved in regulation and conflict resolution in areas where those opposing them are weak: when, for instance, the interests of private industry dominate conflict resolution by defining and interpreting existing laws, this can help cement already existing power discrepancies between heavy industry and weak consumer interests. In such cases, political intervention is required to limit the legal frames of procedural rules relating to the interests of heavy industry. So, proceduralisation, and a stronger focus on autonomy, are not the final solution: '"Inexactness" of legal regulation and increased coordination costs would almost inevitably be side-effects of a "proceduralization" of law.' (Teubner 1987, p. 39).

Conclusion on Mobilising the Law

Generally speaking, the ability to mobilise the law is dependent on having information about the law and competence. In the absence of this, compensatory legal aid is required. Examples of this include legal protection insurance, free legal aid, the collectivisation of implementing the law, and ombudspersons. Juridification of this positive—emancipatory—

variety has potential as a social countervailing power. Compensatory legal aid requires a competent deputy, but also a strengthening of the justice seekers' participatory abilities, so they avoid disenfranchisement (i.e., to achieve inclusion). Compensatory policies are not unlimited. Legal aid projects with a proactive profile are rare, because they demand considerable resources. Proactive legal aid is thus selective; it is used to discover where the real need is.

However, access to the law is not only a problem to do with class. Proceduralisation and more indirect forms of government through the introduction of elements of self-regulation show that there are not only weak justice seekers, but also weak rights. This applies to consumers generally, regardless of their social status. This means that the elements of self-rule in procedural regulations do not hinder, but possibly help cement inequalities of power in the world of producers and consumers.

What can be done in addition to the remedial actions already discussed, in order to improve the abilities and opportunities of (law-dissociated) citizens to mobilise the law? I have presented some proposals elsewhere (Papendorf 2012, p. 261ff.):

- Mandatory training in school
  The law is increasingly complex, and this makes it difficult to mobilise. This is particularly true for law-dissociated citizens. To alter this situation it is important to increase knowledge and understanding at school level, to help pupils to utilise the law where this seems useful as a problem solving strategy.
- Needs thinking must be integrated into legal access for law-dissociated citizens
  The Finnish law theorist Thomas Wilhelmsson introduced the idea of a 'social civil law' (Wilhelmsson 1987). His revolutionary idea was to integrate needs thinking into contract law, where there is often one strong and one weak party. This real difference (despite formal equality) in the contractual relationship would, he argues, be ameliorated by introducing needs-oriented principles giving precedence to the interests of weaker parties in the contractual relationship.

- Increasing the knowledge of certain groups
  The Norwegian women's legal aid organisation, JURK, seeks to provide legal information to minority women. Legal information is given as part of an empowerment strategy to enable them to mobilise legal aid independently. This strategy should be expanded and become mandatory for the immigrant population in general.
- Compensatory legal aid must be extended and expanded. Compensatory legal aid requires both a competent deputy, but also a strengthening of justice seekers' participatory abilities, to protect them from disenfranchisement. Proactive efforts are needed to reach all justice seekers, including those suffering from poverty, drug problems, and discrimination.

Notes

1. *Makt- og demokratiutredningen*, hereafter referred to as 'the research group'.
2. All quotes translated from the Norwegian by the author unless otherwise noted.
3. Originally, the concept of juridification differed from the one commonly used in contemporary debates. Otto Kirchheimer (1928) used the term first, but as a concept relating to political struggle in the labour rights debates in the Weimar Republic. Kirchheimer criticised the ongoing juridification of labour conditions, which led to a neutralisation of former political class conflicts (*ibid.*, p. 596ff.).
4. For a more thorough presentation of the critique, (see Papendorf 2012, p. 31 ff.).

References

Andenæs, K. (2006). Om maktens rettsliggjøring og rettsliggjøringens maktpotensial [On the juridification of power and the power potential of juridification]. *TfS 4*, p. 587ff.

Andenæs, K. et al. (2005). *Kontoret for fri rettshjelp: Retshjælp til ubemidlede. Evaluering av en Oslo-institusjon gjennom 112 år* [The Office for Free Legal Aid: Legal aid for the indigent. Evaluation of an Oslo institution over 112 years]. Oslo.

Blicher, L., & Molander, A.. (2006). Maktutredningens rettsliggjøringsbegrep [The juridification concept of the Research Group on Power and Democracy]. *TfS 4*, p. 601ff.

Brinkmann, J. (1982). *Konfliktsosiologi* [Sociology of conflict]. Oslo: Institutt for rettssosiologi.

Calliess, G. P. (2006). *Systemtheorie*: Luhmann/Teubner. In B. Christensen & A. Fischer-Lescano (Eds.), *Neue Theorien des Rechts* (pp. 57–75). Stuttgart: UTB.

Christie, N. (1977). Konflikt som eiendom [Conflict as property]. *Tidsskrift for Rettsvitenskap, 90*, p. 113ff.

Ericsson, K. (1998). Regler og relasjoner i barnevernet [Rules and relations in the child welfare services]. *Tidsskrift for velferdsforskning, 1*(4), p. 187ff.

Eskeland, S., & Finne, J. (1973). *Rettshjelp* [Legal aid]. Oslo: Pax Forlag.

Feiring, Eli. (2006). Demokratiet og rettsliggjøring av velferdspolitikken [Democracy and juridification of welfare policy]. *TFS 4*, p. 575ff.

Habermas, J. (1981). *Theorie des kommunikativen Handelns. Bind 1: Handlungsrationalität und gesellschaftliche Rationalisierung.* Bind 2: *Zur Kritik der funktionalistischen Vernunft.* Suhrkamp: Frankfurt/Main (3rd ed.) 1985. English translation: *The theory of communicative action, volume 1. Reason and the rationalization of society.* Boston: Beacon Press, 1984. Vol. 2. *Lifeword and system: A critique of functionalist reason.* Boston: Beacon Press, 1987.

Habermas, J. (1985). Dialektik der Rationalisierung. In *Die neue Unübersichtlichkeit* (p. 167ff). Frankfurt/Main: Suhrkamp.

Habermas, J. (1992). *Faktizität und Geltung. Beiträge zur Diskurstheorie des Rechts und des demokratischen Rechtsstaats.* Frankfurt am Main: Suhrkamp. English translation: Habermas, J. (1996) *Between facts and norms. Contributions to a discourse theory of law and democracy.* Massachusetts: MIT Press.

Kirchheimer, O. (1928). Zur Staatslehre des Sozialismus und Bolschewismus. In *ZfP*, p. 596ff.

Luhmann, N. (2014). *A sociological theory of law* (2nd ed.). Oxon: Routledge.

Mathiesen, T. (2005). *Retten i samfunnet. En innføring i rettssosiologi* [The law in society. An introduction to the sociology of law]. Oslo: Pax Forlag.

Nonet, P., & Selznick, P. (1978). *Law and society in transition. Toward responsive law*. New York: Harper & Row.
NOU. (2003). 19 *Makt og demokrati. Sluttrapport fra Makt- og demokratiutredningen* [Power and democracy. Final report of the Research Group on Power and Democracy].
Østerud, Ø. (2006). Makt og urett—kommentar til en rettsteoretisk kritikk av Makt- og Demokratiutredningen [Power and injustice—Comments on a law theoretical critique of the Research Group on Power and Democracy]. *Lov og rett, 45*, p. 106ff.
Østerud, Ø. et al. (2003). *Makten og demokratiet. En sluttbok fra Makt- og Demokratiutredningen* [Power and democracy. A final book by the Research Group on Power and Democracy]. Oslo: Gyldendal.
Papendorf, K. (2012). *Rett for alle? Rettsliggjøring og rettsfjerne personers mulighet til å mobilisere retten* [Law for all? Juridification and possibilities for law-dissociated persons to mobilise the law]. Oslo: Novus forlag.
Röhl, K., & Machura, S. (Eds.). (1997). *Procedural justice*. Aldershot: Ashgate.
Schulze, D. G. (2005). *Verrechtlichung—Deformation oder Performation?* Überarbeiteter Vortrag auf der Tagung "Die Jurisprudenz zwischen Verrechtlichung und Rechtsferne der Alltagspraxis" am 17./18. Juni 2005 in Düsseldorf.
Skjeie, H. (2003). Særuttalelse fra Hege Skjeie [Separate opinion by Hege Skjeie]. In NOU (2003):19. *Makt og demokrati. Sluttrapport fra Makt- og demokratiutredning*.
Stø, E. et al. (Ed.) (2007). *Å få rett—når du har rett. En diskusjon av de frivillige klagenemndene og FTUs effektivitet, nøytralitet og legitimitet* [Being granted rights—When you are right. A discussion on the voluntary complaints boards and the efficiency, neutrality and legitimacy of the Consumer dispute panel]. SIFO. Oppdragsrapport nr. p. 4.
Teubner, G. (1985). Verrechtlichung—Begriffe, Merkmale, Grenzen, Auswege. In F. Kübler (Ed.), *Verrechtlichung von Wirtschaft, Arbeit und sozialer Solidarität* (p. 290ff). Frankfurt/Main: Suhrkamp. English edition: Juridification—Concepts, aspects, limits, solutions. In G. Teubner (Ed.) (1987), *Juridification of Social Spheres* (p. 3ff). Berlin/New York: Walter de Gruyter.
Teubner, G. (Ed.) (1987). *Global law without a state*. Brookfield/Singapore/Sydney: Dartmouth/Aldershot.
Voigt, R. (1980). Verrechtlichung in Staat und Gesellschaft. In R. Voigt (Ed.), *Verrechtlichung. Analysen zu Funktion und Wirkung von Parlamentarisierung, Bürokratisierung und Justizialisierung sozialer, politischer und ökonomischer Prozesse* (p. 15ff). Athenäum: Königstein/Taunus.

Weber, M. (1967 (1960)). *Rechtssoziologie aus dem Manuskript herausgegeben und eingeleitet von Johannes Winckelmann* (2nd ed.), Neuwied am Rhein und Berlin: Hermann-Luchterhand Verlag.

Wilhelmsson, T. (1987). *Social civilrätt. Om behovsorienterade element i kontrakträttens allmänna läror* [Social civil law. On needs oriented elements in the general discipline of contract law]. Helsinki: Juristförbundets förlag.

Open Access This chapter is distributed under the terms of the Creative Commons Attribution 4.0 International License (http://creativecommons.org/licenses/by/4.0/), which permits use, duplication, adaptation, distribution, and reproduction in any medium or format, as long as you give appropriate credit to the original author(s) and the source, a link is provided to the Creative Commons license, and any changes made are indicated.

The images or other third party material in this book are included in the work's Creative Commons license, unless indicated otherwise in the credit line; if such material is not included in the work's Creative Commons license and the respective action is not permitted by statutory regulation, users will need to obtain permission from the license holder to duplicate, adapt or reproduce the material.

13

Outsourcing Legal Aid in the Nordic Welfare States

Ole Hammerslev and Olaf Halvorsen Rønning

Introduction

The Nordic countries have as a common characteristic the ideology of universal welfare. The Nordic welfare states were, largely, built through comprehensive written law, giving all citizens clearly defined rights, and entitling them to receive specific, but equal and sufficient, benefits. Public authorities advised citizens about their welfare rights and ensured they got them. However, the increasing complexity of welfare rights and of regulation, and increasing bureaucracy meant that that poor people in particular, but ordinary people too, had difficulty in naming their social problems legally, and

---

O. Hammerslev (✉)
Department of Law, University of Southern Denmark, Odense M, Denmark

Department of Criminology and Sociology of Law, University of Oslo, Oslo, Norway

O.H. Rønning
Department of Criminology and Sociology of Law, University of Oslo, Oslo, Norway

claiming their rights either from public bodies or in court. Thus, even though legal services in all Nordic countries were based primarily on market assumptions, legal aid schemes became—as part of the universal welfare state ideology—ways to ensure people could claim their welfare rights.

One feature of civil legal aid schemes in all the Nordic countries is this backdrop of the universal welfare state ideology; it is the context in which the legal aid schemes have been understood. This includes, to a certain extent, the ideological component of the schemes, namely that they all have the same social democratic welfare state core. In the earliest stages of the modern legal aid schemes, public legal aid in all Nordic countries was an informally governed, discretionary feature of social security, and could be granted if deemed necessary. The schemes focused on legal aid in court cases. It was to some extent an addition to charitable legal aid, such as that provided by church organisations, for example, but the aid given by such organisations was limited. The next stage came with the development of formal legal aid legislation, from the 1950s onwards. Although the actual implementation of their legal aid acts varied, all Nordic countries enacted welfare state-inspired legal aid legislation, which set up quite generous schemes with the aim to improve legal aid, and ensure access to the courts and legal services for all. Finland was first, passing a new Legal Aid Act in 1953, and, in 1973, developing a more extensive and very clearly welfare state-inspired system. Sweden followed suit in 1972, Denmark in 1974, and Norway in 1980. Such legislation was never passed in Iceland, but a similar act was brought before Parliament. Of these, the Norwegian Act was originally extraordinarily generous: for example, it granted legal aid outside court proceedings to all who met the financial criteria, unless they could not benefit from legal aid assistance. Similarly, the Swedish scheme of the time has been characterised as 'probably the most generous and comprehensive scheme internationally' (Kilian and Regan 2004, p. 247).

The chapters making up this book show how civil legal aid schemes are structured in the modern Nordic welfare states, and demonstrate the different ways the schemes have developed in each Nordic country. The core welfare state component in the public legal aid schemes remains but to a varying degree. The public legal aid schemes are managed as welfare state institutions and have been heavily state-funded. In fact, the Nordic countries are consistently among the nations in Europe spending most on legal aid per inhabitant. Drawing on national reports, we will discuss whether a uniquely Nordic model of legal aid exists. To place the Nordic schemes in the European and international context, similarities and differences between the Nordic countries are analysed by comparing their legal aid schemes and relating them to international legal aid developments. The findings will also be related to discussions about general developments in the welfare state. Through case studies of prominent third sector legal aid organisations and mentoring programmes, we have considered the difficulties involved in reaching marginalised target groups, how third sector institutions have organised legal aid outside the welfare state, and how they help marginalised individuals to name, blame, and claim—to adopt the notions of Felstiner et al. (1980/81)—their rights from public authorities, in particular. Because of a shift in modern Nordic welfare states towards third sector organisations, and the insurance market, third sector organisations have become more important in reaching groups in society with special needs, and are able to manoeuvre in ways that public organisations cannot. Finally, based on these case studies, we discuss how the changing role of the law and the possibility of legal encounters between citizens, and caseworkers, lawyers, public officials, etc. affect the most vulnerable groups in welfare societies.

Legal Aid in the Nordic Countries

We will now, on the basis of the reports on the five countries, make a comparison between legal aid in the Nordic countries and discuss whether it is possible to identify a Nordic model of legal aid.

By international standards, Norway is financially the most generous provider of legal aid assistance per inhabitant. In Chap. 2, Rønning shows that the Norwegian state funds legal aid primarily through judicare schemes, in which paid lawyers in private practice provide legal aid to people who are granted legal aid. Eligibility for legal aid in civil cases is determined by financial criteria, which have to be met to obtain aid in the civil areas listed in the Legal Aid Act. These areas include divorce, social security, immigration, and unfair dismissal. However, the income limits for financial eligibility for legal aid have been stable, although average salaries have increased over time. The scheme only covers legal aid in cases where no other assistance is provided. This limitation mostly rules out legal aid assistance in administrative matters, because public officials are obligated to give guidance, under the Norwegian Administrative Procedure Act. Norwegian legal aid research has criticised the scheme for being too restrictive, and therefore not meeting the legal needs of the population. Many people from the most disadvantaged groups will have frequent legal conflicts with administrative bodies but, under this rule, will be excluded from the scheme. However, in addition to the public judicare scheme, there are quite a few alternative legal aid providers. Some involve the commercial provision of legal assistance, such as legal aid insurance, while some are non-profit initiatives. These are oriented around student legal aid clinics, such as Juss-Buss, described by Hammerslev et al. in Chap. 7, special interest organisations providing legal aid to specific groups such as asylum seekers or drug users, consumer organisations, and labour unions. Some are fully or partly state-funded but managed independently.

In Chap. 3, Schoultz shows how the Swedish legal aid schemes that came into force in the 1970s were part of a universal welfare programme designed to compensate for financial differences by providing comprehensive legal aid via state-financed legal bureaus with more than a hundred public-sector lawyers. However, to reduce spending on legal aid, new legislation changed the system in the 1990s. The reform made legal aid schemes subordinate to private legal aid insurance, and the state-financed legal aid bureaus were closed and replaced by a judicare system. Schoultz demonstrates that this fundamental change meant that the current legal aid schemes went from being tax-funded to being mainly provided through private insurance. The shift towards insurance only covered legal cases conducted in court, and, thus limited the type of legal aid services provided. Legal aid other than for court proceedings is limited, both in terms of legal expenses insurance and of public legal aid. In principle, all legal matters qualify for public legal aid, but the Legal Aid Act excludes things such as debt restructuring, most family law disputes, and the preparation of tax returns, wills, and prenuptial agreements. The legal aid scheme also makes individuals responsible for identifying and naming legal problems, and for paying for legal assistance, which may be reimbursed later. Because of the high cost of legal consultation, which is a prerequisite for applying for legal aid, people get discouraged from seeking advice. Citizens, moreover, face the very real burden of naming a social problem and turning it into a legal issue, in order to apply for legal aid. This transformation process is identified in previous studies as particularly challenging for the most socially disadvantaged groups. The 'cut down' reforms of the 1990s brought back the need for *pro bono* work by lawyers (Regan 2001), in the same way that students' legal clinics developed. The reform of legal aid policy has left some needy groups without any legal help: for example, those with moderate means, who do not have legal expenses insurance, are not poor enough to qualify for legal aid, and not able to afford a private lawyer. The same goes for those with moderate means, who are not eligible for legal aid for work-related problems, and who do not belong to a union.

In Chap. 4, Rissanen shows how legal aid in Finland is organised differently than in the other Nordic countries. Like Swedish legal aid in the 1970s, the current Finnish legal aid system mainly involves public-sector lawyers working in Public Legal Aid (PLA) offices. These offices provide all types of legal aid. In addition to the PLA offices, private lawyers approved by the PLA offices can be funded by the state to represent legal aid clients in court proceedings. The development of the extensive legal aid provision in Finland reflects the welfare state paradigm of equal access to legal aid, irrespective of income. The main reason for supplementing PLA offices with private lawyers was to provide nationwide legal aid, including locations previously not covered by the PLA offices. Rissanen also notes that the PLA offices play an important mediating role between the conflicting parties, thus preventing court proceedings. This extensive public legal aid goes hand in hand with legal aid insurance provided by commercial companies. By comparison with developments elsewhere in the world, the Finnish PLA system has not tightened its legal aid criteria in recent years (regarding, for example, income ceilings or case eligibility). On the contrary, the Finnish PLA system has continued more or less to offer access to justice in a quasi-universal way. With recent budget cuts, however, the number of PLA offices has shrunk, and IT solutions and telephone services are prioritised. The decrease in PLA offices has also meant that a growing number of cases are delegated to private lawyers, but overall, the effects have been slight compared to those in many other European legal aid systems. The main reason that the Finnish legal aid system has been able to maintain its comprehensive coverage is the existence of an efficient, integrated, legal aid model, where the PLA offices offer more holistic legal aid, and private lawyers concentrate on legal disputes.

In Chap. 5, Kristiansen shows that, in Denmark, there has been a long tradition of publicly funded legal aid, alongside voluntary offices and legal clinics. With the expanding welfare programmes of the 1960s the goal was to achieve universal access to justice through public funding, and to cover legal costs when cases were brought to court. In addition, pre-trial legal aid was introduced that gave citizens the right to free legal aid by lawyers. Everyone, irrespective of income and the type of legal problem in question, currently has a right to verbal legal aid assistance, with eligibility to further legal aid assessed on mainly financial criteria. In 2014, however, legal action against public authorities was excluded from extended legal aid: verbal advice, drafting letters, writing complaints, or case handling support in the pre-court phase. Instead, the authorities are obligated to assist citizens, as is also the case in Norway. Legal aid is provided by a mix of non-commercial legal aid offices organised by pro bono lawyers and student volunteers in a form of judicare, where lawyers are remunerated for extended legal aid. In 2007, a reform was introduced that ensured citizens easier access to small-claim courts, in which they could represent themselves, with the help of procedural guidance from the courts. As we will discuss below, this is in tune with the access to justice perspective, but it also places a lot of responsibility on citizens, requiring them to be able to name, blame, and claim their rights without any legal help. At the same time, legal aid insurance took on primary importance, so free legal aid is now only available to those without insurance, or those whose insurance does not cover the case. Kristiansen concludes that government-subsidised legal aid provided by lawyers is, in practice, non-existent for the vast majority of the population. However, a number of new non-profit organisations have developed, such as *Gadejuristen* [The Street Lawyers], as described in Chap. 8. Such organisations as unions and tenant associations provide legal aid to their members, while others offer outreach support to specific target groups, like refugees and abused women.

In Chap. 6, Antonsdottir discusses how, with the legal aid reforms of the 1990s, legal aid in Iceland changed from being a kind of charitable activity supporting the poor and needy, to being the right to access the courts irrespective of financial status. In reality, access to legal aid depends on financial criteria. Moreover, a section of the legal aid bill that lays down whether cases of public or individual interest should be eligible for legal aid has been repeatedly taken out by one political wing, and put back in again by the other. Iceland lacks out-of-court legal aid, which is provided instead by membership organisations or the non-profit sector. In the 1990s, legal expenses insurance was introduced, but it usually failed to cover out-of-court legal expenses. There is no official policy on how eligibility for legal aid is assessed in the light of the level of insurance an applicant has, but, as Antonsdottir points out, policyholders get their legal aid applications rejected.

Legal Aid in the Nordic Countries: A Nordic Model?

This volume makes clear that, as with other general Nordic welfare programmes (Arts and Gelissen 2010; Goul Andersen and Albrekt Larsen 2015), the Nordic countries follow different legal aid models; there are also differences in organisational structure and supply of legal aid. Even though, as discussed above, all the Nordic legal aid schemes have the universal welfare paradigm in the background, the five countries have developed in different directions to compensate for financial cuts, and deal with new requirements for legal aid. Sweden has moved in the direction of a market-based approach, where legal aid is primarily based on insurance. Although the scheme in Sweden was originally based on public legal aid offices, a broad publicly-administered social support scheme, and a strong welfare state ideology, cost cutting measures significantly reduced the state's role in legal aid provision. In consequence, responsibility for ensuring access to legal services was transferred from the state to individuals and the market, via legal expenses insurance. As a result, legal expenses insurance is the main provider of legal aid, and it is up to the individual to approach lawyers and name their legal problems. Finland tries to maintain its opposite position, retaining its welfare state inspired scheme and public legal aid offices. Nevertheless, Finnish legal aid too, is complemented by legal aid insurance and has developed IT solutions, to achieve greater efficiency. Denmark and Norway are most alike in their general legal aid schemes: they represent a middle ground between Finland and Sweden, pursuing neither a broader welfare state approach, nor one that is market-based. The public legal aid schemes continued in Norway and Denmark with comparatively little change, although with some cost-saving measures, and some development of alternative legal aid providers. The challenges facing public legal aid in Norway and Denmark have largely been mitigated by third sector legal aid initiatives. Of the Nordic countries, Iceland has the least generous system, and it consists mainly of out-of-court legal aid based on insurance, membership organisations, or voluntary institutions. Research on welfare states suggests that Finland is exceptional, compared to the other Nordic countries, when it comes to welfare programmes (Kongshøj 2015; Arts and Gelissen 2010), and such a view is further supported by the Finnish legal aid model. Developments in Sweden especially, but also in Denmark and Norway, go against universal welfare state ideology, and represent a reconfiguration of the traditional welfare state. Formerly, legal aid programmes were considered a state responsibility, but they have now been outsourced to the market and the third sector.

One issue common to all the Nordic countries is the focus on budget cuts in the wake of developments in Europe and worldwide. Because of this, the five countries are in the process of bringing their approaches into line with those found elsewhere. On the one hand, except in Finland, there has been a move towards outsourcing legal aid to non-profit organisations based on volunteers or membership. On the other hand, legal aid has been commercialised through private insurance. In most of the countries, legal aid insurance is the main provider of legal aid. Such an abdication of the welfare state to the third sector, and privatisation, have also been observed in other areas of welfare, such as the health system, which has increasingly resorted to private health insurance (Kongshøj 2015).

Another dimension of the move of legal aid schemes towards the third sector and membership organisations is the transformation of professional legal hierarchies. The country chapters indicate to varying degrees that it has become less attractive for lawyers to provide legal aid. This development parallels trends in the UK. In all the Nordic countries, legal aid lawyers earn less than private lawyers—and markedly less than corporate lawyers, whose salaries are determined by the free market. In Denmark and in Sweden, it is difficult to recruit volunteer lawyers to legal aid offices. There are several structural reasons for this. The most important is the tendency for the larger law firms to be concentrated in big cities, and to specialise in business law. This development is clearly seen in the USA, with most specialised lawyers being employed in the major firms (Galanter and Palay 1991). Lawyers from such firms are not equipped to deal with the kind of legal work required in legal aid offices. Changes in legal hierarchies have also been reported in other Western countries (Sommerlad 2001; Heinz et al. 1998; Sandefur 2001; Moorhead 2004). As is shown by Sommerlad, in England, the legal aid worker has gone from being a kind of cause lawyer—a lawyer with a social face—to being a low status hack lawyer with a massive overload of cases. This has an impact on the quality of legal aid. In the Nordic countries, things have not gone that far, but there is a tendency towards a further marginalisation of legal aid workers and disillusionment with public-sector legal aid.

Third Sector Initiatives

One key feature of the development of legal aid in all the Nordic countries is the move towards commercial legal expenses insurance. Another is the development of third sector legal aid initiatives in Denmark and Norway, and to a lesser extent in Finland and Sweden. Such third sector initiatives have striven to alleviate deficiencies in the public legal aid schemes and, in particular, shortcomings in the way these schemes function in relation to the welfare state. Legal aid provided through third sector initiatives comprises a major part of the total legal aid provided in the Nordic countries. In Norway, it has been estimated that they deal with about 250,000 cases annually, while the public-sector scheme provides legal aid in around 33,000 cases. In view of this, the role of third sector initiatives calls into question perceptions of how the Nordic legal aid schemes relate to welfare state ideology. Both the amount and nature of legal aid provided indicate that there are flaws in the Nordic legal aid schemes, since they fail to provide comprehensive and all-encompassing social support. We will now go on to discuss how these third sector organisations work, and manage to reach their target groups in different ways than those used by traditional judicare offices and public legal aid.

Third sector legal aid institutions can be divided into two types. On the one hand, the third sector includes membership groups, such as health organisations, tenants' associations and labour unions. In a welfare state perspective, one consequence of this is that people who have resources—both financial and social—in that they consider joining such organisations—will have easier access to expert legal advice and organisations that can take up the cases. Membership organisations can give a form of outreach legal aid to their members by informing them about legal issues of relevance to them through various platforms and magazines. They can also help their members in the first phases of the naming process, and assist them in making a social problem into a legal issue. Because these organisations work at a very specialised level, they can choose when and how to use the court system for bigger political battles, to promote their specific agendas. To advance their cases against public bodies, membership organisations can use their legal knowledge together with empirical data about the lives of their target group.

On the other hand, we find various smaller organisations—especially in Norway and Denmark—that specialise in providing legal aid to some of the most marginalised groups in society. Legal aid for such people is thus left to third sector organisations and legal clinics, as we have seen in the chapters on *Gadejuristen* [The Street Lawyers] and the Norwegian *Juss-Buss*. Without volunteers and third sector initiatives, many of the most disadvantaged would lack any means to access the legal system. The smaller organisations are highly innovative, but dependent on volunteers and various forms of funding. These third sector initiatives use untraditional methods, such as outreach legal aid work, which is The Street Lawyers' way of handling clients, or focus on particular client groups—Juss-Buss, for example specialises in legal aid for prisoners. Because of this concentration on different target groups, there are different kinds of outreach work. The organisations' knowledge about the intertwined web of regulations affecting the target groups, and their understanding of the working principles of public authorities, as well their close familiarity with the lives and problems of the target clients make them specialists in their fields (Olesen et al. 2017). Outreach legal aid initiatives like The Street Lawyers, or Juss-Buss's prison project, like the membership organisations mentioned above, are very often based on thorough knowledge of their target groups' life situations. They have adopted ways of dealing with marginalised groups that are designed more to meet the users' needs than to fit into specific welfare structures, as is shown by how The Street Lawyers operate. First, they are involved in the initial 'troubles-talks' (Jefferson 1988) where a social problem can be named, blamed, and claimed, and transformed into a legal issue (Olesen et al. 2016). To be able to enter into such talks, the organisations have developed various trust-building techniques to approach their target groups. Second, the organisations take the troubles-talks seriously, and offer to take legal action to claim the target groups' rights from the relevant authority. Outreach legal aid consists of more than legal work: it also involves giving practical advice on navigating bureaucratic systems, providing information about opening hours, and establishing channels of communication by, for example, handing out free cell phones to facilitate contact between the client and the public authorities at the necessary times. Third, organisations such as The Street Lawyers work to empower their user groups by raising their legal awareness and increasing their knowledge of their rights. It can generally be said that the third sector, both volunteer organisations and membership groups, become attuned to their target groups' needs through specialisation and detailed knowledge of their lives.

Legal clinics play a major role as legal aid providers for the poorest people in the USA and in Europe, as Wilson notes in Chap. 11. In the Nordic countries, by contrast, the Norwegian Juss-Buss is one of few legal clinics to be found. The increase in legal clinics in Europe reflects an attempt to educate law students in a more practical manner, and at the same time help vulnerable groups, as happens in the USA, where almost all the nation's 198 accredited law schools have more than one clinic, and almost half of all law students participate in clinical work. Wilson reports that the number of European legal clinics is growing. Although many of the clinics did not begin operations until after 2011, one survey has identified 51 clinics in Western Europe (see also Piana et al. 2013). However, apart from Juss-Buss, Clinical Legal Education is not well integrated into law schools in the way it is in the USA.

Individualisation of Legal Aid

Although many of the welfare laws in the Nordic countries are based on the universal welfare paradigm, there is no requirement that the most disadvantaged should be informed about their rights, and thus enabled to claim them. The literature on legal aid discussed throughout this book clearly demonstrates that legal aid schemes should compensate for this legal deficit, but even though legal aid exists, there is no guarantee that it will reach everyone who needs it. On the contrary, several chapters in this collection show that there need to be interpersonal encounters between the law and the person who needs to claim his/her rights, and that the visibility and attractiveness of these 'meeting points' depends on the resources of the individual person.

As discussed above, various kinds of physical interpersonal legal aid encounters have been developed. Several new ways of delivering legal aid in the Nordic countries have been mentioned in this collection. The chapter on The Street Lawyers and the chapter on ex-prisoners both discuss the process of naming, blaming, and claiming (see also Olesen et al. 2016). Legal aid often needs to be offered even before a legal problem has been identified, because many of the most vulnerable people in society struggle to understand and voice their complex problems and therefore tend to fail to seek legal advice and take legal action. However, efforts to provide outreach legal aid are often hampered by the difficulty of reaching target groups (Mathiesen 1975). One approach to extending legal aid would be by setting up informal discussions to identify the most appropriate way to refer clients to the relevant legal and non-legal systems. The Street Lawyers approach their target group through informal conversations and troubles-talk, as does the Legal Aid Centre described by Olesen. The Legal Aid Centre's gatekeeper-function has proved to be useful in the clients' naming, blaming, claiming process, as increasing numbers of clients use the Centre as a source of referral, follow through on the referral, and take up the relevant referral.

One notable development in the Nordic countries is that, to cut costs, the public authorities' encounters with citizens have been digitalised. In all the countries, except for Finland, legal aid mostly does not cover disputes with public authorities, even though they administer most welfare law.

The rationale behind this is that the public authorities have advisory obligations towards citizens. However, with the introduction of cost-cutting measures, and the drive to make public administration more efficient, several initiatives have begun to offer online services. The most basic of these is the provision of information about welfare rights and procedures online, on the webpages of public authorities. Such information is often very basic, and does not cover more complex cases involving several legal areas. Yet, while there is the intention to provide information on legal rights online, it is still up to the individual to name a problem and transform it into a legal issue. If their life situations are difficult, and they lack resources, people are not usually able to find the right information and act upon it. They need a professional to turn the problem into a legal case. The unintended consequence of the use of IT solutions is that they make it harder for the most marginalised and vulnerable people in society to claim their rights. Advanced online and telephone services, such as those offered by the public legal aid offices in Finland, have the disadvantage that citizens need to make use of the technology, and be able to acknowledge and name a problem in legal terms.

Another issue that is discussed throughout the book is how legal aid relates to welfare rights, dispute resolution, and access to justice. Legal aid in the Nordic countries has been framed as a welfare right, rather than being viewed from the perspective of access to justice. With the creation of the Nordic welfare states after World War Two, the process of juridification accelerated in the Nordic countries, as legislation ensuring people's rights to welfare proliferated. Both the law and decision makers were affected by changes in the welfare state, which—as noted by Weber (1978) in his description of modern law—went from being based on relatively clear rules containing little discretion for the civil servant, to being much more complicated, with the possibility of considerable discretion, and of decisions being based on the views of professionals such as social workers and psychologists, as well as legal experts. With the transformation of the law, other professional groups entered the legal sphere, and new forms of governance in the public sector challenged legal decisions with extra-legal dimensions (Aubert 1976, 1989; Sand 1996; Bertilsson 1995; Hammerslev 2003). Most legal aid outside the courts relates to welfare law, which is getting ever more complex, and opening the way for a greater degree of discretion for case workers and leading to extra-legal complications and professional battles. The extension of written law into hitherto unregulated areas, either through an expansion of the law, or through more detailed regulation of something which was not previously legally regulated can—as Habermas (1987) points out—be seen as society's attempt to protect its citizens against the deficits of capitalism. With the individualisation of legal claims to entitlements guaranteed by welfare law, it becomes the responsibility of the individual to claim his or her rights. However, the institutionalisation of welfare rights through welfare laws individualises claims, even though they address problems of a collective nature. The skills required to claim one's rights are distributed unevenly among different groups in society. Most people need legal aid to turn an acknowledged problem into a claim that can be petitioned under the conditions specified in formal law. As Papendorf argues in Chap. 12, this highlights the bureaucratic and distanced organisation of the law, which makes it difficult to claim rights if you do not know about them, and if you do not have the resources to claim your rights in a bureaucratic welfare system. This means that the welfare rights that should protect citizens needing support actually distance them from the public bodies that should provide aid (see also Papendorf 2012).

In Chap. 10, Johnsen examines how legal aid moves from being a welfare paradigm to one of human rights. The European Union (EU) and the Council of Europe focus on 'access to justice' through the European Convention on Human Rights and the EU Charter of Fundamental Rights. The EU rules, however, can be viewed as being focused on the institutional set up, i.e., on how citizens get access to justice via the court system, without acknowledging that legal aid often concerns basic welfare rights that could be claimed more easily from the relevant authority. Human rights protect citizens from the state, and secure their rights, but legal aid is becoming an individual project to oblige states to follow minimum standards. The welfare paradigm of legal aid may therefore be challenged by individualising rights, which leaves the most vulnerable even more distanced from the law, as Papendorf claims in Chap. 12. He argues that the impact of this shift towards rights legislation has been to link the use of the law to individuals' situations and their ability to mobilise their rights. Satisfying legal conditions entails redefining everyday situations, i.e., living situations have to be recast—or named, blamed, and claimed—in the language of the law by individuals themselves, to be able to approach the system. Moreover, the authorities' solution is to abstract human beings from their situation, to bend them to the rules and treat them bureaucratically. This gives unequal access to justice and leaves little room for welfare with care professionals 'squeezed between growing demands and insufficient budgets', as Papendorf puts it. With greater scope for discretion in the public sector, when citizens are given aid, such extra-legal factors as budgetary considerations and administrators' workloads can become important.

Thus, compensatory legal aid requires not only qualified assistance, but also a strengthening of justice seekers' participatory abilities, so they avoid alienation. Legal aid projects with a proactive profile are rare, because they demand considerable resources, but they have in fact increased in the Nordic countries, through the third sector. However, because the third sector often targets particular groups in society, proactive aid is selective; but nonetheless, it responds to real needs and targets them.

Conclusion

All the Nordic countries have public legal aid schemes founded upon a core welfare state model. Such schemes face the twin challenges of cost and effectiveness. To a varying extent, the public schemes have adjusted the welfare state model in the face of these challenges, but failed to fully meet them. A reconfiguration of the legal aid scheme has thus taken place, bringing in third sector legal aid providers. These are more sensitive to legal aid needs, and consciously strive for better ways to cater for those unable to take advantage of the public schemes. However, the increasing role of the third sector represents a shift away from the traditional welfare state ideology of the Nordic countries and also fails to offer the inclusiveness and all-encompassing effects normally attributed to a well-functioning welfare state support scheme. This becomes even more significant when the move towards the marketisation of legal aid through legal expenses insurance and membership organisations is factored in. These developments take different forms, so no such thing as a Nordic model of legal aid exists.

The area of legal aid might thus be seen as representing a flaw in the Nordic welfare state model. The general social support schemes of welfare states, which are governed by a bureaucratic system regulated by laws and regulations, remain inaccessible to those in most need of support, and the welfare state system itself fails to provide the legal aid needed to access universal welfare rights.

We have shown how welfare ideology focuses on the structure of people's needs, problems, and well-being, and ask how legal expertise can help, whereas the access to justice perspective is mainly concerned with people's rights, and their ability to use a specific institution—the courts—to solve problems. The access to justice perspective focuses less on whether the courts can provide citizens with solutions to their problems in an efficient way. Seen in a welfare perspective, access to justice thus depends on the substantive content of people's rights, and the existence of non-implemented rights that can be made operational through better access to the courts. The access to justice perspective does not solve the actual challenge of transforming a social problem into a legal issue through naming, blaming, and claiming processes.

While even the Nordic states have abdicated responsibility for legal aid, new organisations have taken over. They are organised differently than traditional legal aid offices, and understand the target groups' needs better; they are able to meet their target groups in different settings and help transform social problems into legal problems, so that they can then claim the clients' rights. Thus, as seen in several of the chapters, alternative legal aid providers are innovative: they employ new methods to improve access to legal assistance, based on knowledge of the target groups' needs, the effectiveness of different legal aid strategies, and the workings of the legal system. This might provide a basis for reform of the public system that would produce a public legal aid scheme, which, in keeping with welfare state ideology, would provide access to the law for everyone.

References

Arts, W. A., & Gelissen, J. (2010). Models of the welfare state. In S. Leibfried, F. G. Castles, J. Lewis, H. Obinger, & C. Pierson (Eds.), *The Oxford handbook of the welfare state* (pp. 569–585). Oxford: Oxford University Press.

Aubert, V. (1976). The changing role of law and lawyers in nineteenth- and twentieth-century Norwegian society. In D. N. MacComick (Ed.), *Lawyers in their social setting* (pp. 1–17). Edinburgh: Green.

Aubert, V. (1989). *Continuity and development in law and society.* Oslo: Scandinavian University Press.
Bertilsson, M. (Ed.). (1995). *Rätten i Förvandling. Jurister mellan stat och marknad.* Stockholm: Nerenius & Santerus Förlag.
Felstiner, W. L. F., Abel, L. R., & Sarat, A. (1980/81). The emergence and transformation of disputes: Naming, blaming, claiming. *Law & Society Review, 15*(3/4), 631–654.
Galanter, M., & Palay, T. (1991). *Tournament of lawyers: The transformation of the big law firm.* Chicago: University of Chicago Press.
Goul Andersen, J., & Larsen, C. A. (2015). Hvad er universalisme? In J. Goul Andersen & C. A. Larsen (Eds.), *Den universelle velfærdsstat: Funktionsmåde, folkelig opbakning og forandring* (pp. 13–29). Frederiksberg: Frydenlund Academic.
Habermas, J. (1987). *Theory of communicative action: A critique of functionalist reason* (Vol. 2). Cambridge: Polity Press.
Hammerslev, O. (2003). *Danish Judges in the 20th century: A socio-legal study.* Copenhagen: DJØF Publishing.
Heinz, J. P., Laumann, E. O., Nelson, R. L., & Michelson, E. (1998). The changing character of Lawyers' work: Chicago in 1975 and 1995. *Law & Society Review, 32*(4), 751–776.
Jefferson, G. (1988). On the sequential organization of troubles-talk in ordinary conversation. *Social Problems, 35*(4), 418–441.
Kilian, M., & Regan, F. (2004). Legal expenses insurance and legal aid—two sides of the same coin? The experience from Germany and Sweden. *International Journal of the Legal Profession, 11*(3), 233–255.
Kongshøj, K. (2015). Den nordiske velfærdsmodel: veje til og fra universalisme i Danmark, Finland, Norge og Sverige. In J. Goul Andersen & C. A. Larsen (Eds.), *Den universelle velfærdsstat: Funktionsmåde, folkelig opbakning og forandring* (pp. 159–178). Frederiksberg: Frydenlund Academic.
Mathiesen, T. (1975). Noen konlusjoner om rettshjelp, rettspolitikk og samfunnsstruktur. In A. Eidesen, A. Eskeland, & T. Mathiesen (Eds.), *Rettshjelp og samfunnsstruktur* (pp. 187–206). Oslo: Pax.
Moorhead, R. (2004). Legal aid and the decline of private practice: Blue murder or toxic job? *International Journal of the Legal Profession, 11*(3), 159–190.
Olesen, A., Minke, K. L., & Hammerslev, O. (2016). Det retlige møde. In *Festskrift til Sten Schaumburg-Müller.* København: Jurist- og Økonomforbundets Forlag.
Olesen, A., Nielsen, S. P. P., & Hammerslev, O. (2017). Gadejura – kunsten at fremelske gadefolkets oplevelse af at bære rettigheder. In N. J. Clausen (Ed.),

Festskrift til Hans Viggo Godsk Pedersen (pp. 435–455). København: Jurist- og Økonomforbundets Forlag.

Papendorf, K. (2012). *Rett for alle? Rettsliggjøring og rettsfjerne personers mulighet til å mobilisere retten*. Oslo: Novus forlag.

Piana, D., Langbroek, P., Berkmanas, T., Hammerslev, O., & Pacurari, O. (2013). *Legal and judicial training in Europe*. The Hague: Eleven International Publishing.

Regan, F. (2001). How and why is pro bono flourishing: A comparison of recent developments in Sweden and China. *Law in Context, 19*, 148–162.

Sand, I.-J. (1996). *Styring av kompleksitet. Rettslige former for statlig rammestyring og desentralisert statsforvaltning*. Bergen-Sandviken: Fagbokforlaget.

Sandefur, R. L. (2001). Work and Honor in the Law: Prestige and the Division of Lawyers' Labor. *American Sociological Review, 66*(3), 382–403.

Sommerlad, H. (2001). "I've lost the plot": An everyday story of the "political" legal aid lawyer. *Journal of Law and Society, 28*(3), 335–360.

Weber, M. (1978). *Economy and society*. Berkeley: University of California Press.

Open Access This chapter is distributed under the terms of the Creative Commons Attribution 4.0 International License (http://creativecommons.org/licenses/by/4.0/), which permits use, duplication, adaptation, distribution, and reproduction in any medium or format, as long as you give appropriate credit to the original author(s) and the source, a link is provided to the Creative Commons license, and any changes made are indicated.

The images or other third party material in this book are included in the work's Creative Commons license, unless indicated otherwise in the credit line; if such material is not included in the work's Creative Commons license and the respective action is not permitted by statutory regulation, users will need to obtain permission from the license holder to duplicate, adapt or reproduce the material.

Index

A

Aarhus, 103, 107, 109, 111, 210
Abel, Richard L., 272
Academic capital, 4
Academic credit, 265, 280
Access to justice, 7, 36, 44, 48, 51, 54, 56, 59, 67, 69, 71, 79, 80, 85, 89, 94, 101, 113, 121, 125, 134–136, 158, 159, 194, 227–262, 275, 292, 315, 316, 323–326
Action research, 4, 148, 162
Advokatvakten, 31
Alþingi, 133, 134, 136
American Bar Association (ABA), 272
Andenæs, Kristian 'Kikki', 4, 17, 23, 29, 32, 147, 174, 185, 294, 299
Antonsdottir, Hildur Fjola, 9, 316, 317
Armenia, 251

Asia, 281
Association of American Law Schools (AALS), 273
Asylum
  asylum procedure, 35
  asylum seeker, 16, 28, 32, 35, 55, 84, 86, 88, 95n8, 276, 314
Aubert, Vilhelm, 3, 323
Auðuns, Auður, 140
Australia, 2, 215, 267, 279
Austria, 281
Autopoiesis, 302
Azerbaijan, 251

B

Bailiff, 119, 196, 204, 205, 213
Ban zone, 183, 184
Bandit Radio, 160
Barendrecht, Maurits, 2, 80, 89, 94
Belgium, 281
Bergen, 18

Białystok University, 276
Bills, 108, 127–129, 132, 136, 137, 140, 144n16, 210, 211, 317
Bistandsadvokat, 16
Bologna Process, 275
Bourdieu, Pierre, 154, 196
Bourdieusian, 196
Bradway, John, 268, 269
Brazil, 2
Bureaucratization, 290, 296

C

California, 267, 271, 272
California Rural Legal Assistance (CRLA), 271
Capitalism, 324
Cappelletti, Mauro, 44, 51, 67
Case
  asylum case, 25, 28, 35
  civil case, 26, 28, 43, 46, 78, 125, 128, 133, 142, 235, 237, 239, 241, 254, 265, 266, 313
  debt case, 151
  expulsion case, 151
  immigration case, 20, 22, 25, 32, 36, 151
  matrimonial case, 45
  test case, 162
  tort case, 133
Cause lawyering, 4
Central Europe, 264, 275–280
Charitable organisations, 3, 34, 35, 149, 157
Child
  child custody, 25, 26, 49, 54, 58, 62, 68, 78, 113, 235
  child maintenance, 19, 47, 49, 55, 58, 62
  child welfare, 19, 20, 297
China, 2, 162
Chinese, 277
Christiania, 169, 176
Christie, Nils, 291
Church City Mission, The, 34
Civil
  civil litigation, 44, 235
  civil service, 15
Coercion, 20
Colonization, 295, 296
Communicative action, 154
Conciliation council, 150
Copenhagen, 101, 111, 169–172, 176, 267, 268
  Copenhagen Legal Aid Office, 101, 106
Council of Europe (CoE), 228, 239
Council of Europe's Commission for the Protection and Efficiency of Justice (CEPEJ), 1, 26, 143n12, 228, 239, 247–255
Council on Legal Education for Professional Responsibility (CLEPR), 270
Court
  administrative court, 49, 55–57, 88
  appellate court, 26
  city court, 116
  court hearing, 83, 270
  court of appeal, 49
  court system, 100, 112, 120, 320, 324
  district court, 49, 83, 88, 91

labour court, 57
market court, 57
probate court, 119
public court, 57
specialist court, 49
supreme court, 26, 49, 57, 134, 265, 271
trial court, 266
Crime, 204, 233, 235, 265
violent crime, 21
Criminal
criminal charges, 65, 239, 240
criminal group, 196
criminal procedure, 16, 143n5, 144n17, 244, 246
criminal scheme, 232, 244
Criminological study, 158
Croatia, 162
Cultural issues, 23
Custody, 21, 95n12, 115, 133, 137, 139, 143n13, 246
Czech Republic, 275

D

Danish
Danish National Register (DNR), 206, 207
Danish Parliament, 107
Danish Prison Service, 197
Danske Lov, 100
De-democratization, 295
Defamation, 241, 242
Democracy, 288, 289, 291, 292, 295, 300
Denmark, 1, 3, 4, 7, 9, 34, 99–122, 133, 143n9, 170, 171, 173, 193, 230, 252, 253, 267, 312, 316, 318–320

Disadvantaged groups, 3, 6, 8–10, 16, 22, 29, 35, 36, 148, 152, 153, 158, 159, 162, 193, 206, 298, 299, 314, 315
Divorce settlements, 150
Domestic violence, 16, 19, 20
Drug addiction, 34, 197
Duke University, 269
Durham, 269

E

Eastern Europe, 251, 256, 281
Eastern European, 2
Eckhoff, Torstein, 3
EEA, 289, 293
Empirical knowledge, 161
Employment disputes, 150
England
See United Kingdom (UK)
English, 79, 155, 218n2, 241, 252, 256, 277, 297
Ericsson, Kjersti, 297
Eskeland, Ståle, 4, 5, 16, 17, 23, 63, 69, 103, 148, 193–195, 299
Ethical codes, 23
Ethnic minority, 196
European
European Committee for the Efficiency of Justice (CEPEJ), 26, 143n12, 254, 256, 258
European Convention on Human Rights (ECHR), 36, 239–241, 249, 254
European Court of Human Rights (ECtHR), 36, 55,

European (*cont.*)
    67, 228, 238–248, 254, 257, 258, 293
  European labour movement, 296
  European Network for Clinical Legal Education (ENCLE), 281
European Economic Area (EEA), 86, 143n5, 144n17
European Union (EU), 107, 143n9, 276, 293
  EU Charter of Fundamental Rights, 324
Eviction, 21, 180, 209, 233
Evidence, 50, 57, 82, 111, 113, 121, 125, 183, 184, 189, 257, 274, 279, 288
Ex-prisoner, 7, 9, 193–218, 322
Extra-legal, 177, 323–325

F

Faculty of Law, University of Oslo, 3, 147, 149, 163
Family reunification, 67
Felstiner, William L. F., 155, 216
Field work, 88, 120, 154, 156, 158, 161, 163, 175–178, 183, 321
Finland, 1, 4, 7, 8, 48, 77–94, 228, 230–237, 239, 242–247, 251–257, 312, 315, 317–319, 322, 323
Finnish
  Finnish Bar Association (FBA), 86, 91–93
  Finnish Legal Aid Act (FLAA), 232–237, 244, 246
Forced marriage, 20

Ford Foundation, 270, 271, 275, 278
Foreign nationals, 139
Foreign workers, 33
France, 251, 281
Fri Rettshjelp, 29

G

Gadejuristen, 9, 103, 108, 149, 169–190, 316, 320
Gatejuristen, 17, 34, 171
Gatekeeper, 156, 215, 216, 322
GDP, 27, 89, 132, 143n9
Gellerupparken, 103, 109
Gellerupparkens, 111
Gender discrimination, 67
German, 267, 297
Germany, 48, 251, 281, 295, 296
Globalisation, 295
Gotfredsen, Nanna, 170, 178
Gothenburg, 67
Great Britain
  See United Kingdom (UK)
Greenland, 4
Greenpeace International, 241

H

Habermas, Jürgen, 295
Habermasian, 10
Hammerslev, Ole, 4, 5, 9, 148, 218n1, 314, 323
Health care, 3, 19, 20, 90, 158
Homeless, 4, 33, 68, 108, 170, 172, 176, 183, 202
Human rights, 9, 35, 135, 136, 184, 189, 227, 276, 279, 282, 289, 293, 294, 324
Hungary, 251

Iceland, 1, 7, 125–142, 253, 312, 316–318
Icelandic
  Icelandic Bar Association, 127, 129–131, 134, 141, 142n2
  Icelandic Human Rights Centre (ICEHR), 141, 144n16
  Icelandic Parliament, 135
Immigrant
  immigrant group, 29
  immigrant worker, 4
Immigration, 15, 20–22, 25, 32, 35, 67, 158, 266, 280, 282, 313
Immigration law, 67
India, 267, 279
Indigenous population, 2
Inequality, 292
Inner city population, 29
Institutionalisation, 324
Interdisciplinary, 94
Interventionist, 290, 291, 300, 301, 303
Irish High Court, 240
Istedgade, 176
Italy, 281

J

Jagiellonian University, 276
Japan, 2
Johnsen, Jon T., 3, 4, 8, 9, 16, 17, 23, 31, 32, 45, 47–49, 59, 66, 79, 80, 91, 94, 103, 147, 154, 159, 227, 324
Judges, 4, 24, 57, 88, 89, 129, 130, 155, 241, 257, 266, 268, 293
Judicare
  judicare lawyers, 8, 254, 255
  judicare scheme, 8, 15–17, 25–29, 33, 229, 230, 236, 237, 313, 314
Judicial, 24, 44, 91, 144n16, 186, 232, 235, 236, 238, 240, 242, 243, 245, 248–250, 258, 288, 289
judicial area, 69
Judicialisation, 290, 295
Juridic, 82, 291, 294, 297, 300
Juridification, 3, 9, 287–307, 323
  juridification process, 297, 303
Jurisprudence, 297
Juristjouren, 68, 69, 72n9
JURK, 33, 307
Juss-Buss, 6, 17, 148
Jusshjelpa i Nord-Norge, 17, 33

K

Karelia region, 275
Krakow, 276
Kristiansen, Bettina Lemann, 6, 8, 99, 103, 109, 113, 121, 122n2, 316

L

Latin America, 281
Law
  administrative law, 30, 56, 63, 69, 71, 106, 240
  business law, 60, 93, 112, 120, 282, 319
  common law, 79, 231, 252, 257, 281, 293
  consumer law, 68
  contract law, 110, 289, 306
  criminal law, 34, 68, 69, 110, 254, 265

Law (*cont.*)
  family law, 25, 30, 47, 51, 55, 61–63, 68, 110, 113, 314
  formal law, 18, 300, 301, 324
  health law, 34
  immigration law, 30, 67, 151, 152
  inheritance law, 68, 110
  insurance law, 34, 65
  labour law, 30, 62, 63, 65, 66, 90, 151, 296
  law centre, 231
  law-dissociated, 287–295, 306
  law firms, 32, 50, 59, 65, 67–69, 86, 93, 95n8, 112, 120, 129, 141, 230, 266, 319
  law studies, 68
  materialized law, 298
  regulatory law, 301, 303
  rental law, 110
  social security law, 34
  tax law, 5, 110, 205
  welfare law, 5, 229, 300, 301, 322–324
Law school clinics, 264, 272–274, 280
Lawsuits, 62, 100, 101, 104, 105, 107, 112–116, 118, 121, 130, 132, 136, 298
Lawyer
  family lawyers, 215
  PLA lawyers, 80, 83, 84, 92
  private lawyers, 8, 59, 71, 77, 78, 80, 82, 86–88, 92–94, 253, 267, 315, 316, 319
  private-practice lawyers, 8, 23, 29, 237, 313
  publicly funded lawyer, 16
Legal, 49, 198

legal advice, 4, 8, 9, 17, 34, 49–51, 58, 59, 62, 63, 66–68, 70, 71, 77, 83, 84, 89, 93, 95n8, 101, 104, 105, 107, 108, 110–112, 119, 121, 157, 158, 209, 211, 218n6, 242, 247, 248, 265, 287, 320, 322
legal assistance, 1, 5, 6, 15–19, 22, 23, 25, 27, 30, 33, 36, 37, 45, 46, 52, 53, 55, 58, 59, 65, 66, 84, 90, 94, 100, 126, 133, 135, 140, 142, 148, 160, 195, 198, 205, 207, 213, 214, 232, 236, 242, 245–247, 255, 256, 258, 276, 314, 326
legal assistance aid, 49
legal categorisation, 154
legal consultations, 60–62, 64, 65, 70, 71, 91, 314
legal costs, 44, 51, 65, 89, 129, 130, 200, 201, 204, 210, 230, 231, 235, 236, 316
legal council, 130
legal discussion, 290
legal disputes, 22, 33, 50, 51, 82, 89, 94, 187
legal documents, 67
legal expenses insurance (LEI), 30, 31, 43–46, 48–51, 53–58, 64–66, 69–71, 72n3, 79, 80, 89, 90, 116, 126, 139, 140, 142, 144n19, 314, 315, 317–319, 325
legal framework, 69, 158, 179, 185, 215
legal guardians, 126

legal hierarchies, 2, 318, 319
legal information, 9, 33, 35, 68, 70, 71, 118, 127, 140, 141, 148, 160, 307
legal insecurity, 5
legal institutions, 107, 153, 158, 208, 214, 291
legal interpretation, 129
legal issues, 25, 33, 69, 82, 84, 88, 90, 93, 160, 195, 205, 207–214, 218n8, 231, 232, 266, 314, 320, 321, 323, 326
legal labelling, 154
legal matters, 21, 51–53, 55, 71, 80, 91, 104, 258, 266, 278, 314
legal needs, 3, 4, 6, 8, 16, 17, 21, 29, 34, 35, 148, 161–163, 177, 195, 199, 229, 272, 314
legal position, 99, 100, 102, 105, 110, 119, 211, 305
legal problems, 6, 8, 9, 17, 45, 46, 58, 59, 63, 70, 71, 84, 87, 88, 90, 92, 94, 105, 109, 110, 120, 148, 152, 161, 162, 176–180, 182, 186–189, 197, 203, 206, 218n5, 229, 232–234, 236, 240, 243, 246, 247, 255, 264, 314, 316, 317, 322, 326
legal proceedings, 65, 69, 79, 82, 104, 105, 112, 247
legal professionals, 2, 92, 182
legal protection, 5, 44, 48–51, 56, 59, 62, 70, 91, 238, 298, 299, 305
legal regulation, 205, 290, 291, 295, 305
legal representation, 8, 9, 18, 22, 23, 26–29, 43, 49, 50, 55, 66, 78, 150, 172, 181, 232, 240, 251
legal services, 1, 3, 5, 23, 37n5, 45, 47, 56, 66, 69–71, 77, 79, 86, 90, 91, 93, 94, 129, 140, 195, 214, 228–234, 237, 238, 248, 256, 267–274, 277, 279, 281, 282, 292, 311, 312, 317
legal tactic, 162
Legal aid, 3–8, 45, 58, 78, 80, 92, 93, 194, 195, 231, 314
  alternative legal aid, 7, 8, 15, 16, 29, 31–35, 37, 45, 66, 80, 89–91, 108, 147, 314, 318, 326
  extended legal aid, 57, 176, 185, 187, 188, 216, 316
  Finnish legal aid, 8, 79–89, 91, 94, 230, 253, 315, 317
  Icelandic legal aid, 9
  lawyer-based legal aid, 102, 103, 106–112, 117, 120, 122n4
  Legal Aid Act, 17–24, 27, 29, 30, 43, 46–49, 51–61, 64–66, 71, 77, 78, 86, 87, 299, 312–314
  Legal Aid Authority, 43, 52, 56, 57, 59–63
  Legal Aid Board, 57
  Legal Aid Centre, 215, 216, 322
  legal aid clinics, 3, 4, 9, 15–17, 32–34, 147–163, 268, 269, 279, 314

Legal aid (*cont.*)
  Legal Aid Committee, 128, 130–134, 139, 142, 142n2, 142n3, 144n16
  legal aid council, 27
  legal aid fee, 24, 37n2, 46, 52, 64, 65, 77, 88, 92, 93
  legal aid initiative, 2, 8, 16, 17, 31, 32, 34, 66, 80, 89–91, 108, 149, 153, 158, 214–217, 318, 319, 321
  legal aid insurance, 8, 16, 113–115, 314–316, 318
  legal aid lawyers, 2, 6, 22, 23, 34, 77–79, 318
  legal aid model, 94, 315–317
    mixed legal aid model, 80, 92, 93
  legal aid policies, 35, 36, 44–46, 63, 71, 236, 237, 315
  legal aid programs, 7–9, 63, 151, 157, 266, 267, 271, 272, 274, 281, 282, 318
  legal aid provision, 125, 134, 239, 315, 317
  legal aid research, 8, 9, 16, 48, 102–104, 158, 193, 194, 295, 314
    Nordic legal aid research, 3–8, 194, 195, 231
  legal aid scheme
    Danish legal aid scheme, 8
    Finnish legal aid scheme, 8, 78
    Swedish legal aid scheme, 8, 45, 58, 314
  legal aid system, 2, 8, 9, 36, 77, 79, 88, 92–94, 102, 104, 107, 120, 236, 241, 244, 248, 255
  pre-trial legal aid, 100, 101, 104–106, 109–113, 116, 117, 119, 316
  private legal aid, 78, 101–103, 106–111, 117, 120, 121, 122n3, 314
Legislation, 2–5, 31, 44, 45, 79, 86, 104–109, 112, 114, 125, 127–132, 135, 137, 139, 140, 149, 162, 182, 184, 185, 188, 201, 202, 206, 239, 288–290, 293, 295, 304, 312, 314, 323, 324
Legislators, 99, 289, 290, 296
Libel, 241
Lichtenstein, 251
Lied, Camilla, 17, 34, 149, 170, 171, 179, 181–186, 195
Lithuania, 162
Litigation
  litigation aid, 45, 49, 232, 234, 236
  litigation process, 44, 70, 94
LO (Swedish Trade Union Confederation), 65, 66, 72n5
Lögmannavaktin, 141
London Greenpeace, 241
Lower-class, 193
Luhmann, Niklas, 301–3
Lumpenproletariat, 5
Lund, 68–70
  Lund University, 68

M

Malmö, 68, 70
Marginalised, 4, 5, 169, 287, 313, 320, 321, 323

Market ideology, 229
Mathiesen, Thomas, 3–5, 147, 148, 193, 194, 290, 322
McDonald's, 241, 245
McQuoid-Mason, David, 278, 279
Meese, Ed, 272
Mental health problems, 20, 126, 174
Mexican, 271
Middle ages, 200, 263
Military service, 20
Ministry of Justice (MoJ), 18, 22, 29, 31, 34, 77, 81, 83, 85, 87, 88, 91, 92, 95n9, 95n12, 115, 116, 137, 138, 149
Moldovia, 251

N

Negotiations, 51, 55, 121, 154, 194, 202, 205
Neo-liberal, 2, 132, 135
Netherlands, the, 251–254, 256, 281
New public management (NPM), 2, 178, 189
New York City, 267
New York Legal Aid Society, 267
Nielsen, Stine Piilgaard Porner, 9, 170
Nonet, Phillipe, 301
Non-governmental organisation (NGO), 188, 231, 248, 249, 282
Non-profit organisations, 68, 108, 170, 199, 217, 316, 318
Nordic
    Nordic countries, 1–10, 45, 91, 103, 127, 131, 147, 229, 230, 247, 252, 256, 311–319, 321–323, 325

Nordic model, 7, 9, 10, 312, 313, 317, 325
Nordic studies, 6, 7, 171
Normative, 6, 227, 228, 295, 302
Normativity, 6, 302, 303
North Carolina, 269
Northern Ireland, 251, 252
Norway, 1, 3, 4, 7–9, 48, 66, 126, 152, 162, 228, 230–237, 239, 240, 242–247, 251–257, 281, 288, 291–293, 295, 299, 312, 313, 316, 318–320
Norwegian
    Norwegian Administrative Procedure Act, 22, 314
    Norwegian Association for Asylum Seekers (NOAS), 32, 35
    Norwegian Bar Association, 31
    Norwegian Church, the, 34
    Norwegian legal aid act (NLAA), 22, 232, 233, 235, 246
    Norwegian Ministry of Justice and Public Security, 24
    Norwegian Romani, 4

O

Olesen, Anette, 8, 9, 147, 193, 321, 322
Olomouc, 275
Ombudsman, 90, 143n5, 144n17, 277
Organic solidarity, 303
Organisation for Economic Co-operation and Development (OECD), 66
Oslo, 18, 29, 34, 158, 171, 282, 299

Ø

Østerud, Øyvind, 288, 291

P

Palacky University, 275
Papendorf, Knut, 5, 6, 10, 324, 325
Paradigmatic, 4, 264, 301, 302, 315, 317, 322, 324
Parole, 198, 201–203
Paternalistic, 94
Petrozavodsk State University, 275
Plaintiffs, 44, 127, 128
Poland, 162, 264, 275, 282
Policies, 8, 30, 31, 33–35, 43–46, 49, 50, 56, 63, 71, 80, 89–92, 125, 130, 135, 136, 139, 140, 142, 148, 149, 152, 158, 161–163, 170, 171, 182, 183, 186–188, 202, 204, 219n15, 229–231, 237, 238, 244–246, 250, 255, 289, 294–299, 306, 315, 317
Polish Legal Clinics Foundation (FUPP), 276–80
Political discourse, 183
Political knowledge, 103
Post-prison, 196, 197, 199–203, 210, 211, 215, 217, 218, 218n5
Prisoners, 9, 22, 158–160, 163, 197–204, 217, 218, 242, 266, 320
Prisons, 33, 54, 90, 157–160, 193, 195–198, 200, 202–204, 206, 208, 213, 216, 218n5, 242, 257, 321

Pro-bono, 31, 32, 45, 66, 67, 70, 71, 91, 108, 141, 274, 277, 281, 315, 316
Professional, 174
Professionalisation, 153, 301
Pro-forma, 278
Public
  public authority, 5
  public defender, 46, 53, 65, 111, 266
  public funds, 6, 15, 17, 100, 101, 104, 105, 107–109, 122n3, 128, 130, 132, 136, 142, 232, 256, 316
  public sector, 72n5, 93, 189, 206, 231, 314, 319, 323, 325
Public legal aid (PLA), 3, 8, 15–31, 33–37, 44–46, 48, 50–60, 63–65, 70, 71, 72n4, 77–94, 102, 105, 106, 108, 122, 125, 127, 142, 230, 232, 253, 312, 314–320, 323, 325, 326

Q

Quantitative, 290, 291, 295

R

Radical student movements, 32, 147
Rättsskydd, 43
Reagan, Ronald, 264, 267
Recession, 46, 137
Refugees, 35, 108, 161, 276
Regan, Francis, 44–49, 51, 55, 58, 59, 63, 64, 66, 71, 79, 80, 93, 94, 312, 315

Reoffenders, 196, 198, 200, 210, 212, 213, 218n5
Research Group on Power and Democracy, 288
Retten til juridisk bistand (Johnsen, Jon T.), 16
Rettshjelp (Eskeland, S.& Finne, J.), 16
Reykjavík, 140
Rissanen, Antti, 8, 77, 315
Rønning, Olaf Halvorsen, 15–37, 147, 313
Russia, 264, 275
Russian, 277

S
Saco, 65, 72n7
San Marino, 251
Sarat, Austin, 2, 155, 159, 196, 213, 216, 218n10
Scandinavian, 45, 197
   Scandinavian countries, 100, 288
Scheingold, Stuart A., 2
Schoultz, Isabel, 8, 43, 314
Schulze, Detlef, 294
Scotland, 208, 251, 253
Second wave, 269–70
Selznick, Philip, 301
Semi-structured interviews, 196
Seventies, 3, 4, 9, 18, 32, 33, 45, 101, 103, 107, 109, 162, 229, 269–271, 295, 314, 315
Sexual assault, 16, 55
Sex workers, 9, 170, 172, 183
Shelters, 33, 140, 176

Skårberg, Hanne Hareide, 33, 151, 152, 157, 158
Skjeie, Hege, 293
Smith, Reginald Heber, 5, 193, 267, 269
Social, 179, 201, 206, 207
   social care, 34
   social change, 270
   social distribution, 299
   social exclusion, 59, 159, 207
   social hierarchy, 5, 194
   social injustice, 2
   social insurance, 52, 65, 244
   social integration, 297, 298
   social phobia, 201
   social rights, 294
   social sciences, 301
   social security, 3, 5, 15, 20, 21, 30, 34, 37, 59, 158, 204, 206, 296, 312, 313
      social security benefit, 179, 201, 206, 207
   social structures, 4, 5, 162, 187, 291
Social Democratic Alliance, 133, 135
Socio-economic, 129
Socio-legal
   socio-legal analysis, 16, 17
   socio-legal debate, 125
   socio-legal research, 3, 136
Sociology, 4, 196
Sociology of law, 4, 148, 298
Sommerlad, H., 2, 149, 319
South Africa, 267, 278, 279
Soviet Union
   See Russia
Spain, 281
State budget, 28, 29, 116–118, 135

State-funded, 8, 22, 78, 86, 89, 90, 92, 137, 232, 312–314
Stavanger, 18
Stigamot, 140
Stockholm, 67
Street lawyer method, 171, 174, 185–188
Street Lawyers, The (Gatejuristen), 7, 9, 17, 34, 149, 169–191, 316, 320–322
Studentersamfundets Retshjælp for Ubemidlede, 18, 267
Subpoenas, 105
Substance abusers, 108
Sweden, 7, 43–71, 252, 253, 312, 317–319
Swedish
    Swedish Bar Association, 46, 66, 67, 70
    Swedish citizenship, 67
    Swedish National Audit Office, 48
    Swedish Refugee Advice Centre, 67
Symbolic power, 154

T

Target groups, 5–7, 108, 153, 160, 170–189, 194, 231, 233, 243, 313, 316, 320–322, 326
Tax avoidance, 53
TCO (Swedish Confederation of Professional Employees), 65, 72n6
Teubner, Gunther, 291, 297, 300–305
Theoretical analysis, 4
Trade unions, 53, 65–67, 72n6, 72n7, 90, 104, 108
Trondheim, 18

U

United Kingdom (UK), 2, 5, 208, 215, 241, 242, 245, 251, 254, 259n9, 279, 318, 319
United Nation (UN)
    UN Committee Against Torture, 36
    UN Convention on Civil and Political Rights (CCPR), 36, 37n5, 239, 240, 243
    UN High Commissioner on Refugees (UNHCR), 276
    UN Human Rights Committee, 36
United States of America (USA), 2, 3, 5, 7, 10, 32, 148, 157, 162, 263–282, 319, 321
United States Supreme Court, 265, 271
University of Chicago, 267
University of Copenhagen, 267, 268
University of Delaware, 272
University of Maryland, 273
University of Oslo, 148, 162, 171
University of Southern California, 267
Unlawful dismissal, 15, 151
US Office of Economic Opportunity (OEO), 271, 272

V

Vesterbro, 176, 177, 183
Vietnam, 162

Voigt, Rüdiger, 294
Volunteers, 4, 8, 34, 68, 101, 112, 120, 149, 150, 156, 157, 162, 169, 172, 173, 175, 176, 178, 182, 231, 241, 316, 318–321
von Briesen, Arthur, 267, 268

W

Wales, 2, 208, 251
Washington, 271, 272
Weber, Max, 153, 289, 290, 300–305, 323
Weimar Republic, 296
Welfare
    welfare ideology, 3, 17, 37, 228, 229, 232, 235–238, 246, 247, 255–257, 326
        Scandinavian welfare, 45
    welfare perspective, 227, 228, 233, 326
    welfare policy, 46, 295, 296
    welfare regulations, 100, 229
    welfare rights, 3, 5, 170, 172, 257, 271, 292, 311, 312, 322–324, 326

welfare schemes, 3
welfare workers, 2
Welfare state
    Nordic welfare states, 3, 7, 311–326
    welfare perspective, 320
    welfare state reforms, 3
West Heidelberg, 215
Western Continental Europe, 280
Western Europe, 252, 263, 264, 281, 296, 321
Western European, 1, 228, 251, 281
Wiersholm, 32
Wilhelmsson, Thomas, 306
Women´s organization, 140
World War Two (WWII), 3, 135, 323

Y

Yale, 267

Z

Zealand, 210

The manufacturer's authorised representative in the EU is Springer Nature Customer Service Centre GmbH, Europaplatz 3, 69115 Heidelberg, Germany. If you have any concerns regarding our products, please contact ProductSafety@springernature.com

Printed and bound by CPI Group (UK) Ltd, Croydon, CR0 4YY

23/03/2026

02076678-0001